The Presidencies of

WILLIAM HENRY HARRISON

&

JOHN TYLER

AMERICAN PRESIDENCY SERIES

Donald R. McCoy, Clifford S. Griffin, Homer E. Socolofsky
General Editors

George Washington, Forrest McDonald
John Adams, Ralph Adams Brown
Thomas Jefferson, Forrest McDonald
James Madison, Robert Allen Rutland
James Monroe, Noble E. Cunningham, Jr.
John Quincy Adams, Mary W. M. Hargreaves
Andrew Jackson, Donald B. Cole
Martin Van Buren, Major L. Wilson
William Henry Harrison & John Tyler, Norma Lois Peterson
James K. Polk, Paul H. Bergeron
Zachary Taylor & Millard Fillmore, Elbert B. Smith
Franklin Pierce, Larry Gara
James Buchanan, Elbert B. Smith
Abraham Lincoln, Phillip Shaw Paludan
Andrew Johnson, Albert Castel
Rutherford B. Hayes, Ari Hoogenboom
James A. Garfield & Chester A. Arthur, Justus D. Doenecke
Grover Cleveland, Richard E. Welch, Jr.
Benjamin Harrison, Homer B. Socolofsky & Allan B. Spetter
William McKinley, Lewis L. Gould
Theodore Roosevelt, Lewis L. Gould
William Howard Taft, Paolo E. Coletta
Woodrow Wilson, Kendrick A. Clements
Warren G. Harding, Eugene P. Trani & David L. Wilson
Herbert C. Hoover, Martin L. Fausold
Harry S. Truman, Donald R. McCoy
Dwight D. Eisenhower, Chester J. Pach, Jr., & Elmo Richardson
John F. Kennedy, James N. Giglio
Lyndon B. Johnson, Vaughn Davis Bornet
Gerald R. Ford, John Robert Greene
James Earl Carter, Jr., Burton I. Kaufman

The Presidencies of
WILLIAM HENRY HARRISON
&
JOHN TYLER

Norma Lois Peterson

UNIVERSITY PRESS OF KANSAS

Published by the University Press of Kansas (Lawrence,
Kansas 66049), which was organized by the Kansas
Board of Regents and is operated and funded by Emporia
State University, Fort Hays State University,
Kansas State University, Pittsburg State University, the
University of Kansas, and Wichita State University

Library of Congress Cataloging-in-Publication Data

Peterson, Norma Lois.
The presidencies of William Henry Harrison & John Tyler / Norma
Lois Peterson.
p. cm. — (American presidency series)
Bibliography: p.
Includes index.
ISBN 0-7006-0400-6 (alk. paper)
1. United States—Politics and government—1841–1845.
2. Harrison, William Henry, 1773–1841.   3. Tyler, John, 1790–1862.
I. Title.   II. Series.
E391.P48   1989
973.5′8′0922   dc19   89-5341

British Library Cataloguing in Publication data is available.

Printed in the United States of America
10 9 8 7 6 5 4 3 2

The paper used in this publication meets the minimum requirements
of the American National Standard for Permanence of Paper for
Printed Library Materials Z39.48-1984.

For Lewis Atherton, James L. Bugg, Jr.,
Ruth and Harvey Carter, Elmer Ellis, and
Lloyd E. Worner, in appreciation,
and for Walter V. Scholes, in memoriam

CONTENTS

CONTENTS

FOREWORD

The aim of the American Presidency Series is to present historians and the general reading public with interesting, scholarly assessments of the various presidential administrations. These interpretive surveys are intended to cover the broad ground between biographies, specialized monographs, and journalistic accounts. As such, each will be a comprehensive, synthetic work which will draw upon the best in pertinent secondary literature, yet leave room for the author's own analysis and interpretation.

Volumes in the series will present the data essential to understanding the administration under consideration. Particularly, each book will treat the then current problems facing the United States and its people and how the president and his associates felt about, thought about, and worked to cope with these problems. Attention will be given to how the office developed and operated during the president's tenure. Equally important will be consideration of the vital relationships between the president, his staff, the executive officers, Congress, foreign representatives, the judiciary, state officials, the public, political parties, the press, and influential private citizens. The series will also be concerned with how this unique American institution—the presidency—was viewed by the presidents, and with what results.

All this will be set, insofar as possible, in the context not only of contemporary politics but also of economics, international relations, law, morals, public administration, religion, and thought. Such a broad approach is necessary to understanding, for a presidential administration is more than the elected and appointed officers composing it, since its work so often reflects the major problems, anxieties, and glories of the nation. In short, the authors in this series will strive to recount and evaluate the record of each administration and to identify its distinctiveness and relationships to the past, its own time, and the future.

The General Editors

PREFACE

According to Henry Adams, a perceptive observer of White House occupants, a president should resemble a captain of a ship at sea. "He must have a helm to grasp, a course to steer, a port to seek." Without headway, the ship would arrive nowhere, and perpetual calm was as detrimental to a president's purpose as a perpetual hurricane. He must also, said Adams, listen "with patience" and reply "with courtesy to the leading men of his party," but the president was the one who must steer the ship.[1]

A president who would steer the ship was not what prominent Whigs had in mind when they cast about for a candidate for the 1840 election. Conditions pointed to defeat for the Democratic incumbent, Martin Van Buren, and to ensure this outcome, the Whig party turned, not to its leader, the controversial Henry Clay, but to William Henry Harrison, who with adequate image building, could be portrayed as "the hero of the Battle of Tippecanoe," a military folk legend in the likeness of Andrew Jackson, who so successfully had been elevated by the Democrats to the presidency in 1828 and reelected in 1832. The Whigs, however, did not want their candidate, if elected, to be a strong, hard-headed Jackson-type chief executive. The Democratic general, they contended, had been guilty both of the gross usurpation of powers and of the misuse of the presidential office. Their opposition to his actions had brought about the formation of the conglomerate known as the Whig party.

To many of the party's members, the legislative branch was the body that should govern the nation. This point of view did not originate with them. Colonial experience had made many of the Founding Fathers wary of executive despotism, and the portion of the Constitution dealing with the executive branch was, as Edward S. Corwin has pointed out, "the most loosely drawn" in the entire document. "The executive power," the Constitution states, "shall be vested in a president of the United States of America," but executive power was not clearly defined. The president had the power to make treaties, by and with the advice and consent of the Senate, but his war powers were hazy, as was his responsibility in the conduct of foreign affairs. He could make certain appointments with the advice and consent of the Senate, and he was charged with taking "care that the laws be faithfully executed."[2]

During the Constitutional Convention, James Madison had offered the opinion that the president should be a "restraining hand on an impetuous Congress," and Gouverneur Morris had believed the president should act as "the general guardian of the national interest," but few guidelines had been established.[3] The powers of Congress, on the other hand, were specific and numerous. As president, Madison found he was unable to restrain a Congress that was resolved to exercise its rights. Henry Clay, in the House of Representatives, was more in charge than was the chief executive, and the administrations of Madison and James Monroe saw a decline in presidential leadership.

The decline came to an abrupt halt when Andrew Jackson became president. Accustomed to issuing orders and having them carried out, he tolerated no interference from either the legislative or the judicial branch, and "usurpation" became the rallying cry for the Whigs. So it was that Harrison, who was believed to be amiable and pliable, was nominated and elected. How Clay, the great champion of congressional supremacy, would have viewed the president's powers and prerogatives had he been the victorious Whig candidate in 1840 is a matter of conjecture. Grievously disappointed at having been rejected in favor of Harrison, Clay was determined to control the presidency from the Senate, but during Harrison's brief term in office, there were indications that while Harrison was willing to be reasonable, he did not propose to be Clay's puppet.

The real contest came when Harrison succumbed to pneumonia one month after his inauguration, the first president to die in office, and when Vice-President John Tyler, adhering to his own interpretation of the ambiguous constitutional provision on presidential succession, refused to be considered merely an acting president. Rather, by claiming the office and title, with all its rights and privileges, he established an important precedent. Stubborn, proud, independent, and quite possibly, ambitious, Tyler believed he should discharge the duties and powers of the presidency under the constitutional system of checks and balances. His tenacity in refusing to bow to the dictates of the Clay Whigs, as well as his use of the veto, resulted in a prolonged and bitter collision between the executive and the legislative branches, or, more explicitly, between Tyler and Clay, which rivaled and in some instances exceeded the conflicts during the Jackson administration. Tyler had no cause to fear a perpetual calm. Around him swirled a perpetual hurricane, and although the Clay Whigs expelled Tyler from the party, they failed to prostrate the presidency.

Whereas Clay sought to "head" the president, another eminent Whig, Secretary of State Daniel Webster, treated Tyler with respect, working harmoniously with him and acknowledging the significant part that Tyler played in the conduct of foreign affairs, an area in which the administration excelled. The Webster-Ashburton Treaty was crucial to the improvement of Anglo-American relations. The Treaty of Wanghia gave the United States most-favored-nation status in China and, along with the Tyler Doctrine, which extended the protection of the Monroe Doctrine to the Sandwich Islands, paved the way for the Open Door policy of the late nineteenth century. These and other agreements, plus the interest generated by the return of the Great United States Exploring Expedition in 1842, made the Tyler administration "Pacific-minded."

For a time, Webster and Tyler hoped to create a political middle position, attracting moderates from both parties, but when this failed and when Tyler's desire for election in 1844 led him to court Democratic support and turn to Texas annexation as a popular issue, Webster, who had long been pressured by the Whig party to do so, resigned from the cabinet. Tyler then became a prey for the extreme states' righters, many from his own state of Virginia, who, while attempting to manipulate him, treated him with disdain for what they regarded as his betrayal of their cause. Contrary to Tyler's wishes, the secretaries of state who succeeded Webster (Abel P. Upshur and John C. Calhoun) stressed the slavery and sectional aspects of Texas annexation, thus increasing tensions between the North and the South. Chastised by both Clay Whigs and extreme states' righters and eclipsed by the oratory and charisma of the great men of the period, the achievements of Tyler's presidency often have gone unnoticed.

To understand a presidential administration properly, it obviously must be placed against the background of its time—in this case, of a nation's expanding its boundaries and its international influence, of the greater involvement of the people in the affairs of state, of a country's being terribly in danger of splitting apart. This, too, was a period of numerous reform movements, of abolitionists' demands for freedom for the enslaved, of industrial developments and the ensuing problems of the laboring class, of the rapid unfolding of knowledge in science and technology, of the appearance of great works of literature, of materialism and humanitarianism, of exploration and discovery, of peoples of the North and the South, with different ways of life, who, at an alarming rate, were coming to distrust and dislike each other.

For many years of encouragement and friendship and for their exemplary devotion to teaching and scholarship, my deepest gratitude goes to the individuals named in the dedication. For unfailing assistance and innumerable courtesies during the preparation of this volume, I am indebted to the staffs of the Earl Gregg Swem Library of the College of William and Mary, the Virginia State Library, the Alderman Library of the University of Virginia, and the Manuscripts Division of the Library of Congress. To Jean Buchanan, an intelligent and skillful typist who managed to carry on with good-humored efficiency despite the distance between Colorado and Virginia, my sincere appreciation.

Alamosa, Colorado   *Norma Lois Peterson*

1

THE GROPINGS OF A
GROWING NATION

Hezekiah Niles, the publisher of the highly regarded *Niles' Register*, believed that in the United States there was an "almost universal ambition to get forward." This was a nation of opportunity, where a white man could improve his situation if he so desired, where half the wealthy men over forty-five years of age had started their lives in very humble circumstances.[1] Although blighted now and again by downward trends in the economy, this optimism prevailed during the 1830s and 1840s.

In the three decades prior to the Civil War, numerous European travelers, who came to observe and to criticize or praise what they saw, repeatedly marveled at the energy and spirit of the people. The enthusiasm with which the citizens built towns, cleared the land, and created new industries was impressive. Canals and roads connected regions, hitherto almost unreachable, with centers of commerce. Steamboats provided river and coastal transportation, but the railroads proved to be more rapid and reliable. By 1840, more than three thousand miles of track had been laid, mostly east of the Appalachians.

In twenty years the population had nearly doubled, from 9,638,000 in 1820 to 17,069,000 in 1840. As the population grew, so did the westward movement: into Texas, both before and after it had declared its independence from Mexico in 1836; into Iowa Territory and Wisconsin Territory; and in the early 1840s, at an increasing rate, into Oregon Territory, which was held jointly by the United States and Great Britain. By the mid 1840s, many Americans had become convinced that the nation had a mission to take possession of the entire continent, from the Atlantic to the Pacific. This was its "Manifest Destiny."

In the Northeast there was expansion of another kind—industrial expansion, particularly in the manufacture of cotton textiles. By 1840, cotton mills were employing more than a hundred thousand people, among them a high proportion of women recruited from rural areas of Vermont and New Hampshire. Skills that had been perfected in the creation of machinery for the cotton-textile factories were utilized in the development of other industries: the manufacture of shoes, woolen textiles, agricultural tools, and others.

In Ireland, the Germanies, and Great Britain, there were people who looked to the United States for a better life, or even for survival. Available land or a factory job could provide what they needed, and European immigration accelerated at an astonishing rate. Those who lacked the funds to buy land or move beyond the eastern seaboard settled in coastal cities, often causing resentment as they competed for employment with native-born laborers or those who had arrived earlier. This was especially true during periods of economic depression.

Competition from foreigners was not the only labor problem. Before the great influx of immigrants, harsh working conditions led to attempts to organize trade unions not only to promote better wages, shorter hours, and safer surroundings but also to state their concerns about a broad spectrum of reforms, ranging from public education and the abolition of imprisonment for debt to universal white manhood suffrage and the legal recognition of their unions. The panic of 1837 and the ensuing depression brought widespread unemployment and weakened the workingmen's movement. Hostility toward the more recent arrivals increased.

During the 1840s, the United States witnessed its first substantial outbreak of nativism. It had been simmering for a number of years, and it was directed against immigrants in general, but more pointedly against Catholic immigrants. "Natives" were admonished to combat the "foreign menace" and to "awaken the attention of the community to the dangers which threaten the liberties of these United States from the assaults of Romanism." Rumors circulated about plans for a papal takeover of the nation or of European countries' ridding themselves of their paupers and criminals by dumping them on American shores. Ministers appealed for funds to save the nation for Protestantism. Samuel F. B. Morse took time from perfecting his telegraph to rail against "papal puppets" and to urge the government to shut the gates against further immigration. Protestants must "unite against Catholic schools, Catholic officeholders, and especially against lenient immigrant laws. We must first stop this leak in the ship through which the muddy waters from without threaten to sink us." Congress was swamped with petitions calling for an increase—from the current five years to twenty-five years—in the residency requirements for naturalization.[2]

As anti-Catholic propaganda intensified, certain violent elements in the population were roused to action. During the spring and summer of 1844, mobs burned and pillaged Catholic churches. Few major cities escaped bloodshed and riots; but to their credit, many Americans found such persecution and prejudice repugnant, so they disassociated themselves from such actions. They condemned the church burnings, the inhumane treatment of foreigners, and the lawless activities of the mobs. For a time, nativism declined, but it was by no means dead.

There was a lack of consistency in American attitudes and thinking. During the same period in which Catholics were being harassed unmercifully, the attention of numerous people was focused on man's inhumanity to man and on the general disregard for individual rights. There was concern for the quality of life for blacks, whites, women, children, the mentally ill, and various victims of mistreatment. "In the history of the world," Ralph Waldo Emerson observed, "the doctrine of reform never had such scope as at the present hour."[3] Reformers, however, might condemn slavery and immigrants in the same breath; or they might crusade for the emancipation of blacks but oppose granting them equal rights or allowing them to remain in the United States after they had been freed.

Reform movements attracted a variety of people and developed out of an assortment of motives. Some movements stemmed in part from religious and moral crusades that were carried across vast stretches of the country by men such as Charles Grandison Finney or from more obscure philosophical ferment, such as that in Concord, Massachusetts, where Emerson and other members of the transcendentalist group discussed and wrote about the "spark of divinity" within every human being. Utopian societies—some of European origin but others American, or a mixture of both—were founded to provide mutual help and to serve as models for a new and better society. Some were very peculiar; others, more practical. While not agreeing on the importance or priority of issues, the reformers, in general, raised a number of questions: Was it right for blacks to be held in bondage? Why should laborers not be entitled to better working conditions and a decent living wage? Why should women be regarded as inferior, barred from higher education and the professions? How could the inhuman treatment of the impaired

3

and the mentally ill be justified? Why should equal opportunities not be extended to all, regardless of their status?

Antislavery societies sprang up throughout the North. Among the abolitionists there were arguments over whether the movement should be political or nonpolitical, violent or nonviolent; whether it should insist on no union with slaveholders and call for the secession of the Free States; and whether women's rights should be included in its crusade.

Some antislavery organizations were founded by women: Maria Weston Chapman headed the Boston Female Antislavery Society, and Lucretia Mott established a similar group in Philadelphia. Two South Carolinians, Sarah and Angelina Grimké of Charleston and Beaufort plantation, left their sheltered southern life to travel to Philadelphia to devote themselves to abolition and women's rights. They were the first American-born women to speak in public on these subjects. "We Abolition Women are turning the world upside down," Angelina Grimké announced in 1838.[4]

Theodore D. Weld, Lewis and Arthur Tappan, William Ellery Channing, Henry David Thoreau, Ralph Waldo Emerson, Theodore Parker, and dozens of others wrote, spoke, and acted against the enslavement of blacks; they also extended their efforts to other causes. Some joined Dorothea Dix in her appeal for improved treatment for the mentally ill and the physically handicapped. The rehabilitation of criminals was urged. Parker waged war against capital punishment. Orestes A. Brownson helped found the Workingmen's party and, after its collapse, continued to strive for better conditions for the laboring class. Many of these individuals continued their agitation for reform until the outbreak of the Civil War, but with attention increasingly being centered on the slavery issue.

As antislavery societies multiplied, so did the flood of abolitionist propaganda; this caused vigorous protests from southerners, reacting to what they considered threats to their safety and welfare. Fear of slave uprisings, fomented by the abolitionists' "incendiary materials," gripped several state legislatures. They attributed Nat Turner's insurrection of 1831 to William Lloyd Garrison's abolitionist publication the *Liberator*, the first issue of which appeared on 1 January 1831. Haunted by the thought of another Turner-type episode, the Virginia General Assembly prescribed severe punishment for advocates of abolition and ordered the burning of books, pamphlets, and newspapers that contained inflammatory antislavery doctrines. Harsh and repressive measures were passed by other state legislatures, some of which specified death for the propagators of such materials. There were demands for censorship of the mails.

Even more disturbing to the South were the petitions sent to Congress, urging emancipation of slaves in the District of Columbia. If such action were taken, southerners believed it could be an opening wedge for the emancipation of all slaves by an act of Congress. As petitions became more numerous and strident, southerners in the House and the Senate tried to prevent the petitions from being received or discussed. Many northerners, too, realized that debates on the sensitive topic could endanger the future of the Union.

In the spring of 1836, Henry L. Pinckney of South Carolina offered a resolution in the House of Representatives that "all petitions, memorials, resolutions, propositions, or papers relating in any way or to any extent whatever to the subject of slavery shall, without being printed or referred, be laid upon the table and that no further action whatever be taken thereon." This was the first "gag rule," which was repassed by the House at every session until January 1840, when, after bitter debate, Standing Rule 21 was adopted. Henceforth, until the rule was repealed in 1844, petitions dealing with slavery could not be received by the House or "entertained in any way whatever." John Quincy Adams led the fight for the constitutional right of petition, and abolitionist societies, realizing the enormous publicity advantages for their cause, increased the flow of such entreaties. In the year 1837/38, the American Anti-Slavery Society reported the presentation of more than four hundred thousand supplications to the House and more than three hundred thousand to the Senate for the abolition of slavery in the District of Columbia, against the annexation of Texas, for the repeal of the gag rule, and for the termination of interstate slave trading.[5]

Most of the Democrats and a majority of the National Republicans in Congress wanted to avoid the question of slavery if at all possible, fearful that debating it could lead to the disruption of their parties and could inflame the public. But Pandora's box was wide open, and the subject would not down. As westward migration increased, the touchy matter of slavery in the territories continued to create intense animosity. The Missouri Compromise of 1820, which restricted slavery in Louisiana Territory to the area south of latitude 36°30′, had angered the South. William F. Gordon, a member of the Virginia legislature, voiced the general reaction. Southerners were upset, he said, "not perhaps on account of the value of the territory or the disadvantage of the bargain so much as that it is against principle, & manifests what we consider is a spirit of injustice & want of faith in the Northern politicians, which if yielded to would lead only to farther & more daring & vital usurpations.''[6] With talk about the annexation of Texas and the expansion of the nation to the Pacific, there was uneasiness in both the North and the South about the consequences of a decision to add or not to add more slave territory or slave states to the Union.

Exacerbating the North/South problem was the matter of fugitive slaves. During the early 1840s, an ever-increasing number of slaves sought freedom by fleeing northward. Their recapture and return to bondage fired emotions in the North. The right of the protection or the retrieval of property was sacred to most Americans, but designating a human being as "rightful property" gave many people pause. There was uneasiness about the clause in the Constitution that said "No person held to service or labour in one State, under the laws thereof, escaping into another, shall, in consequence of any law or regulation therein, be discharged from such service or labour, but shall be delivered up on claim of the party to whom such service or labour may be due." According to the Constitution and the Fugitive Slave Law of 1793, the federal government had the authority and the responsibility to return runaway slaves to their rightful owners. This was upheld in the 1842 Supreme Court decision in the case of *Prigg* v. *Pennsylvania*, which disallowed state legislation that interfered with federal enforcement. But federal enforcement was ineffective, and the South demanded better protection for its property. In other respects, however, southerners wanted absolutely no federal intervention in regard to their "peculiar institution." The states'-rights philosophy was most pervasive in the South, but it was not necessarily confined to that region. From time to time, northern states also found the doctrine helpful.

In the country as a whole, there was little meeting of the minds about what kind of a nation the United States should be or how it should be governed. There were pronounced differences, many of which had originated during the early years of the Republic. During the presidency of George Washington these differences had led to the formation of the first two-party system. Secretary of the Treasury Alexander Hamilton was an ardent nationalist who believed a strong central government could curb the excesses of democracy. He favored a diversified economy, but he was convinced that the United States would reach its highest potential as a manufacturing nation. Industrialization was the wave of the future, and it should be supported by a protective tariff.

Also included in Hamilton's plan was a Bank of the United States. Patterned somewhat on the Bank of England, this institution was designed to act as a fiscal agent for the government. It would receive governmental deposits and would issue bank notes, payable on demand in gold and silver; and branch banks would be established in the states. Twenty percent of the bank stock would be owned by the government; the remainder would be sold to the investing public. Of the twenty-five bank directors, the government could appoint five. In a limited way it was a joint venture: the government would help the bank, and the bank would help the government. As stockholders, the rich men of the nation "would be bound more closely to the Federal government." Hamilton made it clear that the bank would be the instrument of the business interests.

Hamilton also had definite thoughts about the position of the chief executive in the governmental structure. These conceptions were unsettling to many who had experienced executive abuses during colonial times and who clung to the Lockean theory of legislative predominance. Hamilton dismissed such fears and was determined to make the executive branch, without question, the controlling force. A successful and efficient government, he argued, "must always naturally depend on the energy of the executive department," and to carry out his responsibilities effectively, the president must have plenary powers. To a large extent, Hamiltonian ideas formed the basis of the Federalist party.

President Washington's secretary of state, Thomas Jefferson, had a different outlook. He was committed to the idea of an agrarian nation with a frugal and simple central government. Although he moderated his views during his second presidential administration, and moreso after the War of 1812, to advocate an equilibrium of agriculture, manufactures, and commerce, he continued to believe agriculture was the great American interest, and he did not wish to see the nation rush into the Industrial Revolution. The quality of life was important, and to him, the best quality was obtainable by those who labored in the earth.

The Jeffersonian Republican party, which developed from this set of values, cherished the compact theory of government. The Republic, it held, was created by a compact among the states. The power of the central government was limited by the tenets of the Bill of Rights and, particularly, by the Tenth Amendment: "The powers not delegated to the United States by the Constitution, nor prohibited by it to the States, are reserved to the States respectively, or to the people."

While Hamilton and the Federalist party favored a broad interpretation of the Constitution, the Republicans were opposed to the idea of reading between the lines of that document in order to increase the power of the national government. Nowhere in the Constitution, they contended, was Congress specifically authorized to create a Bank of the United States. Hamilton, in retort, pointed to Article I, section 8, which gave Congress the right "to make all laws which shall be necessary and proper for carrying into execution" the specific powers and responsibilities assigned to the legislative branch.

Chief Justice John Marshall agreed with Hamilton's principle of broad construction, and many of Marshall's judicial opinions expanded the powers of the federal government. In 1819, in the case of *McCulloch v. Maryland*, he cited the "necessary and proper" clause to pronounce constitutional the second Bank of the United States, chartered in 1816 for a twenty-year period.[7]

Interestingly, as the power of the federal government increased, that of the presidency declined. The Supreme Court Justice Joseph Story observed in 1818: "The Executive has no longer a commanding influence. The House of Representatives has absorbed . . . all the effective power of the country." This condition had developed during the presidencies of James Madison and James Monroe, largely after the War of 1812, when the Federalist party faded away and its members merged with the Republicans. In the new organization the Federalists were successful in making their economic theories and their idea of a strong central government prevail. Times were changing, and to a number of Republicans, progress meant adherence to Hamiltonian ideas. States' righters and those known as Old Republicans, those who clung to their beliefs in agrarianism, were not happy. Even though the period, because of the existence of a single party, has been known as the Era of Good Feelings, good feelings were actually scarce between the opposing factions.

The Federalists failed, however, to sustain Hamilton's desire for a powerful executive. Instead, the Speaker of the House of Representatives, Henry Clay, a Kentuckian, gained the reputation of being the most powerful man in the government. His oratory, magnetism, and charm made him, and consequently Congress, the focal point. Clay informed John Quincy Adams, who was then the secretary of state, that President Monroe "has not the slightest influence on Congress." Henceforth there would not be a man in the United States who possessed less *personal* influence over Congress than the president. "I saw Mr. Clay's drift in these remarks," Adams confided to his diary, "which was to magnify his own importance and to propitiate me in favor of his outfit claim." Given his position, Clay liked the idea of a relatively weak president, but in other ways he leaned toward Hamiltonianism, strongly promoting what he called the American System, a vigorous nationalistic program that included a Bank of the United States, a tariff to promote American industry, and federally supported internal improvements. These would be the creations of Congress.

The practice of having the congressional caucus act as the official nominating body for presidential and vice-presidential candidates also contributed to the growth of legislative supremacy. During the one-party period, the caucus was able virtually to name the next incumbent. Additionally, congressional influence on the cabinet was strong. Members, who frequently were holdovers from the preceding administration, were more loyal to Congress than to the president, and they often undercut presidential policy by dealing unilaterally with the House and the Senate. In cabinet meetings, decisions were reached by majority opinion, the president having one vote; therefore, congressional wishes often took precedence. The chief executive bowed—sometimes gracefully, at other times protestingly—to the will of Congress.[8]

The Era of Good Feelings came to an end with the disputed election of 1824, when five candidates, all from the one party, vied for the presidency: Clay; John Quincy Adams of Massachusetts; William Harris Crawford of Georgia, Monroe's secretary of the treasury; Gen. Andrew Jackson of Tennessee, the colorful hero of the Battle of New Orleans; and John C. Calhoun of South Carolina, secretary of war in Monroe's cabinet, who was in the process of shifting his political philosophy. A nationalist and a supporter of the American System during his earlier career, Calhoun was dismayed by the South's declining position in the affairs of the nation and was soon to become an ardent opponent of Clay and a champion of the southern states'-rights cause.

Crawford, the politicians' candidate, received the blessings of the congressional caucus, but this method of selecting a nominee was becoming increasingly unpopular; so from state legislatures, mass meetings, and local conventions came the other nominations. Calhoun, who was disappointed at not having received the expected presidential endorsement from Pennsylvania, withdrew to seek the vice-presidency. Because of the multiplicity of candidates, no one contestant received a majority vote in the electoral college; therefore, it devolved on the House of Representatives, each state having one vote, to decide among the three candidates who had the largest number of votes: Jackson, Adams, and Crawford. Actually, the contest was between Jackson and Adams. Crawford, who had been incapacitated by a stroke in 1823, suffered a relapse in 1824. Jackson, the front runner in both popular and electoral votes, believed he was the rightful choice of the House, but Clay threw his support to Adams, and the New Englander emerged victorious. Calhoun was elected vice-president over Albert Gallatin, the caucus's nominee.

When Adams made Clay his secretary of state, cries of "corrupt bargain" were numerous and loud. Adams, it was charged, had traded the cabinet position for enough votes to make him chief executive. A bargain most corrupt and unholy had been consummated. Jackson was bitter: "Mr. Clay (*like Judas of old* it is said), *sold himself and his influence* to Mr. Adams, and collected his thirty pieces of silver."[9]

For all his vast experience, Adams was not adept at leadership, and when he tried to exercise his presidential prerogatives, he met with stern resistance from Congress. His four years in office were stormy. Clay, in the State Department, also felt the onslaught of the congressional power he had helped to create.

Out of the anger of the Jackson supporters, at what they conceived to be a miscarriage of the electoral process, grew the Jacksonian Democratic party. The first step toward its organization was taken on Christmas Day, 1826, at Ravensworth in the Virginia countryside, for it was there that Martin Van Buren, a New York member of the House of Representatives, and Calhoun agreed to form a North-South alliance in behalf of Andrew Jackson. There were others at the meeting who understood the ambitious natures of the New Yorker and the South Carolinian and suspected that each was paving the way for his own political future, each preening himself for the presidency, each willing to use Jackson to reach that goal, and each on guard against the other.

Van Buren was anxious for the reemergence of the two-party system: Adams, Clay, and the National Republicans, as they were now called—with their Hamiltonian principles—opposed by the Jacksonian Democrats, who followed the precepts of Jeffersonianism. The Jacksonians would appeal to those on the lower end of the economic scale who now were demanding a right to participate in the political process. Party differences, however, were not very sharply defined.[10]

In 1828 the Democratic party won an astonishing victory, trampling the National Republicans and elevating Jackson to the presidency. Calhoun was reelected to the vice-presidency, this time on the Democratic ticket. But even before the election, fissures had begun to appear in the Democratic ranks when the party's leadership in Congress concocted the Tariff of 1828 to lure to Jackson's side certain doubtful states—New York, Pennsylvania, Kentucky, and Missouri—by including protection for certain items that were important to their economies. Those states that felt plundered by this "Tariff of Abominations" protested loudly. Vice-President Calhoun expressed his distress to James Monroe: "It is always dangerous to see the country divided, as it is, by sections," especially when the measures that caused the division had originated "in the spirit of gain on one side, at the expense of the other." The tariff, he said, was impoverishing the South.[11] During the summer of 1828, Calhoun anonymously penned his *South Carolina*

Exposition and Protest, suggesting nullification as a way for the South to protect itself.

The 1828 campaign changed forever the mode of selecting a president. The electorate was undergoing a transformation. No longer would it be the monopoly of the "rich and well-born." Demands for white male suffrage were being met as a majority of the states moved toward the removal of property qualifications for voting. The exceptions were Rhode Island, Virginia, and Louisiana, but in the rest of the country, participation in elections increased appreciably. In 1824, 36.8 percent of those who were qualified to vote cast ballots; in 1828, the number rose to 57.6 percent. The campaign engendered interest and enthusiasm, particularly among the newly enfranchised. While some found the "Hurra Boys" distasteful—with their demagogic appeals to the "common man," their raucous songs, their banners, and their noisy demonstrations—others welcomed the spirit of the new democracy and the diminution of the role of the gentry. More state offices were becoming elective rather than appointive. In almost all the states, presidential electors were now being chosen by the people rather than by the state legislatures. Gradually, the printed ballot was replacing the voice vote. In the selection of presidential candidates, the congressional caucus was forced to give way to state and national conventions, with their own peculiar characteristics. Political rallies took on the look and feel of glorified picnics, with song, strong drink, and comradery. Above all, in 1828 there was a colorful candidate, Andrew Jackson, with whom the people could identify. By comparison, John Quincy Adams, who was running for reelection, had little appeal. He seemed remote and pallid.

"Of Andrew Jackson," John William Ward has observed, "the people made a mirror for themselves." The folk-hero president became the symbol of the self-made man who could rise from humble beginnings to the highest office in the land. Although the period is commonly referred to as the Age of Jackson, Ward has pointed out that "the symbol was the creation of the times. . . . The age was not his. He was the age's."[12] The political success of the "hero-candidate" was duly noted by the opposition. His presidency was exciting, and newspapers, ever growing in number, capitalized and fed on the public's appetite for information from Washington.

The popular appeal of the Democratic president did not guarantee peace and harmony within the administration. Jackson and Calhoun, both strong-minded individuals, soon clashed over a number of issues. Also, Jackson was persuaded that Calhoun was plotting the disruption of the Union, hence the famous exchange of toasts during Jefferson's birthday dinner in 1830. "Our Federal Union, it must and shall be preserved," thundered the president. "The Union, next to our liberty, most dear," retorted the vice-president. "May we always remember that it can be preserved only by distributing equally the benefits and burthens of the Union."

The Tariff of 1832 did not meet Calhoun's requirements of equal "benefits and burthens." Although in some ways it was more moderate than the Tariff of 1828, that of 1832 still contained the protection principle; so South Carolina moved to declare both tariffs—1828 and 1832—null and void within its boundaries. By now it was widely known that Calhoun was the author of the *South Carolina Exposition and Protest*, which advocated the doctrine of nullification now activated by Calhoun's own state. To Jackson this was proof of Calhoun's desire to dissolve the Union. The tariff was not the issue in the nullification controversy, the president declared; nor was slavery. Disunion and the formation of a southern confederacy were the goals of the nullifiers. Regardless, Jackson wisely postponed his reply to South Carolina's declaration until after the 1832 election. This time, Van Buren, not Calhoun, was Jackson's running mate.[13]

Along with the nullification controversy, Jackson was faced with a struggle over the Bank of the United States. Henry Clay, after serving as secretary of state in John Quincy Adams's cabinet, had returned to his Kentucky plantation, Ashland, until, in 1831, he was elected to the United States Senate. He arrived in Washington in December, primed to do battle with Jackson and, he hoped, to replace him in the White House in 1833. In mid December, 1831, Clay was nominated without opposition by the National Republican convention, which met in Baltimore, Maryland.

In the Senate, Clay defended a protective tariff and introduced a bill to distribute the proceeds of the sale of public lands among the states. Of chief concern, however, was the Bank of the United States. Although the Bank had provided economic stability by the establishment of a sound and uniform currency, its opponents considered it a money monopoly, operated by a few financiers who were immune from either governmental or popular control. Jackson was hostile toward "the monster," believing it had used its influence against him in the 1828 election. But this was not the only reason: he disliked banks of any kind.

The bank's charter was due to expire in 1836, and Clay and Nicholas Biddle, the bank's president, worried about the institution's future. They wondered if it would not be advisable to push for a new charter in 1832, four years before the old one was due to expire. Clay was eager for a controversial issue that would be troublesome to Jackson, and the bank was, indeed, controversial. The Democratic party was not of one mind about the bank, and Clay was certain Jackson would lose votes if he either signed a recharter bill or vetoed it. Urged on by Clay, Biddle agreed to make recharter an issue in the presidential campaign. Daniel Webster, the illustrious and influential senator from Massachusetts, was in agreement; so the bill was pushed through Congress. Among the National Republicans there was confidence that Jackson would not veto recharter during an election year. But reject it he did, and he turned his veto message into a brilliant campaign document, a ringing appeal to the people. He played on class and sectional prejudices, pitting the poor against the wealthy, insisting that the bank was an instrument of the "elite East." If the bank were allowed to continue, it would "make the rich richer and the potent more powerful."[14]

Instead of causing trouble for Jackson, the bank issue contributed to Clay's disastrous defeat. Jackson swept the electoral college, 219 to 49, winning the electoral votes of sixteen of the twenty-four states. With the exception of South Carolina, Jackson did well in most of the South, a result that would not have occurred had he issued his proclamation against nullification before the election. A new political organization, the Anti-Masonic party, which was also anti-Jackson, siphoned some support away from Clay; but the outcome undoubtedly would have been the same without the existence of a third party.

The election over, Jackson turned his attention to South Carolina's nullification ordinance, and in December he issued his proclamation against nullification, secession, and state sovereignty. Many southerners who held no brief for nullification were staggered by what they interpreted as the president's total disrespect for cherished states' rights and his apparent advocacy of a strong national government, controlled by a majority with no concern for minority rights.

There was greater consternation when, in a January 1833 message to Congress, Jackson requested the authority to resort to military force, if necessary, to prevent South Carolina from obstructing the execution of the Tariff Act of 1832 or from attempting to carry out its threat to withdraw from the Union if nullification were not allowed. With the adoption of the Compromise Tariff of 1833, the crisis passed, but serious cracks in the structure of the Democratic party remained. The "Force Bill" was a source of bitter discord.

The discord increased when Jackson took up the issue of the Bank of the United States. Not satisfied with merely vetoing its recharter, Jackson was determined to kill the "monster." It had tried to kill him, he said; now he vowed, "I will kill it!"[15] Therefore, in 1833, against the express desire of Congress to allow governmental deposits to remain in the bank until the charter had expired, Jackson made the surprising announcement that public funds no longer would be deposited in the bank. Shortly thereafter he ordered the transfer of governmental deposits from the Bank of the United States to designated state banks, which became known as "pet banks."

The president had to remove two secretaries of the treasury and appoint a third, Roger B. Taney, before he could find one who would do his bidding. Even to a number of Democrats who had opposed the bank's recharter, the removal of the deposits was a shocking act. Economic chaos was a real possibility, but what disturbed many was the creation of a precedent that gave to the chief executive absolute control over the currency and the capacity to utilize that control to influence elections. This was a frightening prospect. Victory in an election, they said, even as decisive a victory as Jackson had just achieved, did not give a president a mandate to do anything he wished, to act unilaterally, ignoring constitutional provisions for checks and balances.

In December 1833, Clay called upon the Senate to censure Jackson for "open, palpable, and daring usurpation" and misuse of the presidential office. The president, Clay charged, had assumed power and authority not conferred upon him by the Constitution or by statutes; instead, he had acted in derogation of both. The nation, Clay continued, did not want an "elective monarch" who abused the right of veto, made arbitrary appointments, treated the Supreme Court with contempt, and assumed absolute control over governmental funds. The secretary of the treasury should be responsible to Congress; he should not be the tool of the president.

The censure resolution passed, 26 to 20. Voting with the majority were Webster, Calhoun, and John Tyler. Clay rejoiced in the curbing of "executive usurpation," but the victory was short-lived. Loyal Jackson Democrats, who had been either elected or reelected to Congress in 1834, pledged to reverse the censure. Two years later the resolution was expunged from the *Senate Journal* in what was considered by some to be the final blow to congressional supremacy, but the struggle against presidential usurpation continued, and for Clay it became an obsession.[16]

Before Jackson left office, the nation was on the verge of an economic upheaval, because of the irresponsibility of state banks, the overextension of bank notes and credit, and wild speculation. The Bank of the United States also contributed to financial disruption. When Jackson ordered the withdrawal of governmental funds, Biddle struck back, curtailing loans throughout the entire banking system in an attempt to force Jackson to return the deposits. Many members of

Jackson's party urged him to do so. There were near-riots in many cities, but Jackson stood fast.

After the expiration of the bank's charter in the summer of 1836, the Democratic leadership in Congress took steps to formalize, after a fashion, the "pet bank" idea by sponsoring a Deposit/Distribution bill requiring the secretary of the treasury to designate at least one bank in each state as a receiver of governmental deposits. These banks were to perform services for the federal government that the Bank of the United States formerly provided. The legislators, however, elaborated on Jackson's earlier action. A limit was placed on the amount of national funds to be deposited in each bank. This limitation made the creation of additional deposit banks necessary. The number increased from twenty to ninety, making it virtually impossible for the Treasury Department to supervise the soundness of their operations. The distribution section of the bill specified that revenues held by the federal government in excess of $5 million should be distributed among the states in four installments. Jackson did not like the bill, but in many states, distribution was popular. Vetoing the bill could be detrimental to Van Buren's election, and Jackson dearly wanted to be succeeded by his vice-president.

In the West, land sales were out of control. Speculators borrowed money to purchase land, priced it above its actual value, and sold it to eager buyers, who borrowed money from the banks to pay for the property. Bank notes were the medium for the transactions, and they were lent with little or no collateral. The nation was engulfed in worthless paper money; inflation was rampant.

In an effort to stop the disastrous economic spiral, Jackson, in the summer of 1836, issued the Specie Circular, which specified that only actual settlers could purchase public land with bank notes, and the amount of land they could buy in this manner was limited to 320 acres. From speculators, hard money would be required. This caused a run on specie, so there was not enough available to meet the demand. Supplies in state banks were quickly depleted. Gold and silver that had not been hoarded by easterners was drained to the West. Businesses suffered; confidence in banks was weaker than ever. The nation's economy was headed toward disaster.

Out of the turmoil of Jackson's second administration the Whig party emerged. It was a strange political cluster. At its center was the former National Republican party, composed of northerners and southerners who, to varying degrees, supported Clay's American System. They were joined by defectors from the Democratic party: southern states' righters, who earlier had thought Jackson was one of their own and had promoted his election but who now were upset by his response to South Carolina's nullification ordinance; other states' righters who did not approve of nullification but who found the "Force Bill" disconcerting; Democrats who favored the Bank of the United States and were in disagreement with Jackson's veto; those who did not want the Bank rechartered but deplored the withdrawal of governmental funds; those who blamed Jackson for the country's financial troubles or opposed him for a combination of reasons. What they all had in common was a deep antipathy toward the president's usurpation of power.

The *National Intelligencer*, which was fast becoming the primary Whig organ, pointed to the Specie Circular "as a measure of the same arbitrary character as the removal of the public deposits in 1833, emanating from the imperious will of an irresponsible Magistrate." The Specie Circular would, said the paper, "produce a derangement of all the business of the country."[17]

2

"THIS DISCORDANT COMBINATION"

In 1836, the Whigs, facing their first presidential election as a party and uneasy about uniting their various factions, decided against following the recent vogue of holding a national convention. Instead, nominations were made at state legislative caucuses, state conventions, or local meetings. From these bodies, three prime contenders for the presidential nomination emerged: Daniel Webster, who was nominated by the Massachusetts legislature; Hugh Lawson White, one of Jackson's disillusioned former friends and supporters, who was named by a Tennessee anti-Jackson caucus; and William Henry Harrison of Ohio, who was designated by a Whig state convention in Pennsylvania. The Whig strategy was to force the election into the House of Representatives, where, they believed, there would be a better chance of defeating Jackson's hand-picked successor, Martin Van Buren. Thomas Ritchie, the Democratic editor of the *Richmond* (Va.) *Enquirer,* ridiculed the Whig conglomerate: "The Whigs have materials enough to choose from; but the misfortune is that they have also too many persons to please. They have 'too many cooks'—and their broth may be spoiled."[1]

Of the three Whig candidates, Harrison appeared to have the most popular appeal. With a stretch of the imagination, some saw him as a sort of second Jackson, a military man with western experience who possibly could be made to fit the hero-candidate concept, but hopefully he would lack Jackson's "dictatorial" proclivities.

John Quincy Adams, often a harsh critic, earlier had characterized Harrison as a person whose "thirst for lucrative office is absolutely rabid'' and who did not care under whose banner he enlisted to obtain a nomination or a governmental sinecure. Even Adams, however, had to admit that Harrison came from good stock. Born in 1773 in the Virginia tidewater, where his forebears had settled in the seventeenth century, he was the son of Benjamin Harrison, who was an active participant in both the First and the Second Continental Congress, a signer of the Declaration of Independence, and a governor of Virginia.[2] Young William Harrison grew up on the family plantation, Berkeley Hundred, in Charles City County. For a short period he attended Hampden-Sydney College and later studied medicine in Richmond and Philadelphia, but his father's sudden death and his growing dislike for the medical profession caused William to abandon it for a military career.

Assigned to the old Northwest Territory, he saw action against the Indians. In 1798 he resigned from the army, and after filling several posts in the territorial government, he became, in 1800, governor of Indiana Territory, an office he held for the next twelve years. As governor he was ex-officio superintendent of Indian affairs for the territory, a frustrating task. According to his official orders, he was to gain the trust of the Indians, see that they were treated fairly by the settlers, and obtain as much land from them as possible. He often was upset by disregard for Indian rights, yet he negotiated treaties that gained millions of acres for the government. As white settlers pressed into the region, an Indian confederation under the leadership of the Shawnee chief Tecumseh and his brother Tenskwatawa, the Shawnee Prophet, was determined to stop the encroachment. In 1811 Harrison led a force against a Shawnee settlement near Tippecanoe Creek, thus giving political merchandizers, years later, the opportunity to present Harrison to the electorate as the Hero of Tippecanoe.

Also because of the Tippecanoe episode, Harrison attracted the attention of Henry Clay, who was serving his first term in the House of Representatives. There Clay was leader of the ''war hawks'' and was the champion of territorial expansion and national honor. Clay became Harrison's most influential friend and sponsor, and with the outbreak of the War of 1812, Clay obtained for Harrison a commission as brigadier general in the Regular Army and, eventually, full command of the Army of the Northwest.

When the war ended, Harrison returned to his farm, North Bend, near Cincinnati, Ohio, where he had difficulty making an adequate living for his large family. To supplement his income, he sought political office and served one term in the House of Representatives and one in the Ohio legislature. In 1825 he became a United States senator, a position that he held until 1828, when, again through the intercession of

Clay, President Adams reluctantly appointed Harrison as minister to Colombia. Harrison, Adams observed, "has withal a faculty of making friends, and is incessantly importuning them for their influence in his favor."[3] In this instance, Clay's favor was not altogether altruistic. Harrison had tried to convince the National Republicans to adopt an Adams-Harrison ticket for the 1828 election. Clay, with ambitious political plans of his own, thought it better to have Harrison sent out of the country.

After Jackson had defeated Adams, Harrison made friendly gestures to the new administration, but when no appointment materialized, he became disenchanted with the Democrats. During the Jackson years, Harrison's financial burdens increased, and when his name was suggested as a presidential candidate in 1836, he held a modest position as clerk of the Cincinnati Court of Common Pleas.

In 1836 the Whig vice-presidential candidates were selected in the same fashion as the presidential ones, resulting in the emergence of two names: Francis Granger, a former Anti-Mason from New York, and John Tyler. Clay, although he was favorably disposed toward Tyler, felt it more expedient to court the Anti-Masonic segment, so he backed Granger.

In background, Harrison and Tyler had much in common.[4] Like Harrison, Tyler had been born (1790) in Charles City County, Virginia, into a family that traced its American lineage to the mid-seventeenth century and whose members were prominent in the governance of the Virginia colony. After distinguishing himself during the American Revolution, Tyler's father had become a judge of the High Court of Admiralty and the governor of Virginia.

John Tyler was educated at the College of William and Mary; he read law and then entered Virginia politics. At the age of twenty-one he was elected to the Virginia legislature; six years later he represented his district in the House of Representatives; and by 1825 he was governor of Virginia. Then followed nine years in the United States Senate (1827–36), where he made his mark by taking a strong stand against what he construed as Jackson's unconstitutional measures. He approved of Jackson's veto of the Maysville Road bill and the president's decision to oppose the recharter of the Bank of the United States, but he vigorously contested the removal of governmental deposits.

Although Adams referred to Tyler as a "Virginia nullifier," this was incorrect. Tyler did not join Calhoun in advocating nullification as a remedy for counteracting the overcentralization of the government or to ensure the South's influence in national affairs. Rather, Tyler agreed with his fellow senator from Virginia, Littleton Waller Tazewell, that there was no legal or constitutional way of refusing to obey a duly authorized law that had been passed by Congress and signed by the president. If a state found an act of Congress unbearable, it could protest and call upon other states to join in the protest. If this brought no results, the state had the option of seceding. While frightening in its consequences, secession was constitutional; nullification was not.[5]

In 1832, when South Carolina nullified the tariff acts of 1828 and 1832, Tyler believed the state had cause for complaint, but he did not approve of its ordinance. He also did not think that Jackson was justified in calling for the right to use military action to coerce South Carolina into compliance. Because other southern senators who were opposed to the "Force Bill" withdrew from the chamber when their request for postponement of the measure was refused, Tyler's was the only vote cast against the bill. His speech on this occasion was one of the ablest of his career: "I disclaim the policy adopted by her [South Carolina]; all here know that I did not approve her course. [But] I will not join in the denunciations which have been so loudly thundered against her, nor will I deny that she has much cause of complaint."[6]

Tyler and Clay were on opposite sides in regard to the "Force Bill," but they worked together to promote a compromise tariff that served to defuse a dangerous situation. Regardless of their differences on many issues, Tyler's admiration for the Kentuckian was of long standing. Clay, in turn, did all he could to assure Tyler's reelection to the Senate in 1833, largely because of the Virginian's unhappiness with Jackson and his approval of the Clay-sponsored Senate censure of the president for removal of the deposits. This made Tyler, by the spring of 1834, a hesitant states'-rights member of the newly formed Whig party. In 1836 Tyler resigned from the Senate rather than to comply with the Virginia legislature's instructions to vote for the removal of the censure against Jackson.

Yet, Tyler was an outspoken opponent of Clay's American System. His views were well known, and for this reason, many states'-rights Whig southerners regarded him as an acceptable choice for the vice-presidential nomination in 1836. Tyler was endorsed by Maryland, North Carolina, and Georgia, usually in tandem with the first-place runner, Hugh Lawson White. Virginia's states'-rights Whigs also nominated a White-Tyler ticket, but western Virginians preferred a Harrison-Tyler combination. Initially, the Ohio Whig convention leaned toward a Harrison-Tyler ticket, but with the help of Clay, the Anti-Masonic faction was able to replace Tyler with Francis Granger.

To the Jacksonians, the results of the election were surprising. The total popular vote for all three Whig presidential candidates was

736,147, compared to 764,198 for Van Buren. The electoral vote was fairly close: Van Buren, 170; the Whigs, 124. Horace Greeley, a promising young journalist from New York, was sure that the 1836 election was indicative of an overwhelming triumph for the Whigs in 1840. Henry Clay believed this, too, but Daniel Webster, a United States senator from Massachusetts, was more skeptical. Clay and Webster were veterans of many political battles, and both were eager to win the presidential prize. Clay, however, seemed to have the advantage. "The only opposition man who has the slightest chance for the next presidency is Mr. Clay," William Campbell Preston, a United States senator from South Carolina, said to Willie P. Mangum, who was soon to be a United States senator from North Carolina for a second time: "Webster and Harrison are both in his way."[7]

With victory in the air, a group of ambitious and pragmatic younger men were anxious to gain control of the party. Some were former Anti-Masons who had affiliated with that strange organization largely to make themselves known in politics. Their interest was in winning, rather than in advancing a specific program. Coming from key states, they were endowed, at times, with prestige beyond their experience. William H. Seward, who had become governor of New York in 1838, and Thurlow Weed, editor of the *Albany* (N.Y.) *Evening Journal*, were among this group. They were willing to challenge Clay's control of the party, especially his claim to the 1840 nomination. Seward hailed Harrison as the 1840 "candidate by continuation." The impetus that Harrison had gained in 1836 should, Seward contended, carry him victoriously through the next contest. With the right managers, Harrison could be molded into an invincible candidate.[8]

A few weeks after Van Buren's inauguration, the nation's financial structure collapsed. Signs of impending disaster had increased during the last months of Jackson's administration. In March and April 1837, portents had multiplied, and in early May, Philip Hone, a wealthy New York businessman, had noted in his diary that the number of bank failures, largely because of the pressure to exchange paper currency for specie, was so great that he could not keep a record of them. A short time later, banks in most major cities suspended payments in specie. Businesses closed. There were countless bankruptcies. Every level of society felt the impact of the depression. Thousands were unemployed. The number of beggars on city streets rose to alarming proportions.

Horace Greeley of the *New York Tribune* warned the jobless in other cities not to flock to New York, because no work was to be had there. Instead there were riots, protesting high rents and inflated prices for food and fuel; and not knowing where to turn to feed their families, large bodies of men, in desperation, had broken into the city's flour warehouses. Greeley urged the unemployed to leave the city and "go to the Great West." Anything was better than remaining where there was no hope for the future. As the situation became more unbearable, there were fears that a "civic volcano" would explode if relief were not forthcoming. Local communities attempted to provide some assistance, but the depression was more widespread and of greater intensity than anyone had experienced, and programs were inadequate and poorly planned.[9]

In Washington, Van Buren was inundated with advice: rescind the Specie Circular; create an Independent Treasury, where governmental funds would be kept in governmental custody, free from any connection with banks; suspend the distribution of revenue to the states. Clay, of course, recommended the creation of another Bank of the United States, to rescue the nation from complete economic ruin and to restore popular confidence in the government and financial institutions; but this was the last thing Van Buren wanted to do.

In an effort to find some alternative, the president called a special session of Congress. In his message to the session he warned that "again to create a national bank as a fiscal agent would be to disregard the popular will, twice solemnly and unequivocally expressed" (in the elections of 1832 and 1836). The sentiments of a large majority of the people could not be ignored. Depositing governmental moneys in state banks had also created problems. Therefore, Van Buren recommended the creation of an Independent Treasury, a "system most consistent with the Constitution and most conducive to the public welfare." Additionally, he asked for a suspension of the fourth distribution installment to the states, of the issuance of treasury notes to provide for the operation of the government, and for a limited bankruptcy bill.

Van Buren also reminded Congress that there was no way in which direct federal relief could be provided to ease the situations of those who were suffering from the depression. "Such measures are not within the constitutional province of the General Government," and even if they were, their adoption would not promote the real and permanent welfare of those whom they might be designed to aid.[10]

Voicing Whig opposition to an Independent Treasury, Webster argued that the government had a greater obligation to society than merely to take care of its own revenue. It had a duty to provide a sound currency and to stabilize the economy. Divorcing the United States Treasury from these obligations would be disastrous. The people would be left to shift for themselves, abandoned by their government which, under the Constitution, was supposed to provide for their general welfare.

Calhoun, now a United States senator from South Carolina, on the other hand, eventually supported the Independent Treasury measure, made his peace with Van Buren, and again joined forces with the Democratic party. His association with the Whig party had been tentative at best. A number of Democrats, however, preferred to retain the services of the state banks. Arguments were sharp and unpleasant, and the special session failed to adopt the Independent Treasury plan, and it did not pass a bankruptcy bill. The issuance of treasury notes was authorized, and distribution was stopped. As Silas Wright, a leading Democratic senator from New York, observed, the government would have to borrow several million dollars to distribute a "surplus" that no longer existed. This would be ridiculous.[11]

In the spring of 1838, the Specie Circular was withdrawn, and many banks resumed payments in specie. There was a short period of slight recovery, followed by a more devastating panic in 1839, which was occasioned, as Philip Hone believed, "by a premature resumption of specie payments. . . . The blossoms of hope which had sprung up in the brief sunshine of confidence are again blighted by the frosts of suspicion." Prices that were charged for the necessities of life were higher than ever. "How the poor man manages to get a dinner for his family passes my comprehension."[12]

In October 1839, more than eight hundred banks again suspended specie payments, and while bank failures were less numerous than in 1837, the depression was more severe. In the summer of 1840 the Independent Treasury bill finally was adopted, but by then the Van Buren administration had run its course, and the more than three years of bitter congressional debate over the issue had further weakened the Democratic party.

The economic catastrophe was not Van Buren's only source of trouble. He was burdened with a variety of complications in foreign affairs. In January 1838, Secretary of the Treasury Levi Woodbury had lamented to Richard Rush, one of his predecessors in the Treasury Department who was then in England, "We are in the midst of a Florida war [the second Seminole War, 1835–42], a quasi Mexican war—& almost a Canadian war. Besides these, we have our domestic difficulties as to the currency—the keeping of public money—and numerous less exciting topics."[13]

The second Seminole War resulted from Jackson's policy of removing Indians from areas that white inhabitants desired and sending them to the West, a policy that the Florida Indians fiercely opposed. Uneasy relations with Mexico were caused by agitation for the annexation of Texas by the United States, which surfaced periodically. Trouble with Great Britain and Canada had been fomented when Americans had crossed the northern border to aid an insurgent movement aimed at overthrowing British rule. Stemming from this was another diplomatic complication, which had developed when an American steamboat, the *Caroline*, transporting supplies for the rebels, had been boarded and set afire by Canadian militia on the United States side of the Niagara River, killing one American. A greater threat to Anglo-American relations arose from the unsettled boundary between Maine and New Brunswick. This led to the "Aroostook War" and to charges by Maine that Van Buren was not supporting the cause of its citizens.

The president's low-key attempts to deal with these difficulties seemed pale in contrast to Jackson's bombastic outbursts in similar situations. Instead of sword rattling, Van Buren tried to be judicious and diplomatic; this led to accusations of his timidity and lack of aggressiveness in foreign affairs. The spirit of expansion was strong in the land, and Van Buren's desire for peaceful relations with all nations seemed too mild to those who were impatient to push to the Pacific, to push to the Rio Grande and beyond, and to acquire as much territory as possible in both the Northeast and the Northwest.

Capitalizing on Van Buren's troubles, especially the financial crisis, which held center stage, the Whigs busily made plans for the election. Victory appeared more certain with every passing day, but the question as to who was to have the honor of becoming the first Whig president remained unanswered. A Whig congressional caucus finally decided that this time, a national convention would name the party's standard bearer. The choices seemed to be Clay, Harrison, and Webster.

Clay was optimistic about his chances. "Our cause everywhere is making sure and certain progress," he informed Mangum; "my *particular* cause could hardly be improved."[14] Certainly, the Whigs would turn to him, the obvious leader of the party; but Thurlow Weed and others thought Clay had too many liabilities. He had been exceedingly harsh in his defense of the Bank of the United States, a cause that was not considered popular with a large segment of the population. Moreover, Clay had disastrously lost the 1832 election as the National Republican candidate. His ownership of slaves had repelled northern abolitionists. Warnings were voiced about being "stuck in the Clay." On the other hand, Harrison's showing in 1836 had been quite satisfactory, he was not strongly for or against any divisive issue, and better yet, he was a former general who might even be portrayed as a hero.

When the legislatures of Kentucky, Rhode Island, and Maryland expressed a preference for Clay, the Kentuckian saw "an irresistible current" in his favor; but even his sincere supporters were not sure he could win. "Mr. Clay, of course, is preferred by us all," William Alexander Graham, another North Carolina Whig, informed Mangum, but possibly "for the sake of success" the general should be nominated.[15]

In the North, Clay did not receive enthusiastic endorsements. Weed and Seward went so far as to advise Clay to withdraw from the race, but Clay desperately wanted to be the party's candidate in this year of almost guaranteed victory. Hoping to attract a larger following, he moderated, at least in public, his views on the bank and the protective tariff. Tyler was delighted. "When we have differed," he told Clay, "it has been more in construing the Constitution than on fundamental principles." Tyler felt "great solicitude" for Clay's nomination and was sorry that Clay faced party opposition in the North, but this could be surmounted. Tyler was positive that Clay would occupy the White House in 1841.[16]

When Webster realized that there was little likelihood he would be nominated, he made known his preference for Harrison. "My opinion at present is, that our only chance is with General Harrison, and that that is not a very good one," Webster said in March 1839.[17] The following May he wrote a letter, to be released later, withdrawing his own name from consideration by the convention; and then he departed for England.

When the Whig convention met in Harrisburg, Pennsylvania, in December 1839, Harrisonians were there in force. Thurlow Weed, determined to prevent Clay's nomination, arrived with a bevy of delegates for Winfield Scott. Scott, a career military man who recently had been involved in the Indian-removal program and in attempting to avert war with Canada and Britain along the Maine boundary, was an "available candidate." Weed planned to present Scott as an alternative choice, if Harrison failed to kindle enough enthusiasm. In the minds of those who had witnessed Jackson's success, a general could win in a well-staged campaign—if not Harrison, then Scott.

Clay had a plurality of delegate votes, but the Weed-Seward forces cleverly manipulated the adoption of a plan resembling the later unit rule. Instead of allowing each delegate to express his individual preference, a state's entire vote would go to the candidate whom a majority of that state's delegates preferred. In this manner, Clay's advantage was destroyed, and Harrison won the nomination. It had been difficult for Clay to accept the fact that he should not be the Whig candidate in 1836, so soon after his 1832 defeat. However, all through the Van Buren years in the White House, Clay had prepared for the 1840 election. This time, he was certain he would not be passed over; and when he was, he was very angry and bitter. Yet, he urged his followers to work for Harrison, who gratefully thanked Clay for his magnanimity, and Weed pronounced Clay "a truly noble fellow."[18] Such words did nothing to lessen Clay's resentment at having again been rejected by his party. This was deep and lasting, and during the next four years it influenced many of his actions.

As in most political conventions, the selection of the vice-presidential candidate was perfunctory. Not until Tyler became president and clashed head-on with Clay and other nationally minded Whigs did his detractors question how the delegates, if in full possession of their senses, could have chosen John Tyler. There were efforts to explain this "incomprehensible mistake." Some said that Clay earlier had offered Tyler a Clay-Tyler ticket if he would withdraw from the Senate race against William C. Rives, which had deadlocked the Virginia legislature for almost a year. Rives was a member of a group known as the Conservative Democrats—mavericks from the Van Buren wing of the party—and Clay was anxious to lure Rives and as many of his kind as possible into the Whig ranks. Therefore, so the explanation goes, when Clay's bid for nomination failed, the convention named Tyler to the second spot to placate the Clayites. This account is improbable. Tyler had not withdrawn from the Senate race, and it is doubtful that having been denied the presidential nomination, Clay cared a whit about who would become the vice-presidential candidate. Others said Tyler was nominated by default, after Benjamin Watkins Leigh of Virginia, Willie P. Mangum of North Carolina, and several others had refused. According to Weed, "Tyler was finally taken because we could get nobody else to accept." These remarks, it must be remembered, were made many months later, after Tyler had been expelled from the Whig party.[19]

Oliver P. Chitwood, one of Tyler's biographers, believes geographical balance was the main concern in the selection, pointing out that the general committee of the convention unanimously had agreed to select a vice-presidential nominee from the North if Clay were the presidential candidate, or, if the nod went to Harrison, a man from the South would be named. When the convention decided on Harrison, Tyler became the logical choice. He was well known, especially since the 1836 election; he appealed to the states'-rights segment of the party; and he was an admirer of Clay. Also, Virginia was the most populous state in the South, and although Virginia had gone for Van Buren in 1836, the Whigs hoped to capture its electoral votes in 1840. There was some uneasiness, too, about talk of Harrison's possible abolition tendencies, which led John C. Calhoun to wonder how Harrison would be received in the South. Therefore, it was politic for the Whigs to place Tyler, a slave owner, on their ticket.[20] On the whole, however, the vice-presidential selection was not considered of great importance. No president had failed to complete the term for which he had been elected.

The Whigs did not try to formulate a platform, concluding that attempting such an impossible task would only serve to tear the party apart before the campaign. Up to now, it had not been unusual for a party to omit a statement of its policies, but the Democrats, nominating Van Buren for a second term, did have a platform that firmly stated their opposition to the American System, to any interference in the domestic institutions of the several states, and to abolitionists' efforts to induce Congress to take action against slavery, thus endangering the stability and permanency of the Union.

Within both the Whig and the Democratic parties there were strongly held feelings for and against the abolitionists and their tactics. Among themselves, the opponents of slavery could not agree whether or not political action would harm their cause. Some believed that politicians would only compromise the issue. Others saw political pressure as the only resort and tended to associate with the northern Whigs. When there was no sign of the Whig party's official approval of their crusade, some turned to the formation of a party of their own. In 1840 the Liberty party named James G. Birney to head its ticket.

Launching into the campaign, the Democrats railed against the American System; the Whigs blamed the Democrats for the depression and accused them of promoting excessive executive power; the Liberty party's one issue was antislavery. Late in December 1839, Webster returned to the United States and began to campaign for Harrison. After a period of delay, Clay, notwithstanding his painful political wounds, finally began to stump for Harrison and Tyler. "Never," announced the *National Intelligencer,* "has the Whig party been so united." There was an appearance of harmony. Clay, Webster, and Harrison promised to restore prosperity and to regulate the currency, but they offered no specifics as to how these were to be accomplished. Differences among Whigs, said Webster, were not proper topics for discussion.[21]

Clay could not refrain from mentioning the Bank of the United States, but when he did so, he was cautious. Speaking in Hanover County, Virginia, he said he was convinced that there could be no sound currency or faithful execution of the fiscal duties of the government without a Bank of the United States or a similar unit, but public opinion ought to have the controlling influence as to whether such an entity should again be created. If state banks could achieve sound financial health and act as responsible depositories for governmental funds, no one would rejoice more than he. The Democrats scoffed. If the Whigs were triumphant, they charged, a national bank would be high on their agenda.

Until fairly late in the campaign, Tyler made few speeches. No one seemed to think the views of the vice-presidential aspirant were of much significance. Harrison appeared to be in good health. Of course, if elected, he would be older than any other president had been upon taking office. In 1841 he would be sixty-eight. Webster, now more optimistic about Whig success in November, obviously was concerned about Harrison's age, commenting: "If Genl. Harrison lives, *he will be President*," and "His election is certain . . . if an all-wise Providence shall spare his life."[22]

In September and October, Tyler did travel to Ohio, western Virginia, and Pennsylvania. Following the pattern set by other Whigs, he tried to avoid controversial issues, saying he agreed with Harrison on all major points. Harrison's standard statement was that he would bow to the will of Congress on all decisions and that even though he opposed a national bank, he would support it if Congress could find no adequate substitute. But, he added, it really did not matter what he thought. The people would express their desires through Congress, and he would go along with whatever Congress should decide to do.

It is unlikely that Tyler, with his independent temperament, actually accepted this notion of passive assent, but during the campaign, saying he agreed with Harrison was a convenient answer, and it was less dangerous to the outcome of the election than expressing his own feelings. This he learned early in the contest, when a group of Pittsburgh Democrats wrote to him, asking for his views on establishing another Bank of the United States. In formulating his reply, Tyler said he always had considered the creation of such a bank unconstitutional; therefore, a constitutional amendment would be necessary before he would be able to support the reinstatement of the institution. Before sending his reply to Pittsburgh, Tyler submitted it to leading congressional Whigs for clearance. They were upset; and they directed Tyler not to make any comments on controversial subjects. Although his opinions were widely known and long held, he could not answer questions candidly without endangering the "unity and harmony" of the party, but neither could Harrison, Clay, or Webster.[23]

It was better by far to provide the people with diversions from the cares of everyday life than to burden them with serious speeches on banks and tariffs. At one time, Van Buren had observed that "those who have wrought great changes in the world" had succeeded "by exciting the multitude."[24] Unfortunately for his own success, he had not been able to excite the people, but the Whigs, fundamentally a party of big business in the North and large plantation owners in the South, a party that did not really believe in popular rule or in extending the suffrage to the "common man," pitched their appeals in this election mainly to the laborer, the farmer, the frontiersman. Those who managed the campaign had learned much from the 1828 Democratic extravaganza, and they added their own touches. Luck also played a part. When a Democratic journalist mockingly remarked that Harrison was content to sit in his log cabin and drink hard cider, the Whigs were provided with the marvelous idea of plying the crowds with a seemingly inexhaustible supply of the fermented liquid. A Philadelphia distiller, E. G. Booz, enlivened many a gathering even more by dispensing whiskey in cabin-shaped bottles. Everywhere, songs, parades, speeches, coonskin caps, log cabins, and other attention-getting devices touted for president a rather dignified descendant of an upper-class family who did not live in a log cabin or wear a coonskin cap.

The Whigs turned the summer of 1840 into one continual celebration. Crowds loved to sing about "Tippecanoe and Tyler Too," along with numerous other ditties derogatory to Van Buren:

> Let Van from his coolers of silver drink wine,
>   And lounge on his cushioned settee,
> Our man on a buckeye bench can recline,
>   Content with hard cider is he.

Horace Greeley published the most popular lyrics in the *Log Cabin Song-Book*. "People like the swing of the music," he told Weed. Philip Hone maintained that Harrison was sung into the presidency. But underlying the people's enjoyment of the promotional trivia was a sincere hope that a change in party control of the government would bring an end to the depression. "Men wish to see ground for better hope," Webster observed; "General Harrison's election will bring this confidence and this hope of a better time."[25]

Even so, when the ballots were counted, the popular margin was not overwhelmingly in the Whigs' favor. In a tremendous turnout of eligible voters, 80.2 percent, Harrison received 1,275,612 votes, while Van Buren had a total of 1,130,033. Birney, of the Liberty party, managed to get 7,053. In the electoral college, however, Harrison did well. Seven states gave Van Buren 60 electoral votes, while Harrison carried nineteen states with a total of 234. Every large state, with the exception of Virginia, to Tyler's chagrin, went for the general. In the Senate, where the Democrats previously had a majority of 28 to 22, the situation was reversed. There would now be a 28-to-22 Whig advantage. Whig control of the House was likewise assured, with 133 Whigs to 102 Democrats.

Astonishingly, "a coalition of the most diverse elements of American political life" utilized "a campaign of purely emotional appeal" to elect a president "without positive principles or policy, supported by a party which had not ventured to formulate a platform."[26] Thomas Ritchie was bitter: "We may be beaten, but we will not stay beaten. . . . This discordant combination of odds and ends of all political parties cannot long continue. Like the image of Nebuchadnezzer, which was made of clay and brass and various materials, a single stone must shatter it to pieces."[27]

3

THE SHORT MONTH OF
HARRISON'S PRESIDENCY

John Quincy Adams, now sitting in the House of Representatives, his caustic comments sparing few, noted that Harrison was not the choice of three-fourths of those who elected him. "His popularity is all artificial. There is little confidence in his talents or firmness." No halcyon days should be expected, Adams warned, merely the exchange of one set of unsound principles for another. "Harrison comes in upon a hurricane; God grant he may not go out upon a wreck."[1]

Nicholas Biddle, the former president of the Bank of the United States, considered Harrison a nonentity. "The impression I have," he wrote Webster, is "that the coming administration will be in fact your administration."[2] However, Henry Clay, still smarting from the injustice of being passed over for the nomination, was determined to rule without benefit of election. His chance to gain an advantage came in November, shortly after the votes had been counted, when Harrison decided to journey to Kentucky to confer with Charles A. Wickliffe, that state's recent governor, supposedly about a land company. Rumors persisted that Harrison was destined to be Clay's puppet, and the president-elect, sensitive to such statements, did not wish to meet with the Kentuckian on his home ground, explaining that "a personal meeting might give rise to speculations, and even jealousies, which might be well to avoid." Instead, Harrison suggested communicating through a mutual friend.[3] But Clay was not to be deterred. Wickliffe and Clay were political enemies, and Clay did not like the idea of having Harrison meet with Wickliffe while seemingly ignoring Clay. So Clay

31

rushed off to intercept Harrison in Frankfort and insisted that Harrison spend a week at Clay's plantation, Ashland, near Lexington. In this initial test of strength with Clay, Harrison did not stand firm; he allowed himself to be carried off to Ashland. Harrison was a genial gentleman who preferred pleasant relationships whenever possible. In a speech at Versailles, Harrison, in a convivial mood, even said if the Constitution permitted it, he would happily turn the presidency over to Clay and retire to his farm in North Bend, an offer that the senator from Kentucky might have been tempted to accept. Harrison had Clay slated for the State Department, but before the invitation could be offered, Clay made known his desire to remain in the Senate. If Harrison meant what he said about allowing Congress full authority, the Senate, Clay thought, would be a better springboard to the presidency in 1844 than the State Department would be.[4]

Clay had suggestions to make regarding cabinet appointments, but Harrison diplomatically avoided discussing the topic. Nevertheless, Clay did say that his confidence in Webster had been shaken during the last eight years; however, Clay advised Harrison that no Whig president could overlook the Massachusetts senator in creating a cabinet. Harrison, of course, had intended to offer a post to Webster, possibly the Treasury Department, but when Clay decided against taking the State Department, Harrison gave Webster his choice of State or Treasury, hoping that Webster would choose the latter. But Webster selected the more prestigious office and the one for which he felt he had more talent. Harrison also solicited Webster's advice on other appointments and told him to comment "fully and freely" upon "every other subject, whether you occupy a place in the cabinet or not," an option that he did not offer to Clay.[5]

When Clay returned to Washington early in December 1840 for the lame-duck session of the Twenty-sixth Congress, he conveyed the impression that he had the president-elect well in hand. Harrison "now entertains sentiments of warm regard and attachment to me," he confided to his friend Francis Brooke of Virginia.[6] Rumors about what had transpired between Harrison and Clay during their meeting in Kentucky were rife, just as Clay had planned, and there were those who believed that Harrison, by his Versailles speech, had named Clay as his successor in the executive mansion. But the Kentuckian's usually pleasant demeanor was lacking. Descriptions of him at this time invariably contain the words "imperious," "arrogant," "domineering." He taunted Democrats with their defeat, threatening them with the repeal of the Independent Treasury and other measures that had been passed during the days of Democratic control, as well as his plans to oust Francis P. Blair and John C. Rives, of the Democratic *Washington Globe*, as printers to the Senate. Clay declared that Blair had libeled him for years; now it was Clay's chance to retaliate. Obviously, Clay's thoughts already were on the 1844 election, and so were Webster's. They jockeyed for position, but Webster's words and deeds were more temperate.[7]

Both Clay and Webster realized that contributing to the nation's economic recovery would be the most desirable attainment for future political use. Clay intended to do this by spearheading domestic legislation designed to create financial stability. Webster thought diplomacy was the answer. If Anglo-American relations could be improved, British investments and credit would again flow into the country, thus contributing to a healthier economy. Webster's Anglophile bent had been strengthened during his recent stay in England; and as secretary of state, "the premier of the cabinet," he could guide the nation along proper paths. Diplomacy had fascinated Webster for years, and he had dreamed about an appointment to the Court of St. James's.[8]

Harrison arrived in Washington on 9 February, his sixty-eighth birthday, and was greeted by a large crowd. A kindly disposed person, he was, in contrast to Clay, very gracious in victory, and he unassumingly called at the White House for a pleasant visit with President Van Buren. The president, equally gracious in defeat, took his entire cabinet to call on Harrison at Gadsby's Hotel and invited him to dine at the White House. There, Harrison had an enjoyable time exchanging pleasantries with Senator Thomas Hart Benton and other leading Democrats. Van Buren reportedly felt that Harrison was the most extraordinary man he ever had seen. "He talks and thinks with . . . much ease and vivacity. . . . He is as tickled with the Presidency as is a young woman with a new bonnet." For Harrison's convenience, Van Buren offered to vacate the executive mansion prior to 4 March. Harrison was appreciative, but declined the offer. Perhaps it would have made no difference where he lodged, for office seekers beseiged him wherever he went in the city.[9]

Yet, Harrison strolled down Pennsylvania Avenue unattended and seemingly unconscious of the dignity of his position, shaking hands and joking with those whom he met. Unannounced, he even dropped by the Senate chamber. Calhoun was startled when he felt someone tap him on the shoulder and "turning around, lo and behold it was the President-elect." Calhoun thought Harrison did not look well, and he doubted if the man had the necessary strength to encounter the heavy responsibilities that would soon be his. Even in those preinaugural days, Harrison was kept on a perpetual round of receptions, dinners, assemblies, and soirées; and no matter where he went or how he tried to escape, there were office seekers. Inevitably, he made too many promises. Was Harrison aware of the critical condition of the country? Calhoun wondered. "The only hope is that he may be perfectly passive and leave it to the strongest about him to take control. As bad as it may be, it cannot be as bad as the absence of all control."[10]

But Harrison increasingly was sensitive to any hint of his being someone's dupe. His first serious encounter with Clay on this issue arose over a cabinet appointment. Prior to Harrison's arrival in Washington, Webster and other Whig leaders in the city had made suggestions about prospective cabinet members. Clay's primary desire was to obtain the Treasury Department for John M. Clayton of Delaware, a strong advocate of a national bank. Webster countered by proposing that Thomas Ewing of Ohio, who earlier had been assigned the Post Office Department, be shifted to the Treasury. Harrison concurred, leaving Clay very unhappy, even though his fellow Kentuckian and friend John J. Crittenden was named attorney general and John Bell of Tennessee, who was by no means anti-Clay, was to be secretary of war. Thomas Ewing was considered a "stout Clay man," and Francis Granger of New York, whom Clay had earlier endorsed and who was acceptable to Seward and Weed, became the choice for postmaster general. But Clay was not satisfied. Although Harrison had promised the remaining position, that of secretary of the navy, to the South Atlantic states and had asked their delegations to make a recommendation, which resulted in the selection of George E. Badger of North Carolina, Clay was determined to have Clayton in the cabinet. The night before the official announcement of Badger's appointment was to be made, Clay called on Harrison to urge him to change his mind and name Clayton. The meeting became heated, and supposedly, Harrison terminated the interview with the forceful statement, "Mr. Clay, you forget that *I* am the President."[11]

Tyler's advice on selections for the cabinet was neither sought nor given. He hoped that Harrison would be firm and decisive, especially at the onset of his administration, by allowing no intrigue in the cabinet. Tyler's main concern was about the hazardous influence of the "extreme nationalists," who were "too excessive in their notions." However, he expressed this only in private and, as he deemed proper conduct, remained quietly at home in Williamsburg.[12]

With the formation of the cabinet concluded, Harrison also sought a few days' rest and quiet in Virginia. He first stopped in Richmond, where, with Tyler, he watched a parade, made a speech again denying that he ever had been or could ever be an abolitionist, and journeyed on to his ancestral home, Berkeley plantation, where, in his mother's room, he wrote his Inaugural Address, which was later edited by Webster.[13]

Inauguration day was raw and cloudy, as early March often is in Washington. The crowds were enormous, and the parade to the Capitol was more colorful than ever before on such an occasion. Harrison, coatless, with his hat in his hand, rode his favorite horse, Whitey, to the ceremonies. Adams thought the horse was "mean-looking" and the entire affair "showy-shabby, like the campaign." In the Senate chamber, shortly before noon, Tyler took the oath of office as vice-president. His remarks were brief, covering less than a third of a column in the *National Intelligencer*. He was cognizant, he said, of the honor of presiding over the deliberations of the United States Senate, a body committed to guarding and protecting the institutions handed down by the Founding Fathers, from the waves of popular and rash impulses, on the one hand, and from the attempts of executive encroachment, on the other. The Senate, he said, "may properly be regarded as holding the balance in which are weighed the powers conceded to this Government and the rights reserved to the States and to the People." He warned against factionalism—"that destructive spirit which recklessly walks over prostrate rights and tramples laws and constitutions in the dust." If ever partisanship were to find an abiding place within the Senate, the peace and happiness of the people and their political institutions would topple.[14]

Outside the Capitol, Harrison, again hatless and without an over-coat, addressed a crowd of fifty thousand for more than an hour and a half. In general terms, repeating many of his campaign statements, he described how he viewed the presidency, stressing the Whig conception of the office as one of strictly limited powers. The executive should serve only one term, because long continuance in office created a love of power and could lead to despotism. The president should never forget that he was an accountable agent—a servant, not the master. So saying, he renewed his pledge that under no circumstance would he consent to a second term.

The president, Harrison declared, should never intrude upon the duties of the legislative branch. Although he could recommend measures, he should not be considered the source of legislation and should "never be looked to for schemes of finance." The mode of keeping the public revenue should be prescribed by Congress, and the further removed the revenue was from the control of the executive, the more wholesome the arrangement. Harrison did not directly mention the reconsideration of a national bank, but because he was opposed to the Independent Treasury Act, he obviously expected some bank plan to emanate from Congress. Additionally, he voiced his resistance to an exclusively metallic currency and to the assumption of state debts by the federal government.

The president's right to veto acts of Congress should, Harrison thought, be used sparingly and with discretion, but he was not willing to relinquish it entirely. If exercised, it should be to provide just and equitable legislation to all parts of the nation, to guard against unconstitutional measures or hasty legislation contrary to the public will or acts in violation of the rights of minorities. But he added: "It is preposterous to suppose that the President . . . could better understand the wants and wishes of the people than their own immediate representatives."

Harrison's desire for civil-service reform was apparent. He wanted no political purge of governmental employees or any coercion of them in the form of assessments or contributions in exchange for the retention of their positions. He stressed especially that treasury officers should not be removed without cause, and he declared that he would never remove a secretary of the treasury without communicating all reasons for the dismissal to both houses of Congress.

Above all, Harrison wanted peace and harmony among the branches of the government and among the various executive departments, which, he insisted, must be kept within their appropriate orbits. The same standard should apply to the various parts of the Union. "The attempt of one state to control the domestic institutions of another can only result in feelings of distrust and jealousy, the certain harbingers of disunion, violence, and civil war, and the ultimate destruction of our free institutions."[15]

Peace and harmony were elusive commodities. Day after day the White House was crowded with office seekers who blocked the president's path to the cabinet room while swamping him with petitions. Intense and bitter struggles developed over the most lucrative appointments. There were special requests from friends and associates. Webster found that Nicholas Biddle longed to be named minister to Austria. Duff Green, an erstwhile Jacksonian Democrat and a henchman of Calhoun's, desired the mission to Texas. Washington Irving wanted to be consul in Paris. It was difficult for Webster to disappoint them, but so many prior promises had been made. Also, the appointments of Biddle and Green would have caused outcries from both extremes of the Whig party. Extreme states' righters would have been enraged by an appointment for Biddle, and the naming of Green would have been unacceptable to the strong nationalists.[16]

One of the choice political plums was the collectorship of the port of New York, which controlled possibly five hundred jobs, and the struggle over who should fill this post created further animosity between Clay and Harrison. Edward Curtis had the formidable backing of Webster, Seward, and Weed, whereas Clay wanted the appointment to go to Robert C. Witmore, especially because Curtis had worked zealously to thwart Clay's nomination in Harrisburg. To settle the matter, Harrison asked the advice of four cabinet members: Ewing, Badger, Bell, and Granger, who recommended Curtis. Again Clay's anger flared. His recommendations, he declared, were being either ignored or shunted aside. He had no voice in patronage, and he felt isolated from Harrison's inner circle, where Webster seemed to reign supreme.[17]

Clay's angry frustration was evident again when he demanded that Harrison call a special session of Congress to take action on the bank question and other economic issues that, Clay contended, would set the nation on the road to recovery and eventual prosperity. A special session also would give Clay an opportunity to address the nation and reassert his leadership of the party. If the session were not called, he would be in relative obscurity until Congress met in December. But Webster was not in favor of a special session. The Whigs, in his opinion, were still in serious disagreement about many measures, including whether or not a national bank was necessary and, if it were, what kind of a bank should be devised. A modicum of conciliation was necessary prior to bringing the issue to the floors of the Senate and the House, or the party would be torn apart in public before the administration had had a chance to try to prove itself. Webster, of course, was in a comfortable position as the president's chief confidant and spokesman, or so it seemed to Clay.[18]

The senator from Kentucky was not satisfied with anything but immediate action on the extra session, and there was justification for haste. The nation was in a financial crisis, but Harrison hesitated. On 11 March the cabinet vote on calling such a session resulted in three for and three against. The president broke the tie with a negative vote. The impatient Clay then dashed off a high-handed letter to Harrison, in which he pressed for reconsideration of the question of a special session and hinted that inaction made the administration appear to be vacillating. Enclosed with the letter was a draft of the proclamation that Clay thought Harrison should use in calling the session. The president was annoyed. "You are too impetuous," he told Clay, reminding Clay that there were others whom he, Harrison, had to consult, and there was the situation in Tennessee to consider. The Tennessee legislature, presently under Democratic control, was not scheduled to elect United States senators until after the state election in August, an election that the Whigs hoped to win. However, in the event that a special session of Congress were called before August, the current Democratic legislature could convene and elect two members of its own party to the Senate. This was an important factor to keep in mind, because the Whig margin in the Senate was not large; but, even so, Harrison explained, the vote of the cabinet on 11 March was merely preliminary, and the matter of a special session was still open. He concluded his letter with, "I prefer for many reasons this mode of answering your note to a conversation in the presence of others."[19]

The letter sent Clay into a rage. Emotionally upset, he read more into Harrison's reply than was actually there. The president, Clay insisted, had directed him not to visit the White House, not to see him personally, and not to communicate with him except in writing. This was a misrepresentation, but in his perturbed state, Clay was not thinking clearly. He felt humiliated, thwarted, cast aside by the man he had hoped to guide, if not to control.[20]

In what was to be his final letter to Harrison, Clay vigorously denied any intention of trying to dictate policy or appointments. Enemies, he claimed, had poisoned the president's mind against him. Clay denied rumors that he had said Curtis should not be named collector of the port of New York: "I have never gone beyond expressing the opinion that he is faithless and perfidious, and, in my judgement, unworthy of the place"—a seemingly subtle distinction. If Clay could not freely express his opinions, "as a citizen and as a Senator, in regard to public matters," he would have to retire to private life; but he hoped that by remaining a little longer in the Senate, he could be of some service to the country. Coldly ending the letter with, "I do not wish to trouble you with answering this note," Clay said he trusted that Harrison, "whatever others may say or insinuate," would justly appreciate his motives.[21]

The Senate, which met 4 March to confirm cabinet appointments, adjourned on 15 March. As there was no reason for Clay to remain in Washington, he left immediately for Kentucky, not knowing of Harrison's instructions to Ewing to examine the anticipated revenues of the government and then to decide whether operations could continue until Congress convened in December. Ewing's conclusion was sobering. If no action was taken soon, the country would be insolvent within a short period. Thereupon, two days after Clay's departure, Harrison issued a call for a special session of Congress to meet on 31 May, to consider "sundry important and weighty matters," primarily dealing with revenues and finance. In view of the seriousness of the situation, there were those who thought the session should begin weeks before 31 May.[22]

With this settled, Harrison turned to other affairs. The dispensation of patronage, as was to be expected, caused unhappiness in the Whig ranks. Not enough Democrats were removed to make way for the victors. Although himself the recipient of several political appointments, Harrison advocated the reform of the spoils system and opposed the wholesale removal of Democrats without cause. He directed Webster to send to all departmental secretaries a message instructing them to protect governmental employees from various abuses, such as forcing them to support the party in power. However, while they should be free to express their political opinions, civil servants should not "take an active part in attempts to influence the minds of others."[23]

During the campaign the Whigs had vowed to correct these "flagrant Jacksonian abuses," and Harrison took seriously his pledges to improve the civil-service system. A president, he held, was selected to advance the public interest, not to "requite personal favors or gratify personal animosities"; but he was being pressured from all sides to punish Democrats and reward Whigs. To complicate matters, there was controversy within the party as to which Whigs were worthy of reaping the fruits of victory. Willie Mangum was disturbed by what he considered Webster's excessive influence, which made, according to Mangum, "the old Federal clique to the North" more powerful than it had been in forty years. Others thought Webster was "not proscriptive enough." Ewing believed that numerous removals were necessary. For twelve years, he noted, the Democrats had filled offices with their "brawling offensive political partisans, of very low moral standards—their official duties performed by substitutes, or not performed at all. Many defalcations and gross peculation constantly occurring among them."[24]

Harrison was not averse to removing Democrats for just cause. He wanted efficiency and honesty in government, and he visited every department to observe operations. He then called for reports detailing the activities and responsibilities of each office, and he vowed to protect officeholders who were performing their duties well. Nevertheless, innumerable removals were made for political reasons. All the leading Whigs, as well as lesser members of the party, had countless friends to reward. Because his department controlled more positions than any of the others, Postmaster General Granger probably held the record for dismissals. During his six months in office, he ousted seventeen hundred postmasters and boasted that had he remained in the cabinet another two or three weeks, three thousand more would have been gone. For the time being, at least, the creation of a nonpartisan civil

39

service was impossible. The Democrats had been in command for a long period, and the Whigs were hungry.[25]

There were other aspects of his position that Harrison perhaps had not anticipated. According to the Constitution, a president "may require the opinion, in writing, of the principal officer in each of the executive departments, upon any subject relating to the duties of their respective offices." Nowhere does the Constitution either mention a cabinet or direct the president to consult such a body before making a decision. Some past presidents had sought advice from department heads as a group, others had preferred to confer with them on an individual basis or with a select few.

President Washington had expected his department heads to speak only in his name and to "act only with his approval," but he "was not so much the captain of the team as the hub of a wheel from which the departmental spokes radiated." Jefferson had consulted with individual cabinet members on minor matters, but issues of importance had been submitted to all the secretaries. In the gravest cases, he had called them together, and after discussion of the problem, a vote had been taken, with the president counting as one. Jefferson believed the president did have the prerogative of overruling the majority vote, but he considered this an unwise practice.[26]

Between the presidencies of Jefferson and Jackson, as James S. Young has pointed out in *The Washington Community, 1800–1828*, presidential leadership had been weak, and Congress increasingly had exerted more influence over the cabinet than had the chief executive. Some department heads had become disloyal and insubordinate. Congress, through the control of departmental budgets, had encouraged secretaries to conduct business with the legislative branch without informing the president. The loyalty of the cabinet had been further diminished because members frequently had been holdovers from previous administrations and therefore had not been indebted to the incumbent for their positions. Factions in Congress at times supported departmental heads whom the president wished to dismiss.[27]

Andrew Jackson brought changes. The general, who was accustomed to making his own decisions regardless of opposition, had preferred the counsel of trusted friends to that of officially appointed secretaries. In the Harrison administration, the Whig cabinet, appointed with the advice of Webster and other party leaders, had believed it should guide and direct all of the president's actions. According to Attorney General Crittenden, it was right and proper that it should do so. This was in line with the Whig desire to curb or, preferably, eliminate executive usurpation. The president was to preside over cabinet meetings, but decisions were to be reached by the expression of the majority, with Harrison, "first among equals," having one vote.

Occasionally Harrison became restive under this arrangement. One such incident occurred when Webster informed him that the cabinet had selected James Wilson of New Hampshire to be governor of Iowa Territory. Harrison arose in the meeting and announced to the cabinet that "William Henry Harrison, President of the United States, tells you, gentlemen, that by _____, John Chambers shall be Governor of Iowa." Chambers had been Harrison's aide-de-camp and private secretary. Had Harrison's tenure in office been longer, indications are that he would have grown more unhappy and refractory as the cabinet and Congress attempted to limit his executive power.[28] There was not time, however, for such a crisis to develop.

Prior to the election, the Whig press had repeatedly emphasized Harrison's endurance and fine health, as if to assure the nation that this man, older than any other president had been on entering office, would be able to carry out the duties of his position. Harrison was tired when he arrived in Washington, but buoyed by the excitement of becoming president, he was constantly on the move, visiting outgoing Democrats, dropping by all the departments, meeting with hordes of office seekers. The pressures were many, and differences with Clay were disturbing. Insisting on walking about the city on business or doing his own marketing, he ignored the elements, was caught in the rain, and was drenched. A severe cold, which may initially have been contracted during the inaugural ceremonies, led to serious complications, and on 27 March the illness was diagnosed as "bilious pleurisy, with symptoms of pneumonia and intestinal inflamation." After a week's confinement, the president appeared to have improved, but a relapse followed, and shortly after midnight on Palm Sunday, 4 April, a few hours less than a month after his inauguration, he died.

Having no precedents to guide them, the cabinet, with Congress not in session and with Vice-President Tyler in Williamsburg, assumed the responsibility for deciding what actions should be taken. At once they composed a letter to Tyler, informing him of Harrison's death. Webster's son Fletcher, now chief clerk in the State Department, was dispatched to Williamsburg to deliver the message. The cabinet then readied the necessary announcements and sent notifications to governmental officials at home and abroad. A handbill was drawn up, to be circulated and published in the *National Intelligencer*. There was a funeral to be arranged and a procession to be planned.[29]

In the days prior to Harrison's demise, Tyler had received no official notification of the president's illness, and not until 31 March was there any mention of it in the press. On that date, a short statement appeared in the *National Intelligencer,* saying that the attending physician considered the president decidedly improved and that the editors hoped very soon to be able "to relieve the public mind entirely from apprehension of the consequences of this attack." The *Washington Globe* of 1 April was much less optimistic, but no official word was sent to Tyler prior to the arrival of Fletcher Webster early on the morning of 5 April. However, the news did not come as a complete surprise. James Lyons, a Richmond friend who was president of the Tippecanoe Club of that city during the campaign, twice had written to Tyler about Harrison's condition. After conferring with his family, Tyler left immediately for Washington. The trip was made in record time, and he was in the city before dawn the following day.[30]

John Quincy Adams, with kinder words for the dead Harrison than he ever had for the live one, expressed deep sympathy for the president's family, especially for Anna Harrison, who had not accompanied her husband to Washington but was to join him later in the spring. When Harrison's illness became more serious, she had been summoned, but, as Adams noted, "tidings of death must meet her before she can reach this city." Harrison, Adams said, was "amiable and benevolent. Sympathy for his suffering and his fate is the prevailing sentiment of his fellow-citizens."[31]

This was true. Never before had a president died in office, and as word of the tragedy slowly spread throughout the country, outpourings of grief continued for weeks. Newspaper columns were outlined in black, signs of mourning were everywhere, but as Congressman Henry A. Wise of Virginia bluntly observed, had Harrison lived until the special session of Congress, he would have been "devoured by the divided pack of his own dogs."[32]

Harrison never considered himself a great political leader, and the Whigs were under no illusion that he was one when they nominated him. Quite the contrary, he was named because they believed he had the best chance of winning and because, once he was in office, they thought he would be pliable, would follow directions, and would not assert executive powers. But Whig directions often were mixed and contradictory, and Harrison objected to being looked upon as a puppet or a pawn. He did not want to be merely a figurehead. He had no desire to dictate, but he sincerely wished to be recognized as president of the United States, the chief executive of the country. He hoped to right many of the wrongs that he had observed, and he was dismayed by the multitude of people who expected to profit personally from the Whig victory. Clay's high-handed behavior irritated Harrison. Even in the short month of Harrison's administration, there were decided indications that all was not well with the Whig concept of a powerless president.

4

★ ★ ★ ★ ★

THE SUCCESSION

Harrison had been dead for only a few hours when Francis Preston Blair, editor of the *Washington Globe,* expressed his fears to his old friend Andrew Jackson. Clay, Blair said, undoubtedly would now try to seize control of the administration. Would Tyler be his "pliant tool"? "Upon that hangs matters of great magnitude to the country." Blair considered Tyler "a poor weeping willow of a creature" who might resign all to the audacious depravity of the political black leg [Clay]."[1]

Blair's characterization of Tyler was not quite correct. The Virginian was a proud man who had a stubborn streak and was not accustomed to being told what to do. At the age of fifty-one, he was the youngest man, so far, to assume the leadership of the nation. Unlike Harrison, Tyler was neither weary nor ill. He was well educated, intelligent, and experienced in governmental operations. He had never begged for office and had not sought the vice-presidency; therefore, he had fewer political debts to pay than did most politicians. When he arrived in Washington on 6 April, he handled the events of the trying day with firmness and courtesy.

His first order of business was a noon meeting with the cabinet. Unfortunately, there is no record of what occurred, but there must have been a discussion about Tyler's status. In the cabinet message informing him of Harrison's death, he was addressed as vice-president. In his memoirs, a Whig journalist named Nathan Sargent contended that prior to Tyler's arrival in the capital, the cabinet had concluded that he should bear the cumbersome title of "Vice President, acting as President."

However, in Sargent's opinion, this did not "accord" with Tyler's "views and ambitions." Rather, Sargent said, Tyler was "determined to be curtailed of none of the dignities and emoluments of the high office which had devolved upon him." Sargent, an ardent Clay man, was of course not an impartial observer. Writing years after the close of Tyler's administration, he remained bitter about the president's "treachery" in vetoing bills desired by congressional Whigs. Congress, the "supreme organism" in the governmental structure, should never be forced to strike its flag and legislate "at the foot of the throne."[2]

The initial implementation of the ambiguous constitutional provision regarding presidential succession caused no end of disagreement. Article II, section 1, paragraph 6, of the Constitution states:

> In case of the removal of the President from office, or of his death, resignation, or inability to discharge the powers and duties of the said office, the same shall devolve on the Vice President, and the Congress may by law provide for the case of removal, death, resignation, or inability, both of the President and Vice President, declaring what officer shall then act as President, and such officer shall act accordingly, until the disability be removed, or a President shall be elected.

The question was, Did "the same" mean that the office devolved on the vice-president or that merely the powers and duties devolved upon him? Was it possible to separate the powers and duties from the office? Was a special election necessary, or did the Constitution call for one only when both the presidency and the vice-presidency were vacant? Tyler believed the office, which included the powers and duties, devolved upon him, automatically and immediately, as soon as Harrison had died.[3]

For years the quandary that in all probability would inevitably have to be faced had troubled many who studied the Constitution, but no official pronouncement on the subject had been made. In other words, the problem had been anticipated but had not been resolved. In 1825, William Rawle, in his *View of the Constitution of the United States*, had stated his belief that a vice-president would assume the presidential office for the remainder of the current term. If both the presidential and vice-presidential offices were to become vacant, an officer designated by Congress would act as president until a special election could be called. The Presidential Succession Act of 1792 specifically provided for a special election in the event of a double vacancy.

Justice Joseph Story of the United States Supreme Court, in his *Commentaries on the Constitution of the United States*, first published in 1833, also held that a vice-president should succeed to the presidential office and continue therein until the expiration of the term. This interpretation was not accepted by the venerable James Kent, former chancellor of the New York Court of Chancery, who in the third edition of his *Commentaries on American Law*, published in 1836, said that a vice-president could only act as president upon the death or disability of the incumbent.[4]

Others expressed their views, but by 1841 no conclusion had been reached. While members of the cabinet awaited Tyler's presence in the capital, they puzzled over what should be done. Webster asked the clerk of the Supreme Court, William T. Carroll, to send a message to Chief Justice Roger B. Taney, who was then in Baltimore, requesting him to come to Washington to advise the cabinet on the proper constitutional procedure, but Taney refused to do so. In any interaction between the executive and the judicial branches of the government, he declared, "the communication from one to the other ought to be direct and from the proper origin." He did not wish to appear to be intruding in the affairs of the executive branch without a formal request from the cabinet or from John Tyler. Apparently, no formal invitation was issued, although it is difficult to understand why Webster, as head of the cabinet, did not himself summon Taney, rather than delegating that task to the clerk of the Supreme Court.[5]

One might speculate as to what Taney's opinion might have been, had he acceded to the request to advise the cabinet. Taney, a Democrat who supported Jackson's concept of the presidency, held no brief for the doctrine of congressional supremacy, especially as it was being exercised under the heavy hand of Henry Clay. Certainly Taney understood that an acting president would be helpless against Clay's determination to rule the nation from the Senate. Jackson had appointed Taney to the post of secretary of the treasury after two previous secretaries had refused to obey the president's order to remove governmental deposits from the Bank of the United States. Taney willingly carried out Jackson's wish, and after the death of John Marshall, Taney had been rewarded with the chief justiceship of the Supreme Court. While secretary of the treasury, Taney had had bitter controversies with Clay, and when Tyler had voted against Taney's confirmation as secretary of the treasury, Taney and Tyler had become political enemies. Perhaps, under the circumstances, Taney preferred to disqualify himself in resolving the sensitive question of whether, in effect, Tyler or Clay should lead the nation. Later, Tyler and Taney became friends, but for the present, the chief justice felt no affinity for either Tyler or Clay.[6]

With or without a judicial pronouncement, a decision had to be reached quickly. When meeting with Tyler on 6 April, the cabinet concluded that he should take the presidential oath and thereby assume the office, as well as the powers and duties. Possibly it was Webster who brought speculations to an end. Perhaps Tyler was intractable. Whatever the case, the determination was made, and in the presence of the cabinet, Tyler swore that he would faithfully execute the *office* of president of the United States and, to the best of his ability, preserve, protect, and defend the Constitution. Tyler, convinced that the constitutional provision made his succession automatic, thought the procedure extrinsic, but the presiding judge, William Cranch of the Circuit Court of the District of Columbia, believed the oath taking was necessary in order to forestall any doubts as to whether or not Tyler was legally the chief executive. Cranch appended such a statement to the copy of the oath, along with Tyler's objection.[7]

Doubts, however, did persist. Some individuals, such as John Quincy Adams, never were reconciled to the idea of Tyler as president. To Adams, Tyler always was the "vice president, acting as president." Many scholars have agreed. Basing his judgment on Max Farrand's exhaustive study *Records of the Federal Constitution*, Edward S. Corwin, a twentieth-century authority on the presidency and the Constitution, concluded: "It was the intention of the Framers that the Vice President, for whatever reason he 'succeeded' the President, should remain Vice President unless and until he was elected President."[8]

Arthur M. Schlesinger, Jr., in an interesting discussion of the future of the vice-presidency, has set forth the premise that the Founding Fathers proposed the office, not to provide for succession, but in an effort to facilitate the election of a president whose outlook was more national in scope. In the Constitutional Convention, Schlesinger has observed, there was concern that the presidential electors very likely would cast their ballots for persons from their own states; therefore, the decision was made to have each elector vote for two individuals, one of whom, at least, could not be an inhabitant of the same state as the elector. From this method of selection, there was greater possibility that a president of national stature would emerge. The person with the second-highest number of votes would be vice-president. "Both President and Vice President," Schlesinger has pointed out, "would be voted on for the presidency, and both presumably would be well qualified for the office," but first and foremost, the vice-presidency had been created to establish a "valuable mode of election." However, in debates on the issue, the matter of succession was also a consideration.

With the development of the party system and the adoption of the Twelfth Amendment, which stipulated that electors name in distinct and separate ballots their choices for president and vice-president, the vice-presidency became a bargaining chip in the game of politics. Qualifications were insignificant. What was important was how well the candidate could reinforce the ticket.[9]

In providing for the possibility that the House of Representatives would have to decide a presidential election, the Twelfth Amendment alluded to succession. If before the fourth day of March the House had not chosen a president, "then the Vice-President shall act as President, as in the case of the death or other constitutional disability of the President"; but it was not clear whether "act as President" meant that he would be an acting president or that he would succeed to the office.

Writing in 1951 in *Presidential Succession*, Ruth C. Silva concluded that regardless of differences of opinion, the precedent established by Tyler's succession had stood the test of time and had provided for the orderly transfer of the presidency when similar situations had arisen; however, all such transfers of the presidential office were made "by virtue of usage rather than by virtue of constitutional provision." This was true until 1967, when the Twenty-fifth Amendment provided, among other stipulations regarding succession, that "in case of the removal of the President from office or of his death or resignation, the Vice-President shall become President."[10]

Another precedent that was established by Tyler's assumption of the presidential office was the administering of the presidential oath and of dating the beginning of a presidential term from the time of the oath taking, not, as Tyler held, from the moment of his predecessor's death. Thus, the *Congressional Directory* records the inception of Tyler's presidency as 6 April, rather than 4 April.[11]

The decision to claim the presidential office was not Tyler's alone. Webster, with the acquiescence of the other cabinet members, agreed that this was the correct step to take. They were present at the oath-taking ceremony, and no one accused Tyler of usurpation.

Later, on 31 May, at the opening of the special session, Congressman Henry A. Wise of Virginia, in offering a resolution, referred to Tyler as the president of the United States. This touched off a debate on Tyler's correct status. After a heated exchange, the resolution was passed without any alteration in the wording, which signaled the passive assent of the House to the title. On the following day the same matter was brought up in the Senate, where William Allen and Benjamin Tappan, both of Ohio, led a protest against the form of Tyler's succession. Many arguments were heard, but in the end, the Senate voted, 38 to 8, to recognize Tyler as the president of the United States.[12]

This did not terminate the controversy. Discussions continued in the halls of Congress, in the press, and among officials of the government. Behind his back, Tyler was called "His Accidency," and throughout the years, charges that he had "seized" the presidency to satisfy his political and personal ambitions have persisted. Looking ahead to the 1844 election, so the allegations go, Tyler had carried out a "shrewd political manipulation" to wrest Whig leadership from the hands of Clay, believing that the occupation of the presidential office would give him a distinct advantage.[13]

Unquestionably, Tyler was interested in politics, and thoughts of his future naturally must have been on his mind as he journeyed from Williamsburg to Washington to assume his obligations, whatever their essence might be. Perhaps this was when he resolved to become the legally recognized president, but no proof exists, and if such an idea did occur to him, there were other impellents.

Along with others of his period, Tyler considered it a duty for people of "public virtue" to accept responsibilities in government. From time to time this must be done, he insisted, in order to counteract the "mad careers" of immoderate individuals who might threaten the life of the nation. He sincerely believed the Union was in peril. The North, growing in population and therefore in political power, threatened the southern economy with demands for an ever-higher tariff and for more Free States to the west, which would upset the balance in the Senate. The House already was controlled by the North. Above all, the agitation for abolition was most unsettling, but so were the calls for disunion by the extreme state's righters.[14]

In the 1787 Constitutional Convention, James Madison had seen the president "as a restraining hand on an impetuous Congress," whereas Gouverneur Morris had characterized the president as "the general guardian of the national interest."[15] Tyler may have perceived himself in both roles. He was a historically minded man of learning and political experience, fully cognizant of the connection of past, present, and future; and he realized the significance of precedents. He respected the constitutional provisions on checks and balances and therefore did not condone the development of overweening power on the part of either the executive or the legislative branch. If either assumed undue authority and upset the balance, the democratic underpinnings of the government and the nation would be weakened. Tyler did not approve of

Jackson's conduct as president, but neither did he favor congressional supremacy.

These had been Tyler's concerns during much of his political career, but he did not embark on his new position with any sense of hauteur or great confidence. He wrote to William Rives:

> Apart from my apprehension of my want of the necessary qualifications for the discharge of the most important functions of chief magistrate, even under the most favorable circumstances, I am under Providence made the instrument of a new test which is for the first time to be applied to our institutions. The experiment is to be made at the moment when the country is agitated by conflicting views of public policy, and when the spirit of faction is most likely to exist.

Tyler fully realized the difficulties he faced: "Under these circumstances, the devolvement upon me of this high office is peculiarly embarrassing."[16]

One difficult and potentially embarrassing decision was the matter of the cabinet. Should Tyler retain Harrison's appointees? Again, there was no precedent to guide him. Several presidents, some to their dismay, had continued department heads from preceding administrations, while others had appointed entirely new cabinets. Tyler's situation was unique. By inheriting Harrison's administration, had he also inherited Harrison's cabinet? If he had been regarded as merely an acting president, presumably he would have had no option but to retain the department heads; but fully established in the presidential office, perhaps he had a choice. Nevertheless, he requested the secretaries to remain. Harrison's death had brought uneasiness and uncertainty. Appointing a new cabinet would cause additional tensions within the party. "Surrounded by Clay-men, Webster-men, anti-Masons, original Harrisonians, old Whigs, and new Whigs, each jealous of the others, and all struggling for office," Tyler knew he must tread carefully. Creating another cabinet would take time and inflict more bruises. Tyler thought it better to avoid additional bitterness.[17]

This decision did not please extreme states' righters from his own commonwealth. They were dismayed, especially by his having allowed Webster to remain as secretary of state, a man who, thought Congressman Thomas W. Gilmer of Virginia, never should have been appointed in the first place. As early as 1 January 1841, Gilmer had wanted Webster "put into some dark corner, or thrown overboard entirely," calling him "a federalist of the worst die, a blackguard & vulgar debauchee," and a man who, "but for his splendid talents, would be in jail or on some dunghill. He won't do—the men who cling to him can't stand."[18]

Regardless of later accusations, Tyler had no desire to cause an upheaval in the Whig party. He preferred to work, if he could, with the men chosen as Harrison's "constitutional advisers," as the Whigs liked to call the cabinet. He was willing to listen to or even seek out their counsel, but he drew the line at being governed by the majority opinion of the cabinet. He could not, he said, consent to being dictated to on matters of presidential policy. He would be responsible for his own administration.[19]

As noted, Tyler was not consulted in the selection of Harrison's cabinet, and most, if not all, of its members probably would not have received Tyler's approval. He was aware, too, of Clay's desire to control the cabinet, the members of which felt little or no loyalty to the new president. This may have influenced Tyler's refusal to be considered as only one among equals. Despite this independent stand and despite their different views on a number of issues, Webster believed he and Tyler could and should work together to preserve party unity. This would entail holding to a middle position between the extreme states'-rights men, on the one hand, and the Clayites, on the other. Neither group would be easy to manage.[20]

On 7 April, the day of Harrison's funeral, the *National Intelligencer* congratulated the country on the quiet and orderly transfer of the presidency from the hands of one citizen to those of another, and it praised Tyler as a man of honor, talent, and character. "President Tyler is a Whig—a true Whig," the paper announced, "and we risk nothing in expressing our entire confidence that he will fulfill in all their extent, the expectations of the People when they bestowed on him an office from which it was possible, as they knew, he might be elevated to the Chief Magistracy of the Union."[21]

Two days later, Tyler issued an address to the people of the nation, termed by some an inaugural message, although he himself did not designate it as such. It was not long, and it had been written in haste; but, he said, he felt impelled to present to his countrymen "a brief exposition of the principles which will govern me in the general course of my administration." Here, too, was the opportunity for him to announce publicly that for the first time in the nation's history, "the person elected to the vice presidency of the United States has had devolved upon him the presidential office."

Tyler's use of the terms "which will govern me" and "my administration" caused warning flags to go up among some segments of the Whig party. Tyler made no mention of limiting his presidency to one term. This was disturbing. He did not say, as Harrison had said, that Congress knew better than he what the people wanted. However, there were encouraging statements. Tyler promised to give his sanction promptly "to any constitutional measure which, originating in Congress, would have for its objective the restoration of a sound circulating medium, so essentially necessary to give confidence in all the transactions of life." In considering the acceptability of such a measure, he would "resort to the fathers of the great republican school for advice and instruction." What he meant was, he would not forsake entirely his commitment to states' rights, although some who read the message did not interpret it thus. They should have, because he went on to warn against any attempt on the part of the federal government to enlarge its range of powers, lest by so doing, it should disturb the balance that statesmen and patriots who had framed the Constitution had established between the federal government and the states. If factions, intent upon the gratification of their selfish ends, should upset the balance, the bonds of union could be broken.

With the *Caroline* affair and the northeastern boundary controversy still pending, Tyler favored strengthening the army and the navy, but in foreign affairs he hoped to hold to a policy of "justice on our part to all, submitting to injustice from none." He considered it his most imperative duty to see that the honor of the country sustained no blemish.

To quiet the fears of officeholders, Tyler promised not to remove from office any incumbent who faithfully and honestly performed his duties, but if anyone used his position for political purposes, he would be dismissed immediately. In an indirect reference to Jackson's treatment of secretaries of the treasury, Tyler declared that the president should not have the power of appointing and removing, at his pleasure, agents who had been selected for the custody of the public moneys.[22]

The *National Intelligencer* praised the message as a "frank and most satisfying exposition of the opinions and purposes with which he enters upon the important and highly responsible duties. . . . It embraces most of the leading articles of the Whig creed."[23] Whigs in Congress, in the cabinet, and in business and finance tried to reassure each other that Tyler would be faithful to that creed. Early impressions voiced by Webster, Badger, Bell, and others were encouraging. Webster reported that relations with the president were "of the pleasantest kind," and Badger thought the cause of the country was safe in Tyler's hands. "He behaves with much dignity and courtesy, is intelligent and appears to realize what the country expects from his administration." John Bell thought Tyler was conciliatory to all and probably would "help us in keeping out some extremes on both sides." Of course, Bell admitted,

Tyler would have an interest in making himself strong; and no doubt he would cast his eyes on the next election. But he would not disturb the essential Whig policy in a bid for victory in 1844, and he would not have such a passion to succeed himself that he would destroy the harmony of the party. "Things look quite as fine as could be expected just now."[24]

Senator William C. Preston of South Carolina saw things differently. To him, Harrison's death was the first in a "teeming source of political sequences, many of which doubtless cannot be foreseen." He believed there would be a gradual divergence from what might have been Harrison's policies. "The same compass but a variation of the needle. . . . For all Mr. Tyler's sympathies, associations, and habits of thought are southern and State rights." Tyler probably would not intend to deviate. Indeed, he might have a fixed purpose to conform to Whig policies, but Tyler's ingrained beliefs and attitudes would not allow him to stray from his long-held principles. Preston wondered also if the accidental manner of Tyler's accession would diminish his influence as president. If it did and if this resulted in "throwing more power into Congress," the administration could be "stormy and factious, as in the case of a regency."[25]

A regency was exactly what Clay had in mind. Writing to Nathaniel Beverley Tucker of Virginia, he said the Whigs were "in a painful state of uncertainty as to the effect [Harrison's death would have] upon the policy of the government. I can hardly suppose that V.P. Tyler will interpose any obstacle to the adoption of measures on which the Whigs are generally united. Still, his administration will be in the nature of a regency, and regencies are very apt to engender faction, intrigue, etc."[26]

Clay, it seems from this letter, planned to be the power behind the regency. There were those who feared, as did Blair, that Tyler would be "Clay's pliant tool." Others felt this was the way it should be; they happily believed that Clay's position under Tyler's presidency would be more favorable than it might have been during a Harrison administration, for "Tyler is a friend of Clay." Those who were hoping for Clay's rise in favor were, likewise, anticipating Webster's fall from grace. David Lambert, the Washington correspondent for the *New York Courier and Enquirer,* could not imagine that Tyler would "stand by and see the old Federalist, abolitionist, and apologist for the Hartford Convention, drive rough shod over poor Clay."[27]

If the outlook for the Clay Whigs was optimistic, so also was that of the states'-rights southerners. One of the latter, from Virginia's Eastern Shore, was elated that with Tyler in the White House, "*now* the abolitionists & others who would harm us are foiled—that the Constitution & with it the Union will be preserved—and that come peace or war, our Honor is secure & we shall be saved." Nevertheless, he warned Tyler to be on guard, because Tyler was surrounded by many who wanted to be in his place, and he must take care. He should not listen to them. "Act out your Virginia feelings & principles guided by the Constitution & you will be safe."[28]

A great deal of advice came from more prominent Virginia states' righters: Nathaniel Beverley Tucker and Thomas Dew, both of the College of William and Mary; Henry Wise and Thomas Gilmer of the House of Representatives; Judge Abel Parker Upshur of Virginia's General Court; and the agriculturalist Edmund Ruffin. These tried to influence the president in the direction of extreme states' rights. He listened politely but pledged himself to no group. These gentlemen, along with a few others, it has been said, constituted a sort of "Kitchen Cabinet," but, in reality, they frequently offered more advice than Tyler either sought or desired. This was a faction with which Tyler had to deal, but his preference was for a moderation of some of their views.[29]

To add to his difficulties, Tyler knew that unless he was willing to do the bidding of congressional Whigs, his tenure in office was destined to be distressful or brief. Having come only recently into the Whig ranks, he had no power as a party leader, whereas Clay, who wanted to control the government from the Senate, tenaciously held claim to be the Whig's helmsman. Unlike Jackson, who had a flair for appealing to the people for support against Congress, Tyler, low-key and soft-spoken, found this almost impossible. He was not a hero-president. Moreover, his southern plantation background made him anathema to certain segments in the North.

Rumors and suspicions about what kind of president Tyler would be continued to circulate. As early as 20 April, Adams saw an alliance between Tyler and Webster, "a concert of mutual concession between North and South," as a distinct possibility. Tyler's policy, Adams was convinced, would be exclusively shaped to pave the way for his election in 1844, and Webster would aid him, while "Mr. Clay will be left to fight his own battles." A few weeks later, Clay believed there was reason to fear that "Tyler will throw himself upon Calhoun, Duff Green, etc., and detach himself from the great body of the Whig party." In the final analysis, Calhoun's insight was the most perceptive: "[Tyler] is essentially a man for the middle ground and will attempt to take a middle position now when there is none. Such is my fears. If he should[,] all will be lost."[30]

While speculations raged, Tyler tried to find time for personal affairs. He moved his wife, who had been invalided by a stroke several years earlier, and five of his seven children, along with house servants, from Williamsburg to Washington, and by 14 April they had occupied the White House. Tyler found employment for his two older sons— Robert in the United States Land Office; John, Jr., as his father's private secretary. Letitia, the president's wife, was unable to assume the duties of First Lady, but the position was filled most ably by the Tylers' daughter-in-law Priscilla Cooper Tyler, Robert's wife.

Amid the ever-increasing bitterness of political conflict, gracious hospitality was extended to friend and foe alike in a constant series of dinners, balls, and formal and informal receptions. The aged Dolley Madison, a Tyler friend of long standing, advised the youthful Priscilla on the social etiquette of the nation's capital; and Daniel Webster often was on hand to guide her in the choice of food and wine. Events were more elegant and colorful than perhaps ever had been held in the White House, with no thanks to Congress, for during most of Tyler's administration, that hostile body withheld funds for White House expenses, which Tyler was forced to pay from his own pocket, not only for entertainment, but also for heating, lighting, and essential maintenance.[31]

Nevertheless, Adams grumbled that a strict constructionist, such as Tyler purported to be, should have more than a doubt as to "whether the Vice-President has the right to occupy the President's house, or claim his salary, without an Act of Congress."[32]

5

THE SPECIAL SESSION

Events crowded in on Tyler. Like Harrison, he was besieged by hungry office seekers whose expectations of appointments had not yet been realized. But uppermost in the minds of the president, the cabinet, and Whig congressional leaders was the special session, scheduled to begin on 31 May. Clay was anxious. Tyler, Clay well knew, had strong, long-held negative views on the creation of another national bank, the tariff, and other of Clay's favorite projects; but Clay comforted himself with the assertion that Tyler, in accepting the vice-presidential nomination, had "an obligation to stand by and carry out the measures of the Whigs." Clay considered himself the unquestioned spokesman of the party, and he would brook no opposition to the agenda he was prepared to set forth as the Whig program, one that would convince the populace that the real leadership of the nation emanated from the Senate, rather than from the White House. Whether or not Clay actually said, "Tyler dare not resist; I will drive him before me," this was his sentiment; and Harrison's unfavorable reaction to Clay's arrogance had not diminished the senator's determination.[1]

Some Whigs wished to move more cautiously. Both Congressman Millard Fillmore of New York and Secretary of State Daniel Webster had preferred to postpone the special session, thinking that it was premature and that it was likely to cause trouble in the ranks; but Clay's absolute conviction that there would be no improvement in the economy without the rapid enactment of his proposals made Whig opponents of the session reluctant to voice their objections.

Economic recovery was of paramount importance. Shock waves from the panics of 1837 and 1839 continued to shake the nation. A brief flurry of optimism in late 1840 caused a number of banks to resume payments in specie, against the advice of Nicholas Biddle, who warned the banks that if they did this too quickly, they would be like a man who attempts to resume his normal activities before he has completely recovered from his illness "and would almost inevitably suffer a relapse." The relapse came rapidly. Individuals, anxious to obtain specie while they could, caused a run on the banks, including the United States Bank of Philadelphia, which was forced to close its doors in February 1841. This institution had been created by the legislature of Pennsylvania to fill the gap that had been left when the charter of the Bank of the United States had expired in 1836. The former incorporated all the stockholders of the latter and assumed all its assets and liabilities, minus the federal government's deposits, which earlier had been transferred to the Jacksonian pet banks. There were many who did not distinguish between the Bank of the United States and the United States Bank of Philadelphia; therefore, the closing of the latter had a broader psychological impact than the collapse of a state bank would ordinarily have had.[2]

"The situation of the country is most critical," Nicholas Carroll, a New York business leader, lamented to Senator Willie Mangum of North Carolina. "We have had no period resembling this at all. I could not depict the actual amount of suffering here, the extreme destitution of our laboring classes. Business of no kind is healthy or prosperous." Monetary affairs, he reported, were in shambles. There was no building in progress, and manufacturing had ceased or had been greatly reduced. Events of the past three years "had the business world agog." Individuals, businesses, and state governments were engulfed by bankruptcy. Some states could not meet the interest on their debts, and several were forced to default on their loans. Social disorders rocked the cities, Locofocoism—the radical movement in the Democratic party—gathered strength, and soon the Whigs extended the name, in derision, to the entire party. As competition for jobs increased, nativism became more widespread and increasingly cruel.

The populace now looked to the Whigs—whose campaign promises had called for better, rather than bitter, times—to find remedies for the crisis. The restoration of the Bank of the United States and higher protection for American industries were Clay's answers, but where would Tyler stand? Tyler was "known to be a firm, steadfast & true friend to Henry Clay," Carroll reminded Mangum, and "under these circumstances we look forward to the future divested of unnecessary fears."[3]

Throughout April, Tyler was bombarded with advice, especially from his states'-rights associates in Virginia. Nathaniel Beverley Tucker and Abel Parker Upshur sent Tyler a detailed plan for a bank to be created by the states, a sort of fiscal corporation wherein the states would form a federal banking association that would be completely separated from "the hands of the central power." Tyler was interested, but he thought it would be difficult to structure a governing board that would be satisfactory to all the states. Although he promised to ponder the plan, he feared that "nothing short of a National Bank, similar in all its features to that which recently passed out of existence will meet the view of the prominent men of the Whig party." The cabinet was not in any way enthusiastic about the Tucker-Upshur plan.[4]

Because of the brief time that Tyler had to prepare for the special session, he asked Clay if intricate matters, such as the bank question, could be postponed. The session, Tyler suggested, could deal with the relief of the Treasury, which was the most pressing problem. Perhaps the Independent Treasury Act could be repealed and some attention could be given to military defenses, but "as to a Bank, I design to be perfectly frank with you—I would not have it urged prematurely. The public mind is in a state of great disquietude in regard to it. The late exposures at Philadelphia [the collapse of the United States Bank of Philadelphia] have not been calculated to put it at rest." Even if Congress should decide to charter a new national bank, Tyler thought that the division of votes in both houses would be close and that those who were opposed would try to destroy the institution as soon as possible. Such a climate would very likely deter capitalists from investing in the new bank. "Jackson tore the old Bank to tatters," Tyler told Clay, and "his followers will go forth as agitators and the result of their agitation may prove disasterous." Yet if Clay should refuse to defer the question, Tyler requested that he try to avoid all constitutional objections. Tyler himself had no plan to submit to Congress, but should he have reservations about the constitutionality of congressional action, he would have to resolve his doubts accordingly. In other words, he would veto the bill. "I am writing to you in a spirit of frankness," Tyler told Clay. The letter was courteous, and nothing that the president said precluded cooperation between the two men. Clay possibly mistook courtesy for weakness, but the letter was not a weak statement. Rather, it was forthright, and after reading it, Clay knew exactly where Tyler stood.

Clay, however, was resolute. He now erroneously declared that the election of 1840 was a referendum on the bank and said that he had in mind a perfect plan for such an institution. His friends tried to tell him to proceed with caution. The president, Secretary of the Treasury Ewing informed Clay, "speaks of you with the utmost kindness and you may rely upon it, his friendship is strong and unabated." Others pointed out the advisability of having Clay reciprocate the president's cordiality. This, they said, could smooth over at least some of the differences on policy.

On 20 May, Clay left Kentucky for Washington and the special session. Aggravated by Tyler's letter, Clay arrived in an imperious and agitated mood, similar to the one he had been in less than three months earlier, when he had confronted Harrison. He declared: "If the Executive will cordially cooperate in carrying out the Whig measures, all will be well. Otherwise everything is at hazard." The "Great Compromiser" obviously had no intention of considering concessions.[5]

Not all members of the party were in agreement on "the Whig measures." Senator William C. Preston from South Carolina found the bank issue "in truth very distasteful to me. I wish the cup could be passed by—All my habits of thought have been against it, but I suppose it is inevitable."[6] Among other Whig senators who shared this sentiment were William C. Rives and William S. Archer of Virginia, William D. Merrick of Maryland, and Alexander Barrow of Louisiana. The reservations of these senators, along with the slim Whig majority in the upper house, made Tyler's prophecy about a close division of votes on a bank bill, if brought forward at this time, ring true.

Tyler's message to the special session was conciliatory and reasonable; it contained no surprises. The alarming state of the Treasury was his major concern: the secretary of that department had reported that funds, present and accruing, were insufficient to finance the government for the current year. Therefore, Tyler advised Congress, its first priority should be to take immediate action to meet a possible national deficit of approximately $11.5 million. He did not object to "discriminating duties imposed for purposes of revenue," but for the present he did not believe it advisable to disturb the compromise tariff of 1833. Consequently, the issuance of additional treasury notes seemed expedient.

Tyler advocated the creation of a "suitable fiscal agent" that would have increased facilities for the collection and distribution of public revenues and that would be capable of establishing a currency of uniform value. States as well as individuals had been infected with a reckless spirit of adventure and speculation, largely because the public revenue had been removed from the Bank of the United States and placed in irresponsible select banks.

Tyler traced the history of the first and second Bank of the United States. Jackson's veto of the recharter of the second bank was, he contended, fully sustained. Van Buren, likewise, had interpreted the will of the people correctly when he had opposed the rechartering of the bank. But placing governmental moneys in selected state banks was not a proper solution, nor was the subtreasury system, which "does not seem to stand in high favor with the people." In a short period of eight years, he observed, the public successively had condemned three systems of finance: the Bank of the United States, state banks acting as governmental depositories, and the Independent Treasury. It now was necessary to design something more acceptable.[7]

There was truth in Tyler's analysis. The state banks, in which the Jackson administration had placed governmental funds, were poorly managed. State supervision and laws were inadequate to prevent disastrous financial practices, but there were reasons to block the resurrection of the old Bank of the United States. In the past it had used its power ruthlessly, and although Clay touted it as the most important remedy for economic recovery, it, in fact, had been at least partially responsible for the severity of the 1837 panic. When deprived of federal deposits, the bank had contracted its loans more precipitately than necessary and had relentlessly pressured state depository banks to refuse to receive deposits from the federal government. According to the bank's adversaries, if the monopolistic practices of the bank had not been curtailed, it would have used financial manipulations to destroy or severely damage numerous state banks, to influence elections, and, in effect, to control the national government.

While acknowledging the bank's potential to benefit the country economically, seriously concerned Jacksonians and anti-Jacksonians alike saw inherent dangers in the accumulation of excessive financial power in the hands of one institution which could control the fate of the nation. The Independent Treasury, however, which separated the government's fiscal operations from all banks, did nothing to help the faltering economy. The "divorce," as it was termed, deprived the nation of an instrument to stabilize the currency, to assure the availability of capital and credit, and to help prevent catastrophic economic fluctuations. The Independent Treasury also threatened the interests of state banks.[8]

In his earlier letter to Clay, Tyler had warned the senator not to expect him to "come before Congress with mature plans of public policy," especially concerning the bank; and in his message, Tyler did not suggest any resolution of the problem. Rather, he submitted the entire matter to the legislators, "who have come more directly from the body of our common constituents," and promised to cooperate with them in the adoption of a proposal; but he specifically reserved to himself "the ultimate power of rejecting any measure which may, in my view of it, conflict with the Constitution or otherwise jeopardize the prosperity of the country." He considered the veto power one that he could not relinquish, even if he wished to do so, but one that he hoped the Congress would not "call into requisition."

Turning to other issues, the president voiced his approval of distributing to the states the proceeds of the sales of public lands, if such distribution did not deplete the Treasury and thereby force Congress to raise revenue by increasing the tariff above those rates contemplated by the compromise tariff of 1833. The 1833 act called for a gradual reduction of all duties over 20 percent until 1 July 1842, when all duties were to stand at a uniform rate of 20 percent. Tyler considered distribution an efficient remedial measure for the indebtedness of the states. It had much to recommend it, he said, because he did not believe the federal government should assume the debts of the states; but he did not want distribution to be used as leverage to increase tariff rates.

Although Tyler realized the limitations on what Congress could accomplish during a special session, he called its attention to other matters of importance. Something had to be done about the war against the Seminole Indians, which had so long afflicted the territory of Florida. Attention should be paid to the proper means of defending the country, taking into consideration new inventions, particularly the use of steam power upon the oceans, which made the strengthening of coastal fortifications essential. The abominable slave trade, he believed, was now on the increase and must be suppressed. "The highest considerations of public honor as well as the strongest promptings of humanity" required the most vigorous efforts to do so.

In conclusion, the president called upon members of Congress to disinterestedly promote the happiness of the people, to preserve the federal and state governments within their respective orbits, to cultivate peace with all nations, and to abolish all useless expenditures.[9]

A few days later, Secretary of the Treasury Ewing sent to Congress his report on the financial state of the government, including recommendations that the Independent Treasury Act be repealed and that a new fiscal agent be created. Clay had both of these recommendations on his agenda for the special session, along with others he considered mandatory to accomplish before the summer's end: namely, the distribution to the states of the proceeds from the sale of public lands; the upward revision of the tariff to provide additional revenue; a temporary loan to cover the debt created by the previous administration.

Clay had his mind set on what type of fiscal agent he would sponsor, but he followed established procedure and requested the Senate to adopt a resolution calling upon the secretary of the treasury to present to the upper house, "with as little delay as practicable, a plan of such a bank to be incorporated by Congress, as, in his opinion is best adapted to the public service." Several Democrats, along with William C. Rives, objected to the wording of Clay's resolution and asked for a modification, directing the secretary to prepare a plan for a bank or fiscal agent that would be "free from constitutional objections," one that would "produce the happiest results, and confer lasting and important benefits on the country."

Knowing that Clay was adamant about recreating a Bank of the United States, Ewing, along with the president and other cabinet members, had been working on a plan during the last week in May. It was based largely on one that Hugh Lawson White had suggested in the 1830s, a compromise measure, hopefully acceptable to both the Clay Whigs and the states' righters. The proposal called for the incorporation of a bank and fiscal agent in the District of Columbia, an area under the jurisdiction of Congress, acting in its capacity as the local governing body for the area, and in which there would be no question of Congress's constitutional authority to locate such an institution. The bank would be the fiscal agent for the government, and it would be authorized to establish branch banks of discount and deposit in states that would specifically give the bank permission to do so. This recognition of a state's right to bar the establishment of a branch bank within its borders had been omitted from the charters of the first and second Bank of the United States. Included in the new plan, however, were some characteristics reminiscent of the earlier banks. The federal government would subscribe one-fifth of the $30 million of authorized capital. An additional $10 million in stocks would be allocated to the states on the basis of population, and the remainder would be sold to the public.[10]

Tyler was uncomfortable about allowing the proposed fiscal agent to compete with state banks in accepting deposits and making discounts on loans. (Ante-bellum bankers on the state level printed and lent their own bank notes, usually deducting, or "discounting," in advance the interest due them.) Nevertheless, he was willing, at this point, to approve the plan, and he met with Clay to urge him, "in the strongest manner," to support its adoption.

Ewing, in his report to Congress in which he recommended the replacement of the Independent Treasury, made a plea for moderation. The power to incorporate a national bank, he reminded the legislators, "has been questioned by many wise and patriotic statesmen, whose opinions are entitled to consideration and respect." Therefore, it was important, "as far as possible, to obviate objections and reconcile opinions."

Clay had no intention of heeding such admonitions, and he was in a position to exert tremendous influence on his fellow Whig senators. He was chairman not only of the Senate Committee on Finance and of the Committee on Public Lands but also of the Select Committee named to consider Ewing's bank plan, which Clay held up to scorn. A bank "having no power to *branch* without the consent of the State where the branch is located. What a bank would that be!"[11]

Regardless of Clay's attitude, Ewing's proposal mustered considerable support. Businessmen were invited to Washington to discuss the idea, and even though they had some reservations, they promised to do all they could to ensure its success. Joseph Gales and William Seaton, editors of the *National Intelligencer*, the Whigs' own organ, believed the bill to be "well-considered." "We do not say that the Treasury plan is perfect, or even the best that could have been devised," but they thought it came nearer to pleasing a larger number than anything yet presented. Do not hazard the success of a great measure, they warned, "for the mere gratification of a personal wish." To fulfill the country's high expectations for relief from the economic depression, the Whigs must "give up personal predilections, & with a singleness of heart, & under the full sense of the responsibility which rests upon them, UNITE their counsels, fairly & cordially, & make a vigorous effort to revive the country."

Daniel Webster followed this plea with three editorials of his own, published in the *National Intelligencer*. He, too, earnestly appealed for unity. It would, he said, be better to agree on *some* bank, rather than to have no bank at all. In answer to those who argued that the states would not consent to the establishment of branch banks within their borders, he countered, "There is no doubt, that the States, with one or two exceptions, perhaps for the present, & with no exceptions, in a short time, will readily give the necessary assent." The practical difficulty, he thought, would be on the other side. The danger would be that both states and individuals would apply for more branches than would be convenient or safe for the institution to create.[12]

Voices from the South were heard. Duncan Cameron, a prominent North Carolina landowner who was also president of the State Bank of

North Carolina, felt the president's message to the special session was "pretty sane." On the subject of a fiscal agent, Tyler "has gone as far in favor of the conversion as his *former* position in regard to that subject will reasonably allow." Care should be taken, Cameron warned, not to force immediate opposition to the plan by introducing provisions that would be unacceptable to Tyler. "His own good sense, and conviction of what is required by the deranged and suffering interests of the Country, must be relied on for approving such a plan as will correct the evils complained of."

Congressman Edward Stanly of North Carolina thought the Ewing bill would be popular if carried through. "I sincerely hope so for the sake of the country." But he also realized that many Whigs believed that "giving in" to the president, even to the smallest extent on this matter, would mean "giving up the whole ground" and compromising their views on the restriction of presidential authority. Stanly himself did not like the Ewing plan very much, but he thought it better to take what they could get now and amend it later on, if necessary. Having a bank was more important than waging war against Tyler's constitutional scruples. Senator William Graham, also of North Carolina, was confident that the bill would pass, saying the plan would be effective and receive the approbation of the president. "There is however, a high state of excitement and there will be every effort to produce a delay."[13]

The "high state of excitement" extended to critics outside of Congress. Mordecai Manuel Noah, a New York attorney and journalist, now an associate judge of the New York Court of Sessions, believed that not one in a hundred of New York City's Whigs approved of Ewing's plan. According to Noah, Chancellor James Kent, citing a verbal opinion expressed by John Marshall, said a surrendering to the states of the power to establish branch banks would be destructive of the Constitution.

Among business and financial interests there was pressure to locate the bank in Philadelphia or in New York. Washington, they said, was for politics; New York and Philadelphia were for commerce. Others thought the states would not give permission for branch banks and that there would be prolonged battles over the issue. Surfacing frequently was the concern that the Ewing bank would not be strong enough to achieve financial stability.

A bank, national in all its characteristics, was what Clay wanted. This had been the linchpin of his American System ever since its inception after the War of 1812. Jackson's demolition of the Bank of the United States had been a bitter pill. Clay was still suffering from the 1832 election and the 1840 nomination. Clay felt his leadership had been tarnished, and he was trying to reestablish his reputation in the eyes of the party and the public. He seemed almost obsessed with the fear that the adoption of Ewing's proposal (which Clay looked upon as a Tyler measure) would weaken his position. Conversely, if Clay could defeat Tyler on the bank issue, congressional supremacy, under Clay's leadership, would be reinstated. Therefore, Clay persisted in his opposition, and he pressured his followers to do likewise. "He is much more imperious and arrogant with his friends than I have ever known him," Silas Wright, then a Democratic senator from New York, reported to Van Buren, "and *that* you know is saying a great deal." The Washington correspondent of the *New York Herald* wrote that Clay "predominates over the Whig party with despotic sway. Old Hickory himself never lorded it over his followers with authority more undisputed, or more supreme."[14]

Oscar D. Lambert, in *Presidential Politics in the United States, 1841–1844,* has placed the responsibility for the controversy over the Ewing plan on Tyler, who, Lambert says, began his administration with one fixed purpose, to succeed himself in 1844. Therefore, Tyler set out to destroy Clay's leadership, and he used the bank issue in an effort to brush Clay aside, seize control of the Whig party, and take away "Clay's crown."

Clement Eaton, in *Henry Clay and the Art of American Politics,* has expressed the opinion that Clay misjudged Tyler's character and perseverance and that Clay thought the president would yield to the dominant element in the Whig party. If this should happen, congressional supremacy would be secure. Perhaps Clay was hoping to goad Tyler into vetoing a bill that called for a strong national bank. Tyler had been frank in saying, both in his 30 April letter to Clay and in his message to the special session, that he could not sign a bill he considered unconstitutional. Clay had used the "veto tactic" in 1832. Confronting Jackson with a bill to recharter the Bank of the United States four years before the old charter was due to expire, Clay was certain that Jackson would disapprove the bill and was confident that the president would be ruined by a veto.[15]

A person's motivation is difficult to understand and most often can only be surmised. To counter the "duel for the presidency" theory, one can point out that Clay had lashed out at Harrison on several occasions and that Harrison posed no threat to Clay's leadership or to his desire for the executive office. It seems likely that a part of Clay's strategy was to reaffirm the doctrine of congressional supremacy, at least until he himself could occupy the nation's highest office. "Presidential usurpation" had been a stumbling block in the implementation of his policies.

Now the kind of bank he wanted was again in danger because of a president's power to destroy it. Overarching all, however, was the deep-seated struggle between nationalism and states' rights, which touched almost every aspect of American politics and government.

By mid June, Clay had succeeded in getting the Senate's approval for the repeal of the Independent Treasury. The next step was to decide on what type of bank should replace it. While most of the Whigs in the Senate favored a stronger bank than the one proposed in the Ewing plan, the Whig majority was slight, and some were willing to compromise for the sake of harmony. The defection of only a few could prevent the creation of the bank that Clay had in mind. Nevertheless, Clay prevailed upon the Select Committee to set aside Ewing's ideas, and on 21 June, as chairman of that group, he brought to the floor of the Senate the committee's majority report, which recommended the adoption of a bank bill authored by Clay himself.

Clay's bill, as in the Ewing plan, located the bank in Washington, but it was to be incorporated by Congress in its capacity as the national legislature, not as the governing body for the District of Columbia. Branch banks would be established without the consent of the individual states. In speaking in favor of his bill, Clay condemned the Ewing plan as "ineffectual and dangerous." A bank whose operations depended on the will of the states, he declared, would end in chaos and disaster. The federal government, in the exercise of its "necessary and proper" powers, should not have to rely upon the consent of the states.

Although the Whigs had a majority of seven in the Senate, at least five were not firmly behind Clay's bill. Perhaps only the threat of executive usurpation, brought to the fore by a presidential veto, could unite the members of the party in support of Clay's measure. "The Whig party is in a most woeful plight," Mangum lamented, "and there is ground for apprehension that the session will prove abortive," resulting in "disgrace, disaster, and final discomfiture." The cabinet had committed a great error, Mangum charged, in yielding to the Ewing plan. Instead, the cabinet should have "brought the President to the broad Whig platform or to have handed in the seals of office. . . . As a man of honor Tyler ought to resign or accede to Whig principles."[16]

Clay hoped to drive the president in that direction. The Kentuckian's "imperious and arrogant actions in 1841 and 1842," Eaton has contended, "are perhaps the least defensible part of his career." But Clay was not the only one who deported himself in an offensive manner. As the debate continued, there were few tempers that did not become frayed. The Senate sat for nearly seven hours a day, from ten o'clock in the morning until five in the afternoon. Preparations to meet "the momentous questions, which are forced on us in such rapid succession and consultations to produce concert of action," occupied most of the remaining hours, Calhoun complained. He was encouraged to see the Whigs "dispirited and distracted," but he feared they could rally and carry their measure. If they did not succeed in doing so, he thought they would "be utterly broke."

Anger boiled over when, on 1 July, William Rives attempted to amend Clay's bank bill by requiring that individual state legislatures consent to the placing of branches of discount or deposit within their jurisdiction. As a compromise, the amendment also included a provision preventing a state from withdrawing its consent after a branch had been established. This was necessary because of the fluctuations of elections in many of the states. One legislature might give its consent which the next one might repeal, leaving branch banks in perpetual insecurity. If this amendment was agreed upon, Rives assured the Senate that Tyler would sign the bill. Democrats, who were delighted to see internal warfare among the Whigs and who were desirous of keeping the inner-party hostilities going, joined Clay Whigs in voting down the amendment.[17]

Clay redoubled his efforts to gain the support of the recalcitrants for the adoption of his bill. He "lectured, cajoled, and intimidated," but the deadlock remained. "Clay and the Whigs are exerting every nerve to carry their measure," Calhoun reported, "and resorting to the most despotick and unusual rules to accomplish their object, but the resistance, particularly in the Senate, is steady, concentrated, and effective." Most of the Whigs blamed Tyler for the impasse, while others saw Webster as the great source of trouble. "The people never intended by the election of Harrison and Tyler to bring Daniel Webster into power."[18]

What Webster hoped for was a compromise bank, one that would be acceptable, if not precisely desirable, to the Clay Whigs and to the president. Such a bank should at least be tried, he pleaded, and "if it fails Congress will meet again next winter and revise their own work. . . . The season is advancing and the weather is hot—but nothing, nothing should induce Congress to rise, leaving this great work wholly undone." Webster was now convinced that the critical condition of the nation's economy demanded a remedy.

Despite his struggles, Clay could not muster a majority for his bill, so he resorted to delaying tactics by calling for the consideration of the loan bill and the bankruptcy bill, both of which were passed by the Senate and signed by the president. In the meantime, the Whigs caucused to formulate an amendment, purported to be a "compromise." It is difficult to say who actually initiated the idea, but it appears to have been a joint effort on the part of Peter B. Porter (a former congressman from New York) and Congressman John Minor Botts of Virginia, formerly a Tyler friend but now a vigorous Clay man.

The Botts amendment, as it was called, provided for the establishment of branch banks, with state consent—a seeming concession, but with a strange twist. The consent of a state would be presumed, unless at the first meeting of the state legislature held after the passage of the bank bill, the lawmakers were to refuse unconditionally to allow branch banks within their state's boundaries. But there was more. Whenever it should become "necessary and proper" for Congress to do so, branches could be located in states, regardless of the wishes of their respective governing bodies. Once in place, the branch banks could be withdrawn only by congressional action.

Botts showed the amendment to Tyler, who said in a later statement that he "emphatically, unhesitatingly, and unequivocally" rejected it, considering the proposal "supremely ridiculous . . . a contemptible subterfuge . . . a settled and deliberate purpose to evoke the veto." Botts, however, supposedly reported to Clay that the president had said he would approve a bank bill thus amended.[19]

Before the amendment was introduced, the Democrats called for a vote on Clay's bill, but the Whigs quickly moved an adjournment. Preston and Merrick were still wavering, and by convincing them of the president's acceptance of the Botts amendment, it was hoped they would vote in favor of the bill. Calhoun told James H. Hammond of South Carolina: "Could we have gotten the question on the engrossment the day before, the bill would have been lost. Preston and Merrick were brought in to its support the night before the question was put." The amendment passed by one vote, and on the following day, 28 July, Clay's amended bill was adopted by a margin of three votes.

Had Botts deliberately misrepresented Tyler's reaction to the proposed amendment? It cannot be known with any certainty what transpired between Botts and Tyler during the White House meeting. On several occasions, Tyler did not make distinct statements about his views, whether out of courtesy in not wanting to have a confrontation with the person who was presenting an idea or because of an unwillingness to declare himself, believing that by doing so, he might appear to be unduly influencing Congress, thus violating the separation of powers.

It is impossible to say whether Botts misunderstood or misrepresented Tyler, but it is inconceivable that the president, who had strong feelings on the subject of state consent, would have accepted the amendment. Later, Tyler said he had reason to believe that many senators voted for the bank bill under the impression that the amendment relieved the bill from his objections to it. The Virginia senators, Rives and Archer, voted with the Democrats against the bill.[20]

What Tyler considered to be Clay's covert actions angered and disgusted him. His feelings were shared by other Whigs. Reverdy Johnson of Baltimore, one of the great constitutional lawyers of his day, was disturbed by the Botts amendment. "Is it possible that you could not have carried the Bank Bill without the 'compromise amendment'?" he asked Mangum. "To tell the States that they shall be *presumed* to assent to a branch, if they do not *unconditionally* dissent, & that altho' they do *so* dissent, a branch will be fixed upon them in their spite, is to insult their sovereignty." The contradiction, Johnson was certain, would have to be dealt with by the Supreme Court, and he was convinced that the Court would declare that it would be unconstitutional to establish a branch bank in a state that had specifically refused to sanction it. "You," Johnson chided Mangum, "I am sure, must, most unwillingly, have fallen in with the amendment."

Tyler thought Clay had backed him against a wall. If Tyler were to approve the bank bill with the Botts amendment he would be condemned by states'-rights Whigs and Democrats; if he were to veto it, the Clay Whigs would cry presidential usurpation. The Ewing bill, which Tyler maintained was devised to promote peace and harmony, was now said "to have arisen in a spirit of executive dictation, and war is to be made not only upon my opinions, but my motives." Now he was no longer certain that he could even support the Ewing bill.[21]

On 6 August the House approved Clay's bill by approximately a thirty-vote majority, and it went to Tyler for his approval or disapproval. For the ten days allowed him by the Constitution, the president held Congress and other interested parties in suspense—in order to allow passions to cool, he said. Some boasted that they knew what he would do. Thomas Gilmer, claiming to have inside information, was one of these. "*The President* will veto the Bank bill. I know this, and am one of the very few who do know it. . . . He has done me the honor to consult me confidentially about measures and men here, and freely." But Webster saw Tyler as being more cautious: "Tyler keeps his own counsel as to approving or disapproving." Although Webster preferred the Ewing plan, he deeply desired the president's signature on Clay's bill. He feared the great commotion a veto would cause. Publicly, Webster voiced optimism, but privately he realized that the chance for approval was nonexistent, and by 11 August, he had no doubt.[22]

On that day, in a five-hour session, the cabinet tried unsuccessfully to persuade Tyler to sign the bill. On the following day, Tyler's unofficial organ, the *Madisonian*, stated its opinion on the proper relationship between the president and his cabinet. The executive branch, it declared, should be a whole unit, with the department heads acting as sincere and willing exponents of the president's deliberate convictions. Otherwise the administration would present to the world the "absurd spectacle" of a power divided against itself. Taking issue with this point of view, the *National Intelligencer* called it an "odious Jacksonian pretension."

As rumors of an impending veto circulated, Willie Mangum took to his bed, "sick in body & at heart," pleading, "God save the Republic." Ewing and Webster had similar symptoms. The great Whig triumph of 1840 was about to become a hollow victory.[23]

On the eve of the last day allotted to the president in which to make his decision, the congressional Whigs caucused to plan their postveto strategy. In the course of their planning, they gave vent to much bitterness against Tyler and finally resolved to return to the Ewing plan, which the president earlier had sanctioned but about which he now appeared to have reservations. In returning to the Ewing plan, the Whigs expected to place Tyler in an uncomfortable position. If they passed the bill and he vetoed it, they could accuse him of rejecting his own measure, department heads would presumably resign, and Tyler would be without a party. On the other hand, if he approved the bill, the Clay Whigs were confident that it could not succeed, and Tyler would be forced to fall back on Clay's bill. No matter what happened, Tyler would lose face.

By a gentleman of the "strictest veracity," Tyler was told of the evening's scheme, and on the following morning, when Ewing and Bell called at the White House, the president read to them parts of the veto message he was about to send to the Senate. Included were statements strongly encouraging the senators to devise another bank bill on which the executive and Congress could agree. Tyler now wanted to prohibit branch banks from discounting promissory notes. In other words, he was against their making local loans in competition with state banks. This had troubled him in both the Ewing bill and the Clay bill, and the longer he had thought about it, the less he liked it. Cabinet members were pleased that Tyler had not closed the door completely on a bank bill, and they began making plans to accommodate the president's wishes.[24]

When the veto message reached the Senate, the Clay Whigs shouted "treason" and professed to be shocked, even though the action had been very much anticipated. What may have been a surprise in the veto message was Tyler's rejection of the branch banks' right to make local loans. He had made no objection to the inclusion of such a provision in the Ewing bill, but in that measure the states had been given the option of accepting or rejecting branches. Because, in Tyler's opinion, there were other, more blatantly offensive features in the Clay bill, perhaps now he had decided to voice his disapproval of the local discounts as well, infringements on what he considered to be the province of state banks.

In particular, Tyler criticized the provisions of the Botts amendment. He declared that the "unbending, inflexible iron rule" that demanded that the state legislatures act on the establishment of branch banks at their first sessions after the passage of the bank bill, or else consent would be implied, was "the language of the master to the Vassal." It would be "far better to say to the States, boldly and frankly, Congress wills and submission is demanded." Moreover, he refused to approve the assertion that Congress possessed the power to establish offices of discount in a state, not only without its assent, but against its dissent.

If Webster's wish had been granted, the president would have signed the bill, but Webster gamely upheld the chief executive's constitutional right to use the veto power and indicated that all was not lost. New efforts toward agreement should and could be made, but tempers were too short to take up the matter at once. He thought it better to wait until the next session, due to convene in a few months.[25]

Postponement did not appeal to Clay. Even before the veto message was read in the Senate, plans for a new bill were under way. Crittenden took the lead. Having local discount privileges granted to the branch banks appeared to be the item that most troubled Tyler. This, the attorney general ascertained, could be circumvented. Writing a quick message to Clay, he said it was understood (presumably by the cabinet) that the president had conceded to Congress the power of creating agencies or branches with authority to deal in the purchase and sale of bills of exchange and to do all other usual banking business *except* the discounting of notes. It was further understood that if these branches were banned from dealing in local discounts, they could be established without the consent of the states. Would it not be better, Crittenden asked, "to drop everything about the *assent of States*, and making the banking power a mere emanation of congressional authority, exclude it from the discounting of promissory notes?"

True, the Whigs considered the control of local loans absolutely necessary if the bank was to have as one of its objectives the regulation of the nation's credit, but Crittenden envisioned the possibility that bills of exchange could be manipulated to make their function almost indistinguishable from that of local discount. "The moneyed transactions of men will be put into the shape of bills of exchange," he assured Clay. If this failed to work, the bank thus formed could easily be amended by future legislation to include the right to discount notes.

The letter smacked of intrigue and irony. "I pray you to consider this well," Crittenden told Clay, "with all the great consequences which attend it, and do whatever your known liberal spirit of *compromise* and your *patriotism* may direct. . . . The political effect of settling this matter now and *by your means* will be great."[26]

Clearly, there was a "joker" in the bill. The president's wishes in regard to local discounting would be honored, but the practice would be continued under a guise, which the attorney general hoped would escape Tyler's notice. Clay saw great possibilities in the plan. If Tyler were to veto the bill, he could be accused of vacillating, of rejecting his own ideas. If he were to sign it, the Clay Whigs would achieve what they had wanted from the beginning: branches placed throughout the country, without the necessity for state consent, would be able to make local loans by utilizing bills of exchange.

Crittenden wanted Clay to write the bill, but the senator thought this would arouse Tyler's suspicions, and furthermore, if Tyler appeared to be having an important part in the formulation of the bill, the better the intrigue might succeed. Therefore, Clay asked James Pearse, a former Whig congressman from Maryland, to contact Congressman Alexander H. H. Stuart of Virginia and ask him to discuss the new bill with Tyler.

The president received Stuart cordially, and the two Virginians talked about the veto message of 16 August and some aspects of an amendment that Senator Richard H. Bayard of Delaware had proposed in July, one of many alterations to Clay's bank bill that had been considered and rejected. Portions of the amendment appealed to Tyler. The term "agency" was used instead of "branch banks." A euphemism, perhaps, but "agency" conveyed a sense of something smaller than a full-blown bank. Tyler suggested its use in the new bill. Also, he recommended that there be a ban on discounting promissory notes by the agencies and that the institutions be entirely prohibited in states where legislatures already had passed laws precluding their establishment. A Virginia statute forbade the location of "foreign banks" within the commonwealth. To a number of states'-rights Virginians, "foreign banks" included agencies of a national bank. Additionally, Tyler wanted the capital of a proposed central bank reduced to $10 or $15 million dollars, rather than the $30 million stipulated in Clay's bill. Stuart thought that the prohibition clause was undesirable and that the bank's capital might have to be larger than the president's suggested figures. The entire conversation was somewhat vague and unfocused. Tyler had not anticipated the meeting and evidently had been surprised by Stuart's visit. Nevertheless, Tyler naïvely appeared to be enormously relieved to know that there was a possibility of a resolution to his conflict with Clay and Clay's followers. Tyler asked Stuart to work out the details with Webster, but Webster was out when Stuart called, and later that evening the congressman reported to an assembly of Whigs on his interchange with the president. After considerable debate, Congressman John Sergeant and Senator John M. Berrian were delegated, as an informal committee, to see Tyler and make certain that they understood his views.[27]

When they met with the president on the following day, 17 August, and again on the eighteenth, Tyler was withdrawn and evinced little enthusiasm for the proposal. When Berrian and Sergeant, in the presence of Ewing, tried to work out specific points, the president refused to discuss details, saying his veto message was sufficiently explicit to indicate what he would or would not approve. He did not think "it became him" to spell out a bank plan.

Ewing, attempting to clarify, said he understood Tyler would agree to a bank located in the District of Columbia which would have agencies in the several states to perform services required by the government. These agencies could deal in exchange and execute all other functions named in the bill just rejected, except the making of local discounts. The president, according to Ewing, offered no objections, even to the creation of agencies without state consent, provided the agencies did not discount promissory notes.

Meeting with his cabinet shortly after having seen Berrian and Sergeant, Tyler said that his primary concern was the impropriety of conferring directly with members of Congress. Apparently, after Stuart's visit, he began to be uncomfortable, thinking he may have said too much. Tyler told the cabinet that he did not want to be accused of dictating to the legislative branch. He also was afraid that his views could be misrepresented. A majority of the cabinet agreed that it would be better for him to decline all such conferences and, in the future, rely on his department heads, who would provide liaison with Congress.

When Ewing attempted to explain some aspects of the proposed bill, the president was testy and uncharacteristically curt but he seemingly agreed on the right of the agencies to receive, disburse, and transact the public moneys and to deal in bills of exchange without the assent of the states, provided, as Tyler specified, the bills were foreign or were drawn in one state and payable in another. The prohibition against creating agencies where they were forbidden by a previous state law was not mentioned. At least, these were the points that Ewing remembered and later recorded in his diary.

Webster, in his "Memorandum on the Banking Bills and the Vetoes," not dated but obviously written some time later, was more cautious about attributing statements to Tyler. The president, according to the secretary of state, "did not intimate that he desired the assent of the States" to the creation of agencies. However, Webster strongly supported the plan under discussion, and his views seemed to have a favorable influence on Tyler, who asked the secretaries of state and of the treasury to see that the plan was put into acceptable form. In doing this, he warned Webster and Ewing to take care not to commit him or them to anything that could embarrass the president or the cabinet. He did not want Congress either to reject a bill that he was known to support or to ridicule him for now favoring what he had formerly vetoed. Ewing observed that Tyler "expressed great sensitiveness" about how Congress would react. Tyler also specifically directed Webster and Ewing to have the bill introduced in the House rather than in the Senate, and he wanted to see a copy of it prior to its introduction.[28]

Webster and Ewing conferred with Berrian and Sergeant, who, in turn, presented the plan to a committee of Whigs, in which an agreement was reached to have the bill—to be called, at Tyler's request, the Fiscal Corporation bill—introduced in the House. As the wheels of legislation began to turn, Tyler had second, or third, thoughts: he expressed a desire to have the bill postponed until the next session. He said he was bewildered by the various provisions and needed time to collect his thoughts. Webster tried to reassure him. If everyone would stay calm and reasonable, the secretary of state was hopeful that the troublesome bank matter could be settled amicably.[29]

6

THE WHIGS EXPEL A PRESIDENT

Clay was not calm. On 19 August, prior to the Senate's consideration of the veto, he rose to speak. There was no reason, except a political
one, for him to discuss the rejected bill. Everyone knew there was
absolutely no possibility of overturning the veto, but for an hour and a
half, Clay dissected Tyler's message. He challenged the president's
reasoning and ridiculed (albeit with studied courtesy) his statements,
ostensibly in an attempt to vindicate the bank bill, "a measure which
has met with a fate so unmerited, and so unexpected." Clay was not
being truthful. All the senators were aware that the veto was anticipated.

Turning to the Botts amendment, Clay claimed it was a friendly
concession to the president's conscience, one that should have engendered Tyler's appreciation. Every senator who had voted in favor of the
bill, Clay declared, greatly preferred unqualified branching power, yet
they were willing to offer this generous compromise. Again, Clay was
dissembling. Several state's-rights Whigs who had been cajoled into
voting for the bill in no way preferred unqualified branching power.

Some of Clay's most caustic remarks were directed at executive
usurpation. For the past twelve years, Clay maintained, a president,
acting autocratically, had been responsible for the ills of the nation.
Should this be allowed to continue in order to preserve inviolate the
conscience of the executive? If Tyler's scruples would not allow him to
sign the bill, he need not have resorted to the veto. There were
alternatives. He could have allowed the bill to become law without his

signature. Obviously, the country wanted a bank. The election of 1840, a referendum on the entire Whig program, indicated the public's desire for a national bank. These statements, too, were questionable. If the Whigs had been so certain of the electorate's support for their program, why had they not spelled it out in a party platform, rather than hedging throughout the campaign?

Clay pointed to another alternative that Tyler might have chosen—he could have resigned. Not, Clay said, that he meant to intimate that Tyler *ought* to have done so, but, he recalled, Tyler had given up his Senate seat because he could not obey instructions issued by the General Assembly of Virginia. If he could not conform to the wishes of a majority in Congress and in the nation, should not a resignation also have been considered in this instance? "Is obedience due only to the state of Virginia?"

If because of the presidential veto the extra session was unable to stabilize the currency, in the near future "some way will be found to limit and qualify the enormous executive power." He suggested an amendment to the Constitution. Although at this time he offered no specifics, apparently what he had in mind was an amendment that would allow presidential vetoes to be overturned by a simple majority in each house, rather than by the current constitutional stipulation of a two-thirds vote of the House and the Senate.

When William C. Rives of Virginia attempted to defend the president, Clay turned his scorn upon the senator: "I found him [Rives] several years ago in the half-way house, where he seems afraid to remain and from which he is yet unwilling to go." This was a reference to Rives's association with the Virginia Conservative Democrats, before Clay had persuaded him to join the Whigs. In an attempt to woo other Conservative Democrats into the Whig fold, Clay had backed Rives in the Virginia senatorial race, but to the Kentuckian's chagrin, Rives had become Tyler's staunchest supporter in the Senate. Rives, Clay said, defended the president "with all the solicitude and all the fervent zeal of a member of his [Tyler's] *privy council.*" There was a rumor abroad, Clay continued, about the existence of a cabal, "a new sort of kitchen cabinet," the members of which had as their objective the dissolution of the regular cabinet, the breakup of the Whig party, and the dispersion of the special session without its having passed a bank bill. This group, he charged, was small, "wholly insufficient to compose a decent *corporal's guard,*" yet they proposed to form a third party with Tyler at the helm.

Clay went on to accuse the president of pride, vanity, and egotism, vices that were "unamiable and offensive in private life" but that take on "the character of crimes in the conduct of public affairs. The unfortunate victim of these passions cannot see beyond the little, petty, contemptible circles of his own personal interests."[1] The speech was spiteful and rancorous, and it held the absolute attention of the Senate and an overflow crowd in the galleries.

Tyler was hurt and embittered, feelings that were intensified when, on the following day, a letter written by John Minor Botts surfaced and later was published in several newspapers. It was addressed to a coffeehouse in Richmond, a club of sorts, where prominent men in the city gathered and where it was the practice to post letters and other communications dealing with political or public affairs.

Botts's letter, written on 16 August, the day the Senate received the veto message, was a violent castigation of Tyler, who, Botts claimed, was "making a desperate effort to set himself up with the loco-focos [Democrats]; but he'll be headed yet, and I regret to say, it will end badly for him." The bank issue, Botts boasted, would destroy Tyler's credibility with both parties. The Whigs would abhor him for having vetoed their bill, and the Democrats would detest him for having signed a worse one.

Shortly after reading Botts's letter, Tyler appeared in Webster's office, "full of suspicion and resentment," distrustful of almost everyone. He suspected Clay, Botts, and others of using the bank issue to destroy him, of baiting him into rejecting the bill. They wanted no rapprochement, of that he was certain; but they were determined either to force him out of office or, failing that, to make him completely ineffectual. He wanted a vote on the Fiscal Corporation bill, now under consideration in the House of Representatives, postponed.[2]

Webster told Hiram Ketchum, an attorney and leader of the Webster Whigs in New York City: "The President is agitated. Mr. Clay's Speech & Mr. Botts' most extraordinary letter have much affected him. At the same time, there is no doubt that violent assaults are made upon him, from certain quarters, to break the Whigs, change his Cabinet, etc., etc."

On 23 August the House passed the Fiscal Corporation bill by a vote of 125 to 94, and on the twenty-fourth it was sent to the Senate. In an effort to have the bill postponed, Webster enlisted the aid of the Massachusetts senators, Isaac Bates and Rufus Choate. Webster doubted the existence of a sinister plot to entrap the president and destroy his effectiveness, but Botts's "coffeehouse letter," which implied that the Whigs intended to "head" Tyler and place him in an embarrassing situation, had deeply disturbed the chief executive. "A decisive rebuke," Webster advised Bates and Choate, "ought, in my judgment, to be given to the intimation, from whatever quarter . . . and such a rebuke, I think would be found in the general resolution of the Party to postpone further proceedings on the [bank] subject to the next session, now a little more than three months off." The president should not be forced to act either under restraint or out of embarrassment.[3]

Tyler deserved better, Webster contended, for he had "cordially concurred" in a mass of important legislation, more than had been accomplished for many years. The Treasury had been replenished by a $12-million loan, the navy had received appropriations for a home squadron and coastal fortifications, the Independent Treasury had been repealed, the Bankruptcy Act was now law, and the land bill was about to receive the sanction of Congress. Tyler, to his credit, had not faulted any of these measures. This, Robert J. Morgan has observed, may have accounted for much of Clay's hostility toward Tyler. The Kentuckian "could not afford to let John Tyler stand as a good Whig."

Webster's request for the postponement of the bank bill was rejected by Clay. A number of Whigs thought the senator was acting rashly, "hurrying matters to a catastrophe," in Ewing's words, "intending to hasten the new Bank bill upon Mr. Tyler; force him to approve or Veto—in the latter event compel the Cabinet to resign—denounce the Administration, and make himself as head of the Whig party an opposition candidate for the Presidency." Clay exerted extreme pressure on Whigs who even dared hint that Tyler, as president, was due at least a modicum of consideration. More than Clay wanted a bank, he wanted to bring down Tyler, and perhaps Webster with him.

Tyler was distraught. If the bill was not postponed, he felt compelled to veto it. He was now well aware of the "joker" in the Fiscal Corporation bill. Botts's imprudent letter had confirmed Tyler's suspicions that there was a plot to discredit him. Also, he had arrived at the conclusion that the bank, as now proposed, resembled the old Bank of the United States more than he could tolerate. He claimed that he had not been given a copy of the bill prior to its introduction in the House and that his desired prohibition of the creation of agencies in states whose laws forbade them had been omitted. Senator Rives and Congressmen Henry Wise and George Proffit of Indiana warned of a veto unless changes were made in the bill, but they were shouted down.[4]

What the cabinet would do in the event of another veto was a matter of grave concern. Tyler knew he had to provide for the possibility of mass resignations, for even though department heads might have some desire to stand by him, they would not be able to endure Clay's relentless harassment.

There were pressures on Tyler from another source. The so-called Virginia Cabal favored the ousting of the present cabinet and the naming of one more favorable to their ideas. Clay was correct in saying that states'-rights Virginians, plus a few others, were exerting every effort to influence the president. Not all their efforts were successful, however. Tyler listened to his Virginia friends and acquaintances of long standing with his usual courtesy, but for the most part, he followed his own counsel. Yet, their constant presence, in person or in writing, could not help but contribute to his confusion and anxiety when faced with difficult decisions. Henry Wise was certain that he, more than anyone else, had the president's ear. Thomas Gilmer believed *he* was the one to whom Tyler listened most closely. Both were in the House of Representatives and frequently visited the White House. From Virginia, Nathaniel Beverley Tucker and Abel Parker Upshur sent enormous amounts of advice; and when the advice was not heeded, their feelings were hurt. The Clay Whigs, from time to time, accused others of being part of what they called "this nefarious group," but the names of Wise, Tucker, Gilmer, and Upshur surfaced most frequently. In his speech on 19 August, Clay expanded the cabal to a "corporal's guard," which included non-Virginians as well as those from the Old Dominion. George Proffit of Indiana and Caleb Cushing of Massachusetts definitely were considered members of this group, but anyone who dared to voice support, however slight, for the president, found that Clay placed them in this category. Tyler did not regard these individuals as members of a "kitchen cabinet," although Clay persisted in using the term.

When Tyler seriously sought advice, he often turned to Littleton Waller Tazewell, who was regarded by many as one of the great intellectuals of the South. Tazewell and Tyler had served together in the United States Senate, and Tyler had the deepest respect for Tazewell's integrity and stability. Tazewell had not supported the Harrison-Tyler ticket in 1840, and perhaps this made his advice all the more valuable to Tyler, for Tazewell made no demands on the president. Rather, prior to the 1840 election, he warned Tyler about the difficulties that Tyler could encounter as a Whig vice-president: if Harrison was elected, there was more than a possibility that he would not live to complete his term. If this happened, the dominant nationalist faction within the Whig party would insist that Tyler agree to its program. If he did not—if he refused to yield his conscience, judgment, and all else into their hands—he would be violently assaulted, and "fearful combinations" would attempt to force him to resign.

This had all come to pass, and Tyler was beset not only by fearful Whig combinations but also by states'-rights extremists. Wise gleefully informed Beverley Tucker: "We are on the eve of a cabinet rupture. With some of them we want to part friendly. We can part friendly with

Webster by sending him to England. Let us, for God's sake, get rid of him on the best terms we can."[5]

Tyler had not found Webster offensive. In compliance with the secretary's wishes and to the consternation of Tyler's self-appointed Virginia advisors, the president, in July, had sent the name of Edward Everett to the Senate for confirmation as minister to Great Britain. Everett—a Unitarian minister, Harvard professor, editor of the *North American Review,* four-term governor of Massachusetts, a man of anti-slavery principles, and Webster's friend—was hardly the person the extreme-states'-rights Virginians would have selected. Tucker had urged the appointment of Upshur. "Everett will not be confirmed," Wise assured Tucker, but on the last day of the special session, Everett's nomination, solidly backed by the president, was approved.[6]

To the Virginia Cabal, Tyler's independent actions were as offensive as they were to Clay. The president needed "some wholesome lessons on the use of his patronage," Upshur told Tucker, who was commissioned to instruct the chief executive along lines that would lead to "the advancement of the true faith."

During the tense days while the Fiscal Corporation bill was under consideration in the Senate, rumors of Tyler's plans for a new cabinet fairly flew around Washington. Reverdy Johnson, in Baltimore, informed Crittenden of the arrival, on the night before, of a Mr. Hamilton of New York, "almost an intimate of the President's house," who met with Upshur. It was believed that Hamilton was making contacts for possible cabinet appointments. "I lose no time in making this fact known to you," Johnson told the attorney general. If half the reports heard from Washington were true, Johnson felt it was exceedingly improbable that Hamilton's visit could have any other purpose.[7]

Hamilton was not the only one who was looking for prospective appointees. As early as the middle of July, Duff Green had traveled to Kentucky for the purpose of fostering an alliance between Tyler and the Wickliffes, sworn enemies of Clay; but Green probably did this without Tyler's knowledge. Green had an inflated opinion of his own importance, and he often claimed authority that he did not have. In July and August 1841, he claimed to be arranging cabinet replacements. Clay Whigs considered Green dangerous. Originally a Democrat, Green broke with President Jackson over the choice of Van Buren as the heir apparent. Unlike Calhoun, Green did not make peace with Van Buren and return to the Democratic fold, but his personal relationship with Calhoun remained close. Calhoun's oldest son had married Green's daughter.

As the turmoil and stress intensified, accusations increased.

Clayites accused the president of base treachery in scheming to dismiss the cabinet, while some supporters of Tyler charged that Clay was calling upon the cabinet to resign if the Fiscal Corporation bill was rejected by the president, thus placing Tyler in the difficult position of having to name new departmental heads before the adjournment of the special session. If Tyler could not accomplish this, the government would cease to function, and he might be obliged to resign, thus possibly, it was rumored, paving the way for Clay to achieve the presidency in a special election. Horace Greeley of the *New York Tribune* declared that dismissal of the cabinet was *"mediated, planned, and advised, I do not say by Mr. Tyler, but by those who now possess his confidence— months ago, and entirely independent of the Bank collision."*[8]

It is not known how deeply Tyler was involved, if at all, in making overtures to various individuals about cabinet appointments. In late August, however, Louis McLane, who had been minister to Great Britain and secretary of state during the Jackson administration, was summoned to Washington and offered the State Department post in a restructured cabinet. All communications were between McLane and William B. Lewis, a former member of Jackson's Kitchen Cabinet and another of Tyler's gratuitous "helpers." McLane, after deliberating for several days, sent his refusal to Lewis. With aspirations for the presidency himself, McLane did not wish to compromise his standing in the Democratic party by serving in the cabinet of a president who, he was convinced, would soon be without a party.

Maurice Baxter, one of Webster's biographers, thinks it very unlikely that Tyler offered McLane the State Department late in August or earlier, "while Webster was still acting as Tyler's trusted intermediary on the bank question." However, in anticipation of a possible exodus of cabinet members, the president logically could have been looking for a replacement in the event that Webster, too, were to resign.

Chitwood, on the other hand, who has based his conclusions on the words of Upshur and others of the Cabal, is of the opinion that Tyler was giving serious thought to replacing the entire cabinet, whether or not they resigned. Tyler had never been comfortable with his inherited departmental heads, with the exception of Webster, and after the first bank veto, Tyler, encouraged by constant derogatory remarks about the cabinet from the Virginia Cabal, became increasingly distrustful of several, if not all, of the secretaries.[9]

However, great reliance should not be placed on the words of Upshur, Tucker, Wise, and others who often counted on Tyler to follow their instructions when he had no intention of doing so. Behind-the-scenes maneuverings, which were actually conducted by the Cabal, often were attributed to Tyler. Even before Harrison's inauguration, Gilmer wanted Webster's name removed from the cabinet slate, and statements about the treachery and disloyalty of the departmental heads continued to circulate among the Virginia group. Tyler "has not a sincere friend" in the cabinet, Upshur told Tucker in late July. "Webster will adhere to him [Tyler] till he kills Clay, and no longer. Ewing, Bell, Crittenden and Granger will sacrifice him to Clay. . . . Badger is a Federalist, and will not aid him in shaking off National Republican centralism."[10] Remarks such as these, constantly dinned into the president's ears, could not help but make some impact on a man who was already uncertain about the motives of his "constitutional advisors." There is no proof that Tyler had a plan to oust the entire cabinet, but there can be no doubt that the president, anticipating resignations in the wake of a second veto, identified possible replacements, believing this was the only reasonable action to take.

Meeting privately, without the president, to discuss what the future might hold, the cabinet was as uneasy as Tyler was. Webster suffered from insomnia; in his diary, Ewing argued with himself about whether or not he should resign in the event of another veto. On the night of 28 August, in one last effort to reconcile Tyler and the Clay Whigs "under the mellowing effects of a social gathering" and to draw the president "from under the influence of the Virginian clique," Crittenden gave a party. Tyler sent his regrets, but because his attendance was mandatory to the "success" of the festivities, a deputation from the party was sent to the White House to fetch him. When Tyler arrived, all seemed harmonious and friendly, with Clay offering the honored guest his choice of whiskey or champagne. Adams, who left early, was told that Tyler "entered into the spirit of this frolicsome agony as if it was congenial to his own temper," but Adams recorded in his diary, "all this was as false and hollow as it was blustering and rowdyish."

On 3 September the Senate approved the Fiscal Corporation bill, 27 to 22. Rives was the only Whig who voted against it. On the following day, Tyler confided to Ewing, Bell, Granger, and Webster that he probably would veto the measure. This certainly came as no surprise, but sensitive to stories about his bidding for the support of the Democrats in preparation for the 1844 election, Tyler also said he might accompany the veto with a "solemn declaration" that he would not be a candidate for another term. The cabinet members who were present voiced objections to this. Later, in his diary, Ewing sarcastically observed that Tyler "was generally it is true tenacious of his own opinions but on this point he showed great deference to the views of his Constitutional advisers" and decided not to include the disclaimer. The president also indicated that he would severely criticize the bill in his veto message. Webster thought that would be imprudent and below the dignity of the chief executive. The message, he said, should be calm, elevated, and dignified.

Ewing and Webster, trying to induce Tyler to sign the bill, pointed out that another bank veto could mean the ruin of Tyler's reputation and the collapse of his political power. They begged him "to avoid the gulf into which he was about to plunge." They assured him that members of the cabinet were willing to support him if he would but give them ground on which to stand. Clay's hold on the departmental heads was not as great as Tyler might imagine, Ewing and Webster insisted. In fact, they argued, Clay "exacted great sacrifices of his friends and was willing to sacrifice nothing to them." Ewing declared that he and Bell had sacrificed enough to Clay's ambition. If Tyler would sign the bill, all would be well. The administration could go forward.[11]

Six days after having received the bill, Tyler sent his veto message to the House of Representatives. Its tone was mild: "With extreme regret" and "great pain" he felt "compelled to differ from Congress a second time in the same session"; but he declared that the Fiscal Corporation (he now objected to the title) was being created by Congress acting as a national legislature, not as the local governing body for the District of Columbia. Tyler took issue with the ability of the Fiscal Corporation to "indulge in mere local discounts under the name of bills of exchange." Reminding Congress that he had sanctioned all measures passed during the special session with the exception of the bank bills, he asked, "Why should our differences on this alone be pushed to extremes?" "May we not now pause until a more favorable time," when the executive and Congress could cordially unite on a better plan. The message lacked strength of purpose and gave the impression that there were insufficient reasons for the president's disapproval.

Cordiality toward Tyler was not the prevailing mood when all the cabinet members except Granger gathered that evening at Badger's home for dinner. When Webster discovered Clay's presence, he left the house, not wanting to be a party to what he suspected was an arranged meeting between the senator and the secretaries. Although Clay withdrew to another room when the discussion turned to resignations, the fact that he was there gave weight to the notion that Clay had coerced the departmental heads into abandoning the administration in a gesture of defiance and repudiation.[12]

On the next day, 10 September, Bell, Badger, Crittenden, and Ewing informed Tyler that they intended to vacate their positions, and on Saturday, 11 September, they submitted letters of resignation, two days before the close of the session, which was scheduled for Monday, the fourteenth. Webster, although he regretted the differences that had arisen between the president and Congress, could not see "in what manner the resignation of the Cabinet was likely to remove or mitigate the evils produced by them." Such action, he was convinced, endangered the life of the Whig party. He told his colleagues that they had acted rashly and that he intended to follow his own course. He did not like the appearance of collusion "between a Whig Cabinet and a Whig senator to bother the President."

Although Webster consulted with the Massachusetts congressional delegation for guidance in making his decision, he clearly indicated to them his personal desire to remain in the cabinet. He blamed Botts's "coffeehouse letter" for Tyler's rejection of the Fiscal Corporation bill and said the bank issue was not closed. Hope still remained for a compromise bill. His own relations with Tyler, he said, were pleasant, and he offered no criticism of the president. The Massachusetts contingent unanimously advised Webster to continue as secretary of state.

In a letter to the *National Intelligencer,* which was published on 14 September, Webster said that even if he had desired to resign, it would have been unfair not to give Tyler reasonable notice, particularly because of pending diplomatic negotiations with Great Britain. What he did not say was that by resigning, he would, in effect, be placing himself under Clay's domination, something he had no intention of doing. Webster never doubted the efficacy of a national bank, and he had hoped, for the sake of the party, that Tyler would approve one of the bank bills; but he, along with a number of his fellow Whigs, deplored Clay's tactics. Had Tyler been treated with courtesy and respect, Webster believed the president would have been more malleable.

Granger, too, asked for guidance from his state's delegation, but he received instructions to resign. There had been rumors that he would remain in the cabinet, and Webster sincerely hoped this was true. Granger could contribute to a policy of moderation. But on Saturday, 11 September, Granger notified Tyler that he intended to resign; however, he did not submit a written statement until Monday.[13]

Despite the fact that Ewing and others blamed Clay for his "hot haste" in pressing the bank measure and for sacrificing the bank in order to make trouble for Tyler, when it came to a choice of standing with Tyler or with Clay, they cast their lot with the senator, the more influential politician. Several wrote unnecessarily harsh letters explaining their actions, almost as if they were on the defensive and felt compelled to lash out at the president in order to justify their resignations. Ewing set the tone, charging Tyler with having betrayed the cabinet by vetoing a "bill framed and fashioned according to your own suggestion" and one that was loyally supported by the departmental secretaries. Ewing wrote: "Deeply as I was committed for your action upon it, you never consulted me on the subject of the veto message. You did not even refer to it in conversation, and the first notice I had of its content was derived from rumor."

With such a short time available before the adjournment of the session, Crittenden was certain that Tyler would "have hard work to make up a cabinet which will please the Senate"; probably, Tyler would have to nominate "unexceptional individuals" who would not be approved, thus giving him more leeway to "supply the vacancies in the absence of the Senate." The complication in regard to the making of appointments arose from an opinion held by many during this period, Tyler included, that all vacancies which occurred during a congressional session had to be filled before the adjournment of the session. Had the cabinet resignations been submitted after the close of the special session, Tyler would have had more time to consider appointments. This accounts for the eagerness of the Clayites to have letters handed to the president on Saturday, 11 September.

Undoubtedly, Tyler's quick action in producing a list of nominees on Monday morning, the day scheduled for adjournment, surprised and disappointed a considerable number of Clay Whigs, especially because the designated individuals were not all "unexceptional." The *National Intelligencer*, which expressed "regret, mortification, and pain at the breaking up of the Cabinet," had to admit that "the appointments are upon the whole better than could have been expected."[14]

In naming his new departmental heads, Tyler did not, as some anticipated, turn his back on the Whig party. His nominees were all Whigs, but like himself, all except John C. Spencer were former Democrats who had become Whigs because of their opposition to the Jackson regime. They all were reputable attorneys, "very clever and agreeable men," yet not all of one mind.

Perhaps the most interesting among them was Hugh S. Legaré, attorney general designate from the South Carolina planter aristocracy, a Charleston intellectual skilled in jurisprudence. He was also the founder and editor of the esteemed *Southern Review*. An ardent Union man and an opponent of nullification, he had crossed swords with Calhoun during the tariff controversy of 1832/33, calling the senator a demagogue and a self-serving sectionalist. Legaré was not a provincial southerner;

he was a cosmopolite, finely educated in the United States and abroad, well traveled, a master of several languages, and an expert in international law. For opposing Calhoun, Jackson had rewarded Legaré with the post of chargé d'affaires in Brussels, but Jackson's bank policies had caused Legaré to join forces with the Whigs, although he was an "indifferent politician" and certainly never a "party regular," either as a Democrat or as a Whig. Like Tyler, he believed in adhering to his own principles, but unlike Tyler, his financial views leaned more toward capitalistic nationalism. Legaré believed that slavery was detrimental to the South's economy and that planters were impoverished by their inherited burden, but he could suggest no suitable method of emancipation, and he saw only the danger of servile war in the schemes of the northern abolitionists. Legaré was an advocate of Manifest Destiny: he envisioned the expansion of the nation to the Pacific Coast and beyond.[15]

Walter Forward of Pennsylvania, who was named to head the Treasury Department, had been Harrison's choice for first comptroller of the currency. According to Calhoun, Forward, "a tariff man," was promoted to the secretaryship because Tyler was attempting to maintain a middle-of-the-road position and was trying to build a solid base of moderates from both parties. To implement this plan, Tyler considered that Democratic support from Pennsylvania, a key state, was essential.

To placate the more aggressive states' righters of Virginia, Tyler, undoubtedly because of the urging of Tucker and others, selected Abel Parker Upshur for the Navy Department post. This did not upset Clay as much as did the offer of the Post Office Department to Charles A. Wickliffe of Kentucky. Wickliffe, a former state legislator, member of Congress, and governor, was, along with all his clan, anathema to Clay. Also, Wickliffe was said to have close ties to Calhoun, and this appointment, it was thought, might give the South Carolina senator "a finger in the pie."

John McLean of Illinois, who had been a justice of the United States Supreme Court since 1829, was considered for the Treasury Department but instead was offered the War Department. When he declined to accept what he regarded as the lesser of the two positions, Tyler turned to John C. Spencer, secretary of state for New York, whose nomination was encouraged by Seward and Weed.[16]

How the Senate would react to the slate of nominees was the question in many minds. Crittenden claimed no prior knowledge, but thought "the great difficulty will be with Upshur." The speculation proved incorrect. All appointments were approved without difficulty. If Clay had actually staged the cabinet exodus in an attempt to force

Tyler's resignation, it is difficult to understand why the Senate Whigs did not challenge the nominations, unless they viewed Clay's strategy as inappropriate. Only five Whig senators voted against Upshur's confirmation. Clay was not present.[17]

The new cabinet was assembled in record time, and its composition reflected Tyler's desire to steer a middle course. Three members (Webster, Secretary of State; Spencer, Secretary of War; and Forward, Secretary of the Treasury) were from the North, and three (Legaré, Attorney General; Upshur, Secretary of the Navy; and Wickliffe, Postmaster General) were from the South. No one faction was dominant. Upshur and, possibly, Wickliffe were the only states' righters. Webster would be the departmental head upon whom Tyler would rely most heavily. The president thought he had selected the "best material" possible, all of whom were willing to work for the public good.

Senate approval of the nominees did not imply its endorsement of the president. On 3 September, R. P. Letcher, the governor of Kentucky, wrote to Crittenden, advising him on what should be done if mass resignation of the cabinet became a reality. The Whigs, he said, ought to hold a meeting and solemnly censure Tyler, then "transfer and assign him over to the 'Locofocos.' They ought, furthermore, by resolution to declare that no honest Whig should hold office under such a faithless public servant. Then let the Captain 'paddle his own canoe,' assisted by his Virginia friends." Crittenden received the letter on 11 September. On the same day a number of Whigs met and approved Mangum's resolution calling for an address to the people, to explain what had occurred during the special session and why the bank bill had not become law. A committee of eight was named to prepare the address, which would be submitted to a meeting of the congressional Whigs on Monday morning for their consideration.

On 13 September 1841, the day when Congress adjourned, a group, estimated by Webster to be around fifty and by John P. Kennedy, who penned the public Whig declaration, to be between sixty and seventy, duly gathered in Capitol Square to accept the manifesto, which expressed mortification and deep regret over Tyler's conduct. The president was charged with having voluntarily separated himself from members of the Whig party, which no longer "in any manner or degree, could be held responsible for his actions." His undermining of the creation of a national bank was harmful, but what really angered the congressional Whigs was Tyler's thwarting of their determination to control the chief executive and to destroy, for all time, presidential usurpation. Therefore, to secure the nation against future abuses, encroachments, and usurpations by the chief magistrate, the Whig caucus reiterated many of the points voiced during the 1840 campaign: a single term for the incumbent in the president's office, the right of Congress to appoint the secretary of the treasury, severe restrictions on the president's power to dismiss from office, the establishment of a fiscal agent (a national bank), and the adoption of an amendment to the Constitution which would limit the chief executive's use of the veto. Tyler had to be brought to heel; otherwise, there would be three more years of "the same kind of suffering inflicted during the last twelve years by the maladministration of the Executive Department of the government." Twenty thousand copies of the manifesto were printed and distributed throughout the land. In this fashion, Tyler was formally proscribed and expelled from the Whig party.[18]

Webster reported that quite a number of the House and Senate Whigs chose not to attend the meeting, and among those present, there were some who objected to the proceedings but did not have the courage to protest. For a time the party was in disarray. In the House, Stanly from North Carolina and Wise of Virginia came to blows, and a duel narrowly was averted, while Botts from Virginia and Proffit from Indiana exchanged bitter verbal thrusts. The pro- and anti-Tyler controversy was not sectional. Often, southerners lashed out against southerners, and northerners against northerners. Botts charged the president with perfidy and treachery to the party that had elected him, comparing Tyler to Benedict Arnold and declaring, "It is impossible to serve God and Mammon both, so I conceived it impossible to serve Mr. Tyler and my country at the same time." Proffit, in reply , insisted that "from the first meeting of Congress up to this hour, there has been a determination on the part of some gentlemen to create an issue with the President," to "head him—to make him sign a bill which neither his conscience nor his judgment approved," or they had presented him with "the most absurd and evasive propositions . . . with full knowledge that they could not receive his sanction."[19]

Congressman Caleb Cushing of Massachusetts, who was considered a member of the corporal's guard, declared that a "caucus dictatorship" had been established to control the president and "to usurp the command of the government." The Whig manifesto, he pointed out, was affirmed only by a small group of disaffected congressmen. It did not represent majority opinion. This coterie wanted to deprive the president of his constitutional rights and duties, the use of the veto, power of appointment, and any control over the treasury. If they succeeded, the liberties of the people would then be in the hands of a despotic caucus, controlled by "one man." The "one man" to whom Cushing referred was, of course, Henry Clay.

Governor R. P. Letcher of Kentucky, who believed the Whigs were "more firmly united now than ever before . . . the vetoes are a good cement to hold them together," was mistaken. Without question, within the Whig party the battle lines were drawn.[20]

Tyler should have been prepared for the harsh reactions to his second bank veto. The first veto had precipitated vicious speeches by Clay, Botts, and others. Threatening letters had been received, and much of the Whig press had been insultingly hostile. There had been a march on the White House by about thirty noisy individuals, "well fortified with liquor" and accompanied by drums and trumpets. Clay was cheered, while Tyler was hissed, jeered, and burned in effigy.

The second veto brought more blatant and vehement attacks. Hundreds of letters threatened assassination. Editorials in the Whig papers were extremely bitter, especially in the *New York Courier and Enquirer* and the *Richmond Whig*. Flames from a thousand burning effigies lighted the night skies, indignation meetings were held in almost every city and village, "a universal roar of Whig vengeance was heard in every blast." Rumors were circulated that Tyler was ill with "brain fever." In large part, these violent reactions were synthetic, staged by Clay Whigs, who were tenaciously committed to the political destruction of Tyler. In general, the public was apathetic to the need for a national bank.[21]

Shortly after the first bank veto, William Gaston, the strongly nationalistic chief justice of the North Carolina Surpeme Court, who was noted for his fairness and reasonable approach, warned against highly emotional reactions. The president was entitled to justice and toleration. Moderation, Gaston advised, would prevent Tyler from being forced to look for support from men who were unworthy of his confidence and whose schemes would be ruinous to the nation. Gaston believed that Tyler was honest, and it was "no small blessing to a community to have a perfectly honest man in the Executive chair, altho' some of his political notions may be wrong-headed." But if other honest men turned their backs on Tyler, he would have no choice except to seek aid elsewhere, with dire consequences to the country. Webster also deplored the maliciousness of those Whigs in Congress who treated the president with "satire and disdain."[22]

Both Gaston and Webster worried about the sequel to such disruptions within the Whig party. The Union was fragile. Lines separating northern and southern views were not drawn as sharply as they would be a few years hence, but the potential for trouble was present. The extreme Whigs, who exaggerated the difficulties with the president, and the extreme-states'-rights men, who opposed moderation and compromise, were speeding the party along a dangerous road toward factionalism.

Tyler was not blameless. He did not handle the bank issue with aplomb. By not being forthright about what kind of bank he would approve and by not adhering to his own recommendations, he left his advisors and all those who desired to help him in limbo, and he left himself open to the charge of not really intending to accept any bank whatever. He should not have been so prematurely eager to go along with the Stuart-Sergeant-Berrien suggestions for the second bank bill without giving them careful consideration, and if a subterfuge was slipped in, he should have been astute enough to recognize it at the outset.

The displeasure of the majority of the cabinet members was understandable. First, Tyler had accepted the plan for a Fiscal Corporation, then he had become cool toward it. Nevertheless, he had instructed Webster and Ewing to have the bill drawn up but not to commit him to it. After they had carried out his wishes, he had asked to have the bill postponed, and finally, he had vetoed it without consulting the cabinet. These twists and turns, even if there was cause for his uneasiness about the measure, gave his enemies a basis for accusing him of having rejected his own plan. In Tyler's behalf, however, it must be recognized that he was in a very difficult position. Although Tyler was not aware of Crittenden's deviousness, he suspected there was treachery afoot among his constitutional advisors. This contributed to his indecisiveness, which the Clay Whigs used to their advantage.

Tyler knew he stood on the threshold of political destruction, a president without a party and faced with an extremely hostile element in Congress, masterminded by the cleverest politician of them all. Tyler had hoped for definite signs of support from more southern Whigs, but many of them were Clay men, having been won over to the Kentuckian's economic program during the late 1830s. As large producers of staple crops, especially cotton, or as members of a growing urban mercantile class or as promoters of incipient industry, they had developed close ties to the business and banking communities of the North. The panics of 1837 and 1839, the continuing depression, and their desire to improve economic conditions in their region made them aware of the importance of a stable currency, at least a semiprotective tariff, and even federally financed internal improvements. These were practical policies for the future of the South. Additionally, men such as Mangum and Graham of North Carolina, S. S. Prentiss of Mississippi, John Berrien and Alexander H. Stephens of Georgia, to mention only a few, who had political careers at stake, did not want to see their party disintegrate. Following Tyler would lead only to political oblivion.[23]

There were Whigs who truly desired harmony and compromise, but the behavior of Botts and Clay, as well as the constant hounding of the president by an inimical Whig press, widened rather than closed the breach between the president and Congress.

7

★ ★ ★ ★ ★

THE TRYING SUMMER OF 1842

Because of Webster's decision to remain in the cabinet, he was the target of incessant ugly barbs and slurs. John J. Crittenden called him "ignoble" and hoped that although Webster had "faltered for a moment," he would "redeem himself by an abandonment of Mr. Tyler." However, Crittenden warned, Webster must not dawdle. "Time for repentance" was very short; the thoughts and feelings of men were moving on too rapidly to afford him much delay. The former attorney general could not understand why Webster had chosen to stay in the cabinet. "He holds on and looks like grim death."[1]

Ralph Waldo Emerson, encountering the secretary of state on a Boston street, also thought him changed since last he had seen him. Now Webster was as "black as a thunder cloud, and careworn." Despite obvious anguish over his current standing in the Whig party, Webster had no intention of "repenting," of abandoning Tyler, and of joining the Clay bandwagon. "We shall stand steady here, let the storm beat ever so hard," Webster had said to Thurlow Weed of the *Albany* (N.Y.) *Evening Journal*.[2]

Clay's bandwagon was, indeed, rolling. Already the 1844 campaign was under way. Throughout the land, Whig papers touted Clay as the party's standard-bearer. Huge public meetings and demonstrations were staged to convey to one and all the idea that Clay was the hero of the hour and that Tyler, aided by Webster, was responsible for the impasse between Congress and the executive, which was so detrimental to the nation. Clay's disdain for Tyler was unbounded, and he sneered at the president's pledge, in his second veto message, to recommend another bank plan in his first annual message in December. "Having rejected a National Bank and the Sub-treasury," Clay could not imagine what other project "even Mr. Tyler's ingenuity could present."

Yet, less than a month after he had been summarily expelled from the party, Tyler was at work on what became known as the Exchequer Plan. Early in November he sent Tazewell a preliminary description, asking for criticisms and commenting that although other schemes might be preferable, he was forced, "in the present state of parties," to accommodate his views to the one that was most likely to gain the support of the greatest number.[3]

The new cabinet offered assistance and encouragement, confirming John Spencer's observation that Tyler "appears really happy in being surrounded by men he knows and feels to be his friends." It was Spencer, the member with the best grasp of financial matters, who gave the most solid advice, assuring Tyler of the workability and constitutionality of the Exchequer Plan. It would, Spencer said, give the country a perfectly good currency.

Almost a third of the president's annual message was devoted to the financial plan. Unlike the old Bank of the United States, the institution he recommended would not be a private corporation. Rather, it would be a governmental entity under the control of a board composed of the secretary of the treasury, the treasurer of the United States, and three members appointed by the president. The institution's headquarters would be in Washington, D.C., with agencies located in prominent commercial centers or wherever Congress might direct, for the safekeeping and disbursement of governmental funds. The Exchequer would also be authorized to receive individual deposits of gold and silver to a limited amount. The limitation was included in order to prevent disastrous withdrawals from state banks, especially during times of crises, when the Exchequer might be considered a more secure depository. Notes, backed by and redeemable in the gold and silver deposited in the Exchequer, would create a sound paper currency. Outlying agencies also would be able to deal in interstate exchange, subject to regulation by the states in which they were located; but the making of loans, whether through discount or by other means, which would bring the agencies into competition with state banks, would not be allowed.

The president, Tyler told Congress, would have no control over the Exchequer's board. Furthermore, since the institution would be created by statute and not chartered for a specific length of time, Congress could change or terminate it at will. The Exchequer would be "created by law, amendable by law, and repealable by law." Upon Congress's request, the secretary of the treasury would submit the plan for legislative consideration.[4]

The House of Representatives, acting on a motion by Caleb Cushing, chairman of the Committee on Finance and the Currency, made the request. Webster, at Tyler's behest, drafted the bill and the letter of transmittal, the administration's official defense of the plan, and on 21 December sent both items to the House over the name of Secretary Forward, who, it seems, was not particularly adroit. The defense, according to Legaré, was "better than excellent—it was plausible."

The Exchequer, Webster pointed out, would avoid the extremes of both a national bank and the Independent Treasury, and it would present Congress with an opportunity to end the "ardent and intense political controversies" over the bank issue. He wanted the plan to receive fair consideration, as it was "the most likely to be useful to the Country, of anything that can now be suggested." Others agreed. Horace Greeley said he favored its adoption if the president was not allowed to appoint board members, and Thurlow Weed thought Tyler had "triumphed not only over his enemies, but over himself." Weed hoped that God would grant Congress the wisdom to act in a spirit of conciliation, but this was not to be. Even though a few congressional Whigs were disposed to try Tyler's idea, Clay would accept nothing but another Bank of the United States. Certainly, after the bitterness of the previous summer, he had no intention of supporting any presidential suggestions, regardless of their merits, and Webster's strong advocacy of the Exchequer did nothing to endear it to Clay.

Clay swung into action, skillfully using "cunning maneuvers" and the tactic of delay. Speaking on the Senate floor, Mangum bitingly accused Tyler of having designed the Exchequer to attain absolute executive power over the nation's fiscal agent. "Never, never, in the whole history of this Government, has there been witnessed a push so bold." The public could not be allowed to forget the issue of executive usurpation—Clay's main theme for 1844.[5]

Well into 1842, Webster urged approval of the Exchequer. "I am ready to stake my reputation, that if this Congress will take that measure and give it a fair trial, within three years it will be admitted by the whole American people to be the most beneficial measure of any sort ever adopted in this Country, the Constitution only excepted." Action was demanded. It was distressing to hear of the "scorn and contumely with which American character and American credit" were treated abroad. Congress, however, never seriously considered the Exchequer bill. Democrats, who continued to back an Independent Treasury, joined

Clay-dominated Whigs in tabling the proposal, without even the courtesy of adequate debate. The Exchequer was a dead issue. In January 1843 it was voted down.

In his December 1841 message, Tyler again had to address the precarious condition of the Treasury. Of the $12 million loan authorized by Congress during the special session, only $5.5 million worth of bonds had been subscribed. An extension of time for the loan was mandatory, and very likely, consideration would have to be given to supplying the government with additional revenue by raising tariff duties. This, Tyler admitted, would be "a most delicate operation," calling for a spirit of "conciliation and harmony." He had grappled with the difficult and seemingly insurmountable problem in 1833, when, in an attempt to stop the nullification movement and avert possible disunion, he had worked with Clay to devise the Compromise Tariff. This act of "conciliation and harmony" stipulated that beginning on 1 January 1834, all duties over 20 percent in the 1832 tariff bill were to be gradually reduced at two-year intervals, after which there would be two acute reductions. By 1 July 1842, no duties were to exceed 20 percent.

From 1834 through 1841, reductions had taken place as scheduled. These, coupled with the effects of the still-existent depression, had taken a toll on the Treasury. Although throughout his political career Tyler had opposed increases in tariffs, he now had to face the reality of the critical situation. The United States government literally was without funds. If he did not recommend an increase in revenue to replenish the Treasury, he felt he would be derelict in his duty. On the other hand, he knew full well how unpopular this would be among certain segments, particularly in the South. "The tariff will be an apple of discord among the Whigs," Senator William Graham of North Carolina predicted, "and may produce a new explosion in the Cabinet."[6]

The problem was compounded by the Distribution and Pre-emption Act, passed by Congress and approved by the president late in the special session. Commonly referred to as the Land Act, it made permanent the temporary preemption act of 1830 and gave settlers the legal right to stake claims on most surveyed lands prior to purchase and, later, to buy a maximum of 160 acres at $1.25 an acre.

Complications were caused by the distribution provision of the measure. The 1841 act granted five hundred thousand acres of public land to each new state. Ten percent of the proceeds from the sale of this land was to be assigned to the states wherein the lands were located, and the remainder was to be distributed among all the states on a ratio based on their representation in Congress. Ostensibly, the funds were to be used for internal improvements.

Opposition to the bill came especially from southern Democrats, who traditionally were against federally funded internal improvements, whether direct or indirect, and who saw in the distribution plan a ruse to increase tariffs to a highly protective level. Deprived of revenues from the sale of public lands, they argued, the Treasury would be in need of other funds. This would give the protectionists the necessary pretext to call for ever-higher tariffs. In an effort to forestall such a move, southern Democrats, joined by a few southern Whigs and northern freetraders, were able to attach an amendment to the land bill, calling for an end to distribution whenever import duties exceeded 20 percent. In this form the bill became law.

Despite the dire condition of governmental finances, Congress ignored Tyler's plea for increased revenues. Upshur told Tucker: "The hostile influences are innumerable, and it will be wonderful if indeed we resist them all. . . . The situation of this country is more perilous than is generally supposed."[7]

Clay, his thoughts on the 1844 election, undoubtedly was pleased to watch the administration unsuccessfully try to cope with the crisis. Upon returning to the Senate in December 1841, he announced his pending resignation from that body, giving fatigue and ill health as his reasons. No doubt he was tired, and he needed time to prepare, mentally and physically, for the presidential race, which was still more than three years away but was much on the minds of a number of aspirants. Calhoun, his hopes for the Democratic nomination at an all-time high, also planned to resign his Senate seat within another year or so. "The presidential question begins to be a good deal talked about . . . ," he informed his son-in-law; "disorders of the times are turning more & more eyes of the community upon me." Calhoun's opposition to the tariffs of 1828 and 1832 had led him to advocate the doctrine of nullification. In 1842 his views had not changed. Reduction of expenditures, he asserted, was preferable to increasing duties, which would be harmful to the economy of the South. But expenditures already had been dangerously pared.[8]

Early in March, in a special message to the House, Tyler again appealed for financial assistance. Unless War and Navy Department requisitions for March, April, and May were halted, the Treasury would have an "unprovided-for deficit" of more than $3 million. Faced with the unsettled condition of foreign affairs, the country could ill afford to halt works of defense that were now in progress. The issuance of treasury notes offered no permanent relief. Only a revision of the tariff could rescue the Treasury from recurring embarrassments.

When still no action was taken, Tyler, who had tried to avoid telling

Congress what to do, sent a forceful and more detailed message, addressed to both the House and the Senate. The crisis, he said, had to be met with vigor and decision. Additional duties on imports had to be imposed if the ordinary expenses of the government were to be met. In an effort to attract the backing of Whigs from industrial states, he also pointedly mentioned that in addition to increasing revenue, a new tariff would afford "incidental protection to manufacturing industry."

Because it seemed probable that some duties would exceed 20 percent, distribution of the proceeds from the sale of public lands would have to be abandoned. When it was manifestly necessary to increase duties and at the same time to borrow money in order to liquidate the public debt, Tyler believed distribution could not be justified. Rather, the money from the sale of lands should be pledged to pay the interest on borrowed funds. The first and highest objective, he declared, was to establish the credit of the government and to place it on a durable foundation.

Congress ignored the messages and occupied its time with other matters, while Clay, who took little part in the debates, managed the activities or inactivities of the Whigs in both the House and the Senate. Control of the executive remained his chief concern. In anticipation of upcoming differences with the president and again to force the issue of executive usurpation, Clay, in January, moved a constitutional amendment to reduce the vote necessary to override a veto to a simple majority and to eliminate the pocket veto; but the measure never came to a vote in the Senate.

Upshur was convinced that all Clay had in mind was the next presidential election and that the senator and those who were determined to have him elected were attempting to impede Tyler by withholding all necessary funds. If the government could not operate, the people would protest, and their wrath would be turned on the president. Upshur was certain that there had never been so dangerous a party as the ultra-Clay men. Clay was the great obstacle to needed legislation. "When he retires something may be done."[9]

Clay filed his letter of resignation on 23 February 1842, and three days later the Kentucky legislature elected Crittenden, who had been in Washington almost from the beginning of the session, waiting to succeed him. Even after resigning, Clay was reluctant to leave the Senate, so he retained his seat for another six weeks. Finally, on 31 March, he bid an emotional farewell to a packed gallery and Senate chamber. Alexander H. H. Stuart said it was "the most august scene" he had ever witnessed. Even Calhoun wept openly, although he knew, as did everyone else, that this was not Clay's final adieu to public life and although Calhoun also believed that without Clay, many impediments to legislation would be removed.

Crittenden had been anxious to step into Clay's position, but he bemoaned the "inervating effect" that his predecessor's withdrawal had had on the Senate. Clay's leaving Congress, Crittenden said, "was something like the soul leaving the body"; but undoubtedly Tyler, "the Tom Thumb of the scene," would serve as an irritant "to stimulate and excite us." Certainly, the president was good for nothing else. But, Crittenden complained, everything was strange and unsettled: "All seems to be standing still and looking and waiting for events."[10]

Instead of subsiding, the bitterness between Tyler and the congressional Whigs intensified after Clay's departure. Calhoun thought the country had never been in greater danger. The administration was powerless against the stalling tactics of the Whigs. Tyler believed he had made a significant gesture toward conciliation in advocating a higher tariff for revenue and also in recognizing the need for "incidental protection" for industry. He had come a long way. So had Upshur, who was now lecturing Tucker on the necessity of increasing duties: "The free trade men of the South must relax their principles a little. We shall never maintain our specie payments without the aid of our tariff system. The true tariff system is duties *for revenue only*, but so laid as to protect incidentally our home industry as far as can be done." Tucker, who had counted on Tyler to take an adamant stand in favor of all the desires of the extreme states' righters, was bitterly disappointed.[11]

Weeks and months passed without congressional action. The Treasury was empty; governmental workers went unpaid; obligations were not met. Petitions for an increase in the tariff rates flooded the House and the Senate. While the Whigs in Congress refused to act, the Whig press stressed the suffering of the people and demanded the president's resignation.

According to the Compromise Tariff Act of 1833, the final reduction in duties to 20 percent or below was to be in place by 1 July 1842. If this did not occur or if no alternative statute had been passed, there was a question as to whether any revenue could legally be collected after that date. Finally, early in June, a temporary, or "Little Tariff" bill was offered in the House, which extended until 1 August all revenue laws in effect on June 1, "provided that nothing herein shall suspend the distribution of the proceeds of the public lands." Clearly, the intent was to continue rates above the 20 percent level and still retain distribution.

Approved by the House and the Senate, the bill was sent to the president on 24 June. Five days later, after receiving Attorney General Legaré's assurance that the government could continue to collect duties under the old rates, even though the 1833 bill had expired, Tyler sent his veto message to the House. Exigencies of the government, he reminded the legislators, required an increase on imports above 20 percent, but an indispensable condition was the suspension of distribution. Clay and company wanted higher tariffs, primarily as protection for manufacturing interests; Tyler's main concern was the national treasury.

Southern Whigs, Mangum assured Clay, would "go far to gratify" northern and eastern industrialists "if they shall stand by the Land Law—surrender of the Land Law or any faltering on the subject, puts an end to all hopes for the present, of passing any tariff at all." However, there were indications, possibly a hint here and there, that some southern Whigs outside of Congress were only lukewarm in their desire for a protective tariff, but they wanted to be loyal to the party. The situation required delicate handling, and both Letcher and Crittenden worried about Clay's aggressiveness. "Clay must hold his jaw," Letcher told Crittenden; "in fact he must be *caged*—that is the point, *cage him*! . . . I have some occasional fears that he may write too many letters." Crittenden reluctantly admitted to Letcher that Clay was "going ahead like a locomotive."

Crittenden was worried about holding the party together. Writing to Clay from his desk in the Senate, Crittenden voiced his uneasiness. In the past, Tyler's vetoes had engendered enough anger to ensure cohesiveness. "His last veto [29 June] has scored us well," but if Tyler were to reject another tariff-distribution bill, what action should congressional Whigs take? "Shall we pass the tariff, giving up the lands, or adjourn and let all go together?" Crittenden implored Clay to send instructions quickly.[12]

John Minor Botts had no intention of waiting patiently for Tyler to destroy himself with vetoes. On 10 July, Botts introduced a resolution in the House calling for the appointment of a special committee to investigate the president's conduct with a view toward recommending impeachment. This was the first time in the nation's history that such a move had been made against a president.

Crittenden was apprehensive. His enmity for Tyler was strong, but he doubted that at this point, impeachment would be well received, either in Congress or among the people. "Botts' ardor, and the strong personal feelings that are ascribed to him, alarm the more timid and prudent," he informed Clay, warning Clay not to have his name "at all *mixed up* in this matter." To do so would be most unfortunate and injurious.

Clay, however, savored the possibility of Tyler's impeachment, which, given the tendency of events, he thought was inevitable; but he conceded that perhaps Botts had acted prematurely. A vote of "want of confidence" might do for the moment, if there was a resolve among the Whigs to follow it with more stringent measures. Another veto would excite great indignation, consolidate Whig strength, and prevent dissension. Congress could not abandon distribution. That would signal a loss of legislative power, which would be given up to the president, and would expose Congress "to the scorn, contempt, and derision of the people and of our opponents." If Tyler were to veto another tariff-distribution bill, Congress should pass "just such another tariff as he had vetoed. . . . Our friends ought to stand up firmly and resolutely for distribution. The more vetoes the better now! Assuming the measures vetoed are right."[13]

To Mangum, Clay explained his tactics with greater vigor. Gleefully, Clay said he felt "inexpressible satisfaction" from Tyler's "last silly veto." If the vetoes continued, the House ought to consider impeachment. Perhaps the Locos (Democrats) would rally around the president, but the more they identified with Tyler, "the better for us, the worse for them." There should be no thought of adjourning until a good tariff, which included distribution, was passed or until the House had impeached the president. "The Whig party bearded the old Lion [Andrew Jackson], amidst his loudest roars. Surely it will not give way, or suffer itself to be frightened by pranks of a monkey." Clay absolutely refused to surrender distribution. From Kentucky he sent letter after letter to Crittenden and Mangum, always with the same refrain: "Stand up firmly and resolutely for distribution," or the Whig party would be disgraced and executive usurpation would flourish.

Webster, although deeply occupied in diplomatic negotiations with Great Britain, could not ignore the stalemate between Congress and the president. Bad as the situation was, Webster feared it would grow worse unless legislators would listen to counsels of moderation and forbearance. The measures of tariff and distribution should never have been united, he told Isaac Bates. Consideration should be given to introducing a separate bill on each subject: one to repeal the restriction on distribution when the tariff exceeded 20 percent; the other, to raise the tariff. Actually, Webster pointed out, income from the sale of public lands was now inconsiderable, making the matter of distribution of little importance compared with providing the government with sufficient funds on which to operate. Webster favored distribution, but he thought it was unwise to couple distribution with the tariff in the same bill. Opinions on the tariff were too strongly held and "warmly excited."

Nevertheless, when another tariff-distribution bill, called the "Permanent Tariff," was sent to the president on 5 August, Webster urged that it be approved, arguing that the awful state of the country, the springing up of factions in every quarter, the imminent collapse of the Treasury—all demanded a resolution to the revenue problem. He would, he told Tyler, "give almost my right hand if you could be persuaded to sign the bill." The conduct of Congress, he acknowledged, was totally indefensible, but regardless, "in the present state of affairs, I should *sign the bill.*"[14]

Although he regretted Webster's disapproval, Tyler thought the "Clay Congress" left him no choice but to veto the bill. The executive could not surrender the prerogatives of his office and subordinate himself to the legislative branch. In his veto message of 9 August, Tyler again stressed the impropriety of uniting in one bill two subjects that were wholly incompatible in their nature, thus imposing on the president the necessity of either approving that which he would reject or rejecting that which he might otherwise approve—"a species of constraint to which the judgment of the Executive ought not to be subjected." A serious conflict of opinion existed among the states and among the people on the matter of distribution, and the practice of passing a measure that, if standing alone, could not command a majority vote was destructive of all wise and conscientious legislation. It should not be continued. Moreover, a fruitful source of revenue should not be given away while the Treasury was in a state of extreme embarrassment. He called on Congress to reconsider.[15]

Instead of reconsidering, the House, upon receiving the president's message, approved John Quincy Adams's motion to refer it immediately to a select committee of thirteen, with instructions to report the committee's conclusions to the House. Speaker John White, a Clay man from Kentucky, appointed Adams as chairman of the committee and Botts and several other strong opponents of Tyler as members. Thomas Gilmer was the lone loyal Tyler supporter. When the committee's majority report was presented to the House, it was apparent that Adams could not control his indignation over the audacity of an "acting president" who believed he could defy a majority in Congress and claim for himself "an inordinate share in the legislative process. . . . The power to enact laws essential to the welfare of the people has been struck with apoplexy by the Executive hand."

The report harshly condemned Tyler's shortcomings, dating back to the beginning of the special session, and renewed Clay's earlier recommendation that an amendment be adopted to allow Congress to override vetoes by a majority vote of each house. What the congressional Whigs found even more offensive than the vetoes, however, were sentiments that Tyler expressed in two letters he wrote to a group of his supporters in Philadelphia. The first was written in February 1842, and the second was a response to the group's request for a message to be read at a gathering on the Fourth of July. The letters elaborated on the difficulties faced by a vice-president who had succeeded to the presidency "by the dispensation of Divine Providence." Tyler called it "a new and hazardous experiment." A regularly elected president, he explained, came into office at the head of a triumphant party. His will was, for the most part, the law that governed the party. But when Harrison had died and Tyler had inherited the office, he was expected to be "a piece of wax to be moulded into any shape that others pleased." If he refused, "denunciations, the loudest and boldest," were in store for him. If his cherished opinions of long standing clashed with party measures and if he would not "yield honor, conscience, and everything sacred among men," thunders broke over his head and threatened annihilation. Because he would not cravenly bow to the demands of the congressional Whigs, they refused to pass adequate measures to relieve the prostration of private and public credit and the paralyzation of industry. They embarrassed the nation in the eyes of the world. He reminded his Philadelphia friends: "Each branch of the government is independent of every other, and heaven forbid that day should ever come when either can dictate to the other. The Constitution never designed that the executive should be a mere cipher."

It was to these letters, more than to the latest veto message, that the House committee directed the majority report, expressing sorrow and mortification at the presidential thwarting of "their own honest and agonizing energies."

Charles J. Ingersoll of Pennsylvania and James I. Roosevelt of New York, both Democrats, submitted a minority report, and Thomas Gilmer presented a counterreport. Ingersoll and Roosevelt upheld the president's constitutional right to veto bills and to request that they be reconsidered by Congress. Gilmer accused the House of violating tradition and the spirit of the Constitution by referring the veto message to a committee, instead of, as the Constitution specified, entering "the objections at large on their journal and proceed to reconsider the bill." Gilmer reminded the House that the president's veto was not absolute. It could be overridden if there was adequate support in the House and Senate.[16]

Almost without discussion, the House accepted the majority report by a vote of 100 to 80, but the resolution to amend the Constitution failed, 99 to 90. Tyler, in a protest message, noted that for the first time in the life of Congress, the House had referred a veto message to a select committee and that the committee had seen fit to charge him with offenses declared to be impeachable but had stopped short of initiating impeachment proceedings. Tyler said that if the charges could in any way be substantiated, the House, "which has the sole power of impeachment," had an obligation to take such action. It had no choice but to do so. This would give him the opportunity to confront his accusers before the tribunal of the Senate and to demand a full and impartial inquiry into the charges. The ordeal, he admitted, would be painful, but "as it is, I have been accused without evidence and condemned without a hearing. . . . I am charged with violating pledges which I never gave, . . . with usurping powers not conferred upon the President by law, and above all, with using powers conferred by the Constitution from corrupt motives and for unwarrantable ends."

Tyler expressed his resolution to uphold the constitutional authority of the executive to his utmost ability and in defiance of all personal consequences. He declared that what happened to him as an individual was of little importance, but he refused to stand aside and witness the desecration of the Constitution, which he had sworn to preserve, protect, and defend. If, as the majority of the House asserted, checks upon the will of the Congress by the use of the veto would no longer be tolerated, an amendment to that effect would have to be submitted to the people of the states. This was a matter for the voters to decide. Until such time, Tyler said he intended to abide by the law "as it has been written by our predecessors."

Tyler asked that his protest be entered into the *Journal of the House of Representatives*. The request was denied on the motion of Botts, who sardonically presented three resolutions, verbatim copies of the Senate resolutions of 1834, which spelled out reasons for refusing to accept Jackson's formal protest against his censure for the removal of governmental deposits from the Bank of the United States. Tyler and Webster had voted in favor of the 1834 resolutions. However, Tyler thought there was a difference between the circumstances of his protest and that of Jackson's. Tyler felt he was being chastised for disagreeing with the Whigs, while Jackson was accused of violating the Constitution and the law. Whereas Jackson claimed responsibility only to the people and denied that he had any accountability to Congress, Tyler had the greatest respect for checks and balances. He was not trying to dictate to Congress, but he did not want Congress to dictate to him.[17]

As was expected, the vote to override the veto failed. Anger and confusion threatened Whig solidarity. "We are in a state of great embarrassment here," Crittenden lamented to Clay. (Gone was the cry of "the more vetoes the better!") "It is difficult to adopt such a course as will satisfy those who are bent on resistance to the usurpations of Tyler and those who fear the effect of our adjourning without a tariff." Northern Whigs knew they could suffer defeat in the upcoming election if a tariff bill was not passed and approved. Distribution was not their major concern. Night after night the congressional Whigs met to try to arrive at an agreement, but Crittenden was "pretty certain" there would be no solution forthcoming. Clay was determined to retain distribution at whatever cost. As Calhoun observed, the Whigs were in "a sad state of distraction between defeats and vetoes. The western portion refuse to give up distribution for the tariff, & the northern the tariff for distribution. It is uncertain whether the schism can be made up."

Lord Ashburton (Alexander Baring), meeting with Webster on the sensitive Maine boundary issue, wrote to Sir Robert Peel, the British prime minister, about the questionable permanence of the United States government, "thinking it impossible that with so much disorganization and violence, the system could hold together." Webster had no apology for the actions of Congress: "Leading friends of Mr. Clay have regarded nothing of so great importance as the promotion of his election. . . . I do not wonder that enlightened foreigners begin to doubt the permanency of our system."[18]

Faced with dire consequences to the nation and to themselves if they adjourned before providing adequate revenue for the government, and faced with threats from northeastern manufacturing interests to abandon Clay if a protective tariff was not enacted and approved by the president, the Whigs were forced to produce another bill. In the process they disobeyed their leader and eliminated the distribution provision. In general, duties were raised to the 1832 level, to the satisfaction of protectionists and to the dismay of free-trade advocates. Speaker White, true to Clay, twice cast the deciding vote to kill the bill, but he finally gave way, and the bill passed the House by a vote of 104 to 103.

In the Senate, Calhoun took his expected stand against the tariff, but he, too, understood that the revenue crisis had to be resolved. His speech was not vehement; however, he expressed disappointment that some Democrats, especially James Buchanan of Pennsylvania and Silas Wright of New York, had forsaken their party's stand against a return to protective duties. Their favorable votes were understandable. Both senators were from states that had large manufacturing interests. Moreover, Buchanan and Wright realized the logic of Tyler's pleas for increased revenue. The votes of the Democrats were crucial. Without them the bill would have failed. On 27 August the measure passed the Senate, as it had in the house, by one vote, 24 to 23. Some southern Whigs who opposed the tariff bill did so because they were upset by the elimination of the distribution provision. This was true of Berrien,

Graham, and Mangum. Others were uncomfortable with the renunciation of the Compromise of 1833, in spirit if not in letter, and there were those who considered some rates unjust.

Clay's intransigence in insisting upon the advancement of his legislative agenda at whatever cost was disturbing to some party members in the South, but they remained loyal to their chief. Such was the case with Crittenden, who, although outwardly in accord with Clay on all issues, was more of a moderate on the tariff and believed certain schedules that Clay recommended were excessive. When the hemp industry of Kentucky demanded greater protection, Crittenden's concern was that increasing the price of the product would anger the cotton planters, among them some substantial Whigs. Would it tend to send them back into the Democratic ranks? But Clay was firm. "When the Tariff gets to the Senate," he instructed Crittenden, "you and your colleagues are expected to take care of this single Kentucky manufacture." Clay's directives of this nature kept most southern congressional Whigs in line, but not all of them. Only in one instance did Crittenden disobey, when he backed the tariff bill without distribution.[19]

Tyler signed the Tariff Act of 1842 on 30 August, but he used his pocket veto on a separate distribution bill. He had achieved the separation of the two measures, but for his own status it was no victory. He had hoped that moderates of both Democratic and Whig persuasion would rally to his support, perhaps creating a base for a political party of his own, but this had not materialized. In signing the Tariff Act, he had alienated southern Democrats and antiprotectionist Whigs. In frustrating distribution, he had earned the displeasure of others in the West and the South. The Clay Whigs, who had disowned him, grew increasingly hostile. "Is there any other course for me to pursue than to look to the public good irrespective of either faction?" Tyler inquired of Tazewell. Tyler now thought it best to ignore politicians of both parties, but he admitted that it was overwhelmingly difficult for a president to function without a party. Whom could he trust? He had no confidence even in those who seemingly agreed with him. "I have been so long surrounded by men who now have smiles in their eyes and honey on their tongues, the better to cajole and deceive." There was pertinence in Calhoun's earlier prophecy that Tyler was "essentially a man for the middle ground."[20]

During the trying summer of 1842, Tyler was also faced with a difficult situation in Rhode Island. For more than a decade, liberal elements had expressed growing dissatisfaction with the 1663 charter under which the state was governed. It was, they declared, outmoded, and so were the views of the legislative body, the General Assembly, which, under the charter's provisions, could establish qualifications for voting and officeholding. Despite the winds of change that were buffeting the nation, Rhode Island's governing body still restricted the franchise to white male adults who owned property or who paid annual rent in tenancy. Nonfreeholders were excluded from juries and were even prevented from initiating civil suits.

As immigration brought numerous new residents to the state, the number of the propertyless and the discontented was increasing. In Providence, only 6 percent of the population was eligible to vote. Reapportionment, too, was sorely needed. Demographic patterns had changed appreciably since the seventeenth century.

Thomas W. Dorr, an idealistic attorney who was a graduate of Phillips Exeter Academy and Harvard College and was certainly no ordinary rabble-rouser, pleaded with the General Assembly to call a constitutional convention to redress the accumulating grievances. Many other states had seen fit to do so. Some state conventions had adopted significant reforms, while others had been more half-hearted in their attempts; but progress was being made.

Dorr wanted a convention drawn from the people at large. Delegates, he insisted, should not be restricted to property owners, but the General Assembly refused to listen. Reformers from New York reinforced those in Rhode Island, urging them to call a popular convention. In the fall of 1841 this was done, without the sanction of the legally elected state government, and a "People's Constitution" was presented for ratification to all white adult male citizens residing in Rhode Island. The majority approved the constitution.

A few weeks later a convention, sponsored by the established government, drew up a "Landholders' Constitution," which provided more moderate reforms. It was submitted for approval or disapproval to the officially qualified voters, who narrowly rejected it as being too liberal.[21]

In the spring of 1842 the frustrated followers of Thomas Dorr organized an extralegal state government, with their leader as the chief executive. The state now had two sets of officials, one operating under the "People's Constitution" and the other according to the charter. The stage was set for domestic violence, and Governor Samuel King, fearful of insurrection, asked President Tyler for assistance from the federal government, which, under Article IV, section 4, of the United States Constitution, was directed to "guarantee to every State in this Union, a Republican form of government, and shall protect each of them against invasion; and on application of the legislature, or of the executive (when the legislature cannot be convened) against domestic violence."

King informed Tyler that for nearly a year, Rhode Island had been agitated by revolutionary movements. Violence now threatened, and King wanted the federal government to provide armed force to prevent it. Tyler demurred. The intervention of the national government in the affairs of a state was distasteful to him. During the nullification crisis of the early 1830s, Tyler had denounced President Jackson for his seemingly undue haste in summoning military units to use against South Carolina before every other means of meeting the situation had been exhausted. The sword, Tyler declared, should be the last resort.[22]

The Constitution, Tyler advised King, did not invest the president with the power to sanction the use of military force in anticipation of domestic violence within a state. Insurrection had to be actual before protection could be furnished, but Tyler hoped this "painful" but "imperative" performance of his duty would not be necessary. No matter what stand he took, Tyler knew he would be condemned. If he acceded to King's request, he would be accused of turning his back on the powerful suffrage movement. If he refused to assist the established government of Rhode Island, he would be seen as an encourager of lawlessness, a position most alien to his nature.

Wisely, he sought a middle ground. The state government, elected according to the provisions of the charter and statutes, was the legal entity. Congress had recognized it as such by seating its duly elected senators and representatives, and Tyler accepted this as the criterion for "a republican form of government." Fairly or unfairly, state officials had been elected in accordance with the laws of Rhode Island. However, Tyler informed King, this decision was not to be construed as an expression of opinion, favorable or unfavorable, on the state's domestic policy. The adjustment of intrastate differences belonged exclusively to the people of Rhode Island, and Tyler hoped that a spirit of conciliation would prevail over rash councils and that all grievances would be promptly redressed.

In mid May, Dorr and his followers tried to seize and occupy the state offices. King declared martial law and again appealed for aid. Tyler offered more advice. A government, he said, never loses anything by being mild and forebearing to its own citizens. "Why urge matters to an extremity?" If the legislature would authorize King to announce a general amnesty for the rebels and call a new constitutional convention "upon liberal principles," there could be a cessation of difficulties. "I speak advisedly," Tyler stressed, but he almost begged King to try the experiment; if it failed, the use of federal force would be justified.

As the situation became more alarming, Tyler sent Secretary of War Spencer to Rhode Island to evaluate the conditions. He then issued an order to the rebels to disperse within twenty-four hours. If this were not heeded, Tyler said he would call on the governors of Massachusetts and Connecticut to furnish militia to join regular troops in the defense of Providence. When the Dorrites realized that their continued efforts would be thus resisted, they gave up the struggle. Dorr was arrested and sentenced to imprisonment for life, but he was released within a short time. In 1843 a legally sanctioned convention drew up a constitution that provided for white-manhood suffrage. Tyler's policy of moderation had prevailed.

Unfortunately but not surprisingly, the president did not escape censure, and the criticisms leveled at him again exemplified the paucity of moderate feeling in the country. Senator William Graham thought that Tyler, instead of "vacillating," should have acted with the energy President Washington displayed in reacting to the whiskey insurrection. A force should have been dispatched at once. "Dorr is president of an abolition society," Graham pointed out; he believes "a majority without regard to color or condition, have at any time a right to overturn the existing Government, and set up their will in its stead."[23]

Upshur viewed the Dorr movement as "democracy run mad," and Beverley Tucker observed that majority rule made minority rights inconsequential and that "the aimless exercise of [majority] power" would lead nowhere except to "plunder and self-indulgence." George Templeton Strong, a young New Yorker, saw Dorr as "silly, ridiculous, and despicable. . . . I trust he'll be hanged by the neck, though that isn't equal to his deserts. He ought to be put in a bag and carried around the country for exhibition first. I'd give a shilling myself to see the man."

Andrew Jackson, understandably, took an extremely opposite view: "If the President should be weak enough to order a regular force to sustain the charter against the peoples constitution a hundred thousand people would fly to the rescue. . . . The people are the sovereign power and agreeable to our system they have the right to alter and amend their system of Government when a majority wills it, as a majority has a right to do."[24]

In 1844, acting on a memorial from some members of the Rhode Island legislature who accused Tyler of interfering with the suffrage movement in their state, the House of Representatives launched an investigation and called upon the president to submit all documents pertaining to the matter. When Tyler complied, even many of his enemies, including the *National Intelligencer*, expressed approval of the manner in which he had handled the affair. Webster, by then no longer a member of the cabinet, praised Tyler for his discretion and firmness in resolving the problem. Tyler's actions also were upheld a few years later in the Supreme Court decision in the case of *Luther* v. *Borden*.[25]

Tyler would have welcomed such praise and exoneration during the summer of 1842. Like Clay, Calhoun, and at least a half dozen others, he was looking ahead to the next presidential race. Tyler was ambitious, and although not apparently a vengeful man, he must have been human enough to want to roust the Whigs by winning the presidency in his own right in 1844. If he could not form a party of his own, would the Democrats be interested in his candidacy? The possibility was remote, but in Tyler's mind, there was a slight hope. The results of the 1842 election pleased him. In the Twenty-eighth Congress, the House of Representatives would have a substantial Democratic majority. Both Henry Wise and Thomas Gilmer switched parties and were reelected as Democrats. Two other members of the "Corporal's Guard," Caleb Cushing and George Proffit, were not candidates. Unfortunately for Tyler, this reduced his meager following of loyal friends in the House to two. The Whigs retained their narrow majority in the Senate, where Rives was the only Tyler spokesman, and Rives's ardor was cooling.

As the new tariff revenues replenished the Treasury and gave encouragement to business interests, Tyler could feel satisfaction in the improvement of the nation's economy. Some financial experts insisted that the tariff had nothing to do with the beginnings of a return to prosperity, that it was only a coincidence that an upswing had occurred after the passage of the bill. Nevertheless, many gave credit to the Tariff of 1842.

The struggle with the congressional Whigs, the threats of impeachment, the scorn and ridicule were enervating for Tyler. Personal matters also took their toll. "Your mother's health is bad," he informed his oldest daughter early in July. "Her mind is greatly prostrated by her disease, and she seems quite anxious to have you with her." Letitia Christian Tyler died on 10 September 1842. Funeral services for her were held in the East Room of the White House, and for a few days the Whig press suspended its attacks on the president and paid tribute to the First Lady.[26]

8

THE PEACEMAKERS

While hostilities between the president and Congress virtually paralyzed domestic legislation, developments on the international scene held out glimmers of hope in foreign affairs. In England, late in 1841, the government of Lord Melbourne was replaced by that of Sir Robert Peel, and the Foreign Office changed from the administration of the recklessly blustering and insulting Lord Palmerston to that of the mild, diplomatic Lord Aberdeen.

During Van Buren's presidency, animosity between the United States and Great Britain came dangerously close to open warfare. The border dispute between Maine and New Brunswick was the source of the greatest friction. On several occasions, boundary commissions recommended solutions, but none was satisfactory to the citizens of Maine. By 1839 the situation had become ominous. Maine politicians and newspapermen appealed to patriots throughout the country to support the "nation's honor." Local groups were urged to take up arms and march off to claim "their land." New Brunswick's militia was ready to retaliate. Van Buren ordered Gen. Winfield Scott to the troubled area, not to fight, but to try to maintain peace.[1]

The *Caroline*-McLeod affair, which occurred at approximately the same time as the deepening crisis in Maine, increased the danger of war. The British were indignant about the aid given by Americans, of the Hunters' Lodges and other secret groups, to Canadians, led by William Lyon McKenzie, in rebellion against what they perceived as autocratic British rule. The United States countered with protests against the 1837 "invasion" of American territory by Canadians, loyal to the Crown, who were endeavoring to stop the flow of men, supplies, and ammunition from the United States to the rebels.

In the clash of forces, a small steamer, the *Caroline*, which was used in transporting goods to the insurgents and was owned by a United States citizen, was pushed from the American side out into the Niagara River, where it was set afire and sunk. An American, Amos Durfee, was killed. Some time later, Alexander McLeod, a Canadian sheriff who had participated in the fray, boasted about the fact while he was in the state of New York. He was thereupon arrested and charged with arson and murder. The British government, stating that McLeod had acted under orders, demanded that he be released. Van Buren explained that the case was pending in the courts of New York and that the federal government had no power or right to intervene.

Palmerston was not appeased; he threatened dire consequences unless the situation was resolved to British satisfaction. Congress voted $10 million for war preparations and gave the president the power to call for fifty thousand volunteers. A clash was avoided, but the crisis remained. "It is difficult for the twentieth-century historian to realize that the United States and Great Britain were on the verge of a third war in 1841," Samuel Flagg Bemis has maintained; "yet such was the case."[2]

Tyler and Webster were anxious to ease tensions between the two countries. The United States, devastated by the depression, could ill afford a conflict with a major power. Webster was certain that friendly Anglo-American relations provided the key to restored prosperity. Not insignificantly, favorable agreements on several points at issue would undoubtedly lend much-needed luster to the executive branch, and Webster, now discredited in his own party, needed to do something to vindicate his decision to remain in Tyler's cabinet. Therefore, when news reached Washington in late December 1841 that the Peel government desired to appoint a special mission to the United States, the president and his secretary of state were delighted, particularly when they learned that the man who had been named to head the mission, as special emissary, was Alexander Baring, Lord Ashburton, the retired head of the banking house of Baring Brothers and Company, who had many business connections in the United States. His wife was the daughter of the late William Bingham of Philadelphia, a wealthy banker, member of the Continental Congress, and United States senator from 1795 to 1801. For several years, Webster had acted as United States legal representative for Baring Brothers, and since his visit to England in 1839, he considered Lord and Lady Ashburton close friends. Ashburton believed, and Tyler and Webster agreed, that while the material interests of England and the United States "call loudly for peace and friendship," of "infinitely greater importance" was the opportunity to demonstrate to the rest of the world that nations could settle their differences amicably and could cooperate to take steps toward humanitarian goals, such as the obliteration of the slave trade.[3]

The time was auspicious. Edward Everett, the United States minister to England, was a solid and able diplomat in whom Webster had the utmost confidence. The chairman of the House Foreign Relations Committee was John Quincy Adams, and that of the Senate was William Rives. Although Adams held both Tyler and Webster in disdain, his own disposition toward Great Britain was "essentially pacific," and he was averse to "everything irritating in form or offensive language" that would injure the possibility of improving relations with the United Kingdom.[4]

There was reason to be concerned. Anglophobia was strong, especially along the boundaries with Canada (or what were claimed to be the boundaries) and in the frontier regions of the West. National honor was at stake, and there were many calls for the nation to go "to the last extremity" in forcing Britain to comply with American demands. Among certain groups, the hatred of England was endemic, dating back to the Revolutionary War and the War of 1812. Webster had no doubt that the great body of intelligent people wanted a firm and settled peace, but there were agitators, "uneasy and restless spirits," who relished disturbances. There were others who did not desire war, but neither did they want to extend the hand of friendship to the hated British. Such feelings, Webster feared, could spread quickly "under the fanning of patriotic professions."[5]

However, from the better-informed and less-emotional citizens came expressions of gratification for the British initiative to settle differences, many of which had festered too long and, if not solved, eventually and inevitably would lead to armed conflict. If Webster and Ashburton failed to find common ground, it was questionable whether there would ever again be such a favorable opportunity. Lady Ashburton assured Webster of her husband's good will and implored Webster "to meet his advances with the same friendly feeling he carries toward you." The special mission, she said, was "thrust upon him as the person most zealous in the cause of America, & most sanguine as to the possibility of settling the long pending difficulties between the two countries."

Lady Ashburton need not have worried. Her husband, who arrived in early April 1842, was received enthusiastically by a majority of those in government, by the press, and by crowds of people wherever he appeared. Webster had no reservations about the Britisher's sincerity in desiring to remove all causes of uneasiness. Webster was sure "no better selection could have been made to carry out the mission."

Unfortunately, Ashburton's initial observations about conditions in the United States were bleak. The financial situation was disastrous, he reported to Aberdeen. The administration appeared incompetent, and the country seemed to be torn by "conflicting interests." The government was at a standstill: the only apparent activities were the president's vetoing of bills and in turn, the Senate's rejecting of his appointments. Ashburton wondered how long such a government could survive.[6]

Another worry was how the Senate, the body with the responsibility of accepting or rejecting a treaty, would react to an agreement concluded by an administration that it scorned. Albert Gallatin, the aged diplomat and cabinet member of the Jefferson era, had given Ashburton due warning; however, Gallatin also said there was no reason to believe that Tyler and Webster, left to themselves, would be intractable on any subject.[7] But how possible was it for Tyler and Webster to be left to themselves?

The McLeod issue was a case in point. During his few weeks in office, Harrison had sent Attorney General Crittenden to Albany to see if he could arrange for the release of McLeod. Governor William H. Seward had steadfastly refused, holding that the state's legal process must be respected. He was almost certain that McLeod would be acquitted, but if a pardon were granted prior to the trial, public resentment would be great. "Public sentiment," Seward declared, "demands that the law should have its due course." Neither the president of the United States nor the king of England, acting upon his own knowledge, could enter a court of law and dictate its proceedings.

When Tyler inherited the problem, he also encouraged Seward to drop the prosecution, which was a difficult stand for a states'-rights southerner to take and which was embarrassing, because Seward accused Tyler and Webster of attempting to interfere in the affairs of the state of New York.

McLeod's trial was scheduled for October 1841, allowing for several months of contention between the federal and state governments. Seward claimed he was "answered by ribaldry" when he tried to communicate with the president. Webster charged that Seward was as "savage as a meat ax" about the entire matter. McLeod's acquittal ended the hostile exchanges between Albany and Washington and lessened the threat of war with Britain, at least over McLeod, but several points concerning the *Caroline* episode remained unresolved. These, along with many other difficulties that were irritating to the two countries, became detailed topics of discussion between Webster and Ashburton during the long, hot, and humid summer of 1842.[8]

Their talks were informal, as were many of their written exchanges. Webster was encouraged. "A pair of more friendly negotiators never put their heads together" was his optimistic report. Calhoun saw Ashburton as a plain, sensible, well-disposed gentleman, whose approach to the troublesome matter of the British "invasion" of American territory was frank and practical.[9] Canadian rebels, Ashburton explained, had taken refuge in the state of New York. From there, aided and abetted by men, ammunition, and supplies from the United States, the rebels had occupied Navy Island, a Canadian possession, on which they had mounted twelve pieces of ordnance within easy firing distance of the Canadian shore. Rebels also fired at the Canadian side from an American island.

"Supposing," said Ashburton, "a man standing on ground where you have no legal right to follow him has a weapon long enough to reach you, and is striking you down and endangering your life. How long are you bound to wait for the assistance of the authority having the legal power to relieve you?" The expedition that had been sent to capture the *Caroline* had expected to find her anchored off Navy Island, but when they discovered that she was moored to the American shore, they moved against her anyway. There was no premeditated plan of violating the jurisdiction of the United States. "The necessity of so doing arose from altered circumstances at the moment of execution."

What was perhaps most to be regretted, Ashburton admitted, was that some explanation and apology for the incident had not been made immediately in 1837. He thought the United States and Great Britain were perfectly in accord on the general principles of international law applicable "in this unfortunate case." Ashburton did not intend this statement to be taken as an apology, but Webster chose to regard it as such, and the dispute over the *Caroline* was ended by an exchange of letters. The subject did not become part of the treaty, as both diplomats agreed on the advisability of keeping the final document as uncluttered as possible. The more items covered, the greater the danger of the treaty's being rejected as one faction or another would challenge specific sections.[10]

The major thrust of the treaty was the settlement of several segments of the boundary between the United States and Canada. The northeastern-boundary controversy involved not only the very volatile matter of the line between Maine and New Brunswick but also the proper border at the head of the Connecticut River in New Hampshire and along the incorrectly surveyed forty-fifth parallel, the dividing line between Quebec and the states of Vermont and New York. In 1827 the northeastern-boundary controversy had been submitted to the king of the Netherlands for arbitration, but the suggested compromise had been unacceptable to the United States Senate and most definitely to the state of Maine.

These were not the only geographical issues to be considered by Webster and Ashburton. The water communication from Lake Huron through Lake Superior to the Lake of the Woods never had been made final. Some skirmishes had occurred in these areas, but none as vigorous and emotional as those in the Northeast. In reality, then, the entire boundary between the United States and Canada, from the source of the St. Croix River in the east to the "most northwestern point" of the Lake of the Woods, was to be discussed and, it was hoped, agreed upon. Initially, the negotiators anticipated settling their nations' conflicting claims to the Oregon Territory, but this proved to be too complicated to resolve along with so many other intricate matters. The task they faced was momentous, one that the peace commissioners in 1783, with their inadequate maps and lack of geographical information, had not been able to settle for all time.

Months before the British initiated the special mission, the Maine-boundary dispute was high on Webster's agenda. As secretary of state it was impossible for him not to be seriously concerned about a situation that was inflammatory enough to involve the nation in war. In late 1840, Maine's legislature requested the governor to expel British troops who were then occupying the Madawaska area, which was claimed by both Maine and New Brunswick. By the spring of 1841, when Webster took office, the states of Alabama, Indiana, and Maryland had voiced support for the expulsion and had petitioned the federal government to take action to drive the British from "American soil." This, they declared, was a matter of national honor. Some members of Parliament interpreted the request of the Maine legislature as a declaration of war and therefore called upon the ministry to take retaliatory measures.

If the boundary controversy ever was to be resolved peacefully, a compromise had to be reached. The sticking point was Maine's unyielding claim to the entire disputed territory—approximately twelve thousand square miles—and the state's demand that its constitutional right to the protection of the federal government against foreign invasion be respected. No settlement with Great Britain could be concluded without

Maine's consent. Maine was intransigent about its claim to the entire area, and Britain was determined to have its share.[11]

Assistance came from an interesting and unexpected quarter. In the spring of 1841, Francis O. J. Smith—a Maine politician, attorney, and newspaper publisher—approached Webster with a "new mode" of attacking the problem, a propaganda campaign to convince the citizens of Maine to accept a negotiated compromise. His tactics were those of a modern-day Madison Avenue public-relations operation. He and several assistants would quietly mingle with Maine politicians, pressing the idea that it would be to the state's benefit to be more flexible on the matter of land claims. More importantly, Smith would strive to "adjust the tone and direction of the party presses, and through them, of public sentiment, to the purpose so desirable of accomplishment." This, Smith declared, would eliminate years of awaiting the fruition of "the circuitous artifices" of diplomacy.

Earlier, in the 1830s, Smith had tried but failed to convince Van Buren of the futility of initiating negotiations "at the wrong end of the dispute." They had to begin with Maine, rather than with Great Britain, for if Maine refused to agree with settlements made between Washington and London, the entire effort would be useless. Tyler and Webster saw merit in Smith's argument and agreed to pay him $3,500 a year, plus expenses. Smith also thought "it would not be unreasonable" to expect a liberal commission if an agreement with Great Britain was finalized.

Given the state of relations between the president and the legislative branch and given the need for stealth in propagandizing Maine, asking Congress for funds seemed to be out of the question; therefore, Smith's remuneration came from the president's secret account, established by Congress in 1810, "to cover contingent expenses in dealing with foreign nations on matters which could not be 'made public' without injury to the public interest." Smith's enterprise did not fall exactly within the scope of the congressional statute, but in their eagerness to achieve a peaceful ending to the boundary dispute, Tyler and Webster decided to stretch the rules.

Tyler also again had to stretch his conscience in regard to states' rights. Smith's plan to "meddle" in the affairs of Maine was not in accord with the president's view on how a sovereign state should be treated, but Maine's persistence in demanding all of the disputed territory was jeopardizing international relations. In the Maine case, as in the McLeod–New York situation, Tyler and Webster believed they must consider the greater good of the entire country. If one state took a stand that could endanger the rest of the states by involving them in war with a foreign power, that state had to be brought into line, and it would be better to do so with propaganda than by a show of force. Webster had no trouble with this course of action, but it undoubtedly caused Tyler some pain.

Smith made good use of the *Portland* (Me.) *Christian Mirror,* a religious journal that had a wide circulation throughout New England. Three editorials, signed "Agricola" and entitled "Northeastern Boundary, Why Not Settle It?" appeared in the *Mirror,* carrying the message that compromise was the only alternative to war and urging the citizens of Maine to petition their state government to agree to negotiations. The editorial staff of the *Portland East Argus,* of which Smith was part owner, was won over. The paper had a larger circulation than the *Mirror,* especially outside of Maine, and papers from Chicago to Richmond, Virginia, reprinted *Argus* editorials calling for an agreement on the boundary. Howard Jones, in his study on the Webster-Ashburton Treaty, did not consider Smith's plan "a mere program in propaganda." Smith's newspaper articles, Jones has contended, "were fair, equitable, and above all practical."

By the time of Ashburton's arrival, Maine's seemingly stony stance had begun to weaken. Yet, Webster realized that no agreement reached in Washington would be acceptable in Maine unless the state actually had a part in the process. Therefore, he notified Governor John Fairfield that the United States was about to begin negotiations with Great Britain. If a settlement failed, another arbitration (to which Maine had strong objections) was likely; this would entail additional surveys, hearings, and reports, which possibly would consume seven or eight years. With Ashburton's unenthusiastic acquiescence, Webster then took the unprecedented step of inviting Maine to appoint commissioners to participate in the Washington negotiations. The same invitation was extended to the governor of Massachusetts. Until 1820, when Maine became a state, it had been a part of Massachusetts which, under the separation agreement, still held a half interest in unappropriated lands in the disputed area. Massachusetts, however, had never objected to a compromise settlement.[12]

To further impress upon Maine the advisability of agreeing to concessions, Webster used a map of the disputed area, which had been found by the Harvard historian Jared Sparks while he was engaged in research in the Paris archives of the French Foreign Office. The map, about which he informed Webster early in 1842, supposedly was one that had been used by Benjamin Franklin during the Paris peace talks of 1782 and 1783. Sparks first had found a letter written by Franklin to the Comte de Vergennes, France's foreign minister, stating that Franklin had indicated on a map, by "a strong red line," the boundary between Canada and the United States that had tentatively been agreed upon by the peace commissioners. Sparks then located the map he believed to have been Franklin's. To Sparks's surprise, it established Britain's right to all of the territory in question. It was a 1746 d'Anville map, and because the Paris commissioners had used a Mitchell map, this, unknown to Sparks, was not the red-line map that Franklin had referred to in his letter to Vergennes.

Webster was not shocked by Sparks's discovery. In 1838 he had purchased a 1775 Mitchell map, which had formerly been owned by Baron Friedrich von Steuben. No one knew how von Steuben had come by it, but the boundary, also marked in red, was the same as on the map discovered by Sparks. Webster had chosen not to make this knowledge public.

There appeared to be a profusion of red-line maps. One found in the London State Paper Office also supported the British claim, but Aberdeen and Ashburton did not use it to press their advantage, undoubtedly thinking there was no proof that the red lines indicated anything more than preliminary boundary discussions. Months after the Webster-Ashburton Treaty had been finalized, another map, this one supporting American claims to the entire land area, surfaced in London. Ashburton had not known of its existence, but Palmerston had. It had come to the latter's attention in 1839, and he had sequestered it in the Foreign Office. This was not the end of the map saga. Several others were found, one as late as 1933.

Webster was uncertain about the validity of the maps that were known to him, and he did not want the British to see them until after agreements with Ashburton had been concluded. However, he was not averse to using them, whether they were authentic or not, to his advantage in convincing Maine authorities that a compromise would be in their best interest. If they refused, they could lose all. Therefore, in May 1842, Webster sent Jared Sparks on a "confidential errand" to confer with Governor Fairfield, who immediately saw the significance of the red lines and agreed that arriving at a "fair adjustment" was the practical thing to do. Ashburton, too, used extraordinary means to persuade Maine to cooperate; he invested approximately £3,000 (about $14,500), most likely for propaganda purposes. The historian Frederick Merk has expressed the opinion that it is not possible to know to whom the Ashburton money was given but that "both Webster and Ashburton were undoubtedly guilty of improper use of secret funds."[13]

Nevertheless, a "fair adjustment" was difficult to achieve. The Maine commissioners were not inclined to relinquish any part of their claim without a struggle. Ashburton became impatient. "These gentlemen," he complained to Webster, "take their departure from the presumption that the whole territory belongs to them, and that they are benevolently giving us a certain portion." They were "obstinate and unmanageable," and Webster seemed either unable or unwilling to force them to be reasonable. Moreover, Ashburton found the Washington climate unbearable. "I contrive to crawl about in these heats by day & pass my nights in sleepless fever." He did not believe he could outlive "this affair" if it was prolonged much further. "I had hoped that these Gentlemen from the North East would be equally averse to this roasting. Could you not press them to come to the point and say whether we can or can not agree?" He did not see why he should be kept waiting while Maine and Massachusetts settled their accounts with the national government. He was ready to go home, but Tyler entreated him, in the strongest manner, to remain until the major causes of friction between the two nations had been dispelled. If Ashburton were to leave, the president feared that relations with Britain would be more critical than they had been prior to the attempt to improve them.[14]

After several days of meeting privately, without the commissioners from Maine and Massachusetts, Webster and Ashburton in mid July arrived at an agreement on the northeastern boundary. The United States received 7,015 square miles (4,489,600 acres) of the territory in question, and the British 5,012 square miles (3,207,680 acres). Among other important concessions, the United States was granted the unrestricted right to use the lower St. John River for commercial purposes. This was of great importance, because settlers in Maine's interior had no other way of transporting their forest and agricultural products to market. Ashburton also agreed to accept the validity of the boundary from the Connecticut River to the St. Lawrence River, as previously surveyed, despite the fact that the survey had inaccurately placed the forty-fifth parallel south of its correct location. The United States had built an elaborate fort at Rouses Point on Lake Champlain. Had this concession not been made, the fort would have been lost. Webster considered this agreement worth the surrender of any territory to which the United States may have had a rightful title, and he urged the Maine commissioners to accept the terms. The president, he said, felt the deepest anxiety for an agreement that would preserve national honor and at the same time respect the rights of the states. No better compromise could be reached. Reluctantly, the men from Maine, encouraged by those from Massachusetts, consented.[15]

With the northeastern boundary seemingly settled, Webster and Ashburton turned their attention to the demarcation line from the channel between Lakes Huron and Superior to the Lake of the Woods, a much less complicated matter than the Maine–New Brunswick border. Neither nation thought the territory of great value. Considered most important was the transportation route for the fur trade. Having achieved what he wanted most in the Northeast, land over which Britain could have built a military road from Quebec to the Bay of Fundy, Ashburton was willing to be generous in what was referred to as the "northwestern section." The United States acquired Sugar Island, claimed by both countries and located in the present Sault Sainte Marie Canals between Lake Huron and Lake Superior. Its strategic position and twenty-six thousand acres of fine soil made it a considerable prize.

In establishing a water boundary, with mutual rights of navigation, along the Pigeon River, Rainy Lake, and Rainy River to the Lake of the Woods—together known as the Grand Portage—Ashburton conceded to the United States extensive lands in what is now northern Minnesota. Although both England and the United States were aware of mineral deposits in the region, neither had any conception of the vast veins of iron ore beneath the surface. Discovered in the 1870s, the rich Vermilion Range was entirely within the land relinquished by Britain, and the equally valuable Mesabi Range was partially so. The remainder of the Mesabi Range was in territory that had already been a part of the United States prior to the 1842 settlement.[16]

In two other matters under discussion, the sensitive topic of slavery loomed large, almost to the point of disrupting the entire mediation effort. One involved the American brig *Creole*, which, in late October 1841, had sailed from Hampton Roads, Virginia, bound for New Orleans with a cargo of tobacco and approximately 135 slaves. On the evening of 7 November, off Great Abaco Island in the Bahamas, 19 of the slaves had seized control of the vessel; murdered 1 of the slave owners; wounded the captain, the first mate, and 2 of the crew; and sailed the brig into the British port of Nassau. Authorities there imprisoned the mutineers and, acting under the provisions of the British Emancipation Act of 1833, liberated the slaves who had not been involved in the uprising, encouraging them "to go beyond the power of the master of the brig or the American consul at Nassau." The consul requested that the slaves who had been accused of mutiny and murder be extradited to the United States; but instead of complying with the request, the governor of Nassau awaited instructions from England.

Prior to Ashburton's arrival in Washington, Webster, through Everett, had protested to the British government. The *Creole*, Webster insisted, was on a completely lawful voyage. The cargo consisted of merchandise that belonged to American citizens and of slaves, who were recognized as property by the Constitution of the United States in those states that condoned the institution. The *Creole* was not transporting slaves to British territory. The brig had been forced, against the will of the captain and the crew, into Nassau harbor. Under such circumstances, the comity and hospitality of nations required that the authorities there, in any manner possible, aid the vessel to resume its voyage and that they return the mutineers to the United States for trial.

During their spring and summer meetings, the *Creole* incident vexed Webster and Ashburton. British and American abolitionists pressured their respective governments to uphold the liberation of the *Creole* blacks. Webster was keenly aware, too, of southern reactions to what was said or done about the incident. It was, indeed, a matter of a "delicate nature"; in Ashburton's opinion, it created greater difficulty than any other of the differences between the nations. To save the overall negotiations, Webster tried to take a middle-of-the-road position. Realizing that the climate of opinion in England would not allow the British government to return the liberated blacks to bondage, he did not make such a demand. Rather, he insisted on compensation for the slaves who had been freed and for the "pirates and murderers." At the same time he clearly stated his opinion that the mutineers should have been delivered to the American consul in Nassau.[17]

The request for compensation brought loud outcries from militant abolitionists and "other friends of freedom" in Massachusetts and elsewhere. Britain, they said, could not retreat from its emancipation policy and, "on every consideration of justice and moral right, ought not to acquiesce" in demands for compensation. Slavery and the slave trade, whether foreign or domestic, should not be condoned and protected by the United States government.

Allowing black murderers to escape punishment, southerners countered, encouraged slave uprisings. "If we may not safely sail on our own coast, with our slave property on board, because Great Britain may choose to deny our right to hold property in slaves," Calhoun warned, "may she not, with equal propriety, extend the same rule to our cotton and other staples?"[18]

Attorney General Legaré, while he affirmed the law of property as applied to slaves, attempted to minimize that aspect of the controversy by basing his opinion on international law. The main point at issue, he stated, was the involuntary nature of the *Creole*'s entry into Nassau's harbor. Without any intention of landing slaves on British soil or of violating British municipal law, the *Creole* had been forced into port. Furthermore, the slaves were not on British soil; they were on an American ship; and an American ship was, in effect, American soil.

Additionally, a vessel that was compelled by weather or any other overruling necessity to take refuge in the port of another nation was not subject to the municipal law of that nation; it was subject to the rule of international law.

The *Creole* controversy came at an especially sensitive time. In the United States, nerves and emotions had been worn thin by violent debates over slavery which had erupted in the House of Representatives almost simultaneously with the beginning of the Webster-Ashburton discussions on the *Creole* affair. Although centering largely on the right of petition and the gag rule, the heated exchanges in the House inevitably encompassed the *Creole*, and Joshua R. Giddings, an abolitionist from Ohio, offered a number of resolutions condemning the coastal slave trade and exonerating the black mutineers.

Legaré feared a "terrible pother" among a majority of southern representatives and senators if "there be nothing forthcoming under hand and seal," providing reparations for the freeing of the *Creole* slaves. "They may," he warned Webster, "make common cause in the Senate with the malcontents on the Boundary question, & fling the whole work into the river—which were a thousand pities."[19]

Personally, Ashburton wanted to offer reparations, but he was not authorized to do so, and because no extradition agreement existed between Britain and the United States, returning the mutineers for trial was deemed to be impossible. The absence of an extradition policy also bothered Governor Seward, who was often faced with the problem of having Canadian criminals flee to New York or of having ones from his state make their way to Canada. Without resort to extradition, both governments were thwarted in their efforts to bring the guilty to justice, but even so, Seward considered demands for the return of the *Creole* slaves, including those who had committed acts of violence, "miserable and unmanly." No law or constitution, he argued, could convert human beings into chattel, and slaves who had escaped from their masters should not be forced to return to bondage. Ashburton, too, was specific in ruling out the extradition of slaves who sought freedom in Canada or in other British possessions. Tyler's concern was of a different nature. Would British authorities, considering the act one of self-defense, refuse to surrender a slave who had killed his master and then escaped? Ashburton thought Tyler had become "sore and testy" about the *Creole*.

After detailed discussions, Webster and Ashburton agreed that murder; assault with the intent to commit murder; piracy; arson; robbery; and forgery were all extraditable crimes and should be so recognized by an article in the treaty proper. Other matters arising from the *Creole* incident were dealt with in an exchange of letters in which the diplomats acknowledged that their main objective was the prevention of occurrences of a similar nature. Britain promised to instruct colonial governors not to interfere with American vessels driven by weather, accident, or violence into British ports, but Britain warned that in other circumstances, there would be no relaxation of the British Emancipation Act in their West Indian or other colonies. With the exception of a few words in Ashburton's correspondence, Tyler found the exchange of notes "entirely acceptable." In 1853 an Anglo-American claims commission awarded $110,330 to the owners of the slaves who had been liberated by the British. The conclusion was that the *Creole*'s voyage had been legal according to the laws of the United States and that the ship had been driven unavoidably into the port of Nassau, where it should have been subject to the tenets of international law.[20]

Another subject of a "delicate nature" was that of the African slave trade, a humanitarian concern of significant dimensions since the early days of the American nation and even during colonial times. As soon as was constitutionally possible, the United States, on 1 January 1808, had prohibited any further importation of slaves. On the same day, Great Britain had banned all African slave traffic in its colonies. Later, under the Emancipation Act of 1833, England had moved to keep slave ships, British or otherwise, out of its territorial waters; and it had used its great naval power to stop suspected "slavers" off the coast of Africa or elsewhere, by boarding and searching suspicious vessels.

To the United States, which had vivid memories of British impressment of American seamen prior to and during the War of 1812, "visit and search" was anathema. Unfortunately, the United States, which had a limited naval force, either did not or could not enforce the 1808 law with diligence. Because the United States refused Britain the right to visit and search American ships and because the United States infrequently did so itself, slave traffickers from other countries often flew the United States flag while engaged in the nefarious trade. The United States, by refusing to cooperate with Great Britain or to assume the responsibility for the enforcement of its own prohibitory law, was, in effect, aiding and abetting the illegal activity, although Congress repeatedly passed stringent statutes against the trade and in 1820 declared that it was piracy, punishable by death.

Nevertheless, extreme Anglophobia prevented the Senate from approving treaties designed to provide closer cooperation with Great Britain in suppressing the trade. From time to time, the United States informally worked with England and other European nations, as well as with those of South America, in stopping "slavers," but Congress was unwilling to pass laws that would allow the seizure and detention of ships that were flying the stars and stripes, even when they were known to be carrying slave-trading equipment. According to the nation's courts, the only acceptable proof that a vessel was a "slaver" was the presence of slaves on board. Obviously, the government's attitude toward the slave-trade problem reflected its agonizing ambivalence toward the entire issue of slavery.

In December 1841, Sir Robert Peel and Lord Aberdeen proposed the establishment of an international organization to combat the trade. The result was the Quintuple Treaty, concluded by Austria, Great Britain, France, Prussia, and Russia, in which the five nations agreed to mutual rights of visit and search and declared the slave trade piracy, subject to trial in the courts of the signatory nations. Aberdeen entreated the United States to join in the effort, and Edward Everett believed the country should. "Is it out of the question for the United States to come into agreement with the Five Powers?" he inquired of Webster. "There surely can be nothing derogatory to our honor in making common cause with them in this way. How would our interests suffer?"[21]

But a storm of protest arose against such an idea. Suspicions of British motives were voiced. "England has much more than a work of benevolence in the suppression of the slave trade," Duff Green warned Calhoun. England, Green said, found it impossible to maintain its commercial and manufacturing superiority because of its inability to raise cotton and sugar as cheaply in India as it could be produced with slave labor in the United States; therefore, the United Kingdom was making war on slavery and the slave trade in an effort to increase the cost of producing raw materials in the United States, Brazil, and Cuba. If this were to happen, England could sell the products of her East India possessions to continental powers at prices below those charged by the United States. Calhoun agreed. The policy of England, he was certain, was "to get control of the commerce of the world by controlling the labour which produced the articles by which it is principally put in motion. Humanity is but a flimsy pretext." The United States was the greatest obstacle to Britain's "great scheme of ambition"; hence the desire to undermine America's strength by destroying its southern labor force.

One of the most vigorous and vocal opponents of the United States involvement in the Quintuple Treaty was not a southerner; it was Lewis Cass, a Michigan Democrat who was an intense Anglophobe. Appointed minister to France by Van Buren and allowed by Tyler to remain in that position, Cass, as Webster observed, had his eye on the next Democratic presidential nomination and intended "to make great political headway upon a popular gale." Protests against participation in the

Quintuple agreement poured from Cass's pen. Much to the dismay of Peel and Aberdeen, Cass succeeded in convincing Louis Philippe of France to reject the treaty. Webster was "nearly overwhelmed" with letters and pamphlets from Cass and from Henry Wheaton, minister to Prussia, also a holdover Van Buren appointee.

Supreme Court Justice Joseph Story thought the Quintuple Treaty had been "exceedingly well drawn and most carefully weighed," and he deplored the "intermeddling" of Cass and Wheaton, fearing they would embarrass the negotiations with Ashburton. Webster pointedly assured Cass that the administration, while it was "resolved to fulfill all our duties respecting the abolition of the African slave trade," had no intention of surrendering any shred of national interest or national honor. In Tyler's opinion, a large portion of American opposition could be overcome if Parliament officially would announce the abandonment of impressment.[22]

Ashburton supported this view, but Aberdeen, although he privately admitted that impressment never would be renewed, informed Ashburton that it was a "very different thing to abstain from exercising a Right we possess, and officially to abandon that right." At the heart of the matter were conflicting views on the right of naturalization. The United States held that citizens of other nations, after a period of residency in the country, could change their allegiance and become American citizens. However, according to British law, this was not possible. British citizenship was perpetual, indelible, and indissoluble; and during time of war, regardless of naturalization in another land, any British-born male of military age was expected to serve the Crown. Therefore, impressment could not be renounced. British opinion would not allow it. American opinion demanded nothing less. As to the matter of visit and search, it was so violently opposed by the American public that Webster decided it was better to avoid discussing the subject with Ashburton. Aberdeen attempted to distinguish between the right of visit—merely to determine a vessel's true nationality—and the right of search, which was a purely belligerent right; but the subject was too sensitive to allow for calm deliberation.

Finally, acting on Tyler's suggestion, the two diplomats agreed upon a system of joint cruising squadrons off the coast of Africa. Each government was to maintain a naval force of not less than eighty guns to "enforce, separately and respectively, the laws, rights, and obligations of each of the two countries, for the repression of the slave trade." Although the squadrons were to be independent of each other, the two goverments, upon mutual consultation, could order them to act "in concert and cooperation" as exigencies might arise. Britain and the

United States also agreed to urge all nations to close their markets for African slaves "effectually at once and forever." These stipulations became articles 8 and 9 of the treaty.

The official document contained no mention of impressment. As in the case of the *Creole* and the *Caroline,* an exchange of notes was considered the better method of at least recognizing serious differences on which, for the present, no solution was possible. Communicating with Ashburton "in the spirit of peace," Webster reiterated Secretary of State Thomas Jefferson's dictum that "the simplest rule will be that the vessel being American shall be evidence that the seamen on board are such." After the passage of fifty years, Webster advised Ashburton, this was still the principle maintained by the government of the United States. "In every regularly documented American merchant vessel the crew who navigate it will find their protection in the flag which is over them." The practice of impressing seamen from American vessels could not be tolerated. According to assurances received from Aberdeen and Peel, Ashburton was certain that his government did not intend to renew the practice, but he also was aware that the prime minister was determined not to stir public opinion by announcing its discontinuance.

On this note of mutual understanding, Webster and Ashburton concluded their negotiations and signed the treaty. Two days later, on 11 August, it was submitted to the Senate meeting in executive session. Despite that body's deep and bitter controversies with Tyler over domestic issues, few believed the treaty would be rejected. "It removes," said Upshur, "every possible cause of dispute with England for years to come."[23]

Others were less optimistic. Senator Thomas Hart Benton of Missouri, at his bumptious best—or worst—led the fight against acceptance. Too many questions, he charged, had been left unsettled, and because of those omissions, the nation at some future date would find itself with no alternative but war. Additionally, he accused Webster of "needlessly and shamefully" giving up territory that was rightfully American, and he admonished the West to be aware of this, because the Oregon question remained to be settled. Hoping for a consolidation of southern and western opposition to the Webster-Ashburton agreement, Benton urged the South to beware of the exclusion of the *Creole* issue from the formal settlement. Because the seriousness of freeing slaves who were guilty of insurrection and murder was not addressed, Santo Domingo style uprisings in the South were more likely to occur, "excited from London, from Canada, and from Nassau."

Calhoun, while agreeing that the *Creole* case should have been addressed officially by an article in the treaty, spoke in behalf of ratification: "Peace is the first of our wants in the present condition of our country. . . . If we have not gained all that could be desired, we have gained much that is desirable, and if all has not been settled, much has been—and that not of little importance." Webster deeply appreciated the "very handsome manner" in which the senator from South Carolina supported the treaty.

William Cabel Rives, chairman of the Foreign Relations Committee, reported favorably on the document and skillfully guided the Senate toward ratification. Webster anticipated approval, but the final vote surprised him. "The work is done, 39 to 9!" he excitedly announced. This exceeded by seven votes the necessary two-thirds. Of the nine who had voted in opposition, eight were Democrats. The only Whig holdout was Charles M. Conrad of Louisiana.[24]

Webster was enormously thankful to all who had worked for the treaty's success, but his special gratitude went to Tyler for his "steady support and confidence." "Your anxious and intelligent attention to what was in progress," he told the president, had been invaluable. Webster acknowledged Tyler's supervision of every step of the negotiations. "I shall never speak of this negotiation, my dear sir, which I believe is destined to make some figure in the history of the country, without doing you justice."[25]

For once, the president, the cabinet, and the Senate had worked together to accomplish a significant goal, and Tyler was justly proud of the diplomatic achievement. If during the eighteen months of his presidency nothing had been attained but the treaty, the administration, he contended, deserved at least a small share of praise "as a set-off to the torrents of abuse so unceasingly and copiously lavished upon me." Yet, in spite of the fact that the Senate Whigs almost unanimously approved the treaty, the party withheld all accolades from the president. Rather, he was scorned publicly during a Whig dinner at New York's Astor House, which was held in honor of Lord Ashburton prior to his departure for England. There, a toast to Queen Victoria was cheered with gusto, while one to Tyler met with "ominous silence." No one except Lord Ashburton and his entourage stood to honor the president. Peace had been preserved, Anglo-American friendship had been strengthened, commercial connections had been encouraged, but Tyler received no credit from the Whigs.

However, a mass meeting of thousands of New York citizens protested the discourteous and disdainful treatment of the nation's chief executive. Banners proclaiming "An Insult to the President Is an Insult to the Nation" were carried in a procession. Philadelphians, likewise, adopted resolutions censuring those Whigs who had acted with such petty vindictiveness. There was bitter pleasure in Upshur's observation that what the Whigs termed "our weak and vacillating administration, so far at least . . . has done well."[26]

9

★ ★ ★ ★ ★

PACIFIC-MINDEDNESS

The approval of the Webster-Ashburton Treaty, which is formally known as the Treaty of Washington, did not quiet its opponents. They were often aspiring politicians who saw an opportunity to attract attention by giving vent to their opinions. Chief among them was Lewis Cass, the United States minister to France, who took issue with the idea of allowing the United States to enter into an "entangling alliance" with Great Britain in the operation of the joint cruising squadrons. Cass stood for the policy of isolation. Webster believed that cooperation with other nations was mandatory for future peace and prosperity. Cass also protested the "sin of omission" in not demanding an absolute British renunciation of the right of search. Such a renunciation, Webster replied, was unlikely to be any more "effectual than the Chinese method of defending their towns by painting grotesque and hideous figures on the walls to frighten away assailing foes." Repeatedly, Webster was forced to remind Cass that the duties and privileges of a minister abroad did not include making formal remonstrances and protests against the proceedings of the legislative or executive branches in the United States upon subjects for which Cass had no responsibility. Such actions, Webster wrote, caused the president considerable concern.[1]

The Democratic diplomat acquired a sizable following, and he returned to the United States in December 1842 to a hero's welcome. Invited to address the House of Representatives, Cass was given a standing ovation, and when he traveled through Pennsylvania, New

York, and Massachusetts, he was hailed as a great defender of national honor, much to Webster's annoyance. The Whig press enjoyed Cass's negative remarks about the Tyler administration, so much so that Mahlon Dickerson, a New Jersey Democrat, felt compelled to question Cass about his party affiliation: "The manner in which your nomination is mentioned by some of the Whig papers, is such as to excite a suspicion . . . that you favor Whig principles. I take the liberty of asking from you such explanation of your views . . . as shall be entirely satisfactory to your political friends."[2]

Senator Benton of Missouri, while not an avowed candidate for the presidential nomination, charged that Webster had used Sparks's red-line maps, as he had in Maine, to convince wavering senators that the United States could lose all the disputed territory if the treaty were not ratified before Britain discovered the existence of the maps. Therefore, said Benton, the approval of the treaty was secured "out of doors" in an irregular manner. But despite Benton's outbursts, Webster thought Senator James Buchanan of Pennsylvania was more wrathful and mean about the treaty than anyone else was. As a member of the Senate Foreign Relations Committee, Buchanan denounced Webster for having failed to sustain the American claim to all the territory in question in the Maine–New Brunswick dispute. The United States title to the land clearly was evident, Buchanan maintained, but Webster had willingly relinquished it in an unsuccessful attempt to foster friendly relations with Britain. Buchanan also believed that Webster should have obtained reparations from the British for the *Creole* and the *Caroline* incidents and that the secretary of state should have been skilled enough as a diplomat to force Britain to abandon its policy of impressment. The Webster-Ashburton Treaty, Buchanan declared, was "an unqualified surrender of our territory to British dictation," so he voted against it.

Throughout the years, such criticism has continued. Samuel Flagg Bemis, in the first volume of his work on John Quincy Adams, *John Quincy Adams and the Foundations of American Foreign Policy*, has maintained that Webster "achieved a diplomatic triumph—against his own country"—by "willfully relinquishing millions of acres of good American territory of the state of Maine." This, Bemis has claimed, was done for selfish reasons. Webster desperately craved to be appointed as minister to England. If he could settle the outstanding disputes between the two nations, he would be *"persona gratissima"* in London; therefore, he did everything possible to conclude the treaty; in the process, he made unnecessary concessions.

In his second volume, *John Quincy Adams and the Union*, Bemis has somewhat tempered his remarks, by admitting that while the Webster-

Ashburton Treaty "may not have been an ingenuous piece of diplomacy or domestic politics, . . . it was certainly a consummately clever device for securing Anglo-American peace." However, Bemis has not found Webster guiltless of "skullduggery" in the use of Sparks's red-line map and the use of secret funds to dupe the Maine authorities. Bemis has also accused Webster of collusion in allowing Ashburton to invest more than $14,000 in persuading Maine to accept a land settlement.[3]

Skullduggery was only one of the many things that Benton found offensive about the treaty. Even more serious to him was the matter of the "pretermitted subjects," the ones intentionally disregarded in the official document: namely, impressment, the "outrage" of the *Caroline*, the liberation of American slaves aboard the *Creole*, and of greatest moment, the failure to settle the Oregon question. In the summer of 1842, Benton's son-in-law, John Charles Frémont, returned from his first exploring expedition, a scientific investigation and mapping of South Pass, on the Oregon Trail, and of the Seedskeedee and Wind River Mountains. On the highest peak in the Wind River Range, Frémont raised a flag to signal the advent of Manifest Destiny. The settlement of United States claims to Oregon could no longer be deferred, Benton roared at his fellow senators. "Our people are beginning to go there!"[4] Actually, the trek to Oregon had begun, at least in modest proportions, some time earlier.

Since the late eighteenth century, when Robert Gray, in his ship the *Columbia* out of Boston, had explored the great river that he named in honor of his vessel, the United States had maintained a claim to the vast Oregon Territory. The British, through the voyages of Capt. James Cook, George Vancouver, Sir Alexander C. Mackenzie, and others, had asserted their rights to the area. During the presidency of Thomas Jefferson, the overland expedition of Meriwether Lewis and William Clark (1803–6) included explorations of the Snake River Valley and of the lower Columbia. Several years later, John Jacob Astor, a prominent American fur trader, established a settlement called Fort Astoria. The competition between Astor and the British Hudson Bay Company was fierce. Rival settlements sprang up, and controversies over land owner-ship intensified. In 1818 an Anglo-American Convention agreed upon a ten-year joint occupation of Oregon Territory. This was renewed in 1827 for an indefinite period, with either party having the option of terminat-ing the agreement on a year's notice.

Spain to the south and Russia to the north also were interested in Oregon. According to the Adams-Onís Treaty of 1819, the United States and Spain agreed upon the forty-second parallel as the southern boundary of Oregon Territory, and Spain relinquished any right to land north of that line. In 1824 and 1825 the United States and Great Britain concluded treaties with Russia, establishing the southern boundary of Russia's territory in North America at fifty-four degrees, forty minutes. Therefore, Oregon Territory, jointly occupied by Britain and the United States, encompassed an area from the Rocky Mountains to the Pacific Ocean and from the forty-second parallel on the south to fifty-four degrees, forty minutes, to the north. It included what are now the states of Oregon, Washington, and Idaho and the Canadian province of British Columbia. Periodically, attempts were made to decide what part of the territory belonged to the United States and what part to Britain, but no mutually acceptable solution could be reached. The United States offered to settle for an extension of the forty-ninth parallel, which was its boundary with Canada from the Lake of the Woods to the Rocky Mountains. Britain was willing to accept the forty-ninth parallel, but only until it intersected with the Columbia River. From there they wanted the boundary line to follow the river to the Pacific Ocean. This was not acceptable to the United States; it needed a deep-water port, which neither the Columbia River nor the coastal area to the south could provide. The only suitable harbor was to the north, between the Columbia River and the forty-ninth parallel, in an estuary, Puget Sound, accessible through the Strait of Juan de Fuca. The United States would agree to nothing less.

By 1842 the situation was becoming critical. Americans were moving westward at an increasing rate. The destination for most of them was the Willamette Valley, a journey of more than two thousand miles along the Oregon Trail, from Independence, Missouri, to the Oregon "utopia," as it was advertised. Although the Willamette Valley was located south of the Columbia River, Oregon fever was on the rise, and expansionists and American settlers were demanding a proper settlement of territorial rights, hopefully during the Webster-Ashburton discussions.[5]

Another incident that focused attention on the Oregon Territory during the summer of 1842 was the return of the Great United States Exploring Expedition, after an absence of four years. The timing of its reappearance, although coincidental, was auspicious. The expedition's flagship, the *Vincennes*, under the command of the strange and brilliant Charles Wilkes, arrived off Sandy Hook, New Jersey, on 10 June, completing a voyage of 87,780 nautical miles. During the "magnificent voyage" the globe had been circumnavigated, the continent of Antarctica had been located, the Pacific had been crisscrossed, and the western coast of North America had been explored. For the Oregon enthusiasts, the last was of greatest importance. Among his numerous reports,

Wilkes wrote a special one on Oregon, which the Tyler administration suppressed, not wanting to arouse hostility toward Great Britain during the sensitive Webster-Ashburton negotiations.

Wilkes's views and recommendations, however, became public knowledge. He advised his government to uphold its claim to all of Oregon, all the way to fifty-four, forty. If it did not, "a storehouse of wealth in its forests, furs, and fisheries" would be sacrificed. He advocated the military occupation of the area. If the United States did not act, it was very probable that California eventually would throw off the lax Mexican control and unite with Oregon to form a state "that is destined to control the destinies of the Pacific." Wilkes also verified what was already known—namely, that the Columbia River was not navigable for deep-drafted ships because of treacherous sand bars. One of the expedition's vessels, the sloop *Peacock*, was lost off Cape Disappointment on the Columbia River, while attempting to negotiate a passage through the shoals.

Public accounts of Wilkes's reports stimulated American interest in both Oregon and California. Perhaps Ashburton and Aberdeen thought the time was too emotional for reasoned negotiations on the topic. Ashburton's major concern was the Maine–New Brunswick boundary. The Foreign Office had not given him adequate information on the background of previous Oregon discussions or authority to relinquish any territory north of the Columbia River. Faced with the strong probability of a stalemate, Webster and Ashburton, with many other problems to solve, decided to defer the Oregon question to a future time.[6]

Nevertheless, because of their desire to have a harbor on the Pacific, Webster and Tyler decided to sound out Ashburton on another possibility. Would Great Britain be willing to use its influence to induce Mexico to cede a portion of the California coast, including San Francisco, to the United States, either by purchase or by the assumption of Mexican debts owed to American citizens? If this "tripartite plan" were to succeed, the United States would be willing to relinquish its claim to the area above the Columbia River. Ashburton replied that Great Britain could take no active part in such an arrangement, but he believed there would be no objection to the plan, "provided the cession by Mexico were voluntary." As he told Aberdeen, he did not anticipate any significant "American lodgment on the Pacific" for many years. The Indians, he said, were there in great force and would serve as a barrier to westward expansion.

Waddy Thompson, the United States minister to Mexico, encouraged the idea of purchasing the San Francisco coastal area. California, he said, was "destined to be the granary of the Pacific," and he thought it conceivable that Mexico might be persuaded to cede both California and Texas to the United States in return for the assumption of Mexican debts. This was wishful thinking, but Thompson persisted. The acquisition of California, he suggested to Tyler, would temper the North's opposition to the annexation of Texas. Rumors of French and British designs on California and Texas caused some anxiety in Washington, but for the moment there was more concern for Oregon, except on the part of southerners and a few northerners, such as Nicholas Biddle, who had invested heavily in Texas land. Tyler and Webster were not concentrating on Texas in 1842. Webster vehemently opposed annexation, and Tyler's involvement in the issue would come later.[7]

Webster was not bothered either by Wilkes's prophecy that California would declare its independence from Mexico, annex Oregon, and form a separate state or by Texan President Sam Houston's dream of expanding his republic's control over California and Oregon. Webster considered Oregon "a poor country." If the United States could establish a port on the Pacific coast, Webster did not find the idea of a separate republic objectionable. His ideas were those of the Whigs, who viewed with alarm the possibility that the United States would grow excessively large, too extensive to be governed properly. But in this the Whigs were out of step with exuberant citizens who saw their futures in the West. Democrats, as Major L. Wilson has concluded, were primarily interested in the quantitative expansion of American society through space, while the Whigs were concerned with its qualitative progress through time. The Democrats, who were preoccupied with the development of an agricultural empire, championed Manifest Destiny, while the Whigs placed their faith in internal improvements and economic development. To the latter, these were more promising for the future than was expansion. "The territory of the United States is already large enough," was Clay's pronouncement; "it is much more important that we should unite, harmonize, and improve what we have than attempt to acquire more."[8]

In criticizing Webster's "tripartite plan," Frederick Merk has seen it as a "flight from reality." The Senate would never have accepted it, and those who wished to enlarge the country would have considered it a betrayal of the nation's destiny. Webster, Merk has contended, "incredibly misconceived the appetite and determination of American expansionists." If the plan had become a part of the Webster-Ashburton Treaty, the entire agreement would have been rejected.

Additionally, the Mexican government had no intention of ceding a portion of California to the United States. There was a strong element of pride in Mexico's refusal to even discuss it. Ever since the Texas rebellion against Mexican rule and the creation of the Lone Star Republic in 1836, Mexico had chafed over the participation of Americans in military actions on the side of the Texans. The latest episode, in the spring of 1841, was the Santa Fe Expedition, which involved a number of young American adventurers who had joined a force of Texans in a march on Santa Fe, hoping to detach that northern territory from Mexico and bring it under Texan control. The attempt was a fiasco; the results were the surrender of the expedition to the Mexican garrison, the execution of a number of prisoners, and the transporting of the remainder to Mexico City. Webster spent many a weary hour negotiating the release of United States citizens. Mexico, naturally, deeply resented these incursions, as well as the desire on the part of many Americans for the annexation of Texas while Mexico still considered the region as its own.[9]

Mexico was disturbed, too, by the growing American enthusiasm for the acquisition of California. In both countries there was an undercurrent of hearsay about a United States plot to seize the territory and of an impending war between the United States and Mexico. John Quincy Adams thought Waddy Thompson's dispatches "insolent, insulting, and contemptuous" in their attitude toward Mexico; Adams believed Webster evinced much the same spirit. Unfortunately, the spirit soon became tangible when, acting on a rumor that hostilities between Mexico and the United States had broken out or were about to do so, Commodore Thomas ap Catesby Jones, commanding the United States Pacific Squadron, sailed from Peruvian waters northward to the California coast and, on 19 October 1842, captured Monterey and hoisted the American flag. However, on the following day, Jones received dispatches revealing that no war existed with Mexico. He immediately lowered the flag, apologized, and left the harbor after hosting a banquet for the "conquered" of the previous day. The Mexican government accepted the apologies and Thompson's explanation that Jones had acted without authorization, but suspicions of American aggression persisted. Jones was never censured officially, although he was relieved of his command. In many quarters there was disbelief that an officer of the United States Navy would take such rash action without specific orders. John Quincy Adams, suspecting that Upshur might have had a hand in the affair, searched the messages and documents relating to the seizure of Monterey, but he found no incriminating written instructions from the secretary to Jones.[10]

California was high on the list of territories desired by the expansionist element, which included numerous members of Congress and a few in the executive department. Tyler and Webster, however, chose to move cautiously, not wanting to disturb the improving relations with Great Britain, but it was difficult to control the hotspurs, among whom was Lewis Linn, Benton's fellow senator from Missouri. For years, Linn brought up Oregon at every opportunity. In January 1841 he introduced a Senate resolution calling upon the president to give England notice of the termination of joint occupation within the specified year's time. The resolution failed to pass, but discussions clearly indicated a growing impatience with the deadlock over a settlement. A large territory was at stake, more than forty times the disputed area in Maine. Linn and other westerners frequently pointed out the State Department's concern about Maine and its apparent lack of interest in Oregon.

After the ratification of the Webster-Ashburton Treaty, Linn redoubled his efforts, thus touching off a vigorous Senate debate over his bill to provide for the erection of stockades and blockhouses along the Oregon Trail and to grant 640 acres for each white male settler over the age of eighteen who would settle on Oregon land and cultivate it for five years. The bill also included the creation of a territorial government over Oregon, including all the land north of the Columbia River to the forty-ninth parallel. Needless to say, the bill failed, but it caused considerable excitement.[11]

To moderate the enthusiasm for expansion, Webster tried to divert attention to possibilities of expanding the nation's commercial prowess. In this he indirectly received help from the Wilkes Expedition, which returned with tales of far-off exotic lands and of fabulous goods available for export from the East Asian markets, thus stirring interest in lands way beyond Oregon and California and lending support to Webster's desire to make the Tyler administration "Pacific-minded." In Webster's opinion, commercial development was preferable to building a great colonial empire, and he carefully shaped American foreign policy to foster the opening of trade relations with as many countries as possible. This would enhance the economic well-being of the nation (including the New England merchant fleet) and gain international respect for the United States.

Prior administrations had devoted little or no attention to outposts in the Pacific, such as the Hawaiian Islands (known as the Sandwich Islands), but northeastern merchants and missionaries were influential there well in advance of any serious interest on the part of the United States government. When American-sponsored Protestantism led to persecution of island Catholics, France intervened and, from the Hawaiian monarchy, obtained promises of religious equality for Catholics, along with trade concessions. This alarmed American sugar planters and other commercial investors who did not want the strategically located and lucrative area to be controlled by a European power, or several powers, so they entreated their government to become involved.

Webster was opposed to claiming Hawaii as a United States possession or even making it a protectorate, but he believed it would be advisable to announce to the world the vital interest the United States had in the future of the islands. He put this in the form of a message which Tyler sent to Congress on 30 December 1842, announcing a policy that became known as the Tyler Doctrine.[12]

The Tyler-Webster message stated that because of the location of the islands and the course of the winds, almost all ships that traversed the Pacific stopped at the Sandwich Islands. However, whaling vessels from the United States were most dependent on the islands' harbors. In fact, by 1842, five-sixths of all ships that dropped anchor in the waters of the Hawaiian kingdom flew the stars and stripes. Moreover, the amount of island property that was owned by American citizens far exceeded the investments of other nationalities. The government of Hawaii was weak, "just emerging from a state of barbarism," and the United States was determined that the rights of this community, "existing in the midst of a vast expanse of ocean," be "strictly and conscientiously regarded." There was no wish to impose exclusive control over the small kingdom or to obtain any special advantage, the message continued; but if any other nation attempted to take such actions, there would be a "decided remonstrance" on the part of the United States. In essence, the principles of the Monroe Doctrine were thus extended to the Sandwich Islands.

In the same message, Congress was asked to authorize funds to send a commissioner to China for the purpose of concluding a commercial treaty with that nation. At the close of the Anglo-Chinese Opium War in August 1842, Britain, by the Treaty of Nanking, exacted from the Chinese government the right to trade in four additional ports. Previously, foreign traders had been allowed only in Canton. Britain also acquired Hong Kong and was paid an indemnity of $20 million. There seemed no doubt about which Western power was destined to control the vast markets of the Far East. To Webster, the exclusion of the United States from this valuable trade would be disastrous. Americans, he insisted, must have equal access to Chinese ports that were open to the British, along with the same commercial rights.

Ever since 1784, when the *Empress of China*, six months out of New York, had shown the first American flag in the harbor of Canton, vessels out of Boston, Salem, and New York had plied the Chinese trade, carrying mixed cargoes to the coasts of Oregon and California, where they traded goods for furs and hides to sell in Canton. There they purchased teas, silks, Canton china, and other luxury items, many of which still grace the homes of New England. "Many a Boston family," Samuel Eliot Morison has said, "owes its rise to fame and fortune to the old Nor'west and China trade." This was what Webster saw threatened by British imperialism, which was significantly apparent in the Treaty of Nanking.

Although after the Opium War, China gave vague promises that the United States would have the same trade advantages as the United Kingdom, Webster wanted a treaty. So did Tyler, who earlier had assured an American missionary that he, Tyler, "had his eye fixed upon China, and would avail himself of any favorable opportunity to commence a negotiation with the Celestial Empire." Not until the final day of the Twenty-seventh Congress, however, did the legislators authorize the mission to China. In arguing against the proposal, Benton viciously attacked the president and the secretary of state. The mission was unnecessary, he said. The United States had traded with China for generations without a treaty. Why did the president now think it mandatory to ask for "forty thousand dollars to enable one of our citizens to get to Peking, and to bump his head nineteen times upon the ground, to get the privilege of standing up in the presence of his majesty of the Celestial Empire?"[13]

Despite the protests of Benton and others, the bill was approved, and Edward Everett was named to head the delegation. This gave Benton another basis for denunciation. Webster, he declared, had created the China position in order to remove Everett from London so that Webster himself could become minister to England. There is no proof that this was Webster's intention. He denied it, and if this was what he wanted, he was disappointed. Everett refused to accept the China post; instead, he remained in England. While Congress was not in session, Tyler named Caleb Cushing as commissioner, envoy extraordinary, and minister plenipotentiary to the Chinese Empire. It seemed fitting that a man from Newburyport, Massachusetts, should be assigned the task of officially concluding a trade treaty with China. Fletcher Webster was to act as Cushing's secretary.

Tyler and Webster went to great lengths to prepare the delegation for its task; they solicited all the information on China they could possibly obtain. In late March, Webster sent out a circular, asking for opinions and suggestions from "intelligent persons" who had personal acquaintance with China or who had been engaged in trade with that country. Many responded, including John Murray Forbes, a prominent Boston merchant, who gave both advice on proper · etiquette and information on Chinese culture and military technology as well as on commerce.

In his instructions to Cushing, Webster stressed the peaceful intent of the mission. First and foremost, Cushing was to be a "messenger of peace." His primary objective was to secure the entry of American ships and cargoes into the Chinese ports that were open to Great Britain on terms as favorable as those enjoyed by English merchants. He was to make certain that the Chinese government realized that the United States was a powerful nation, worthy of respect. Cushing was to do nothing that might seem to the Chinese to imply any inferiority on the part of the United States. While taking pains not to give offense, he was to avoid the "*Kotou*," or kowtow, a Chinese practice of touching the forehead to the ground, signifying submission or servile compliance.[14] Cushing's mission was successful. In July 1844 the first bilateral agreement with China, the Treaty of Wanghia, was signed; it gained most-favored-nation privileges for the United States. Thereafter, with the advent of the great clipper ships, commerce between China and the United States soon flourished.

The Tyler Doctrine and Webster's instructions to Cushing clearly defined United States interests in the Pacific and served as precedents for the Open Door policy of the late nineteenth and early twentieth centuries. Along with the Webster-Ashburton Treaty, these were Webster's greatest achievements as secretary of state in the Tyler administration.

10

★ ★ ★ ★ ★

THE PRESIDENT, THE CABINET, AND THE WHITE HOUSE

Unlike many presidents, Tyler did not act as his own secretary of state except on rare occasions. He gave Daniel Webster a relatively free hand and trusted him; as a result, they worked well together. Only the Texas-annexation issue and Tyler's flirtations with the Democratic party, in a bid for the 1844 election, came between them. Even then, the parting was friendly. This warm relationship is revealed in their numerous exchanges of notes and letters. They made suggestions to each other and compared their reactions to various matters under consideration. "I have deemed it best to enclose to you the accompanying letter from Govr. [William H.] Seward and also my reply," Tyler wrote to Webster in the fall of 1841. "Please read the reply and if you see nothing to object to give it to Gov. Seward's address." When Henry Stephen Fox, the cantankerous British minister to the United States, "threatened consequences" unless the case of Alexander McLeod was withdrawn from the New York court, Tyler sent Webster "some thoughts which occur to me on reading Mr. Fox's two notes." Tyler's tone invariably was courteous: "I send you your admirable letter with one or two suggestions, which you may incorporate or not," or "What say you? Is the objection well founded?" At another time: "Do turn your mind to this and let me have your views tomorrow."[1]

The communications also indicate Tyler's close attention to detail and the time he spent reading documents and considering what should be done. Always his intention was to act in consultation with his secretary of state. Webster, in turn, generously praised the president's contributions, but Webster's successors were not as cordial. Abel P. Upshur and John C. Calhoun were uncompromising in pursuit of their goals, so they were highly critical of Tyler, at least behind his back, when in their estimation he did not act quickly enough or did not completely agree with their modes of operation.

Tyler regarded the secretary of state as the head of the cabinet; he depended on the secretary to call cabinet meetings and to keep other department heads aware of their responsibilities. As a general rule, Tyler held regular Wednesday cabinet meetings, often interspersed with special sessions. At the meetings he asked for reactions to messages he intended to send to Congress and for opinions on problems and policies. Throughout his presidency this was his practice, even during the period when he had a hostile inherited cabinet. But while Tyler wanted to hear their views, the final decisions were his. He believed he alone was responsible for all official actions, and although department heads might differ with him, they should be committed to carrying out his policies. If the executive branch was to be forceful, it had to act as a unit.[2]

Changes in cabinet personnel were numerous. Including those appointed by Harrison, there were four secretaries of state, four secretaries of the treasury, five secretaries of the navy, four secretaries of war, three attorneys general, and two postmasters general. Naturally, some secretaries were more outstanding than others. With the exception of Webster, Harrison's appointees did not stay in office long enough to prove their worth. Three members of Tyler's cabinet died in office: Abel P. Upshur, Thomas Gilmer, and Hugh Legaré. James M. Porter (War Department) and David Henshaw (Navy Department), who occupied positions for several months as recess appointees, failed to receive Senate confirmation. In selecting them, Tyler deviated from his usual insistence upon competence and, instead, made the choices solely for political reasons. Excluding Walter Forward, the secretary of the treasury, Tyler's first cabinet (those appointed in the fall of 1841, plus Webster) was the best qualified of his presidency, with Webster heading the State Department; Upshur, the Navy; John C. Spencer, the War Department and, later, the Treasury Department; Attorney General Hugh Legaré; and Postmaster General Charles A. Wickliffe.

Initially, Tyler had a strong commitment to civil-service reform, and he instructed his cabinet that although he wanted them to exercise their own discretion in appointing and removing employees in their departments, he wanted no removals to be made for purely political reasons. The Whig party, of course, was not happy with this pronouncement, and his order was less than scrupulously observed. As Tyler became more anxious about his political future, his own idealism faded rapidly. "We have numberless enemies in office and they should forthwith be made to quit," he directed Secretary of the Treasury John C. Spencer in the spring of 1843. "In short the changes ought to be rapid and extensive and numerous." Postmaster General Wickliffe, Tyler suggested, could provide many names. Attention also should be paid to United States marshals and attorneys, and care should be taken that new appointees would support the administration. "We must be cautious and never appoint any other than a well known friend."[3]

Both Oliver P. Chitwood, Tyler's biographer, and Leonard D. White, in his study on administrative history, have contended that Tyler, like Andrew Jackson, had a "Kitchen Cabinet," a small group of close friends on whom he relied for advice. According to Chitwood, this aggregation included Thomas Dew and Nathaniel Beverley Tucker of the College of William and Mary; Duff Green, a newspaperman, promoter, and political hanger-on; Virginia Congressmen Thomas Gilmer and Henry Wise; Virginia's Senator William C. Rives; and Congressman Caleb Cushing from Massachusetts. It is true that the Virginia extreme states' righters who were named by Chitwood *offered* Tyler much advice. At the beginning of his presidency, they were delighted to have "their man" in the White House. They counted on him to carry out their wishes, and when he did not do what they expected of him, they became angry, felt betrayed, and considered him a traitor to the states'-rights cause. Only Wise, among the Virginians named, remained completely loyal, but because of his lack of judgment, his emotional outbursts, and his habit of posing as the person who knew exactly what the president thought and what he intended to do, Wise's loyalty was of dubious value to Tyler.

Many found fault with Tyler's predilection for placing in governmental positions family members and other relatives who were in need of employment, albeit, for the most part, the posts were insignificant. Circumstances made some nepotism almost unavoidable. Until 1857, when Congress finally saw fit to provide funds for a private secretary and a few other positions in the White House, such as a messenger and a steward, individuals who constituted the president's "official household," according to the appropriations act, the president was forced to turn to his family for assistance. This had been the practice since the administration of George Washington. Therefore, it was not out of the ordinary for Tyler to employ his son John as his private secretary, but perhaps it was out of the ordinary for Tyler to dismiss John, in September 1844, for inefficiency.

Tyler, however, carried nepotism too far. Thomas Cooper, a former actor who was the father of Tyler's daughter-in-law and was a "staunch Van Buren Democrat," became the military storekeeper at the Frankford, Pennsylvania, arsenal from 1841 to 1843. When Congress, to annoy the president, abolished the position, Tyler nominated Cooper as surveyor of the Port of Philadelphia, but the Senate refused to confirm the appointment. From 1841 to 1844, Robert Tyler, the president's eldest son, worked in the Land Office in Washington. Daughter Letitia's husband, James Semple, was named a purser in the United States Navy. Two nephews, John and Floyd Waggaman, received minor appointments, one in the Treasury Department and the other as a diplomatic courier. Two brothers-in-law were given more lucrative posts—N. N. Miller as second assistant postmaster general; and Alexander Gardiner, a brother of Tyler's second wife, became a clerk in the United States Circuit Court for the Southern District of New York. This appointment was arranged through the joint efforts of John Nelson, Tyler's attorney general, and Samuel Nelson, chief justice of the New York Supreme Court, who was named to the United States Supreme Court shortly before the close of Tyler's administration.[4]

Perhaps, in his own mind, Tyler could justify these appointments. His son John and his daughter Letitia were having marital difficulties which possibly could be mitigated by more favorable financial situations. John, of course, was receiving his salary from his father, not from governmental funds. Success in the law had eluded Robert, so he needed encouragement. Tyler could tell himself that these did not constitute an indiscriminate passing out of plums to his family. Positions were found for them out of kindness, to fill a pressing need for each individual; nevertheless, it was nepotism. But then, Webster's son Fletcher was chief clerk of the State Department, while Secretary Spencer employed his daughter's husband in the Treasury Department. There were many other examples of a practice that appeared to be regarded as standard procedure.

Without a White House staff, Tyler spent untold hours attending to tasks that could have been handled by administrative assistants. He regularly was at his desk by sunrise, sometimes earlier, working by candlelight. At nine he breakfasted with his family; then he continued his official routine which, as he explained to Robert McCandlish, a Williamsburg friend, consisted of, "first, all diplomatic matters; second, all matters connected with the action of Congress; third, matters of general concern falling under executive control; then the reception of visitors, and dispatch of private petitions." At three-thirty in the afternoon he dined and later took some time for exercise, most likely horseback riding, as Tyler was an excellent horseman. He took care of "miscellaneous employments," directions to departmental heads, and the signing of documents; and after dark, he again received visitors socially, "apart from all business, until ten at night, when I retire to bed. Such is the life led by an American President. What say you?—would you exchange the peace and quiet of your homestead for such an office?"

Being kept so busy had its benefits. "So unceasing are my engagements that I rarely hear anything of the abuse of the malignants who are perpetually assailing me." One of the "madcaps," Tyler told Mc-Candlish, "talks of impeachment. Did you ever expect to see your old friend under trial for 'high crimes and misdemeanors'?" Tyler said he pleaded guilty to a variety of high crimes: of sustaining the Constitution, of arresting the lavish donation of revenue to the states at a time when the Treasury was bankrupt, of daring to have an opinion of his own. Because he would not bow to Clay, he was abused, "in Congress and out, as a man never was before—assailed as a traitor, and threatened with impeachment. But let it pass. Other attempts are to be made to head me, and we shall see how they will succeed." Congress was so engrossed in attacking him, he said, that after "more than seven months in session," it had accomplished nothing.[5]

White House social obligations added to the burdens of the presidency and must have been enormously taxing, physically as well as financially. During the first eight months or so of the Tyler administration, a reception was held every evening. But because this proved to be too great a strain on the family, by the first part of 1842 these were limited to twice a week, on Thursdays and Saturdays. While Congress was in session and during the "fashionable season," the White House was the scene of twice-a-week formal dinners, which were attended by dignitaries from the diplomatic corps, the cabinet, and Congress. Once a month there was a public levee, and on New Year's Day and the Fourth of July the doors were opened to the general public.

A correspondent of the *New York Herald* who attended many of these functions praised Tyler's "natural courtesy, simple dignity, and the manner in which he put his guests at ease." The good taste and fine breeding of the president and his family, it was said, made a favorable impression on all present. From April 1841 until March 1844, Priscilla Cooper Tyler, Robert's wife, charmed even the most disagreeable guests. John Quincy Adams, who was not usually given to compliments, was full of praise for the way in which Lord Ashburton was entertained. "The party at the President's house last evening," he wrote in his diary on 12 June 1842, "consisted of about a hundred persons, invited by Mrs. Robert Tyler. . . . There was dancing in the now gorgeously furnished East Room, and an elegant supper. The courtesies of the President and Mrs. Robert Tyler to their guests were all that the most accomplished European court could have displayed." For once, Adams failed to refer to Tyler as the vice-president, acting as president.[6]

Letitia Christian Tyler, the president's first wife, left her private quarters only on one occasion, to attend the wedding of their daughter Elizabeth and William Waller on 31 January 1842. She died the following September. The Tylers had nine children, two of whom died in infancy. At the time of Mrs. Tyler's death, five of the seven were married. Alice, aged fifteen, and Tazewell, twelve, lived in the White House, as did Robert, his wife, Priscilla, and John. In the interval between the Robert Tyler's departure from Washington in March 1844 and the president's second marriage the following June, Letitia Tyler Semple acted as the White House hostess. After Tyler's marriage to Julia Gardiner, gatherings in the White House became more lavish, the dancing more daring, and the events more talked about.

Only infrequently did Tyler leave his duties for brief respites at Old Point Comfort on Hampton Roads, or his plantation on the James River. On even rarer occasions, he went to the Virginia Springs. While in Washington, the majority of his waking hours were devoted to the business of being president. He was aware of what was transpiring in each department of the executive branch, but during the uproar over the bank, the Treasury Department occupied a large part of his time. After the bank became more or less a dead issue, his attention increasingly was focused on the State Department, whose achievements constituted the centerpiece of the Tyler presidency.

In accomplishments or attempted accomplishments, the Navy Department, under the leadership of Abel Parker Upshur, ranked second to the State Department. Tyler selected Upshur, a planter, attorney, judge, and southern apologist from Virginia's Eastern Shore, after the departure of the Harrison appointee, George E. Badger. Although Upshur was not a waterman by profession, all dwellers on the Eastern Shore, a narrow peninsula that juts out between the Atlantic Ocean and Chesapeake Bay, had an affinity for the sea and were acquainted with its problems. The *Richmond Whig* thought Upshur was "entirely too extravagant in his admiration of John C. Calhoun" to be a member of the cabinet.[7] Later, Tyler found this to be very true.

When Upshur assumed responsibility, the navy was in poor condition. "Bad management and injudicious legislation have reduced the Navy to a state of confusion and disorder never before witnessed," Lt.

Matthew Fontaine Maury, a young Virginian who was interested in studying ocean currents and other scientific phenomena of a maritime nature, wrote in 1841. Established in 1815, the Board of Naval Commissioners had outlived its usefulness. President Jackson had proposed that it be abolished, but Congress had taken no action. Holding to its "small-navy policy," Congress had refused to allocate sufficient funds to sustain adequate naval power, thus causing the United States to fall significantly behind several European nations. Upshur called for expansion, modernization, and reform. He was convinced that in a short time, the country would expand to the Pacific coast and beyond. A two-ocean navy would be needed to protect coastal waters and American commerce. "Trade," he told Congress, "is never secure unless it can, at all times and in all places, appeal for support to the national flag; and it ought to feel that it is safe wherever that flag is displayed." The navy had to become larger and more modern, and it needed reorganization.

Upshur made an impassioned plea for an increase in naval appropriations. Suspicious that Britain, a maritime power second to none, was seeking to drive American commerce from the seas, Upshur asked for funds to build a navy at least one-half the size of England's. Tyler strongly supported the request, but in Congress, the "inland opposition," led by Senator Thomas Hart Benton of Missouri, argued against it, terming it excessively extravagant. Commercially minded Whigs favored a larger navy, whereas inland Democrats opposed it; so the administration was forced to accept a compromise.[8]

While the House of Representatives was wrangling over the appropriation request, Upshur began to use funds that were already at his disposal to repair and make seaworthy a number of vessels, some of which had been inoperative for years. His primary projects were to convert the navy from sail to steam and to continue experiments on the use of the screw propeller. The side-wheeler was found to be too clumsy to maneuver. For two decades, Upshur declared, the lack of an adequate and continuing naval policy, arguments over sail versus steam, and congressional indifference had been responsible for the navy's receiving "little more than a step-mother's care"; but the Board of Navy Commissioners and much of the service had a sentimental attachment to sailing vessels. James Kirke Paulding, who had served as secretary of the commission before becoming secretary of the navy under Van Buren, wrote in 1839, "I will never consent to let our old ships perish, and transform our Navy into a fleet of sea monsters." James Fenimore Cooper, the author of a two-volume *History of the Navy of the United States of America* that was published in 1839, felt the same way; he vigorously denied that steam could ever supplant sail in the conduct of naval warfare. "Like most novel and bold propositions, this new doctrine has obtained advocates, who have yielded their convictions to the influence of their imaginations, rather than to the influence of reflection." Perhaps steam could "be made a powerful auxiliary of the present mode of naval warfare," but steam would probably not replace it. Upshur was convinced otherwise, however. In addition to steam-powered naval ships, he recommended the building of steam-powered merchant vessels that could easily be converted to ships of war if the need should arise. He pushed for the adoption of Paixhans guns, which fired explosive shells. Extensive use of them would necessitate the construction of iron warships with less potential of burning to the water line.

Upshur had other objectives in mind. He wanted a naval academy, similar to the army's West Point, to provide proper training for officers; an increase in the size of the Marine Corps; an adequate building and proper equipment for a depot for charts and nautical instruments; the replacement of the Board of Navy Commissioners by five bureaus, each one to be headed by a professional naval officer. Then there was the problem of rank. The navy had only three grades: captain, commander, and lieutenant, whereas the army had nine. The highest naval rank allowed by Congress was that of captain, and the number of these was severely limited. Promotion was almost stagnant. Furthermore, there were embarrassing situations when the highest-ranking United States naval officer, no matter how senior, invariably had to yield precedence to admirals of the naval forces of other nations, both at sea and at social functions ashore. Another morale problem was created by the appointment of more midshipmen than could be placed on active duty. Many appointments were political favors. In other cases, prominent families often used their influence to have troublesome sons placed in the service. There was no screening process, another good argument in favor of a naval academy.

Upshur's recommendations met with stiff resistance in Congress. Some legislators were amazed that such sweeping changes could emanate from a man who was known as an ultraconservative on most political and social matters. Questions of possible ulterior, even sinister, motivation arose. Was it Upshur's plan to place the navy under the control of officers from slave states? After all, Tyler and Upshur were Virginians, as were the president of the Navy Board, two members of the House Naval Affairs Committee, and two members of the House Ways and Means Committee. As the rumors circulated, so did fears, real or feigned, that the navy would be taken over by southern officers committed to sectional interests, to nullification, or even to disunion.

The House Naval Affairs Committee approved a bill creating the ranks of admiral, vice-admiral, and rear admiral; but the bill never reached the House floor, and it was not introduced in the Senate. The recommendation to establish a naval academy received little support from Congress or from senior naval officers. The place to train an officer or a sailor, the latter contended, was at sea, not in a classroom.[9]

Congress was somewhat more receptive to recommendations on departmental reorganization. The Board of Navy Commissioners was disbanded, and the five bureaus were created. Only one of the bureaus, that of provisions and clothing, was to be headed by a civilian; the others were to be headed by naval officers. In 1844, Tyler made a political appointment to this position—Isaac Hill, a former senator from New Hampshire; and when Hill had failed to gain Senate approval, a naval officer had become bureau chief. From that time on, with only a variation or two, all bureau chiefs in the Navy Department were naval officers. However, this did not constitute a unit, as did the army's General Staff.

The secretary of the navy was granted a chief clerk, and the clerical staff was increased from seventeen to twenty-six, to manage a naval and civilian complement of about ten thousand, along with vast and complicated equipment, ships, and bases. While Congress accepted other reorganization ideas, it voted insufficient appropriations to implement them.

Funds for the construction of ships, although inadequate, did allow for the building of some steam-driven iron warships. At least, this was a beginning. In 1842, Upshur ordered work to begin on the world's first iron steam warship to be driven by a submerged screw propeller, which would allow the engine and the boiler to be located below the water line and thus be less vulnerable to enemy fire. The ship was to be christened the USS *Princeton*.

The Twenty-seventh Congress also provided a $35,000 appropriation for the Depot of Charts and Instruments. The bill did not include funding for astronomy, science, or research, as Upshur had hoped, but planners of the depot's new building managed to obtain some equipment and facilities for these purposes, and by 1844 the United States Naval Observatory, which later became known as the National Observatory, was an integral part of the Depot of Charts and Instruments. John Quincy Adams was pleased. As president he had been ridiculed for having tried to get Congress to finance an astronomical observatory, "a lighthouse of the skies," he called it. Now it was a reality, "smuggled in," as he said, "under the mask of a small depot for charts." Young officers who were interested in technology were encouraged by Upshur's openness to new ideas and his quickness in praising those who were working to improve the naval service.[10]

Personnel of all grades and ranks were grateful for the social reforms that were set in motion during the Tyler administration. Richard Henry Dana's *Two Years before the Mast*, which depicted a horrible flogging aboard the brig *Pilgrim* in 1839, awakened its readers to the unwarranted harsh punishments that were being inflicted by tyrannical captains on sailors under their command. Between 1840 and 1843, numerous articles appeared, many written by Maury, calling for reforms.

The acceptance of change was slow in such a tradition-bound branch of the service. Levi Woodbury, who had been secretary of the navy during Jackson's administration, had recommended that badges of disgrace be substituted for flogging whenever the situation seemed suitable. But when Commander Uriah P. Levy availed himself of that suggestion, he found himself, in April 1842, facing a hostile court-martial. Undoubtedly, Levy's "badge of dishonor" was unique, or at least uniquely placed. Not wishing to inflict corporal punishment on a teen-age sailor for mimicking an officer, Levy ordered the lad tied to a gun while a small amount of tar and parrot feathers was applied to his bare backside. For this, Levy was charged with "scandalous and cruel conduct, unbecoming an officer and a gentleman." Flogging, it was held, would have been less cruel. Levy was found guilty and was sentenced to be dismissed from the navy.

When the finding reached Tyler for his signature, the president disagreed, but instead of repudiating the entire sentence, he reduced it to a twelve-months' suspension. Perhaps he concurred that the "badge of disgrace" used on this occasion was not the type to which an officer and a gentleman should resort, but dismissal from the naval service was too-severe a punishment.[11]

The case of the *Somers* mutiny was another matter, one that caused the president considerable anxiety. In the summer of 1842, the *Somers*, an experimental school ship for naval apprentices, put to sea. Because of complaints about the incompetence of numerous naval officers who were ruining discipline and destroying morale, the decision was made to place prospective officers aboard a training ship, under the watchful eye of a respected captain. The *Somers* was commanded by Master Commandant Alexander Slidell Mackenzie, a brother-in-law of Commodore Matthew Calbraith Perry's, under whose supervision the *Somers* had been built. Mackenzie was reputed to be a man of "calmness, gentleness, and refinement." This was not true of some of the young men on board. One in particular, Philip Spencer, was an incorrigible nineteen year old who had a long history of troublesome behavior. He also was the son of Secretary of War John C. Spencer. Young Spencer reacted belligerently to the rules and regulations applied during the training course, and on the return passage from Africa he instigated a plot, involving a number of others, to kill the officers, capture the *Somers*, and turn her into a pirate ship. When Mackenzie became aware of the brewing mutiny, he had Spencer and two other ringleaders incarcerated and, subsequently, executed. Although a court of inquiry exonerated Mackenzie of any wrongdoing, Secretary Spencer demanded that he be tried for murder by a civilian court. As a compromise, Secretary Upshur ordered a court-martial.

For nearly four months, beginning in December 1842, proceedings of the court of inquiry and the court-martial were the chief topic of interest throughout the country. According to Samuel Eliot Morison, "No case of the century, prior to the assassination of President Lincoln, aroused as much interest and passion." Well-informed people disagreed on whether or not there had been justification for Mackenzie's harsh and irreversible judgment. Capt. Robert F. Stockton refused to serve as a member of the court-martial, saying he already had made up his mind that Mackenzie should hang. Richard Henry Dana, certainly no advocate of cruel punishment, believed Mackenzie had acted properly. So did Charles Sumner, an idealistic young attorney from Massachusetts, who wrote an account of the case for the *North American Review*. But James Fenimore Cooper, in his *Review of the Proceedings of the Naval Court*, portrayed Mackenzie as a "jittery, incompetent martinet."

Members of the court-martial voted to acquit Mackenzie of the charges of murder, oppression, and illegal punishment. Upshur confirmed the verdict and, at a cabinet meeting, recommended that the president approve the decision. Secretary Spencer, almost incoherent with anger, pressed Tyler to order a new trial. Upshur objected, maintaining that the conclusions of the court-martial had to be respected. Furthermore, Upshur argued, Mackenzie could not be placed in double jeopardy by being tried a second time on the same charges, using the same evidence. The two cabinet officers, it was reported, came to blows, and only the intervention of the president prevented serious injury.

Tyler had no power to order another trial. He could, as noted in the Levy case, reduce a sentence or completely dismiss it, but he could not either prescribe punishment for someone who had been acquitted or order that the person be tried again. In considering the Mackenzie verdict, Tyler decided to take a middle position; possibly, under the circumstances, this was his only choice. He allowed the verdict to stand, but without his signature; however, during the remainder of his time in office, Tyler refused to assign Mackenzie to another command. Spencer's repeated attempts to have Mackenzie indicted in civilian courts all failed.[12]

The Somers mutiny destroyed the apprenticeship system, and because an alternative was needed, within a few years the United States Naval Academy came into being, its creation undoubtedly hastened by the Somers affair.

Like all of the departmental heads, Upshur complained about having to spend too much time on trifling details when he wanted to work on broad policies. An undersecretary or an assistant secretary was needed. Yet, Upshur enthusiastically and unstintingly poured all his energy into improving the naval service. Later, when he became secretary of state, these compulsive characteristics were directed toward achieving the annexation of Texas.

The War Department in some ways was more complicated than the Navy Department. The secretary had to contend with the General Staff, composed of an adjutant general, an inspector general, a quartermaster general, a commissary general, and a paymaster general—all army officers—and a commanding general with the rank of major general. The position of commanding general was created after the War of 1812, and attempts to abolish it had come to naught. While a member of the Senate, William Henry Harrison had defended its retention. In the Navy Department there was no admiral to contest the decisions of the secretary, but the War Department was torn by controversy over whether the General Staff should answer to the commanding general or to the secretary of war. An article in the North American Review explained the problem. Secretaries of war could ''go out and come in with each season . . . yet the military establishment and the national defense . . . remain the same.'' The permanency in the military command and in the General Staff gave them a feeling of independence and superiority over the civilian who happened to be in charge for the moment. From 1841 to 1861, the commanding general was Winfield Scott, a man with ''a sharp temper and a too ready pen,'' who had no liking or respect for President Tyler.[13]

Tyler's first secretary of war, John C. Spencer, however, was a match for Winfield Scott. Spencer, the secretary of state for New York under Governor William H. Seward, was thought to have a Clay following when Seward and Thurlow Weed recommended Spencer for the cabinet post. They hoped this would heal some of the Whig factionalism in their state, which had been caused in part by their refusal to endorse Clay for the presidential nomination in 1840, but Spencer turned out to be his own man. He toadied to no one, he fulfilled his duties with efficiency, and he was helpful to the president in many ways. Philip Hone has described Spencer as "stern, uncompromising, obstinate in temper, determined and energetic in action, and with talents equal to any effort which his feelings may prompt, or his duty call him to execute." He could be as haughty and difficult as General Scott. John Quincy Adams referred to Spencer as "The Potentate."[14]

Reflecting the general public's distrust of a standing army, the number of career officers and men was kept small, "little more than a nucleus around which to rally the military force of the country in case of war," Tyler reported to Congress. "In all cases of emergency the reliance of the country is properly placed in the militia of the several states." In 1842, after the close of the second Seminole War, the size of the Regular Army was reduced from more than 12,000 to 8,163. These forces were scattered in small posts, mainly along the western and southern frontiers. Tyler and Spencer were sensitive to the danger of potential hostilities with Great Britain or Mexico, which would necessitate bringing regiments up to their full complement and remounting the corps of dragoons, which had been dissolved by act of Congress.

The personnel of the War Department consisted of the secretary, his chief clerk, and several additional clerks. A few civilian employees also were assigned to the military offices of the General Staff. The department was as simple and undeveloped as it had been during the administration of George Washington. Along with its responsibility for the army, the War Department had numerous other duties, such as the general area of Indian affairs, including the removal of Indians from lands desired by settlers, the Pension Office, the resolution of veterans' land claims, and road building. In the years before the Civil War, the department made great contributions to road building in the West.

During the 1840s the War Department also was the collector of weather information. Beginning in 1817, various local agents made weather observations in a haphazard fashion. Local registers of land offices in different parts of the country were required to send daily reports on temperature, wind, rainfall, and other data to the commissioner of the General Land Office, Joseph Meigs, who additionally asked for information on the migration of birds, storms, meteors, and anything else that could "increase the physical knowledge of the country." The surgeon general of the United States also ordered all hospital surgeons to take weather observations and keep climatological records. In 1841 the Patent Office became interested, as did Maury in the Navy

Department, in connection with Maury's work on Atlantic winds and currents.

In 1842, James P. Espy, the author of *The Philosophy of Storms*, became the official meteorologist of the War Department, and he began to systematize the gathering of information. He enlisted the aid of the general public as well as the most professionally prepared, and he announced the availability of a form for keeping records, which he would send to anyone in the United States, Bermuda, the West Indies, the Azores, and Canada who was willing to participate. His plan was to compile the data on large skeleton maps and, by using "appropriate symbols," to track changes in the weather. Newspaper editors, he suggested, could be of great service by mentioning the time of the greatest violence of large storms and the direction of the wind or changes in its direction. All information was to be sent to the Office of the Surgeon General at the War Department. The State Department cooperated by authorizing Espy to solicit data from ministers, consuls, and other diplomatic and commercial agents of the United States who were stationed in foreign lands. All the accounts were carefully collated. Within a few years the telegraph was utilized to speed the collecting process. [15]

In addition to his duties as secretary of war, Spencer frequently was called upon to advise the president on financial matters. Walter Forward, who became secretary of the treasury in 1841, after Thomas Ewing had resigned, was incompetent. He had, as Caleb Cushing observed, an "inveterate habit of procrastinating" or doing nothing, "by which the Department has been disgraced ever since he entered it, and by which it is now in a pitiable condition of delay and disorder." Tyler was forced to turn to Webster and Spencer for help in matters that should have been handled by the secretary of the treasury. Finally, in 1843, Forward was persuaded to resign. Cushing thought he was in line for the position, and Tyler thrice nominated him, but the Senate refused to confirm. Spencer, then, was moved from the War Department to the Treasury. His successor in the War Department was James M. Porter, a recess appointment, who failed to receive Senate approval. William Wilkins of Pennsylvania was named, and he spent most of his tenure in the department aggressively championing the annexation of Texas. [16]

Because the bank issue was no longer under discussion, Spencer, as secretary of the treasury, could turn his attention and expertise to balancing the budget. By November 1843, Webster was able to inform Joshua Bates, a partner in the London banking house of Baring Brothers and Company: "There is no kind of doubt, that the President will be able to communicate to Congress a very favorable state of things regarding our public finances. The receipts at the Treasury have been larger than anybody expected. U.S. Stocks, I should suppose, would rise still higher, when the President & Mr. Spencer shall have made their showing."[17]

In his annual messages of 1843 and 1844, Tyler expressed pleasure that in all departments "nothing has been left undone which was called for by a true spirit of economy or by a system of accountability rigidly enforced." The greatly improved condition of the Treasury, he said, should receive "general congratulations." By the time Spencer left office in the spring of 1844, the budget had been balanced, due in part to the increased revenue collected under the 1842 Tariff Act; there had been a significant reduction in the public debt; trade and commerce had improved; and it was no longer necessary to resort to the issuance of large amounts of treasury notes. In fact, there was now a surplus in the Treasury, and the currency had reached "a state of perfect soundness."

The United States Coast Survey also came under the jurisdiction of the Treasury Department. Since 1816 it had been directed by Ferdinand R. Hassler, who had operated as a law unto himself and who had objected to the government "yoke fitting to his neck." On Hassler's request, John Quincy Adams had introduced Hassler to Spencer, the new treasury secretary; and Adams had immediately perceived "the seeds of conflict already germinating between two proud spirits, which bodes no good to the progress of the Coast Survey." Hassler at once informed Spencer that the survey's work was scientific and therefore must be conducted on scientific principles. "The Potentate [Spencer] answered in a subdued tone of voice, but with the trenchant stubbornness of authority, the laws must be obeyed." Thus, said Adams, "the pride of science clashed with the pride of place."

When Hassler died, in the fall of 1843, he was replaced by Alexander Dallas Bache, a brilliant scientist who was the great-grandson of Benjamin Franklin. Bache proved to be more flexible, and congressional appropriations increased. By 1854 the entire coast from Maine to Florida and from Florida to the Mexican border had been surveyed, with only an eighteen-inch error, which occurred near Cape Hatteras.

Before and after Spencer left the cabinet, Tyler nominated him to the United States Supreme Court. On both occasions the Senate failed to approve the appointment. Spencer was succeeded in the Treasury Department by George M. Bibb of Kentucky. The first cabinet that Tyler appointed was regionally balanced, with three members from the North and three from the South, but after the appointment of Bibb, only one northerner remained, William Wilkins of Pennsylvania, a northern man who had many southern interests.[18]

The post of attorney general was not a full-time position. Whoever filled it was expected to continue his own law practice, so he was paid only half the salary that other cabinet members received. He was, as Michael O'Brien has noted in his biography of Hugh Legaré, "to all intents and purposes, a lawyer kept on permanent retainer to advise and represent the government of the United States before the Supreme Court." Ideally, the attorney general served as "the conscience of an administration."[19]

Harrison's appointee, John J. Crittenden, was a Clay man, clever, able, and very partisan. Hugh Legaré, Tyler's choice after Crittenden's departure, possessed the qualifications of an exemplary attorney general. George Ticknor, the brilliant scholar of Spanish literature who, until 1835, was a member of the Harvard faculty, regarded Legaré as a man of remarkable powers. Legaré, Ticknor said, belonged to the Union party in South Carolina, "for his views are too broad and high for any faction. . . . We have few men like him, either as scholars, thinkers, or talkers. I knew him very well in Edinburgh in 1819, and thought him then an uncommon person; but it is plain he has taken a much higher tone than I anticipated."[20]

As attorney general, Legaré represented the administration in eleven cases before the Supreme Court, none of which was of great consequence, but he performed well and was praised by Chief Justice Roger B. Taney and Justice Joseph Story. As legal advisor to the executive branch, Legaré actively upheld federal and presidential prerogatives and did what he could to strengthen Tyler's position. He advised the president that it was within the latter's power to make ad interim appointments while Congress was in recess. Congress, he held, had no right to stand in the president's way of doing so and thereby create an interregnum in government. The Constitution gave the Senate "only a negative and secondary agency in appointment to office." Therefore, it could not assume a discretionary power that was assigned to the chief executive. During the tariff-distribution battle in the summer of 1842, Legaré came to Tyler's aid by overruling Secretary of the Treasury Walter Forward's opinion that in the absence of a new tariff law, revenues could not continue to be collected under the 1833 act. Legaré said they could, thus allowing Tyler to veto a bill he considered inadvisable, without depriving the Treasury of needed funds.

Between Tyler and Legaré there was fondness and respect. Legaré, in O'Brien's words, "came to be almost Tyler's best man." He tried to convince others, including Ticknor, of Tyler's fine qualities, but Ticknor, writing to the historian William H. Prescott in August 1842, expressed his skepticism: "Tyler will, I think, take a full loco-foco [Democratic] cabinet, and sail on a sea of glory to the end of his term, when he will disappear, and never be heard of afterward. In six months [after he leaves office] it will be a matter of historical doubt whether such a man ever existed."[21]

When the attorney general died suddenly in the summer of 1843, he was, along with his other duties, acting as head of the State Department, an ad interim assignment he had accepted when Webster had resigned. John Nelson, a native of Frederick, Maryland, who followed Legaré as attorney general, was a Democrat with Virginia ties, having graduated from the College of William and Mary in 1811. Tyler knew Nelson from his younger days and, writing to him privately shortly after Legaré's death, urged him to accept the position. It would be, Tyler said, "of deep interest to myself." Nelson had served as a Maryland member of the House of Representatives in the Seventeenth Congress, and in 1832, Jackson had appointed him chargé d'affaires to the Two Sicilies, after which Nelson had returned to his law practice in Fredrick. Nelson, like Legaré, was a moderate who performed his duties well and was loyal to the president. For a brief period after the death of Upshur and before Calhoun took over the State Department, Nelson acted as ad interim secretary of state.

Charles A. Wickliffe, postmaster general, was the only 1841 Tyler appointee to remain in the cabinet until the end of the presidency. Although Wickliffe had a reputation for being arrogant and opinionated, he and Tyler eventually became good friends. This was due in part to the close friendship between Julia Gardiner, who in 1844 became Tyler's second wife, her sister Margaret, and the Wickliffe daughters, Mary and Nannie. The Wickliffes, Margaret remarked, were a lovely family who "had remained long enough at their home in Kentucky not to be easily contaminated by mingling with the worldly." But Wickliffe was no stranger to Washington. For five consecutive terms (1823–33) he had represented his Kentucky district in the House of Representatives. Prior to his cabinet appointment, he had served his state as lieutenant governor and governor.[22]

The Post Office Department, which was supposed to be self-supporting, was plagued with problems. In addition to continual indebtedness, it was faced with having to extend services to greater and greater distances, thus causing easterners to complain about having to pay high rates in order to subsidize western deliveries. Because postage, which was based on a combination of the distance a letter had to travel and the number of sheets of paper involved, usually was collected from the recipient, many people resorted to crafty ways of avoiding payment. A traveler, before leaving home, might say he would send a letter telling of his safe arrival. When the message appeared at the post office, a member of the family would look at the outside of the letter and refuse to accept it, knowing the traveler had reached his destination. At times, symbols that were written on the cover would convey information to the addressee, who would return the letter unopened and refuse to pay the postage. Large amounts of unclaimed mail accumulated in local post offices. Frequently, the postal service was circumvented completely. Letters would be entrusted to stagecoach drivers, railroad employees, or private citizens who were traveling to desired destinations.

The public, which was unhappy with the postal service, demanded reform. During Van Buren's administration, Postmaster General Amos Kendall had struggled with restructuring and reorganizing the department. Rumors of a postal-reform program in England had intrigued him, and in 1840, he had sent George Plitt, a career postal employee, to London to study and report on the program's successes or failures. The Plitt Report, while it was too late for Kendall's use, became available to the incoming Whig administration.

Francis Granger, Harrison's postmaster general, who was busy removing Democrats and appointing Whigs to local postmasterships, had no time to consider the Plitt Report. Wickliffe, however, found the information interesting, especially the material dealing with reductions in British postal rates. While there had been an increase in the number of letters mailed, less revenue had been collected, but the English government regarded the plan as a necessary social reform. Congress, however, was not willing to support a rate reduction that might create a larger deficit in the Post Office Department.

As a result, the early 1840s witnessed a rapid growth in private mail companies, largely intercity, which delivered mail more quickly and at lower rates than did the United States postal service. By 1844, more than forty such companies operated in Boston alone. Some offered service between New York and Boston, and one, Hale and Company, covered the area between New England and Washington, D.C., with a branch service to Buffalo. In 1842 the City Dispatch Post of New York introduced deposit boxes, which were placed in convenient locations and were advertised in the newspapers. Another of its innovations was the adhesive postage stamp, which became very popular. Postage was paid in advance, which saved much trouble and confusion, and within a few months, the United States postal service in New York was in danger of being driven out of business. The competition concerned Wickliffe. He contacted the New York City postmaster and directed him to initiate procedures to purchase the City Dispatch Post. This was accomplished, and the company became the United States City Dispatch Post. ''United

States" also appeared on the stamps, but as yet there was no plan to issue federal postage stamps on a nationwide basis.

By the close of Tyler's administration, 14,183 government post offices were in operation, an increase of 715 since 1840. Late in 1844, Wickliffe again requested a reduction in rates. A deficit remained, but it was diminishing. In his last annual message to Congress, on 4 December 1844, Tyler asked Congress to give the request serious consideration. He also strongly urged authorization for a line of naval steamships to transport mail between the United States and certain foreign ports on a regular schedule.

On 27 January 1845, Senator William D. Merrick of Maryland introduced a bill to reduce postal rates. The post office, he said, was "a most important element in the hand of civilization, especially of a republican people. . . . Every nook and corner of this country should be visited by its operations." This was echoed in the House of Representatives by John Patterson of New Jersey. What institution, except the postal service, he asked, "is so calculated to awaken the ambition of the people to become educated as the cultivation of the taste for epistolatory correspondence . . . ?" On 3 March 1845, the last day of Tyler's presidency, Congress passed the Postal Reform Act, to become effective on 1 July 1845.[23]

The act also recognized the importance of a new form of communication, the electromagnetic telegraph, the "last and most wondrous" invention "of this wonder-teeming age," which had been demonstrated with great success in Washington in 1842. After several refusals, Congress, in 1843, appropriated $30,000 to finance a telegraph line between Washington and Baltimore, to be built by Samuel F. B. Morse; but it rejected the idea of purchasing his invention. The larger question was whether or not Congress should adopt a recommendation made by the House Committee on Commerce—namely, that the government should "seize the present opportunity of securing to itself the regulation of a system which, if monopolized by a private company, might be used to the serious injury of the Post Office Department." Morse favored the governmental ownership of the line, and in 1844 it was placed under the jurisdiction of the Treasury Department, although it was managed by Morse. Under the Postal Reform Act, the Post Office Department assumed responsibility. This arrangement lasted for a year, during which time the telegraph line was opened for commercial use. In 1846, Congress decided to turn the line over to private ownership.[24]

This, indeed, was a "wonder-teeming age," with technological developments in many areas. Adams complained that the people of the nation, and certainly many members of Congress, did not realize the importance of promoting science and research. Although the government did support some projects that were designed to advance knowledge, it often did so grudgingly and sporadically. This was true in regard to the United States Exploring Expedition, the most extensive and elaborate scientific endeavor undertaken by the United States government during the years before the Civil War. Operating under the auspices of the United States Navy, the expedition involved naval and civilian scientists from every conceivable branch of the discipline. Never before had such an array of talented Americans collaborated in a quest for knowledge. The vast collections of materials gathered by members of the expedition were overwhelming. Unfortunately, no preparations were made to receive the mass of plant and animal specimens, illustrations, and maps. For a time they were housed inadequately in the Patent Office, where amateurish handling destroyed many of them. Finally, in 1846, Congress created the Smithsonian Institution, but a structure was not completed for nearly another decade. As William H. Goetzmann has pointed out, "the results of the expedition were larger and more complex than anyone could have imagined and they far outran the intellectual resources of the country."[25] For the most part, the American people were more interested in technological developments that would make life easier, material goods more readily available, and the country more closely bound together by improved transportation and communication.

Coexisting with pride in progress and hope for the future, however, was the deepening anxiety over the problem of slavery and how it would affect the fate of the nation. Abolitionists were becoming increasingly strident in their demands for emancipation. William Lloyd Garrison and his followers were calling both for the North to separate from the South and for the rejection of the Constitution because it acknowledged the institution of slavery. Garrison wrote in 1842: "We affirm that the Union is not of heaven. It is founded in unrighteousness and cemented in blood." Editorials in his paper, the *Liberator*, called for peaceful separation, and the masthead carried the motto "No Union with Slaveholders."[26]

In 1843 and 1844, as the issue of Texas annexation gathered momentum, threats of disunion were hurled more vigorously from both sides of the Mason-Dixon line. Southerners who favored annexation, and there were many, warned that the South would secede unless Texas was added to the Union. From the North came the same warning, in the event Texas was annexed. The days of the gag rule were waning, and fears mounted about what would happen when the slavery debate was unleashed in Congress.

11

★ ★ ★ ★ ★

MODERATION GONE AWRY

"If between them," Richard Current has written, "Webster and Tyler had succeeded in making a middle party go, it might have eased some of the sectional strains which were to culminate in civil war."[1] Perhaps; but if this be true, where should the blame fall for the failure of moderation? Would a middle party have emerged if Webster had remained in Tyler's cabinet to steer the president along the narrow road between extremes? Was Clay's extreme Whig position too strong to be countered? By the summer of 1842, was Tyler so bent on becoming a presidential candidate that he courted any faction he thought would possibly offer him support, thus giving Webster no choice but to leave the administration? Was Tyler unable to withstand the pressure from the extreme states' righters?

For remaining in Tyler's cabinet after the wholesale resignation of department heads and the expulsion of the president from the party in September 1841, Webster was assaulted unmercifully and in the most venomous fashion by the Clay press and by the Kentuckian's faction in Congress. Initially, Webster defended himself, saying he wanted to stay in office until he could bring Britain and the United States to the negotiating table. When this had been accomplished, the Whigs renewed their demands that he sever all ties with the despised Tyler. R. P. Letcher, the governor of Kentucky, wrote in sardonic anticipation to Senator Crittenden: "I am anxious to see what Webster will do or say when he leaves the cabinet. If he has one grain of common sense left, he will give the *Tyler concern a hell of a kick* and fall into the Whig ranks and swear he is now and always was a true Whig."[2]

For a man of Letcher's persuasion, falling into the Whig ranks meant marching to Clay's beat, and this Webster refused to do. He considered himself as important in the party as Clay, if not more so, and did not intend to subordinate his aspirations to those of the Kentuckian. However, because of his stand, Webster lost status in the party, even in his home state. This became obvious during the late summer and fall of 1842 when, against his repeatedly expressed wishes, it was apparent that Massachusetts Whigs were about to name Clay as the state's choice for the 1844 nomination.

This, Webster insisted, should *"by no means"* happen. It would be foolhardy for the state convention to commit itself to anyone at this early date, because "events of magnitude are constantly unfolding." Next year would be soon enough to endorse a candidate. Declaring for Clay now would be premature. Moreover, Webster considered such a move insulting to him and to the president. It would indicate approval of Clay's atrocious behavior in Congress and would very likely give Massachusetts Democrats the victory in November. To nominate Clay or to pledge the Whigs of the state to him "would be little short of insanity."

The state convention disregarded Webster's advice and, instead, followed that of the industrialist Abbott Lawrence, a Clay man, who had set out to undermine Webster's leadership in Massachusetts. The convention endorsed Clay and called for a "full and final separation" from President Tyler. Presumably, if Webster continued in the cabinet, now that Anglo-American relations had been solidified, he, too, would no longer be considered a Whig.[3]

Two weeks later, Webster had an opportunity to respond to this obvious threat. Several thousand Bostonians gathered in Faneuil Hall on 30 September to honor the secretary for his part in concluding a treaty with England. In introducing the guest of honor, the mayor of Boston made an indirect reference to Webster's future, saying, "we know that he who has so nobly maintained his country's honor may safely be intrusted with his own." Yes, Webster replied; in the present distracted state of the Whig party, the proper course for him to pursue should be left to his own choice: "I am, Gentleman, a little hard to coax, but as to being driven, that is out of the question." He was a Whig, and he would always be one. If there were those who would expel him from the party, "let them see who will get out first."

Webster reminded those assembled that the Whig party, from its inception, had been composed of different opinions and principles of every political complexion, and it could endure only with a spirit of harmony and conciliation, of union and sympathy. Unless it wished to plot its own destruction, it had to heal, not widen, the breaches that existed within its ranks; and the healing had to include the betterment of relations with the president. Webster highly praised Tyler for having helped to guide the treaty to a successful conclusion, "for the unbroken and steady confidence reposed in me through the whole progress of an affair not unimportant to the country, and infinitely important to my own reputation." Webster's plea was for moderation: "I believe that, among sober men of this country, there is a growing desire for more moderation of party feeling." Well-meaning members of both parties should unite to uphold the institutions of the nation and carry them forward.

Adams believed that Webster's speech had been "bitter as wormwood to nearly the whole of the Whig party and sweeter than honey to the radical Democracy." Its entire purpose had been "to propitiate the Democracy, and to split up the Whigs, and out of the two fragments to make a Tyler party." Adams further observed: "The signs of the Tyler party are much stronger than I could have imagined."[4]

In the fall elections the Whigs suffered disastrous defeats. While in the Twenty-seventh Congress the composition of the House of Representatives was 133 Whigs to 102 Democrats, the Twenty-eighth Congress would have 142 Democrats, 79 Whigs, and 1 independent (reapportionment had reduced the number of representatives elected). In the Senate the Whigs maintained their narrow majority. Massachusetts Democrats, as Webster predicted, made a good showing. Abbott Lawrence's gubernatorial candidate, John Davis—who was also the state convention's choice for Clay's running-mate—was defeated, although very narrowly, by a Democrat, Marcus Morton. Massachusetts Democrats made significant gains in the congressional races.

Webster believed the rout was due to the "violence and injustice which characterized the conduct of the Whig leaders." The party was in shambles, "broken up and perhaps never to be united"; and the fault was Clay's. If it had not been for dissensions between Congress and the president, "respecting matters which all now admit were of no importance," Tyler's administration, Webster lamented, would have been highly popular and the Whig party would have prospered. In the more than two years that Tyler had left to serve, it would still be possible for him to gain the public confidence. "A vast portion of the moderate & disinterested, will join in support of the President; & there is reason to think some portion of the other party, composed of persons of like character, will take a similar course."

Without a doubt, Webster wished for the emergence of such a moderate coalition, but it is questionable that he truly believed it would become a reality. Even if it did, how many of the moderates would rally to Tyler? During the tariff-distribution controversy in the spring and summer of 1842, while Webster was engrossed in diplomacy, hostilities between Tyler and the Whigs intensified. The *Madisonian*, Tyler's official paper, reported the existence of a conspiracy among the extreme Whig members of Congress to force the president's resignation; and the *National Inquirer* informed its readers that Tyler intended to dissolve the cabinet, either by forcing some members to resign or by removing them. Webster placed no credence in reports from either side. He told Everett: "The truth is, the friends of Mr. Clay, some of them, seek to embarrass the President in all things, to the extent of their power. This causes resentment in him, & between their factious spirits & his resentment of what he regards as intended insult, no one can tell what may happen to the public interest."[5]

A president without a party, who was desperately seeking support, was making what Webster considered unsuitable appointments, many from the Democratic party, in an attempt to create a following. During the summer there was a great outcry over the dismissal of the collector of the port of Philadelphia because, it was alleged, he would not discharge a number of presumably antiadministration Whigs under his supervision to make room for Tyler supporters. If the State Department ever became the object of such Tyler tactics, Webster feared that the damage to America's foreign policy would be inconceivable. In public, he expressed complete confidence in Tyler, but in private he was ambivalent. Late in August, just a little more than a month before his Faneuil Hall speech, Webster confided to Everett that he did not expect to remain in the cabinet much longer. Personally, he and the president were "on the best of terms," and he did not intend to leave his post abruptly or to join the hue and cry against Tyler when he did go. But Webster told Everett that he could not stay if Tyler continued to move toward the Democratic party.

Yet Webster stayed on, possibly in the hope that Tyler would nominate him as minister to the Court of St. James's, if Everett could be encouraged to accept another post, or failing that, perhaps Webster could be named to head a special mission to England to settle the Oregon question. At any rate, Webster did not want to appear to be harried out of the Tyler administration by his detractors in the Whig party.

The president gave no indication of wanting Webster to leave. In fact, Webster believed Tyler would be reluctant to have him resign. Tyler needed bolstering, and the secretary, in late 1842, despite his professed concern about "bad appointments," wrote editorials for the *Madisonian*, in which he urged the public, Congress, and the press to give the president a "fair chance." Webster recommended that the Twenty-eighth Congress, which would convene on 4 March 1843, should reconsider the merits of Tyler's Exchequer Plan. A Clay-type national bank, in his opinion, was passe. But ignoring Webster's advice, the House Ways and Means Committee rejected the exchequer idea without waiting for the Twenty-eighth Congress. The House accepted the committee report by a vote of 193 to 19.[6]

The lame-duck session of the Twenty-seventh Congress (5 December 1842 to 3 March 1843) outdid even the "trying summer of 1842" in turbulence and spitefulness. Almost every statement that it made and almost every item that it proposed, insignficant though they might be, led to partisan speeches, name-calling, and accusations of one kind or another being hurled at the president and the secretary of state. Because of Tyler's ill-advised attempt to curry favor through the use of patronage, the most frequent charge against him, the one that carried the most weight, was that of having violated his own stated policy on civil-service reform. He was accused of having removed Whigs from office without cause in order to fill positions with those who would help him satisfy his "lust for office," and his frequent appointment of family members brought charges of gross nepotism.

The introduction of the bankruptcy-repeal bill gave rise to a three-week debate, the violence of which had not been surpassed in the history of the Congress. The outrage was directed, not against the bill, but at the "crimes and misdemeanors" of the Tyler administration. Cushing, one of the few Tyler followers who remained in the House, tried unsuccessfully to stem the flow of denunciations, but was himself upbraided unmercifully. Because of his loyalty to the president, the Whigs earlier had forced Cushing's decision not to stand for reelection.

Congressman John Minor Botts of Virginia thought the time was auspicious to press again for Tyler's impeachment. Botts introduced nine resolutions, a list of the president's alleged wrongdoings, including the "gross usurpation of power," the "wicked and corrupt abuse of the power of appointment to office," and the "arbitrary, despotic, and corrupt abuse of the veto power"; he then proposed that a committee be named to investigate the charges and to recommend impeachment. The House rejected the motion, 127 to 83. This did not signify a softening of hostilities toward the president. Most Whigs thought the case against him was not strong enough, and to have him tried and acquitted would devastate the party. The best course to adopt, Philip Hone concluded, was to forget impeachment. Let Tyler "serve out his time, and go back to Virginia, from whence the Whigs have bitter cause to lament they ever called him forth."[7]

Tyler, however, was determined to do more than "serve out his time." A few weeks after the defeat of Botts's resolution, he made the strongest statement made thus far by a chief executive on the president's right to use discretion in complying or refusing to comply with congressional requests or demands for information from the executive branch. In most cases there was no difficulty in supplying the desired papers or documents, but from the beginning of the Republic, presidents had occasionally found it necessary to withhold information. Twice during the previous year, Tyler had done so.

In February 1842 the House of Representatives had requested all correspondence relating to the Maine boundary negotiations with Great Britain. In most instances, Tyler replied, he had preferred to give "Congress and the public information affecting the state of the country to the fullest extent consistent with propriety and prudence," but on the subject specified, he regretted that he must claim the right, exercised by other presidents before him, to refuse the request. Negotiations were, at best, in their initial state. Ashburton would not arrive in the United States for more than another month. The divulging of any material at this early date clearly would be detrimental and dangerous to the public interest. Tyler also could have told the House, as Washington had done in 1796, that the request was an invasion of the treaty-making power which the Constitution reserved to the president and the Senate.[8]

In March 1842, Tyler refused a House call for the names of any members of the Twenty-sixth and Twenty-seventh Congresses who had been applicants for office and for the details of their applications, whether they had applied in person or through friends, and, if the latter, whether the friends made their recommendations in person or in writing. The request was a strange one; it undoubtedly stemmed from rumors about Tyler's intention to remove disloyal Whigs and replace them with Democrats.

In denying the request, Tyler lectured the House on its misapprehension of its duties and powers in respect to appointments, a subject that was none of its affair. Applications for office, as well as letters or conversations on such subjects, were not, he reminded the congressmen, official proceedings. They did not become so unless the president, upon nominating an individual, should deem it proper to lay such materials before the Senate. Not until a nomination had been made did an appointment become an official act, a matter of record, which, at the proper time, was made known to the House and to the country. The Senate, not the House, had the constitutional responsibility for accepting or rejecting a nominee. Applications were confidential, and divulging information about a person who was not appointed would serve no purpose.

There was, Tyler contended, a more important consideration underlying the matter: the president's obligation to defend the executive branch against encroachments on its "powers, rights, and duties." The appointing power had been conferred by the Constitution on the chief executive, "by and with the advice and consent of the Senate." Nowhere in the document had the House been given the right "to hear the reasons which an applicant may urge for an appointment to office under the executive department." Any assumption of such duties or responsibilities by the House would be "dangerous, impolitic, and unconstitutional."[9]

There were other cases. Some requests were irresponsible or obviously designed to harass the president, others were legitimate. Tyler complied with a majority of them. He did so in January 1843 by sending to the House the information concerning an executive investigation of frauds in land sales to the Cherokee Indians. However, highly irritated by the House's apparent inclination to badger him, he used this occasion to deliver his vigorous defense of the right of executive discretion. This was in answer to what Tyler considered to be the arrogant and arbitrary behavior of the House during the summer of 1842, when it passed a resolution requiring Secretary of War Spencer to produce several reports on the Cherokee-land-fraud investigation. Spencer, at the president's direction, refused; and he submitted carefully detailed reasons for doing so. The materials desired by the House, Spencer explained, contained information that, it was supposed, would become the subject of negotiations between the War Department and delegates of the Cherokee nation. If the information were made public, the negotiations could be endangered. Moreover, an investigation was in progress, and charges had been made by ex parte inquiries. Persons who had been implicated by these charges had not as yet had the opportunity to reply to them.

The refusal precipitated a six-day debate, after which the House adopted a resolution stating that it had the right to demand from the executive branch any information in the latter's possession relating to subjects on which the House was deliberating. The president was then directed to produce all data on the Cherokee matter, from any source whatever.

Tyler waited until January 1843 to make his reply. After reminding the House of Spencer's reasons for not delivering the requested materials, Tyler firmly challenged the House's assertions that the executive was bound to submit to the House "demand" and that the president did not have the authority to exercise any discretion in reference to "the nature of the information required or to the interests of the country or of individuals to be affected by such compliance." The president, Tyler pointed out, was directed by the Constitution to "take care that the laws be faithfully executed." This included an obligation to inquire into the manner in which all public agents performed their duties. If the president were not able to use discretion in the dissemination of information collected in investigations, an inquiry could be arrested in its first stage, and those who were under suspicion could elude detection. "To require from the Executive the transfer of this discretion to a coordinate branch of the Government is equivalent to the denial of its possession by him and would render him dependent upon that branch in the performance of a duty purely executive."

Tyler maintained that some information which the executive branch acquired was privileged and that as in a court of law, "the general authority to compel testimony must give way in certain cases to the paramount rights of individuals or of the Government." There were, he said, reasons why the president at times had to insist on confidentiality. Primarily, these were to protect ongoing investigations, to protect informants and innocent people, and to protect the nation and the public interest. If the president could not exercise this right, a vindictive Congress could use information that it had extracted from the executive branch to do "incalculable and irremediable injury to innocent parties by throwing them into libels most foul and atrocious. Shall there be no discretionary authority permitted to refuse to become the instruments of such malevolence?"

Tyler did not claim absolute executive control over information; he claimed only the right of discretion, and that only in certain cases; but the line between absolute control and the right of discretion is a fine one. When the administration's abuses needed to be exposed, as the House noted, the president should not have the power to suppress evidence. Neither the legislative branch nor the executive branch is immune from malevolence or vindictiveness, and during a period of pronounced mutual distrust, this constituted a serious quandary.

Nevertheless, in this instance, all papers that were either known or supposed to have any relation to the army's investigation of alleged land frauds were transmitted to the House. The reasons for having declined to do so earlier, Tyler explained, had ceased to exist. The death or removal out of the country of those who needed to be called to testify made it wholly impracticable to pursue the matter. Additionally, Tyler reminded the House about a recent congressional prohibition of payment of accounts connected with any inquiry, except military and naval courts-martial or courts of inquiry, unless special appropriations had been made, which virtually denied to the executive the ability to complete ongoing investigations or to conduct future ones.[10]

Apart from sparring with the president, Congress marked time. Domestic legislation was at a standstill and would remain so for the balance of Tyler's administration. In the political arena, however, there was a flurry of activity. In state after state, Whig conventions nominated Clay, but his candidacy did not go completely unchallenged. Winfield Scott, general of the army, thought there might be a chance that the Whigs would turn to him, especially if Clay's health were to deteriorate. "When an early hard liver begins to break up," he commented to the Pennsylvania attorney Thaddeus Stevens, "there is no possibility of recuperation." Obviously, disloyalty to his commander in chief bothered Scott not at all. His letters soliciting support were filled with snide remarks about the man in the White House. "Removals and putting in relatives and corrupt hacks are the order of the day," he told Crittenden. "A Tyler man? I'll cut my throat first." But the general's candidacy petered out.

For a time, the Supreme Court Justice John McLean, encouraged by antislavery Whigs who had no faith in Clay, toyed with the idea of making a bid for the nomination. The movement went nowhere, but Clay Whigs were disturbed enough to dangle the vice-presidential possibility in front of both Scott and McLean.

Every once in a while there was momentary interest in Webster. The reluctance of Ohio abolitionists to support a slave owner prompted Alphonso Taft—the first member of the Ohio Taft family to command national attention, the father of William Howard Taft—to ask Webster, in the spring of 1843, if he would consider being a candidate. Clay, Taft said, was unpopular in Ohio. From the abolitionists' viewpoint, "the free states have not had their proportion of the great offices under the General Government." Moreover, Clay had done more than any other person to make the barbarous practice of dueling respectable, and Clay's "denunciatory course" toward President Tyler also weighed heavily against him. "Clay cannot combine this great Whig family," of that Taft was certain, but somehow he thought Webster could. The idea of Tyler's candidacy "is regarded as preposterous. . . . It is sincerely regretted by men who wish Mr. Tyler no harm, that he is now presented before the people as an expectant for the next Presidency."[11]

In early February 1843, Calhoun thought Tyler was "striving to build up a party," but "politics and parties are becoming more confused." Prospects of a third party surfaced several times during Tyler's administration. Extreme states'-rights advocates, especially in Virginia, saw a third party as a possibility as soon as Tyler had taken office. If Calhoun and his followers, together with anti-Jackson Whigs and northerners with southern views, few though they might be, could create a party, they perhaps could muster enough strength to influence the passage of legislation that would be more compatible with states'-rights policies. In this manner they could circumvent domination by a northern majority bent on centralization. With luck, Tyler could lead the party to victory in 1844. Edmund Ruffin—a Virginia agricultural reformer, the publisher of the *Farmers' Register,* and an extreme sectionalist—saw merit in the idea, as did William Campbell Preston of South Carolina. "What a destiny for Tyler," was Preston's remark to Nathaniel Beverley Tucker. After a few months, however, the idea of Tyler as the champion of such a movement faded.

The difficulty was that Tyler and the die-hard states' righters did not agree on the composition of a third party. Tyler was not convinced that a formal organization of the type envisioned by Ruffin, Tucker, and others was the answer. What Tyler and Webster had in mind was a coalition of moderates from the Whig and Democratic parties. States' rights would be honored, as would nationalism, but the key would be balance and compromise. Neither group would achieve all it wanted, but the Union would prosper as sectionalism would cease to be a primary force. There would be no fight to the death, such as that engaged in by the Clay Whigs and the radical states' righters.

Tyler wanted his colleagues in Virginia to see the reasonableness of this, but they did not. Their approach, they contended, was the correct one, and they distrusted Webster, whom Tyler relied on to bring the moderate Whigs into an alliance. For a time after he joined the cabinet, Upshur outwardly seemed somewhat inclined toward moderation, but this was short-lived. Nevertheless, Tyler continued to place his faith in an alliance of moderates, and after witnessing the Whig losses in 1842, he began to believe that a third party with a middle-ground approach might be feasible. If nothing more, it could serve as a makeweight, offering its support to whichever of the two major parties would be willing to do the most for the public good, but obviously Tyler did not rule out the possibility of being nominated by such a party. His pride, which had been severely bruised by congressional hostility and the Whig press, needed rehabilitation. He wanted his good name to be exonerated.[12]

However, with no assurance of the successful launching of a third party or of its effectiveness once initiated, Tyler also explored his chances of returning to the Democratic fold. In January 1843 he sent Mordecai Manuel Noah, the editor of the *New York Weekly Messenger,* to Richmond to sound out Thomas Ritchie, the editor of the *Richmond Enquirer* who was also Virginia's leading Democrat, on the prospects of Tyler's becoming a presidential candidate on the Democratic ticket.

Although Ritchie was more gracious about the president than were the great majority of Whigs, saying Tyler was a man of integrity who often supported Democratic policies, Ritchie gave Noah no encouragement. "There appears a determination in the party to do justice to those [Democrats] who were unfortunate in the conflict of 1840," Ritchie said, "and to reinstate them in power, in proof of unwavering confidence in their principles." In other words, Ritchie, a Van Buren man since the early 1830s, intended to work for the New Yorker's nomination. Of course, Ritchie conceded, if Tyler could fairly obtain the nomination in the convention, he would consider it his duty and pleasure to support him as the Democratic candidate; however, Ritchie saw little prospect that this would happen.

Noah appealed to Ritchie's pride as a Virginian and a southerner, but to no avail. "It is all a mistake," Ritchie replied, "to suppose that the south is so clannish and so wedded to the support of a southern president that the claims of northern, western, and eastern men are to be discarded. If anything, I think Georgia and North Carolina would prefer a northern president who has no hostility to southern institutions; at least, I think this is the case in Virginia." Ritchie also gave Noah a bit of unsolicited advice for Tyler: if the president was trying to build a party of his own, he should not depend on patronage. An established party might find it helpful in attracting support, if it was used discreetly, but "patronage alone could never build up a party for any man."

Upon hearing Noah's report on the meeting, Tyler quickly denied any expectation of nomination or election, "although some of my friends are sanguine"; nevertheless, his actions contradicted his denial. His increasing use of the power of appointment was disturbing to those who had believed in his earlier views on civil-service reform. In Virginia, Littleton Waller Tazewell was upset. Tyler, he said, "is now obviously seeking to buy popularity by the use of his patronage."[13] Democrats, many of whom had few qualifications or less than sterling characters, appeared to be the chief beneficiaries.

Notwithstanding Ritchie's pessimistic assessment of Tyler's possibilities, the divisiveness within the Democratic party was enough to give Tyler a glimmer of hope. Calhoun was desperately seeking the nomination, while the Van Burenites were ardently opposing him. Anti–Van Buren Democrats who disliked Calhoun were split among Richard M. Johnson, James Buchanan, and Lewis Cass, none of whom, for the present, was inclined to give way. Perhaps Tyler thought he could serve as an alternative choice if no one leader were to surface. In the columns of the *Madisonian,* his nomination by the Democratic party was openly promoted, and because the president often advised the editor, J. B. Jones, on the paper's policy, it is doubtful that the advocacy was done without his knowledge.

Whether Tyler's future lay with a third party or with the Democrats, one thing seemed certain: the sensitive Texas-annexation issue would figure prominently in whatever Tyler might do. Since 1836, when Texas had declared its independence from Mexico, the old Virginia clique of Gilmer, Upshur, Tucker, and Wise had been determined to add Texas to the Union. When Tyler inherited the presidency, the time appeared opportune. In September 1841, it was to Tucker that Waddy Thompson of South Carolina appealed for aid in obtaining the appointment as minister to Mexico. Thompson had no doubt about the importance of Texas to the "success of the South," a point he had made with increasing diligence while serving in the House of Representatives during the Jackson and Van Buren administrations. Thompson reminded Tucker: "I was the first man to raise my voice in favor of Texas. It was on my motion that its recognition was authorized by Congress." When Tyler appointed Thompson, Upshur rejoiced, jubilantly writing to Tucker: "I am sincerely glad that Thompson has obtained the mission to Mexico. This looks better than I had hoped for."[14]

With such great enthusiasm among his associates, it was small wonder that in October 1841, Tyler approached Webster with a tentative suggestion of acquiring Texas by treaty. "Could the North be reconciled to it, could anything throw so bright a lustre around us?" he asked. Webster's cool reception of the idea made Tyler bide his time, but Texas was not forgotten. As Thompson made his way to his post in Mexico, he voiced the hope that through Tucker or Upshur, Tyler would send him "pretty strong instructions on the subject." Thompson told Tucker: "There is some difficulty in these instructions coming through the Secretary of State. Mr. Tyler's own views are up to the hub."

As Texas fever mounted, rash statements inflamed sentiments on both sides of the issue. In late Janaury 1842, Henry Wise impetuously announced to the House: "Let one more northern state be added to the Union and the equilibrium is gone—gone forever—unless by adding Texas, the south can add more weight to her end of the lever." Again, in mid April, in a violently injudicious speech, he accused England of desiring either to possess or to control Texas in order to emancipate the area's slaves and to plot the dissolution of the Union. This outburst was occasioned by a motion, made by a congressman from New York, to strike the salary of the minister to Mexico from an appropriations bill because, he charged, Thompson's appointment had originated in a design to annex Texas. Because Lord Ashburton had recently arrived in the United States, Wise's speech was particularly ill advised, and measures were taken to suppress its publication. Nevertheless, John Quincy Adams insisted upon quoting extensively from Wise's harangues in order to point out the "sinister motives" of the "slave-power conspiracy." The country was rife with rumors of conspiracies. In addition to the slave-power conspiracy, there was the British conspiracy, the northern conspiracy, and the administration conspiracy. But the slave-power conspiracy, fueled by Adams and the northern abolitionists, drew by far the most attention; and the sectional crisis deepened.

While Wise was speaking in the House, Gilmer was busily writing editorials in favor of annexation. Unlike Wise, however, Gilmer took a broader view: he stressed the benefits that the acquisition of Texas could bring to the entire nation, not merely to the South. Markets would be opened for manufactured goods and agricultural products of all non-slaveholding states, markets that would not have the restrictions and disadvantages of foreign competition.[15]

This was more in accordance with Tyler's approach to annexation. If he intended to make a try for the 1844 election, he needed an issue, but one whose appeal was not based on sectionalism. Also, after considering himself a peacemaker in the Webster-Ashburton negotiations, Tyler did not wish to antagonize Great Britain or to appear to be advocating hostilities of any kind. Expansionism was sweeping the country, and Tyler thought the annexation of Texas should be looked upon as just another aspect of Manifest Destiny. If it could be coupled with a favorable settlement of the Oregon boundary and, possibly, the acquisition of California or, at least, a "window on the Pacific," the cry of sectional favoritism might be stilled; but the injudicious arguments of the rabid proslavery annexationists overshadowed any attempts at more rational or realistic overtures.

Unfortunately for Tyler, the extremists were considered by many to be part of a "Tyler circle." They were the same people, for the most part, who had been labeled as members of the Virginia Cabal. However, these individuals, including Secretary Upshur, were impatient with Tyler. His stand on states' rights had fallen short of their expectations, and in 1842 and 1843 he appeared to be reluctant to plunge into the Texas matter with the enthusiasm they desired. In 1842 he twice rejected Texan

President Sam Houston's proffer of annexation, fearing that the Senate would not ratify the treaty at this time. To countenance the explosive issue in the midst of the Webster-Ashburton talks or while the ratification of the treaty was pending in Parliament was unthinkable, especially in view of all the charges that were being made against Great Britain concerning its "sinister conspiracy" to interfere in Texas.

The extremists blamed Tyler's caution on Webster and Everett. They were New Englanders, and Everett was thought to be an abolitionist. When Everett was appointed to the diplomatic post in London, Upshur was beside himself. "The present condition of the country," he told Tucker, "imperiously requires that a Southern man and a slave holder should represent us at their court." How could Tyler, "reared and living in lower Virginia fail to see this?" To appoint a Bostonian, an abolitionist, was abominable, inexcusable. There was no accounting for it unless it was a concession to Webster. "Let this be as it may, if Tyler has any party at all, it is that party [the Virginia states' righters] which he treats on all occasions with utter neglect."[16]

Perhaps it was to mollify Upshur and his friends that Tyler, in the fall of 1841, sent Duff Green as an unofficial agent to France and England, ostensibly to report on affairs in Europe and to explore the possibilities of a loan to the United States to combat the nation's serious deficit. It was a strange and unwise choice. Green, who had an overly inflated ego, considered himself a "master manipulator" and an expert in international affairs. In reality, he was an irresponsible and dangerous person to have abroad at this or any other time, but particularly during the delicate meetings between Webster and Ashburton. Green was a Calhoun man. His daughter was married to Calhoun's son, but their political ties were more important than the relationship by marriage. During the nullification crisis of the early 1830s, Green, then editor of the *United States Telegraph,* had given his complete support to the South Carolinian and thereby had broken with Jackson. Although Green had not followed Calhoun back into the Democratic party in 1840, they were close personal friends. During the 1840 election, Green had campaigned for the Whigs. Believing a victory was guaranteed, he anticipated receiving a lucrative post. He claimed responsibility for having placed Tyler on the Harrison ticket, but Green was an inveterate credit grabber. With the Whigs victorious, he was among those who had besieged Harrison, wanting his share of the fruits of the triumph; but he had been unsuccessful in his bid for the Texas mission. This had not deterred him, and when Tyler had become president, Green had still been waiting in the wings, hoping for some kind of appointment. In all probability, Calhoun, through Upshur, suggested Green for the European assignment, and although Green went as Tyler's personal representative, he kept Calhoun and Upshur as well, if not better, informed of his "observations" than he did the president. Green's deep desire was to see Calhoun in the White House.[17]

In France, Green joined with and encouraged the United States minister, Lewis Cass, in his Anglophobic diatribes, and throughout 1842, Green sent letter after letter to Calhoun, Upshur, and Tyler, warning of devious British plots against the United States. His communications to the press, which predicted war with Britain and urged the United States to prepare, were even more alarming; they caused public consternation both in the United States and in England. At times, Tyler was shocked by Green's information, which led Tyler to feel that perhaps Cass and Green could be correct in their assessments. Webster, however, was able, in large part, to counteract Green's influence on the president. Of course, Cass's motivation for causing a stir was common knowledge. He had been "bitten by the presidential bug." Webster sternly informed Cass of Tyler's displeasure in regard to the minister's attitude toward the Webster-Ashburton Treaty and his public utterances on the subject: "The President is not a little startled, that you should make such totally groundless assumptions of fact, and then leave a discreditable inference to be drawn from them."

Understandably, Edward Everett, as minister to England, was incensed by Green's interference in diplomatic affairs between the United States and Britain. "I have already given you some notion of the way in which Genl. Green has constituted himself a sort of special envoy to the English and French governments," Everett complained to Webster. Green, Everett said, was engaged in unauthorized intrigues; he had conducted interviews with Lord Aberdeen, Sir Robert Peel, and François Pierre Guillaume Guizot, France's foreign minister. Everett trusted that men of experience would not be misled by any "representations of unauthorized private individuals."[18]

In the early winter of 1842, Green returned, purporting to be carrying home projects of treaties between the United States, Great Britain, and France, "drawn up in concert with M. Guizot and Sir Robert Peel." "You will be able to form your own opinion," Everett disgustedly told Webster, "as to the probability that persons at the head of the governments of France and England, would commit themselves in this way with an unauthorized private citizen of a foreign state." Everett said he had reason to believe Green contemplated returning to London, "and may try to make the President think that he has done and is able to do, good. . . . Nothing would do us more injury" than to give European nations the impression that the United States government "countenanced proceedings so irregular and (according to all European notions) unwarrantable."

With this information at hand, it is inconceivable why Tyler again, in the spring of 1843, sent Green back to England as a "private citizen" on special assignment, to "hold consultations with persons possessing interests in trade & commerce" and to pave the way for a reciprocal commercial treaty. "I have high regard for the General," Tyler wrote, informing Everett of Green's return to England, "& will be obliged to you to assist him in furthering his objects so far as you can consistently do."[19]

According to diplomatic protocol, any communication to a minister abroad should come from the secretary of state, but in this instance, Tyler by-passed Webster, whose resignation was expected momentarily. Everett, who was baffled by Tyler's action, bitterly complained to Webster, who, four days out of office, commiserated with Everett: "I told him [Green] he could do nothing, officially or semi-officially. That any such thing, besides being useless, [would] be disrespectful to you. I fear the President's notions are not strict enough, on such points; but he has the highest regard for you, & always speaks of you in the kindest manner. Yourself & Irving [Washington Irving had been appointed minister to Spain in February 1842 and served until 1846] are the principal monuments of *my* administration of the Department. It is well the appointments were made when they were. We were then all 'going,' as the phrase is, for honor and renown."

Webster, disillusioned and bedeviled from all sides, resigned as secretary of state on 8 May 1843. For months while Webster was agonizing over his decision, Nicholas Biddle had pleaded with him to remain in office. "Do not leave your present position," Biddle remonstrated; "if you do, you descend." But Webster was uncomfortable. In addition to watching his status in the Whig party crumble with every passing day, he now believed Tyler was anxious to have him leave. Henry Shaw, a former congressman from Massachusetts, told Webster in February that Tyler "would feel relieved if you should resign your place." Shaw, during a conversation with the president, concluded, although Tyler did not directly say so, that Webster's continuance in the cabinet stood in the way of Tyler's receiving the confidence and support of the Democrats.[20]

Shaw's evidence was insubstantial, but Webster was now unsure about Tyler for other reasons. Webster told Biddle: "The President is still resolved to try the chances of an *Election*. This object enters into everything, & leads, & will lead, to movements in which I cannot concur. . . . He has altogether too high an opinion of the work which can be wrought by giving *offices* to hungry applicants.'' Personally, between Webster and Tyler there was ''entire good will,'' but every day the secretary expected measures that he could not condone. ''I must, therefore, leave my place. It seems inevitable. Who will take it, I know not; or what is to become of us all, I know not. I fear a confused & unsatisfactory scene is before us.'' If the president were not a candidate, they would get along very well together, Webster sadly told Everett.

Although the editorial in the *National Intelligencer* on Webster's resignation, written by Webster himself, was more flattering to the secretary than to the president and even though the two men disagreed on Texas and a few other issues, they remained personal friends until Webster's death in 1852.[21]

The ad interim appointment of Legaré, who also retained his post as attorney general, did not displease Webster, who told Everett: ''He is an accomplished lawyer, with some experience abroad, of Gentlemanly manners & character, & not at all disposed to create, or foment, foreign difficulties. I think at present the President could not have done better.'' Legaré was not as kind about his predecessor, complaining that he found ''a general indolence, incapacity & want of conscientious duty'' in the State Department and intimating that Webster, during his last months in office, had been somewhat neglectful of his duties, upset, no doubt, by the actions of the president and by his differences with the Whig party.[22]

Legaré was an advocate of Manifest Destiny, and his expansionist views included Texas. However, like Webster, he was also enthusiastic about opening the markets of China to United States trade and about the important part to be played by the Hawaiian Islands in the development of American influence in the Pacific. Tyler was comfortable with Legaré as secretary of state, and for five weeks, the routine work of the department went forward efficiently.

In June, Tyler and several members of the cabinet were scheduled to travel to Boston for the dedication of a monument commemorating the Battle of Bunker Hill; they were to stop en route in Baltimore, Philadelphia, New York, and Providence. Legaré, who was busy with the duties of two offices, was to follow later, going directly to Boston.

The Tyler entourage, as it passed through the various cities, was greeted with parades, crowds, speeches, and other gala events. The Whig press played down the ebullience touched off by Tyler's visits, but seeing a president was a rare occurrence, and as George Templeton Strong recorded in his diary, Tyler was received with ''fuss and parade enough to make him comfortable, it's to be hoped. . . . Everybody stared at the President much as they would have stared at the Emperor of China and displayed about as much enthusiasm and good will toward him as if he had actually been that potentate."

In Boston, Webster was to make the dedication address for the Bunker Hill monument. John Quincy Adams had been invited to attend and sit on the platform but had declined. "Upon this pageant," he complained, "has been engrafted another, to bedaub with glory John Tyler, the slaveholder, who is come with all his court, in gaudy trappings of mock royalty, to receive the homage of hungry sycophants, under color of doing homage to the principles of Bunker Hill martyrdom." Adams termed the event a burlesque, "the mouth-worship of liberty from the lips of a slavebreeder." Adams would have been even more cynical had he known that another of Tyler's reasons for visiting Boston was to confer with David Henshaw, who was working hard to undermine Van Buren's support in Massachusetts. Henshaw may have been promised patronage in return for efforts on the president's behalf, but Henshaw was really a Calhoun man.[23]

Upon arriving in Boston the day before the 17 June celebration, Legaré became so violently ill that he was unable to attend the ceremonies. His condition quickly worsened, and on 19 June, after intense suffering, he died at the home of his friend George Ticknor. His death was attributed to an intestinal obstruction or to bilious colic. Adams eulogized Legaré as "an amiable man, by far the best of the President's present associates."[24]

Unfortunately, Tyler had lost another moderate advisor, and he now was faced with filling two important cabinet posts, secretary of state and attorney general. This was an unpleasant prospect because earlier, in March 1843, he had encountered difficulties with the Senate in replacing Walter Forward, a less-than-competent secretary of the treasury, whose resignation had been anticipated for months. As Forward's successor, Tyler had nominated Caleb Cushing, but Cushing's numerous speeches in defense of the president, his policies, and his vetoes, had created considerable enmity toward him in both houses of Congress. Also, control of the Treasury Department was coveted by the legislative branch, and it would not do to have a member of the "corporal's guard" at its head. Tyler, however, was determined. When, during the closing hours of the session, the Senate rejected Cushing by a vote of 27 to 19, the president immediately resubmitted the nomination. This time the vote was 27 to 10. Tyler refused to concede defeat, and for the third time on the same day, Cushing's name was sent to the Senate. The answer was decisive. Cushing was voted down, 29 to 2. Tyler then had asked approval to move Spencer from the War Department to the

Treasury, and the Senate, by a majority of one vote, had agreed. Cushing finally had to be satisfied with the mission to China.

Prior to adjournment, the Senate also thrice rejected the nomination of Henry Wise as United States minister to France to replace Lewis Cass, who returned home filled with presidential aspirations. In nominating Wise, Tyler was partially acceding to Upshur's expressed desire to have southerners in charge of the nation's diplomatic affairs in both France and England.

After Congress had adjourned, Tyler appointed James M. Porter, a Democrat from Pennsylvania, as secretary of war and moved Upshur from the Navy Department to the State Department. Regardless of Upshur's strong personal views on the positive good of slavery, his ardent sectionalism, and the influence that these had on his determination to annex Texas, he had been restrained in his public utterances on the subjects. He had been an exceptionally efficient and far-sighted secretary of the navy; he had instigated many reforms in the building of naval vessels, in improving conditions aboard ship, and in encouraging scientific experiments.

To replace Upshur as head of the Navy Department, Tyler considered the appointment of Matthew Fontaine Maury, a young Virginian of decided promise whom Upshur had named superintendent of the Depot of Charts and Instruments. Tyler did offer the place to another naval officer, Capt. Robert F. Stockton, who refused it. Inadvisably, the president then turned to David Henshaw, the Massachusetts politician with whom he had conferred in Boston. Henshaw's reputation was questionable, as were his qualifications for the position. He was a former druggist, railroad promoter, and collector of the port of Boston under the administrations of Jackson and Van Buren.

With the naming of John Nelson of Maryland, another Democrat, as attorney general, Tyler had a full complement of secretaries, but instead of the quasi-Whig cabinet appointed in September 1841, the cabinet of 1843 was composed of three Whigs: Upshur (a Whig in name only), Spencer, and Wickliffe (a wavering Whig); and three Democrats: Porter, Henshaw, and Nelson. Among the Democrats, only Nelson had qualifications of merit. Tyler also tried to take care of one of his political friends who, politically speaking, had fallen on hard times. Early in June, Tyler appointed George Proffit of Indiana as envoy extraordinary and minister plenipotentiary to Brazil, and Proffit quickly departed to assume his duties.[25]

Congress was not in session, so these were all "vacation," or ad interim, appointments, subject to Senate scrutiny when the Twenty-eighth Congress convened in December. The president, of necessity, apparently had set aside his earlier scruples about making appointments in the absence of the Senate. The cabinet replacements indicated a shift away from a middle-of-the-road position and clearly reflected the influence of Upshur, who, unknown to Tyler, was already promoting Calhoun for the presidency.

In Boston, Webster was distressed by Tyler's cabinet choices. After much hesitation, Webster wrote the president a "private & entirely confidential" letter, warning him that someone was giving him bad advice. Naming Democrats, especially those "governed by mere selfishness & greediness for office," did not in the least conciliate the party. There was absolutely no evidence that the Democratic party meant to support the president's personal interest. "Out of the fullness of the heart, the mouth speaketh, & I must repeat, therefore, my conscientious belief, that without the exercise of decision & firmness in rejecting solicitations for change, your substantial & permanent fame as President of the United States, is in no small peril."[26]

Undoubtedly, with the departure of Webster, any moderation in the Tyler administration had gone awry, but sadly for the country, it likely would have done so in any event. Moderation was not compatible with the milieu.

12

TEXAS: MISINFORMATION, RUMORS, AND SECRECY

With Abel P. Upshur heading the State Department, the Texas movement gained momentum, and Duff Green, the itinerant unofficial American envoy, was elevated to almost oracular status. Suspicious of Britain and distrustful of Everett, Upshur placed full reliance in reports sent by the "London agent." Invariably, Green said what Upshur wanted to hear. Southern interests, the secretary was convinced, were Green's prime concern. John Quincy Adams thought so, too, referring to Green in public as "the United States ambassador of slavery in London." Without Daniel Webster to disregard or temper his exaggerations and distortions, Green was more dangerous. Yet, to Upshur, Green was "a man of great intelligence and well versed in public affairs. Hence I have every reason to confide in the correctness of his conclusions." Tyler, however, was more skeptical, certainly more so than he appeared to be in April, when he wrote to Edward Everett asking him to assist Green in contacting persons who were interested in trade and commerce. By July, Tyler had become more wary, and again writing directly to Everett, he specifically informed the minister that Green was "invested with no authority whatsoever" to speak in the name of his government. The president wanted Everett to be "perfectly explicit" in notifying Prime Minister Peel of Green's limited position. Any proposals or statements that came from Green were, Tyler said, "the emanation of his own mind."[1]

During the spring and summer of 1843, Green constantly warned about a British plot to abolish slavery in Texas, not from any humanitarian motivation, but in the hope of checking the expansion of the United States and fostering the dissolution of the Union. With a few alterations from time to time, Green's scenario, which was accepted by Upshur, went as follows: Britain would encourage Texas, with promises of interest-free loans and support against Mexico, to emancipate all slaves in the Lone Star Republic. With Texas a free area, runaway slaves from the United States would seek sanctuary there. American slave owners would attempt to recover their property. Border incidents would occur, but the government in Washington, increasingly controlled by the North, would refuse to aid the slave owners. The South would have no choice but to secede from the Union. Thus, Britain would succeed in thwarting the growth and development of, and actually in weakening or destroying, a strong competitor in manufacturing, commerce, and international influence.

According to Green, the British chargé in Texas, Charles Elliot, had promised his government's "warmest support" to the Lone Star Republic in its struggle with Mexico, plus an interest-free loan to pay for the emancipation of the twelve to fifteen thousand slaves within Texas. Green reported, "from a source entitled to the fullest credit," a plan for the organization in England of a company that would advance a sum sufficient to pay slaveholders for all the slaves in Texas. The company would be reimbursed with Texas land.

Green was not reticent about telling Tyler what he must do. Tyler was to instruct Everett to confront Aberdeen and demand answers to these charges, and Tyler was to direct Aberdeen to appoint commissioners to negotiate a commercial treaty with the United States. "If England refuses a commercial treaty—& offers to guarantee a loan to abolish slavery in Texas—we can be at no loss for her motive." Tyler then must go before the country with a proposal to annex Texas, taking the ground that annexation was the only means of preventing Texas from falling into the hands of "English fanatics." Green was positive that the entire object of the British government in relation to slavery and the slave trade was to control the commercial world. Tyler had no alternative. He must go before the next Congress on the issue of annexation. "Rely on what I tell you. It is to become the question which will absorb all other questions." These were similar to the ominous reports that Green had sent during his 1842 stay in England.[2]

Stories about British conspiracies in regard to Texas also had reached Tyler in early March 1843 through Isaac Van Zandt, Texas' chargé d'affaires in Washington. Van Zandt, informing Texas' secretary of state, Anson Jones, said Tyler might be ready to make a move on the subject of annexation, but Webster was very much in the way. "I think it likely that Upshur will succeed him, and if he does, it will be one of the best appointments for us." Tyler, Van Zandt thought, was cautious because of the considerable opposition to annexation, especially in the North; but if the president concluded he could politically profit by the move or could secure ratification, he would "make the treaty as early as he can" after the departure of Webster.[3]

There was no doubt about Tyler's interest in acquiring Texas. He thought it would be the crowning achievement of his administration, but he was concerned about the timing of the move in relation to the settlement of the Oregon question, and with reason, he feared that the Senate would reject an annexation treaty. On the other hand, he believed the Texas issue could help him in his bid for election in 1844.

The pressures on Tyler were great. Upshur, Green, Gilmer, Wise, and others of the so-called Tyler circle were resolved to add Texas to the Union by whatever means necessary, and they wanted the next president to be John C. Calhoun, who had resigned from the Senate in the spring of 1843 to prepare for the campaign. To achieve their ends, they played "fast and loose" with Tyler, who naïvely was unaware of what was happening. Secretly, his "trusted and confidential advisers" were keeping Calhoun informed of everything that was going on in the Tyler administration.[4]

The Texans also used various artifices in an attempt to force a commitment from the president. They often fed information to Green, who passed it on to the Washington government and to Calhoun. Ashbel Smith, Texas' minister in London, gave Green the word about the "British loan." He had heard it from Stephen P. Andrews, a young abolitionist who had come from Massachusetts to Texas.

In the summer of 1843, Andrews was in England for the purposes of raising funds to purchase and emancipate Texas slaves and of enlisting the British government's assistance in the project. Before leaving the United States, Andrews and Lewis Tappan, a wealthy New York abolitionist, had called on Adams, requesting letters of introduction. Adams, explaining that there was no one of prominence in England to whom he felt free to write, declined, but wished them well, with the admonition that the sincerity of the Peel administration in the antislavery cause was not to be trusted. However, Adams encouraged Andrews to make the effort, saying the freedom "of all mankind depended upon the direct, formal, open, and avowed interference of Great Britain to accomplish the abolition of slavery in Texas."[5]

When Andrews attended the world convention of the British and Foreign Anti-slavery Society, he talked with Aberdeen and other British politicians, who listened politely to his plan; but the foreign secretary made no promise of a loan. This would have been impossible for him to do without proper authorization. Additionally, pledging such assistance to a young man who had no official standing would have been highly improbable under any circumstances. Yet, according to Smith, Andrews had assured him that a loan had been promised. Without verifying it, Smith gave this account to Green and to his government in Texas; Smith did not say it came only from Andrews. A few weeks later, after hearing Aberdeen's explanation of the meeting, Smith had to send a retraction to his secretary of state.

The official position of the Republic of Texas, Smith told Aberdeen, was complete opposition to any move to abolish slavery therein, and Andrews, he said, was in no way authorized to speak for the Texas government. While some individuals in Texas might be disposed toward emancipation, they were not numerous. Smith asked if there was any truth to the rumor that Her Majesty's government planned to reimburse or compensate slave owners who freed their slaves.

Aberdeen resorted to his stock answer: the British government wished to see slavery abolished everywhere, including Texas, but it had no intention of interfering improperly in the affairs of that republic. However, he refused to bind his government with a pledge never to consider a loan to enable slaveholders to emancipate their slaves. In diplomacy, one never said "never." He asked Smith to communicate to the Houston administration the position he, Aberdeen, had expressed regarding no improper interference in Texas, "to the exclusion of such as the enthusiastic imaginations of the antislavery conventionists might attribute to him." Smith concluded that the Peel government had no sinister designs on Texas. "British policy in relation to slavery is declared to the world, and the good or ill consequences to Texas are not taken at all into consideration."[6]

Nevertheless, Smith, as a very strong advocate of annexation, was not above spreading propaganda in an effort to frighten the United States into moving on the issue. A month earlier, probably at the instigation of Green, Smith had written directly to Calhoun. Smith expressed his sincere belief that Great Britain's ultimate purpose was to make Texas a refuge for runaway slaves from the South and eventually to turn that republic into "a Negro nation, a sort of Hayti on the continent," under the protection of the British government.[7]

President Sam Houston may have been using similar tactics. Angry about having been rebuffed by the United States and exasperated by Tyler's inaction, Houston told Charles Elliot that if the Peel administration was interested in preventing the United States from acquiring Texas, the best way would be to use its influence to persuade Mexico to recognize Texan independence. In mid June, Houston proclaimed an armistice with Mexico, as a first step, it was hoped, toward opening talks with that country. On 6 July, Anson Jones, Texas' secretary of state, instructed Van Zandt to notify Secretary of State Upshur about Houston's decision to discontinue any further consideration of annexation. British pressure had brought a truce between Mexico and Texas, and Houston preferred to await the development of "events now in progress." Although not for American ears, Jones told Van Zandt that Mexico's recognition of Texas' independence could simplify annexation. The United States, in absorbing Texas, would then not have to be concerned about fomenting a war with Mexico.[8]

The British intervention greatly upset Green and Upshur. They sent urgent dispatches to William S. Murphy, the American chargé in Texas, who reported that Upshur was "fired anew" with determination to bring the annexation issue to a head. The situation became more sensitive when, in the House of Lords, on 18 August, Aberdeen responded to a question about what the British government was doing to stop the sale of slaves from southern plantations in the United States to those in Texas. The matter was raised by Lord Brougham, a Whig who opposed both slavery and the slave trade and who was a political opponent of Aberdeen's. The foreign secretary tried to structure his reply in a manner that would neither offend the antislavery British public nor unduly alarm the United States. He began by announcing the armistice between Mexico and Texas, which had been arranged with the help of Great Britain, and he said he was willing to continue his country's good offices until a firm peace could be established. Further, he reiterated his usual statement: namely, that the entire world knew the position of the British government on the subject of slavery—that it desired to see slavery terminated everywhere eventually. The Aberdeen-Brougham exchange was reported in the *London Morning Chronicle* on the following day.[9]

The general nature of Aberdeen's statements, the American proannexationists insisted, indicated that he had something to hide, he was not revealing all. Britain, they were certain, did intend to interfere in Texas, using humanitarianism as a ruse; but the real reason was not a noble one, and there seemed to be enough truth in their accusations to convince some doubters. Certainly, Britain had no wish to see the United States expand its domain to include the strategically located Lone Star Republic, an area that was capable of raising, with slave labor, cotton and other products to compete with those produced by British colonies. Green consistently argued that the implementation of the British Emancipation Act of 1833 had caused an economic depression in the British West Indies. Free labor was more costly and less efficient than slave labor; therefore, Britain was anxious to encourage abolition elsewhere—in Texas, Cuba, Brazil, and the American South—in order to eliminate the advantage of the slaveholding areas. The continued use of slave labor in the South, Green contended, gave the United States superiority, especially in cotton production; and the British meant to combat this. Through the cultivation of cotton in India and by keeping Texas independent and under British influence, as well as by working for the abolition of slavery in the South, the Peel government planned to create a cotton monopoly. This would cause havoc in the southern states and ruin the northeastern textile industry.[10]

With this information at his command, Upshur increased his efforts to obtain Tyler's approval to pursue a Texas-annexation treaty. Tyler was concerned. "We have intelligence derived unofficially, but yet from a reliable source," he informed Waddy Thompson in Mexico, that Britain's mediation to resolve hostilities between Texas and Mexico was based on "proposed stipulations in the highest degree detrimental to the United States." The "intelligence," of course, had come from Ashbel Smith through Green. Understandably, Britain's diplomacy was conducted with its own self-interest in mind, but Tyler, in spite of referring to Green as a "reliable source," was worried lest the information that Green had given to him was intended only "to awaken a new course of action on the part of this government," that it was "designed simply to make this government take strong and decided grounds."[11]

Thompson's ardor for annexation had cooled. This undoubtedly was why Upshur and Calhoun agreed on the advisability of sending Benjamin Green, Duff Green's son, to Mexico as secretary of the legation. Thompson needed bolstering. Calhoun thought Duff Green himself should also go to Mexico in some official capacity. Upshur replied that he could not employ another person at the legation, but

> this does not prevent me from complying with your request in regard to the Genl Green of whom you write. As the Department does not *need* a bearer of dispatches, it cannot *pay* anything for that service; but it is a very common practice to give citizens whose interests strongly require it the facilities which are afforded by being made the bearers of dispatches by simply entrusting to them a letter or jacket of papers. . . . This is always done in cases which clearly require it. Genl Green's case appears to be of this sort.[12]

Duff Green, who was still in England, did not go to Mexico at this time; but the idea was not abandoned. Already Green was looking beyond

Texas, to the acquisition of California.

By mid September, Tyler still had not given the go-ahead for offering treaty negotiations to Texas. Upshur, restive and anxious, repeatedly approached Van Zandt with almost frantic appeals for the rescinding of Houston's 6 July decision to suspend annexation considerations. Upshur told Van Zandt that he, Upshur, did have Tyler's permission to ascertain the annexation views of members of the Senate and to "prepare the minds of the people." And Upshur was confident that a definite proposition could be forthcoming before Congress convened in December. Upshur urged Van Zandt to send a special messenger to Texas with this information, but Van Zandt did not think a special courier was necessary unless a positive proposal was being offered. This Upshur said he was unable to do at this date.

There was no doubt, Van Zandt told Anson Jones, of Upshur's sincerity, "but whether he will carry out the measures indicated or not, it is impossible to tell. My own opinion is that from the situation of political affairs here, it is hard to know what, or whether any move will be made on any particular question, until you have seen the step taken." He was almost positive that the administration contemplated making an annexation proposal but "that they will do it is at best uncertain." Van Zandt was no neutral observer. He was as anxious as Upshur was for annexation to become a reality. "I have left untried no means," he told Jones, "which I thought calculated to advance or promote this object."

Not until 28 September 1843 did Upshur instruct Everett to contact both Aberdeen and Ashbel Smith in an effort to clarify British designs toward Texas. The president, Upshur said, was reluctant to accept as true the reports of British hostility toward the United States. Upshur, relying heavily on information from Green, then proceeded to give his own opinion to Everett regarding British plans for abolishing slavery in Texas, the United States, Cuba, and Brazil and regarding the dire consequences of these actions, which would eventually result in a race war and the final extermination of the blacks. Everett was directed to find evidence of a British plot that could be used as documentation to accompany a treaty of annexation when it was presented to the Senate.

Without waiting for what he hoped would be Everett's verification of a British conspiracy, Upshur launched a vigorous propaganda campaign against Great Britain, publishing anonymous editorials in the *Madisonian,* with "Designs of the British Government" his constant theme. He also accused John Quincy Adams and the abolitionists of preferring partisan principles to national unity and of weakening the nation with threats of secession if Texas were annexed; and he charged

Adams with hypocrisy, because, as president, Adams had tried to purchase Texas from Mexico.[13]

Although, according to Upshur, Tyler had given him permission to "prepare the minds of the people," the president was not convinced of British knavery. "I presume you have heard from Mr. Upshur on the Texas question," R. M. T. Hunter of Virginia wrote to Calhoun on 10 October. "If so you know the grounds upon which he is disposed to press it. From my conversation with him I inferred that the President was a little doubtful as to the expediency of pressing it."

Six days later, and before receiving a reply from Everett, Upshur approached Van Zandt again, saying he was ready to begin negotiations as soon as the Houston government had given Van Zandt the authority to discuss terms. Van Zandt urged his government to allow him to do so, saying that at no time since annexation had first been considered had there been so many circumstances favorable to ratification by the United States Senate. "The late declarations of Lord Aberdeen in the British Parliament," he was sure, made the Texas question "one of vital importance to the slave holding states." This time, Van Zandt believed the offer was significant enough to send word to Jones by special courier. Claude H. Hall, Upshur's biographer, has said that Tyler did not share Upshur's enthusiasm for "pressing the issue" and that Upshur's "impatience and temper threatened to get the better of his diplomatic good sense."

It is unlikely that Tyler, by 16 October, had given Upshur permission to present Van Zandt with a definite offer to begin treaty talks. Several years later, Tyler recalled having taken this step only after having heard from Everett in November. This seems more probable, because on 26 October, Upshur voiced to Tucker his impatience with and disdain for the president, who continued to insist that the secretary of state pursue consideration of the Oregon boundary in conjunction with Texas annexation, partly to make annexation more palatable to the North and also to give his administration another achievement to its credit.[14]

Upshur informed Beverley Tucker: "I am engaged in settling the Oregon boundary question, imprudently forced upon me prematurely—and in procuring the annexation of Texas to the Union. This last is the great object of my ambition. I do not care to control any measure of policy except this; & I have reason to believe that no person but myself can control it." This, Upshur said, was the only reason he was remaining in the cabinet, the only reason he was allowing himself to be involved "in the odium which awaits this administration." As soon as annexation had been accomplished, he perhaps would want to go to

England or France as minister. Southern men should be in both courts, especially in England, and "why should such a station be refused, merely because an obnoxious President confers it?" The presidency, Upshur reasoned, belonged to the public, not to the man who occupied the position. If an appointment was refused because it was tendered by a particular "functionary," this would imply that the office belonged to the individual.

At Tyler's insistence, Upshur did explore the possibility of talks with Great Britain about Oregon. Everett said Aberdeen was willing to appoint a new minister to Washington, Richard Pakenham, "a conciliatory person" who had the authority to open negotiations for a boundary settlement, possibly along the forty-ninth parallel. But to Upshur, the annexation of Texas was *the* issue of the era: the destiny of the nation depended upon it. Sarcastically, he thought he could make the matter so clear that "even the Yankees" would support it. "They are you know," he told Tucker, "an 'uncommon moral & religious people' & greatly opposed to the sin of slavery since they ceased to carry on the slave trade," but if they could be shown how profitable annexation would be for their commerce and manufacturing, Upshur knew that their greed quickly would overcome their concern for the slaves.[15]

Everett's reply to Upshur's dispatch of 28 September was unavoidably delayed until early November, because of Aberdeen's absence from London and because of the death of Everett's daughter on 21 October. Nevertheless, in the interim, Upshur, very likely without authorization, and Van Zandt, definitely without permission from his government, proceeded with treaty discussions.

When Everett's report did arrive, it was too moderate for Upshur's taste. Everett said Aberdeen had assured him that the British government at no time promoted abolition in Texas or made emancipation a condition for a loan to that republic. The only mention of the issue of slavery in Texas, according to Aberdeen, was made in advising Mexico to recognize Texas' independence, with the hope that abolition would be included in the peace agreement. In seeking information from Ashbel Smith, Everett learned how Smith had been misled by Andrews and how, after his visit with Aberdeen, Smith had modified Andrews's account.

Everett had doubts about the Peel government's enthusiasm for abolition; he reflected that "though all England is now unanimous in the general principle that the whole influence of the Government & Country is to be used against the slave trade and slavery, there are diversities of opinion and feeling as to the degree to which the end is to be promoted either by legislation or diplomacy." There were those who were willing to go to great lengths, he admitted, but they did not belong to the party in power. "It was not, as you are well aware, by this party that emancipation was carried out in the West Indies," he pointedly reminded Upshur. Perhaps the United States had cause to be on guard against British designs, but there did not appear to be any immediate danger from that quarter.

Everett—the Anglophile and friend of Aberdeen—may have been too trusting; on the other hand, Green may have exaggerated the "British conspiracy." Everett preferred to accept Aberdeen's assurances. Upshur placed his reliance on Green's unofficial reports and discounted Everett's more placid accounts as coming from a New England abolitionist who was in sympathy with British policy. Yet, interestingly, Everett was not opposed to annexation. Northern opposition to joining Texas to the United States, he wrote in his diary, was overrated. The fortunes of slavery probably would not be affected by either annexation or nonannexation. There were other more potent forces at work. "Meantime, were it not better that Texas should be attached to the United States?"[16]

In answer to Upshur's 16 October offer to discuss annexation, Sam Houston's government refused Van Zandt permission to proceed. There was now, Jones wrote on 13 December, a good chance that Mexico would recognize Texas' independence; this had been brought about by the good offices of Britain and France. This intervention, Jones explained, had been gratuitously and unconditionally given, and although Texas was free to take any course it wished, for the present it would be impolitic to relinquish the possibility of an agreement with Mexico for the uncertain chance of annexation to the United States. If Texas were to agree to a treaty, only to have it rejected by the Senate, Texas would be in an untenable position. By signing the treaty, it would have foregone the diplomatic support of Britain and France; and if the Senate were to fail to ratify the treaty, the United States very likely would return to its previous attitude of apathy and indifference toward Texas, leaving that republic without a friend and leaving its problems with Mexico unresolved.

Houston and Jones did not completely close the door. Van Zandt was instructed to inform Upshur that whenever the Congress or the Senate of the United States, by a resolution, would authorize the president to propose a treaty of annexation, the proposition would be submitted immediately to the representatives of the people of Texas and would promptly be responded to by the Houston administration.

If Houston and Jones conspired to frighten the Tyler administration into action, they were operating with finesse. According to Jesse S.

Reeves, "Houston's and Jones's ruse of scaring the United States was entirely successful." Reeves might have added the names of Ashbel Smith, Duff Green in London, and Van Zandt in Washington, all of whom were involved in conjuring up alarming rumors.[17]

Weeks before Jones's letter of 13 December was received or even before it was written, Upshur and Van Zandt had secretly begun to draft a treaty. "Mr. Upshur informs me—in the strictest confidence, however, except to you," wrote Virgil Maxcy, a Baltimore supporter, to Calhoun, "that the terms of a treaty between him and the Texas minister have already been agreed on and written out, and the latter only waits for instructions from President Houston which are expected in two to three weeks." If Houston should refuse to allow Van Zandt to proceed with the negotiations, Maxcy continued, Upshur thought Van Zandt, who was convinced of the almost unanimous desire of the people of Texas, could possibly be induced to sign the treaty without instructions from his government. Van Zandt could then return to Texas and "throw himself on the protection of the people." Maxcy contended that Tyler was now ready to submit the treaty to the Senate, and if Van Zandt did not have the firmness to sign it, Tyler planned to find some other mode of bringing the matter before Congress. Upshur believed annexation was the only issue that had enough force to rally the South to the support of a southern states'-rights candidate and to weaken Clay and Van Buren so much that the election would devolve upon the House of Representatives, "where the southern states would not dare to vote for Mr. V. B. and C. [Clay]."

Maxcy told Calhoun that while Tyler still hoped he would be the southern candidate, "Upshur considers you as the only one that can be taken up." After the president's annual message to Congress, Upshur wanted Calhoun to come out strongly with his views on Texas. According to the plan, Maxcy would write a letter to Calhoun, making inquiries about his stand on annexation; Calhoun would answer; and the letters would be published.

By contrast, no one apparently encouraged Tyler to present his views. In his annual message, the president made no direct reference to annexation. The omission surprised friend and foe alike and puzzled the press. On 30 November, Webster had written to Everett: "We anticipate a recommendation from the President in his forthcoming message, of the acquisition of Texas. Such was his purpose a week ago. Yesterday, it was rumored here, that he began to doubt."[18]

Perhaps because of the secret ongoing treaty talks between Upshur and Van Zandt, Tyler, if he knew about them, decided that it was better not to make an official statement. Andrew Jackson thought the president prudent and wise to keep silent until a signed treaty had been sent to the Senate. "Any other course would bring down upon him the abuse of J. Q. Adams and associates, and perhaps injure the negotiation." Or it could have been that Tyler's advisors—those who, while professing friendship for him, were supporting Calhoun—could have convinced him of the expediency of excluding any mention of annexation, while they were encouraging Calhoun to come out as its champion. The political conspiracy was both real and well organized. If Calhoun expected to take the nomination away from Van Buren at the Democratic National Convention, Upshur, Green, Gilmer, Tucker, and others of like mind saw the urgency of placing the South Carolinian at the forefront of the Texas movement.

Early in the fall of 1843, even Henry Wise joined the Calhoun camp. In September a letter from Wise was read at a dinner in honor of R. M. T. Hunter, which was attended by members of Virginia's Calhoun central committee. In his communication, Wise mentioned secret negotiations that, it was expected, would lead to a treaty of annexation and revealed that a letter by Jackson urging annexation, written a year earlier, would soon be published in an effort to influence public opinion.[19]

Calhoun, when informed of Wise's action, was grateful. He wanted more Virginians on his side. "It is important to keep Virginia right," he advised Gilmer during the summer. By September, Calhoun told Hunter that he was pleased "to hear that Gilmer is right. It is important that Wise should go with us. His letter to your dinner was kind. I read the proceedings at the dinner with interest."

In December, Hunter confirmed and added to Wise's disclosures. From a *"source entirely reliable,"* Hunter had learned that an annexation treaty would be sent to the Senate within the next few months. "Nothing but Houston's refusal can prevent it (as I am informed) and it is supposed that he *dare* not *refuse.*" Hunter said that Van Zandt was "anxious for the treaty and will probably be easy to satisfy that there is a chance for its ratification." Not more than two men in the Congress knew about the "real state of the case"; therefore, Calhoun should be guarded in writing to his friends about it.

In the light of future developments, perhaps the most revealing statement and question in Hunter's letter to Calhoun were: "It will be something if we can really make an issue with the antislavery feeling and arouse the public mind to its importance. Can this be done?" If slavery could be made the issue, Hunter foresaw many benefits for Calhoun. It would force him "again upon the theatre of public action let the question terminate as it might. . . . Could the South look to any other man to conduct it through such a crisis?"

Six days earlier, Gilmer likewise sent word of the treaty to Calhoun. "I will say to you that negotiations have been commenced, the object of which is to annex Texas to the Union." Gilmer wanted Calhoun to speak out on the topic, but unlike Hunter, Gilmer believed annexation should be characterized as "a great American question," not as a local or sectional issue. It should have "a national aspect."[20]

Calhoun's backers used other tactics to advance his cause. They maneuvered Tyler into making political appointments that would be advantageous to Calhoun. "Out of political innocence," Charles Sellers has noted, Tyler "turned federal patronage over to as mercenary a band as has ever been assembled in the history of American politics."[21] With Upshur, Henshaw, Porter, and Wickliffe in cabinet positions that allowed them to make innumerable political appointments, Calhoun's managers dispensed offices with a free hand. Despite all these efforts, Calhoun did not receive the necessary support from state Democratic conventions. In setting the date for the national convention, Calhoun's supporters did win out over those of Van Buren, who wanted an early meeting, in December 1843, while the followers of Calhoun pushed for late spring of 1844. However, in the crucial matter of how delegates were to be selected, the Van Buren machine held firm, favoring the selection of delegates by state conventions, with instructions to cast their votes as a unit. Calhoun wanted to have the delegates limited to the number of electors to which each state was entitled, chosen by districts within the states and allowed to cast their votes individually at the national convention.

Until early fall, 1843, the Calhoun faction was optimistic, but the failure of a number of state conventions to declare for him, plus the bitter disappointment of seeing control of the organization of the House of Representatives taken over by the Van Buren forces when the Twenty-eighth Congress convened in December, caused Calhoun to conclude that he should not allow his name to go before the Democratic National Convention in May. This did not mean that he had given up all hope. There remained the remote possibility of running as an independent candidate, not perhaps with a chance of victory, but to use whatever political influence he might have for the benefit of the South.

Rumors of Tyler's withdrawal from the presidential contest circulated. Van Zandt reported this to his government. "Mr. Tyler, having withdrawn from the contest for the Presidency the question [of annexation] neither is nor will be considered in reference to him." Van Zandt did not reveal the source of his information. Tyler had not withdrawn. Instead, he was stubbornly clinging to the frail hope that somehow the Democratic party might turn to him. If this did not happen, he, like

Calhoun, had a vision of being sponsored by some nebulous third party. Yet, he had no organization and no prominent followers whose endorsements might have made some slight difference. Even his "friends" were against him. In January 1844, much to Tyler's dismay, William C. Rives, who had been Tyler's most staunch supporter, often his only one in the Senate, made a public declaration in favor of Clay. This was a most hurtful blow.[22]

While striving for the Democratic nomination, Tyler chose not to make war on Van Buren or on any other aspirant. He wanted to maintain a "lofty attitude." "It is legitimate," he told George Roberts, editor of the Boston Times, "to argue that I am more available than Mr. V. B. or Mr. C. [Calhoun] and to prove, what the sequel will demonstrate, that the one you advocate [Tyler] is the only person the Democrats can elect, to compare the present condition of things with what it was in 1840 and to exhibit the benefits already secured to the country and those in prospective." The administration, he insisted, should be placed above the contests of personal factions. To an unknown correspondent he said much the same thing: hold off on attacking Van Buren; let the Van Buren and Calhoun factions "fight it out"; direct your fire at Clay, who "broke up the Whig party for his own selfish ends."[23]

Upshur was positive that the Texas issue would focus the presidential spotlight on Calhoun. To engender more interest in annexation, Upshur let it be known that the United States, in acquiring Texas, would assume all debts owed by that republic. Texas bonds and treasury notes, which had fallen to below ten cents on the dollar, would be funded at par. Gen. Thomas J. Green, a former land commissioner of Texas, quoted Upshur as having said this was "a chance for a magnificent speculation." "Mr. Upshur used these words to me," Green asserted. Robert Johnson, a Galveston agent for Thomas Gilmer, was pleased to be able to purchase, for his client, notes at a few cents on the dollar.

Nicholas Biddle's interest was aroused by possibilities of economic gain. He owned substantial tracts of land in Texas. With annexation, their value was certain to increase; therefore, he was most solicitous in giving Tyler advice. The glory of Jefferson's administration, Biddle reminded the president, had been the purchase of Louisiana; Madison's great achievement had been the War of 1812; Monroe's pride had been the acquisition of Florida. Reserved for another chief executive was the brilliant accomplishment of enlarging the empire by the annexation of Texas. Biddle's friend Daniel Webster would not have appreciated this letter.[24]

With the coming of the new year, prospects for annexation grew brighter. Upshur interpreted the Senate's confirmation of his appointment as secretary of state as an indication of its willingness to ratify an annexation treaty. Surely, knowing his strong position on the matter, the senators would have seized the opportunity to get rid of him had they been opposed to annexation; of this he was convinced. Nelson's appointment also was accepted, but those of Henshaw and Porter, ad interim secretaries of the Navy and the War departments, were rejected, along with several lesser "vacation" appointees, all of whom lacked the necessary qualifications for their offices.

Gilmer replaced Henshaw as head of the Navy Department. Tyler still looked upon Gilmer as a trusted friend. Upshur considered Gilmer an excellent choice. William Wilkins, another Pennsylvania Democrat, was named to head the War Department. His qualifications far exceeded those of Porter. During the 1830s, Wilkins had served in the United States Senate and as minister to Russia, and when appointed to Tyler's cabinet, he was a member of the House of Representatives. An ardent exponent of expansion and annexation, he was pledged to speak for that cause in Pennsylvania and other northern states. Other members of the cabinet's Texas contingent (Upshur, Gilmer, and Wickliffe) were from the South. Wickliffe, it was said, would "do right" by Calhoun in placing proven adherents in post offices throughout the land. There was no doubt where Gilmer and Upshur stood.[25]

Upshur told W. S. Murphy, the United States chargé d'affaires in Texas, that by mid January 1844, more than two-thirds of the Senate would be willing to ratify an annexation treaty. Upshur gave the same information to Van Zandt, promising him, as soon as the treaty was signed, that a large United States naval force would be assembled in the Gulf of Mexico and along the coast of Texas, as well as military protection along its borders, to guard against trouble from Mexico. Upshur's promise of military aid was not given in writing, however. He was aware of the delicacy of assuring Texas of such support without congressional approval.

Before the Texas government had received Van Zandt's letter containing this information, Houston had decided to grant permission to move ahead with the negotiations, because Mexico had given no indication that it would recognize Texas' independence. Unaware that most aspects of a treaty already had been agreed upon by Upshur and Van Zandt, Houston appointed Gen. James Pinckney Henderson as special agent to assist in the proceedings.

The future looked bright for Upshur. Not only had Texas agreed to consider a treaty, but Great Britain, at the behest of Everett, had decided to appoint a new minister to the United States, Richard Pakenham, who had instructions to explore acceptable grounds for settling the Oregon boundary. Pakenham arrived in Washington on 12 February 1844, and on 24 February, he arranged his first conference with Upshur. Henderson's departure from Texas, unfortunately, did not move with such rapidity, but Upshur and Van Zandt nevertheless proceeded with the treaty. By the evening of 27 February, all that was lacking was Henderson's perusal and the necessary signatures. Upshur looked forward to presenting the treaty to the Senate, possibly in a package with an Oregon settlement.[26]

13

"MR. TYLER'S
ABOMINABLE TREATY"

As secretary of the navy, Abel Parker Upshur had a favorite project: the building of the world's most up-to-date iron warship—a steam frigate, driven by a screw propeller instead of a paddle wheel. Capt. Robert Stockton, who was in charge of the undertaking, kept the secretary informed about every phase of the procedure, from the designing of the engines and the propeller by the Sweden-born engineer John Ericsson to the ship's performance during trial runs. No bit of information was too insignificant for Upshur's attention.

Named the USS *Princeton* in honor of Stockton's hometown, the ship was replete with Ericsson's innovations, including twenty-four pivoting 42-pound carronades and two giant Paixhans-type guns, one at the bow, the "Peacemaker," and the other, the "Oregon," at the stern, each of which was capable of being turned from side to side. The Oregon was equipped with three iron bands around the breach, a precaution against bursting. The Peacemaker, constructed according to Stockton's specifications, was the largest gun ever forged from wrought iron. It had a 15-foot barrel and supposedly was able to withstand an explosion of 50 pounds or more of powder. When tested at the Staten Island proving grounds, each gun could hurl 212-pound projectiles more than three miles, shattering targets of iron and wood that were stronger than the hulls of the most stalwart frigates. The *Princeton* was the pride of the navy, and Stockton, who was anxious to display this paragon of ships, brought her up the Potomac River in mid February 1844.[1]

For several days, governmental parties were taken on short cruises, during which the vessel's remarkable attributes were revealed, including the firing power of the guns. But the best was yet to come: on the night of 27 February, a public reception was held in the East Room of the White House. The chief topic of conversation was the gala excursion scheduled for the following day. Special invitations had gone out to several hundred people, important personages in the capital: the president, his cabinet members and their wives, members of Congress, ranking officers of the army and the navy, the diplomatic corps, and the cream of Washington society, including the inimitable Dolley Madison. David Gardiner of East Hampton, New York, along with his two daughters, Margaret and Julia, were also included. Gardiner, an attorney who had served in the New York legislature, was a wealthy gentleman of leisure who enjoyed taking his wife and daughters to Europe and to Washington to view the political scene. During the winter of 1843, young Julia Gardiner had attracted the attention of the recently widowed president, and for months he courted her assiduously, proposing marriage as early as February of that year. Julia, however, had not yet agreed.[2]

The large and excited group boarded the *Princeton* on the morning of 28 February. In an area below deck, which had been transformed into a salon, refreshments were served. The atmosphere was festive. Colorful flags flew from every rope and yard, and numerous barges surrounded the ship, in readiness to escort her down river.

Upshur was proud of his part in the creation of the *Princeton*, and Thomas Gilmer, who had been secretary of the navy for a little less than two weeks, was pleased to see what a fine vessel he had under his charge. He visited every part of the ship, asking questions about its structure and functions. Only twelve days earlier he had informed a friend, "Well! I am Sec. of Navy!! for better or for worse—God only knows how it will turn out." Undoubtedly looking ahead to possible war with Mexico, he thought the Navy Department "*may* become one of very great responsibility in a short time."[3]

At one o'clock the *Princeton* weighed anchor and proceeded in the direction of Mount Vernon. To the delight of the spectators, the Peacemaker was fired twice, thundering over the waters of the Potomac. Later in the afternoon the guests adjourned to the salon to partake of a lavish meal, enlivened by numerous champagne toasts. As the ship approached a long and vacant stretch of the river, there were requests to have one of the guns fired again. Stockton agreed and many went on deck to observe. Tyler was detained below.

As the curious crowded forward, the Peacemaker was readied. Senator Thomas Hart Benton, standing with Upshur and Gilmer to the left of the gun, was told he would have a better view from the right side, so he moved, but his companions remained on the left. There was a short demonstration to show "the ease and precision" with which the Peacemaker's direction could be changed, then the gun was pointed down river. Benton opened his mouth to lessen the shock of the detonation. He watched "the hammer pulled back—heard a tap—saw a flash" and fell unconscious to the deck. The breech had split wide open. The explosion had blown inward. Fragments of iron were hurled with great force into the assembled onlookers. Clouds of black smoke enveloped the ship. Twenty feet of the hull were torn away. There were screams, frantic calls for the physicians who were on board, and confusion everywhere.

When Benton regained consciousness, he saw "two seamen, blood oozing from their ears and nostrils, rising and reeling," and "Commodore Stockton, hat gone and face blackened, standing bolt upright staring fixedly upon the shattered gun." Debris and carnage littered the deck. The bodies of Upshur, Gilmer, Virgil Maxcy, Commodore Beverley Kennon, Tyler's servant Henry, two seamen, and David Gardiner were lying near the wreckage of the guns. The survivors were transferred to other vessels and were taken ashore, but Tyler, Secretary of War William Wilkins, and a few others remained on board until the dead had been removed. On Friday, 1 March, thousands of Washingtonians filed past the caskets of the victims as they lay in state in the East Room of the White House. Funeral services were conducted there on the following day.[4]

Stunned by the tragedy, Tyler was nevertheless forced to turn immediately to the restructuring of his cabinet. At this critical juncture in the annexation procedures, he thought it was essential to name a secretary of state who would be both sympathetic to the cause and able to conduct affairs in an efficient manner. In the meantime, he asked Attorney General Nelson to assume the duties of that office. Henry Wise believed it was mandatory to place the State Department in "safe Southern hands," and to him, the only conceivable choice was John C. Calhoun, "the one man left who was necessary above all others to the South in settling and obtaining the annexation of Texas." Wise might have added that Calhoun also had been fully briefed on the treaty stipulations that Upshur and Van Zandt agreed upon.

Considerable controversy surrounds Tyler's appointment of Calhoun. Wise claimed responsibility for having maneuvered Tyler into a position in which he had no choice but to offer the cabinet post to the South Carolinian. Before breakfast on the morning of 29 February, according to Wise's account, he contacted Senator George McDuffie of South Carolina and asked him if he thought Calhoun could be prevailed upon to accept the State Department post. Wise told McDuffie to write to Calhoun immediately, telling Calhoun that his name would probably be sent at once to the Senate. Assuming that the offer had come from the president, McDuffie complied. Wise then went to the White House and informed Tyler, who angrily remonstrated, saying Calhoun was not his choice. After regaining his composure, however, Tyler realized that he had been presented with a *fait accompli,* so to avoid embarrassing Calhoun, McDuffie, and Wise, he reluctantly agreed to make the appointment.

A number of historians have doubted Wise's story; several have stated that Tyler, on two previous occasions, had offered the State Department to Calhoun, who had declined. Therefore, they have said, the president, who obviously wanted Calhoun in the cabinet, would not have objected to Wise's interference. There appears, however, to be no substantiation for the alleged earlier offers. Duff Green, who possibly was even more unreliable than Wise, was the source of several of the stories, at least one of which Calhoun himself denied. "There was no foundation for the rumor of my going into Mr. Tyler's cabinet," he informed Green on 31 August 1842.[5]

Frederick Merk, in "A Safety Valve Thesis and Texan Annexation"—a paper that was first read at the annual dinner of the Massachusetts Historical Society in 1960, was published in the *Mississippi Valley Historical Review* in 1962, and was republished in *Fruits of Propaganda in the Tyler Administration,* 1971—has stated that Calhoun was forced on Tyler by Wise. However, in *Slavery and the Annexation of Texas,* which was published in 1972, Merk accepted Charles M. Wiltse's repudiation of Wise's story. Wiltse bases his conclusion largely on Duff Green's testimony. Richard K. Crallé, Calhoun's friend who edited *The Works of John C. Calhoun,* believed Tyler had offered the State Department to Calhoun "some years previously," but Crallé provided no specifics. James Gordon Bennett, in the *New York Herald* of 9 March 1844, said he had "every reason to believe" that Tyler had wanted Calhoun as secretary of state at the time of Webster's retirement. Duff Green, in a letter to Calhoun dated 29 September 1843, indicated that the office was open to Calhoun any time he wanted it; but evidence for this is lacking.

Tyler's biographer Robert Seager II has said: "On two earlier instances he [Tyler] had blocked movements seeking to elevate Calhoun to the cabinet." Seager has contended that Calhoun was the last person Tyler wanted in the cabinet. Oliver Chitwood, who is usually skeptical of Wise's reliability, states "It was to the officious meddling of Henry A. Wise that Calhoun owed his appointment." Chitwood quotes John Tyler, Jr., as having said his father "never entirely forgave Wise for his presumptuous blunder." However, Robert Barnwell Rhett, in a letter dated 25 October 1854, informed Richard Crallé, who was writing a life of Calhoun, that when Tyler had first quarreled with the Whigs, he had offered Calhoun the State Department, "with a carte-blanche as to the Cabinet."[6]

Quite likely, Calhoun's name had surfaced every time there had been a change or a rumor of a change in the State Department. Many other names also were speculated upon, and whether or not Calhoun actually was offered the position on these occasions is open to question. Tyler was not an admirer of Calhoun's. During the 1830s, when Tyler and Tazewell had represented Virginia in the United States Senate, they were wary of Calhoun's extremism and his ambition. Neither Tyler nor Tazewell had been followers of the South Carolinian, and when Virginia's governor, John Floyd, had wanted to launch a "Calhoun for President" movement in 1832, they had refused to be a party to the plan and had deliberately absented themselves from all Richmond festivities in Calhoun's honor. The Virginia senators had disagreed with Calhoun, too, on the doctrine of nullification, believing it to be clearly unconstitutional and unworkable.[7]

Perhaps the most significant indication of Tyler's probable reluctance to name Calhoun secretary of state in 1844 was the president's deep desire to have annexation considered a national issue, not as acquisition of territory solely in the interest of the South. Tyler, who was as concerned as Calhoun was about the deteriorating position of the South in the Union, believed this was not the time to focus on the problem. Annexation required the support of the entire nation. Calhoun tended to emphasize the sectional and slavery aspect; Tyler tried to minimize it, while stressing the economic and strategic values.

Unlike Calhoun, Tyler did not advance the positive-good theory of slavery, and he never, at least publicly, attempted to justify the peculiar institution. Nonetheless, even though he regarded it as an evil that had been inflicted upon the South, he made no effort to terminate the practice or to free any of his own slaves. He wished sincerely, as Robert Seager has noted, "that slavery would just go away somehow, quietly and without fuss," but he brooked no outside interference with the South's labor system. Rumors of British plans to emancipate Texas slaves disturbed him, and he looked upon the activities of northern abolitionists with horror, believing that their propaganda could encourage a terrible servile insurrection. Regardless, he did not want protection of slavery to be a focal point in arguments over annexation. If it was, ratification would fail.

In spite of these reservations and possibly against his better judgment, Tyler sent Calhoun's nomination to the Senate. Graciously informing Calhoun of the appointment, Tyler clearly let him know that his acceptance would mean an end to his, Calhoun's, current presidential aspirations. "While your name was before the Country, as a prominent candidate for the Presidency, I could not have urged this request without committing alike an offense to yourself and many others," but since Calhoun's friends had withdrawn his name from the race, it was possible to offer him the post.

On the day before Calhoun's nomination was sent to the Senate, Tyler met with the Texas chargé d'affaires, Isaac Van Zandt, to press for quick action on the treaty. Van Zandt informed Anson Jones, secretary of state for the Republic of Texas, "The President stated he was very desirous to have the treaty concluded at once and by Mr. Nelson the Attorney General who is Secretary of State ad interim, that he preferred he [Nelson] should do it instead of the gentleman [Calhoun] to whom he intended to offer the permanent appointment." Tyler wanted Nelson and Van Zandt to have everything ready for Henderson's signature the moment Henderson arrived in Washington, which Tyler hoped would be very soon. To Tyler's disappointment, however, the special envoy did not appear until the end of March, almost at the same time as Calhoun took up his duties in the State Department.[8]

In the weeks between the Senate's confirmation of Calhoun's appointment and his appearance in the capital, it was obvious that the secret negotiations between Upshur and Van Zandt were no longer secret. Word of the "already negotiated" treaty had passed from one member of Congress to another. Webster became aware that something was afoot several weeks before the *Princeton* disaster. While in Washington attending to cases before the Supreme Court, Webster had a conversation with Upshur, who, in expressing his disgust with Tyler, said "he [Upshur] would not continue in office a fortnight if he had not a particular object to accomplish." Upshur did not elaborate on what the "particular object" might be, but Webster felt "the chill of Texas" go through him. A few days of probing confirmed Webster's fears. Negotiations were under way. Now, in March, fearing that the stealthily designed treaty was about to be presented to the Senate, Webster renewed his stand against annexation. At Webster's urging, Robert C. Winthrop of Massachusetts introduced antiannexation resolutions in the House. Adams, too, offered a resolution calling upon Tyler to furnish information as to whether or not he had instituted or engaged in a negotiation for the annexation of Texas. In his diary, Adams railed against "slave-envenomed motives" and "the great slave-power conspiracy," and his son, Charles Francis Adams, took up the antiannexation cause in their home state. The Massachusetts and New York legislatures passed resolutions against annexation. Within the Whig party there were fears that there would be an irreparable split between the Conscience Whigs of the Northeast and the Cotton Whigs of the South. In New England there was distress among those who counted on a continued relationship between their textile industry and the cotton producers in the deep South. The choice between a moral commitment to abolition and the desire for economic gain was difficult.[9]

Throughout the nation—in the press, in town meetings, in legislative assemblies, on street corners, in correspondence, and in private conversations—the issue of annexation was argued. The strain on the national structure of both of the major political parties increased daily. Alexander H. Stephens, at this time a loyal Georgia Whig, saw the annexation project as "a miserable humbug got up as a ruse to distract the Whig party at the South." Some southern Democrats, he believed, could be using it to bring about the dissolution of the Union.[10] But Texas had great appeal to many inhabitants of the lower South, who exerted tremendous pressure on southern Whig representatives in Congress.

Within the nation there were wide divisions of opinion. There were expansionists, who were eager to extend the boundaries of the United States as far as possible, even if this meant the addition of more slave territory. That was of secondary importance, at best, in fulfilling the country's destiny of acquiring more and more land. The antislavery faction very vocally opposed annexation. It would be better, they said, to see the Union dissolve than to increase the strength of the proslavery element. There were those who wanted Texas but dreaded the consequences: namely, a possible war with Mexico and perhaps even with Britain and France, the splitting of the political parties, or the breakup of the Union.

It was to this last group—the hesitants, mainly northern Democrats—that Robert J. Walker addressed his arguments. Walker was a native of Pennsylvania who, in his mid twenties, had migrated to Mississippi, where he had become a slave-owning planter and a United States senator. Slavery, he held, would disappear in due time, because it was an unprofitable labor system. Therefore, it was unreasonable and impractical to allow a doomed institution to interfere with the expansion and growth, in power and wealth, of the United States.

In a lengthy letter written in late January 1844 and published in early February, Walker advocated the annexation of Texas and all of Oregon. The "something for each section" premise included new markets for manufactured goods for the Northeast and, for the Anglophobes, the pleasure of thwarting British ambitions. If Texas were allowed to become a British dependency, the Gulf of Mexico would be under British control. From Canada, Texas, Oregon, the gulf and the oceans, the presence of the British Empire would menace the United States. Considerations of this danger should override any anxieties about the extension of slavery, particularly because slavery was a self-destructing, inefficient, careless, and ignorant labor system, employed in growing crops that were ruining the soil of the South.

Walker maintained that clinging too long to an unprofitable system had brought economic catastrophe to many areas. This was evident in the upper South. With annexation, planters of that area happily could rid themselves of their burden by selling their slaves to developers of the "rich soil of Texas." The movement would be gradual, but within twenty years, Walker predicted, Delaware and Maryland would have no slaves. This would occur in all the border states and, eventually, throughout the entire South. As soon as Texas lands had become exhausted, as they inevitably would, planters there would be forced to liberate their slaves. The free blacks would then move southward, into Mexico and into Central and South America, where they would find "a blessed haven of refuge" among other "dark-skinned" people. Without turmoil, slavery would disappear from the United States. Moreover, the dreaded racial problem, which many anticipated in the wake of emancipation, automatically would be eliminated. The acquisition of Texas would have provided a safety valve for the preservation of the nation.

Conversely, if annexation should fail, the British would dominate Texas and insist on the emancipation of slaves there. In the United States, when southern lands were depleted and therefore masters had no choice but to liberate their "people," where would the freed blacks go? They would flock to the cities of the North, causing problems of staggering proportions. Instead of finding a safe haven, they would be subjected to exploitation and discrimination, and they would become an onerous problem for the North.

Walker played on northern racial fears and prejudices, as well as on northern antislavery feelings. But the abolitionists rejected a thesis that would postpone emancipation until a vague future period, and some of them objected to Walker's portrayal of the Negro as an inferior being, incapable of succeeding in a free society. Southerners of the positive-good persuasion also took issue with Walker. To them, slavery was the correct and natural labor system. The idea that it would self-destruct was preposterous.

Because Walker's letter was ignored by many newspapers, he had it printed in pamphlet form. Thousands of copies were sent throughout the country, and by March the letter was causing heated discussions, focused largely on the slavery issue. What part Tyler had in promoting Walker's letter is not known. Frederick Merk has contended that Tyler appealed to Walker for help in influencing northern public opinion in favor of annexation. This might have been true, because with the defection of Rives, Walker had become the administration's defender in the Senate. His uncle, William Wilkins, was Tyler's secretary of war.[11]

However, available evidence indicates that Tyler wanted to use a simple "benefit to the nation" theme in annexation propaganda—one that would stress the commercial and strategic importance of Texas. He believed any mention of the slavery issue, no matter how it was presented, would inflame emotions and destroy the possibility of ratifying the treaty. It was better, he thought, to concentrate on expansion as a bold, positive, and optimistic manifestation of the nation's destiny. This would arouse the pride of the people. "So far as it can be determined," Robert Seager has stated, "Tyler never endorsed Mississippi Senator Robert Walker's comforting 'safety valve' theory." Walker himself denied having had any influence on Tyler. The president, Walker said, listened to his suggestions, but was "no captive."

For leaders of the Democratic party and the Whig party, the entire subject of annexation, not just the slavery issue, caused grave concern. In Richmond, Virginia, Thomas Ritchie, who was being inundated by letters in favor of acquiring Texas, worried about Van Buren's reaction. "Unless there is great imprudence or folly," one writer warned, "Van Buren will be reelected, but if he goes against Texas (which I deem impossible) all is gone." Ritchie agreed; he hoped that in time, Van Buren also would be convinced of this. Ritchie wanted to be loyal to Van Buren, but the pressure from Virginia Democrats was strong. They wanted Ritchie's *Enquirer* to announce its support for the Texas cause. Ritchie sent the above warning on to Silas Wright, New York's leading Democrat and Van Buren's friend. Two days later, Ritchie's paper published the year-old Jackson letter that advocated annexation in the most cogent terms.[12]

Clay, who was on an extensive tour of the South, reported to Senator Crittenden that there was "no great anxiety for the annexation here at the South as you might have imagined." Clay said he would reserve for his arrival in Washington, sometime in April, the question of whether or not he would make a statement on the matter. Most Whigs, especially those from the southern states, thought he should tread softly; they did not want him to make any comment on Texas, at least not for the present.

In Washington, few other topics received much attention. "Full half the time there is no quorum in the House," Adams complained. The only time the Senate was bestirred was when Tyler sent a nomination for its approval. That of John Y. Mason, a Virginia Democrat, as secretary of the navy, met with no opposition. For a brief time there was some confusion over the appointment. Initially, Mason refused the position, so the offer was extended to James K. Polk, a Tennessee Democrat. Polk, who believed he was in line for the vice-presidential spot on the Democratic ticket, was not interested, but before his refusal had been received in Washington, Mason had changed his mind and accepted the post. An embarrassed Tyler had to ask an intermediary to notify Polk that the offer to him had to be withdrawn.[13]

The naming of Mason and Calhoun did not change the party structure of the cabinet. Both Upshur and Gilmer had severed their affiliations with the Whig party. Only two northerners remained as department heads—Secretary of the Treasury John C. Spencer, a New York Whig; and Secretary of War William Wilkins, a Pennsylvania Democrat. Spencer was no longer happy as part of Tyler's administration, dominated as it was by southern Democrats. Additionally, he had never forgiven the president for having refused to set aside the navy court's acquittal of Captain Mackenzie and to order another trial.

Tyler tried to find a different place for the discontented Spencer. When Justice Smith Thompson of the Supreme Court died, the president, in January 1844, after having considered, for obvious political reasons, both Van Buren and Silas Wright, appointed Spencer. Smith Thompson was from New York, and according to custom, his replacement should be from the same state. Before joining the cabinet, Spencer had had an outstanding reputation as a New York attorney. There was nothing wrong with his qualifications, but because he had accepted a cabinet post after the Whigs had renounced Tyler in the fall of 1841, Clay directed that Spencer, along with several other nominees for various positions, be rejected because they were not "true or faithful or honest" Whigs. Political considerations, rather than qualifications, were made "a test for Judicial preferment." Certainly this was true in Spencer's case. The Clay Whigs considered Spencer a traitor to their cause; they were determined not to have him on the Court. In any event, they believed the appointment should be made by the next administration, which, they were certain, would be Clay's.

Before Tyler could fill Thompson's place, another justice died—Henry Baldwin of Pennsylvania. James Buchanan was offered the seat, but declined; and Tyler had no success in selecting someone who was acceptable to the Senate. Not until more than a year later did the senators approve the appointment of Samuel Nelson, chief justice of the New York Supreme Court, whose credentials were impeccable, to replace Thompson. The Baldwin position was left for the next administration to fill. Out of six nominations to the Supreme Court, all during the last months of the Tyler presidency, only one was accepted; this gave Tyler the dubious distinction of having more of his appointees to the highest court in the land rejected than any other president, before or after.[14]

The Senate also refused to confirm the appointment of George Proffit as minister to Brazil, even though he had served in that capacity since June 1843. Interestingly, when Tyler then nominated Henry Wise, the Senate approved. Whig senators, who three times had rejected Wise's appointment to the legation in France, seemed more than willing to send him out of the country if he was assigned to an inferior station; but still they voted for him with repugnance. As minister to France, Tyler named Senator William D. King, an Alabama Democrat. Fearing the hostility of France and Britain when the Texas treaty was made known, Tyler wanted to have a strong proponent of annexation representing the United States in France. King departed immediately and arrived at his new post in June 1844. As Upshur had urged, a southerner was now ensconced in Paris.

This was considered important, because the Texas question involved more than controversies within the United States. International diplomacy and the nagging possibility of war with countries that were considerably stronger than Mexico called for careful handling. Calhoun realized this as he assumed his duties on 1 April 1844; he at once moved forward with annexation, conferring with Henderson and Van Zandt about the treaty draft that Upshur had left on his desk on the evening of 27 February. They found no reason to make any basic changes. Texas, according to the agreement, was to enter the Union as a territory and then would be able to apply for statehood, as one state or several, under the stipulations of the United States Constitution. The public domain of Texas was to be transferred to the federal government, which, in turn, would assume Texas' public debt. No territorial boundaries were specified, and slavery was not mentioned. The boundary matter was left to future negotiations, and it was assumed that the issue of slavery in Texas was covered by the clause in the treaty that secured general property rights to the citizens of Texas. Van Zandt and Henderson noted that, under the Constitution, slaves were recognized as a species of property.[15]

A major concern of the Texas government was protection against possible hostile action on the part of Mexico and what the United States intended to do about it. There was some confusion. Upshur had promised military aid after the signing of the treaty, but in mid February, William Murphy, in his eagerness to ensure Houston's continued approbation of annexation, went beyond Upshur's declaration and, in writing, promised assistance prior to the signing. He did not stop with promises; instead, he took upon himself the ordering of a naval vessel, the United States schooner *Flirt*, to proceed to Vera Cruz and discern whether or not Mexico was preparing for an invasion of Texas. The captain of the *Flirt* also was to alert other United States naval vessels in the area and request them to sail between Vera Cruz and Galveston, keeping an eye out for Mexican military activity.

Before Murphy's letter informing Upshur of the steps taken reached Washington, the *Princeton* explosion had occurred. Tyler, dismayed by Murphy's audacity, ordered Acting Secretary of State John Nelson to reprimand the chargé. The president "regrets to perceive, in the pledges given by you," Nelson wrote, "that you have suffered your zeal to carry you beyond the line of your instructions, and to commit the President to measures for which he has no constitutional authority." As a "measure of prudent precaution," however, naval and military forces could be concentrated in the Gulf of Mexico and on the southern borders of the United States, but the president could not permit the government of Texas or Murphy to "labor under the misapprehension that he [Tyler] has the power to employ them at the period indicated by your stipulation."[16]

Many Americans, both in and out of government, expressed fears that annexation would precipitate a war with Mexico and possibly with England and France. If word of pledges of protection to Texas were to become public knowledge, war anxiety would increase. More important, Congress was very sensitive about its perceived constitutional authority to authorize the deployment of the armed forces. True, the Constitution contained gray areas on this subject. According to some interpretations, legislative and executive responsibilities could overlap. But during this time of great distrust of presidential power, Tyler had to proceed with care and to avoid putting assurances of aid in writing.

The treaty was signed on 12 April, with Calhoun renewing Upshur's pledge of protection, saying army units would be concentrated at Fort Jessup, with additional forces standing by at Fort Towson, New Orleans, and other locations near the Texas border. Ten or twelve naval vessels would be in the Gulf of Mexico. Although Calhoun gave these assurances orally, Van Zandt and Henderson "reduced them to writing in his presence and by his consent" and then read them back to him. "Much more passed between Mr. Calhoun and ourselves on this subject," the Texans reported to Anson Jones, "calculated to assure us that everything would be done by the United States to protect Texas from the aggressions of Mexico, but which we cannot now mention."

Discussions between Calhoun and Van Zandt and Henderson dwelt at length on the ratification of the treaty by the Senate. The earlier optimistic outlook of Walker, Upshur, and others now gave way to doubt. Nevertheless, before the Texans agreed to sign the treaty, Tyler assured them that in the event of its rejection, he would send to both houses of Congress a message, recommending "in the strongest terms" the annexation of Texas, not as a territory, but as a state, under the provision of the Constitution that authorized Congress to admit new states into the Union. This procedure would require a simple majority vote in each house, rather than the two-thirds majority of the Senate that would be needed for the ratification of a treaty.[17]

After the treaty had been signed but before it was sent to the Senate, Calhoun tried to dispel fears of war with Mexico should annexation become a reality. The threat of hostilities, he felt, could stand in the way of ratification; therefore, he talked several times with Juan Nepomuceno Almonte, Mexico's minister to the United States, to explore the possibility of Mexico's accepting a financial settlement to compensate for the loss of Texas and to endeavor to explain how crucial it was for the United States to annex Texas in order to prevent British intrigue in that area. Calhoun sent conciliatory dispatches to Mexico by special messenger, hoping for a signal of approval before the Senate voted on the treaty. However, as word leaked out that the signed treaty was being held in the State Department, Calhoun decided that he could no longer delay turning it over to the scrutiny of the Senate.

Historians have had trouble in understanding why, if Calhoun really was concerned about ratification, on 18 April he wrote a letter to Richard Pakenham, the British minister in Washington, in which Calhoun defended slavery as "essential to the peace, safety, and prosperity" of the South and described blacks as inferior beings, who were infinitely better off under the paternalistic care of a slave owner than they would be as free persons.

The letter was in reply to a dispatch from Lord Aberdeen, sent to the British minister in the United States and dated 26 December 1843. The contents were intended to be conveyed to the American secretary of state. When Pakenham arrived in Washington in February 1844, he discovered that Aberdeen's message had not been communicated to Upshur. Pakenham thereupon read the dispatch to the secretary and then sent him a written copy of it. Had Upshur lived, he probably would have responded, but Acting Secretary Nelson did not, either from a lack of time or because he thought an answer was not necessary. When Calhoun found the dispatch in the State Department office, he decided to reply with vigor, centering his attention on Aberdeen's statement about his government's abolition policy.

Actually, what Aberdeen had said was not new. He had merely elaborated more fully on his response to Lord Brougham's question in the House of Lords on 18 August 1843 regarding Britain's intentions toward slavery in Texas. Aberdeen's tone was courteous, not hostile. He admitted that his government had pressed Mexico to acknowledge the independence of Texas, but it had done so with "no occult design, either with reference to the slavery which now exists, and which we desire to see abolished in Texas." It was well known to the United States and to every other nation, Aberdeen explained, that Great Britain desired and was "constantly exerting herself to procure the general abolition of slavery throughout the world." But in attempting this, Britain would do nothing in a secret or underhanded manner. "We should rejoice if the recognition of that country [Texas] by the Mexican Government should be accompanied by an engagement on the part of Texas to abolish slavery eventually, and under proper conditions"; but Britain did not intend to exercise improper authority on either Mexico or Texas. "We shall counsel, but we shall not seek to compel, or unduly control, either party. So far as Great Britain is concerned, provided all other States act with equal forbearance," Mexico and Texas were at liberty "to make their own unfettered arrangements," in regard to slavery or any other matter.

Calhoun informed Pakenham that when Aberdeen's letter was shown to Tyler, the president had expressed appreciation for the British government's disavowal of any intention to disturb the internal tranquility of the slaveholding states, but he had regretted that Great Britain for the first time had officially announced its abolition policy.

Calhoun did not stop with this statement. Britain, he continued, could do whatever it wished in its own colonies, but when Britain interfered with other nations, "whose safety or prosperity may be endangered by her policy," those nations, of force, had to take measures to protect themselves. This, said the secretary, was precisely what the United States intended to do in relation to Texas, a small nation that could not withstand British pressure for emancipation, and he informed Pakenham that a treaty of annexation had been concluded and agreed upon by the United States and the Republic of Texas, which would, without delay, be presented to the Senate for ratification.

By annexing Texas, the United States, Calhoun declared, was protecting its own safety and happiness. If abolition were forced upon Texas, the domestic institution of the slaveholding states of the Union would be endangered, and tranquility would be destroyed. It was the "imperious duty of the Federal Government, the common represen-tative and protector of the States of the Union, to adopt, in self-defence, the most effectual measures" to avoid such a calamity. Annexation was perhaps "the only means of guarding against the threatened danger."

In addition, Calhoun launched into a long defense of slavery, quoting statistics to prove how much better blacks lived under slavery and how many more deaf, dumb, blind, insane, and idiot blacks there were in the North as compared with the South. This was due, he contended, to the wretched conditions under which free Negroes in the North lived. Abolition, "so far from being wise or humane," would be a calamity to the entire United States, and especially to the race that it was the avowed object of Britain's policy to benefit.

Pakenham refused to enter into a discussion with Calhoun on the pros and cons of slavery, but he did express dismay that Aberdeen's remarks, which had been intended to allay the anxiety of the United States over Britain's intentions in Texas, had instead been used to assign "to the British Government some share in the responsibility of a transaction [the annexation of Texas] which can hardly fail to be viewed in many quarters with the most serious objection."

In a lengthy second letter on 27 April, Calhoun explicitly stated that annexation "was made necessary in order to preserve domestic institu-tions placed under the guarantee of their respective Constitutions, and deemed essential to their safety and prosperity." Pakenham chose not to continue the exchange; he merely responded that the communication had been received and transmitted to Her Majesty's government.[18]

On 22 April, the treaty (which made no direct mention of slavery), along with associated documents and correspondence—all selected by Calhoun and including his 18 April letter to Pakenham—were sent to the Senate under seal of secrecy. Tyler's letter of transmittal again stressed the importance of the treaty to the entire nation—the incalculable advantages to be gained for the North and the West in commerce, agriculture, mining, manufacturing, and industry of all types. For the

South it offered peace and tranquility against efforts to disrupt them. The federal system, Tyler assured the Senate, was capable of encompassing additional territories and admitting new states. The nation would only grow stronger. He urged ratification, but Calhoun's letter destroyed any chance there might have been for acceptance of the treaty. Northern expansionists who favored annexation could not support Calhoun's reason for implementing it.

The opponents of annexation seized upon Calhoun's letter to Pakenham as proof that the issue was a sectional one, fostered to benefit the South and to perpetuate and extend the institution of slavery. Calhoun's reasons for writing the letter have long been a subject of speculation. Charles Wiltse believes that Calhoun wanted only to stop the British government's encouragement of northern abolitionists, that Calhoun did not mean to endanger the annexation treaty by focusing on the slavery issue, and that his letter to Pakenham never was intended for publication. However, a man of Calhoun's political experience should have been aware of the implications of his action.

Jesse Reeves's theory is that Calhoun "used the tools of diplomacy" for a political purpose. In writing the letter to Pakenham, he really was directing it "over Pakenham's shoulder to the American people," using the threat of the "fancied [British] Menace" to excite the American public. But David Pletcher has raised the question why, if Calhoun intended the message as an aid to annexation, he stressed the controversial slavery issue instead of concentrating on general Anglophobic fears that might have garnered support from various sections?[19]

George Poage thinks Calhoun wanted his letter to initiate a general debate with the British government over slavery, hoping this would alarm southern Whigs and bring them into a sectional bloc under his leadership. Their votes were necessary to ratification, but as yet, they remained loyal to Whig policy and seemed oblivious to the growing danger to their "way of life."

To William R. Brock, "all evidence suggests that Calhoun knew what he was doing and calculated the odds." Early in March, weeks before Calhoun had discovered Aberdeen's letter, he lamented the disunity in the South: "We must show as fixed a determination to defend our property and our safety, as the friends of the tariff and the abolitionists do to assail them." From what he had read in the *National Intelligencer,* Calhoun was convinced that southern Whigs would vote against the treaty unless they could be alerted to the impending destruction of their slave property, which would be brought about by British intrusions in Texas. The protection of slavery had to be made the central issue of annexation. This would be a test, not only for southern

Whigs, but also for northern Democrats. This was the time to announce to the world "that the United States was committed to the general support of slavery."

Writing to Richard Crallé in mid March, Dixon H. Lewis of Alabama, one of Calhoun's most ardent supporters, called annexation "the greatest question of the Age" because of the political power that could accrue to the South: "It will unite the hitherto divided South, while it will make abolition & treason synonymous & thus destroy it [abolition] in the North."[20]

Calhoun thought it was important to discover exactly where the North stood: "If our safety and the great interest we have in maintaining the existing relation between the two races in the South, are of no estimation in the eyes of our northern friends—if they see neither insult nor danger, in the Declaration of the Earl of Aberdeen, in reference to that relation, in connection with Texas, it is time we should know it. If they are insensible or blind to our danger on that vital point, they may rest assured we are not." If the North would not defend the South when the latter's safety was at stake, there was something wrong, and "not a little ominous to the duration of our system."

In his dual review of Merk's *Slavery and the Annexation of Texas* and *Fruits of Propaganda in the Tyler Administration*, Sydney Nathans has offered the opinion that Calhoun wrote the letter to Pakenham in an effort to assure the passage of the treaty. Like Upshur before him, Calhoun felt an urgent need to "rouse the South," shake it out of its lethargy, make it realize the vulnerability of slavery. He "expected his defiant letter [to Pakenham] to provide a *British* counterattack on both slavery and annexation, and thus to create an international incident that might have made annexation a patriotic necessity. But the British proved 'too wise.'"

Senator Benton was certain that Calhoun's "strange diplomatic dispatch" had been written explicitly to disgust northern senators. The whole annexation business, Benton maintained, had been conducted with a double aspect: one looking to the presidency; the other, to disunion. Duff Green's alarms, sent from England, were links in the chain of events, the object of which was to elevate Calhoun to the presidency. When the desired ground swell of support did not materialize, defeating the treaty was necessary in order to give secessionists a reason to call for the creation of a southern confederacy, presumably with Calhoun at its head. Benton, of course, could not be considered unbiased in his opinions. He vehemently disliked both Calhoun and the idea of annexation.[21]

Washington Globe editor Francis Preston Blair also believed the defeat of the treaty would furnish Calhoun with a pretext for uniting the entire South under his leadership and for urging the slaveholding states to leave the Union and form a southern confederacy. Calhoun "wantonly" made annexation "a sectional instead of a national question," Blair told Jackson, "to defeat the measure and make it ground of collision between north and south. . . . I sincerely believe that Calhoun and his old Junto of conspirators are more than ever anxious to separate the south from the north. They want Texas only as a bone of contention."

Pletcher has noted that if disunion was Calhoun's motive, he was being "disloyal to his chief, his party, and his country. Whatever his reasons, he acted recklessly, but with characteristic self-righteousness." However, if credence can be placed in Calhoun's letters to his friends and family, there was nothing he desired more than that the Senate ratify the treaty, but he wanted the treaty accepted because, according to national policy, property in slaves must be protected. The entire nation should present a united front in acknowledging this. "It is to us a question of life and death," he told James Hammond, governor of South Carolina. "Strange as it may seem, Benton and his wing object to the admission [of Texas] among other things, because in my letter to Mr. Pakenham, I should dare to place the issue where it does!" Calhoun told his daughter, Anna Clemson, that he regarded annexation as a vital question. "If lost now, it will be forever lost; and, if that, the South will be lost, if some prompt and decisive measures be not adopted to save us."[22] He did not explain what "prompt and decisive measures" he contemplated. In placing the slavery issue in the forefront of the annexation debate, contrary to Tyler's wishes, Calhoun was being disloyal to the president. If, in the event the treaty was rejected, Calhoun's next step was to be the creation of a southern confederacy, he was, indeed, being disloyal, not only to the president, but to the nation.

With the treaty in the Senate, the storm that had been brewing for months broke in all its fury, especially after the treaty and its accompanying documents had been published in the *New York Evening Post*. Senator Benjamin Tappan of Ohio, in violation of the rules of the Senate when it was meeting in executive session to consider the treaty, was responsible for the exposure. He was not as ardent an abolitionist as was his brother Lewis. Nevertheless, Benjamin leaned in that direction, and he was indignant about the secrecy in which the treaty was to be discussed in the upper house. He thought it was preposterous to consider annexation without public debate, so he defied Senate rules by sending the materials to Lewis in New York. Lewis, at first, was hesitant about giving the information to the *Post*. He consulted Albert Gallatin, an early champion of freedom of the press, who encouraged Lewis to go ahead. Therefore, early in May, readers of the *Post* knew exactly what the treaty contained, and they also knew how Calhoun viewed annexation. Other newspapers quickly reprinted the information. The public, which heretofore had relied on rumor, now had facts to ponder.

To complicate the pondering were letters from Clay and Van Buren, considered by almost everyone to be the contending presidential candidates, even though nominating conventions were yet to be held. Their letters were published on 27 April—Clay's in the morning *National Intelligencer*, and Van Buren's in the evening *Washington Globe*.

In previous months, as word about annexation negotiations spread throughout the country, both gentlemen were mightily disturbed. Clay did not think "it right to allow Mr. Tyler for his own selfish purposes, to introduce an exciting topic, and add to the other subjects of contention which exist in the country." This would only promote discord and dissatisfaction. In the past, Clay had not been opposed to adding Texas to the Union. Quite the contrary: "The appetite for Texas was from the first a Western passion stimulated by no one more greedily than by Henry Clay," Adams remembered. Now, however, Clay wanted to base his campaign primarily on internal issues: the tariff, distribution, and presidential usurpation, as well as his own "heroic fight" against it. Clay was convinced that he had unlimited ammunition to use against Tyler, which, because of Tyler's recent relationship or attempted relationship with the Democrats, would be of great benefit to the Whig cause.

As differences of opinion over annexation became more intense, Van Buren's political aspirations were endangered more than Clay's were. Sectional divisions over Texas were more serious in the Democratic party than in the Whig party. Before the issue had become so heated, Van Buren's nomination had been considered a certainty. Delegates from three-fourths of the states were pledged to him, and the Whigs were delighted with the prospect. Without a doubt, Clay could defeat the New Yorker. The Whigs only hoped Van Buren would be able to "stand up" until nominated. "He is too weak to run," Letcher told Crittenden; "he is like Baillie Peyton's steer, which was so poor and weak it had to be *held up* to be shot."[23]

In March 1844, Congressman W. H. Hammet of Mississippi, an unpledged delegate to the Democratic convention, which was scheduled to meet in Baltimore on 27 May, wrote to Van Buren, questioning him about his views on annexation. Queries also had come from others, and several of Van Buren's friends advised him not to express an opinion on the subject, but he decided that the time had come to speak out. He drafted a reply to Hammet and sent it to a few of his supporters for their reactions. In the letter, Van Buren said that while he believed the United States had a constitutional right to annex Texas, he did not think the danger of foreign interference in that republic was so serious that immediate action was necessary, nor would delay mean, as some contended, that the area would be permanently lost to the United States. Annexation should be postponed. Present conditions could cause a war with Mexico, and he questioned how this would damage America's reputation: "Could we hope to stand perfectly justified in the eyes of mankind for entering into it?"

James K. Paulding, who had been secretary of the navy during Van Buren's presidency, was among the first to react to the letter. He confessed that his fingers itched a little to get hold of Texas, but he thought Van Buren's hesitation was on the "side of law and justice, not to say expediency, for the acquisition might after all, cost more than it's worth." However, he wondered whether Clay would make a clear-cut statement on the issue or find some way to dodge it. Paulding thought it was a pity Van Buren could not avoid the subject, for there were pitfalls no matter what he said. Paulding doubted the wisdom of having a presidential candidate commit himself on questions of foreign affairs before an election. But Benton, Silas Wright, and several others believed Van Buren's letter should be published, and they rushed it to the *Globe* before Hammet had had a chance to read the message, which was addressed to him. Unfortunately, the letter was complicated and overly long, which caused most readers to give up before they had reached its substance.[24]

Clay, still on his southern tour, was trying to decide if he should make known his views on annexation. Crittenden kept Clay informed about developments in Washington, so Clay knew about the signing of the treaty on 12 April. While traveling through the South, Clay had increasingly become convinced that enthusiasm for annexation among southern Whigs was not strong. When he reached Raleigh, North Carolina, he conferred with Governor John Morehead, George Badger, and Edward Stanly, showing them a letter in which he set forth his position. With their concurrence, Clay forwarded the letter to Crittenden, with the request that it be published in the *National Intelligencer*. He felt it his duty, Clay told Crittenden, to present his opinions to the public. Crittenden was not convinced that this was advisable, but Clay was adamant. "I am perfectly confident of the ground which I have taken," he wrote a second time to the senator; "I cannot consent to *suppress* or *delay* the publication." Public sentiment, Clay admonished

Crittenden, was everywhere sounder than in Washington, and he was certain that he was in tune with public opinion. Clay rarely doubted that "his wishes and those of the people were identical." Van Buren, Clay believed, also was opposed to annexation; therefore, in a political contest between the two of them, it would not become a subject of conflict. They could avoid the matter entirely. Albert D. Kirwan, Crittenden's biographer, believes that when Clay and Van Buren met at Clay's home in the spring of 1842, they could have reached an agreement that they would ignore the Texas issue in the 1844 campaign. However, no proof of such an accord has been discovered. Those who think such did occur refer to the alleged arrangement as the "Treaty of Ashland."[25]

Crittenden reluctantly delivered Clay's letter to the *Intelligencer*. It was shorter than Van Buren's, but it was also more ambiguous. If the question of annexation could be presented without the loss of national character or the hazard of foreign war, with the general concurrence of the nation but without any danger to its integrity, and without the payment of an unreasonable price, Clay thought annexation could, at some time, be considered.

At one point in the letter, Clay predicted the eventual creation of an independent republic of Canada. "With the Canadian republic on one side, that of Texas on the other, and the United States, the friend of both, between them, each could advance its own happiness." In conclusion, however, Clay left a loophole by saying that he considered annexation, at this time, dangerous and inexpedient and that it was not encouraged by general public expression. Did "at this time" mean he would favor it at a later date, or did his portrayal of the United States as a friend of the republics of Canada and Texas indicate his preference for continued Texas independence? Many interpreted Clay's opposition to annexation "at this time" as meaning "not just yet."[26]

What could be said with certainty was that both Van Buren and Clay had voiced their opposition to immediate annexation. On the other hand, James K. Polk, who was making a bid for the Democratic vice-presidential nomination, answered an inquiry about his stand with an unequivocal advocacy of "immediate re-annexation." The idea of "re-annexation" was gaining popularity. Texas, it was claimed, had been part of the Louisiana Purchase, but it had been relinquished to Spain in the Adams-Onís Treaty of 1819.

In the Whig convention, which met in Baltimore only a few days after the Clay and Van Buren letters had appeared in the Washington papers, Clay's opinions caused not a ripple of dissension. He was nominated unanimously and by acclamation. The Whig party appeared to be united, strong, and confident of victory. The Clayites delightedly anticipated the departure of a Tyler who would be devastated by the defeat of the treaty that he hoped would be the crowning glory of his administration.

Van Buren's plight was quite different. There was a month between the publication of his letter and the opening of the Democratic convention on 27 May—time for party members to consider the consequences of his statements or for rumors and false interpretations to circulate. Immediate annexationists trampled one another in a frenzy of activity, demanding that Van Buren be abandoned and deciding who should replace him as their candidate.

No one was more upset about Van Buren's statement than Thomas Ritchie, whose *Richmond* (Va.) *Enquirer* had long and loyally supported the New Yorker and the alliance between the Albany Regency and the Richmond Junto. Ritchie's influence was felt beyond the borders of Virginia. For weeks he had warned leading Democrats, both in the North and in the South, of disaster to the party if Van Buren did not openly urge the ratification of the treaty. Now the damage had been done. The *Enquirer* was swamped with communications from irate proannexation Democrats who condemned Van Buren's letter. All carried a similar message: the party needed a candidate who strongly favored annexation. Van Buren had yielded to abolitionist influence. His name had already brought and would continue to bring defeats in local as well as national elections.[27]

In Virginia the ever-vigilant Calhoun Central Committee called for a new state convention to pledge support for the South Carolinian. This, Ritchie was determined to avoid. He quickly convened a meeting of the Shockoe Hill (Richmond) Democratic Association, and he introduced a resolution calling for immediate annexation and for the release of Virginia delegates to the Baltimore convention from their commitment to Van Buren. On 5 May, Ritchie sent to Van Buren, via Senator Silas Wright of New York, a bundle of the protests that he had received from party members, along with a personal letter that, he said, gave him as much pain to write as any that had ever come from his pen. "The last ten days," he told Van Buren, "have produced a condition of political affairs, which I had not believed possible." No longer could Virginia be counted in the Van Buren camp. Obviously, although he did not directly say so, Ritchie wanted Van Buren to withdraw. Read the letters, Ritchie advised, "and judge for yourself" how the party was reacting. Something had to be done at once; some decision had to be made. If the "jarrings" were to continue, the party would break up, which would "insure beyond the probability of a doubt, the triumphant election of the most profligate politician perhaps in our country"—namely, Henry Clay. The Whig party, "this strong party in favor of a strong candidate," was united "with bands of iron." The situation was distressing, indeed!

Van Buren, hurt and disappointed, ignored the hint that he should withdraw. Without responding to Ritchie's letter, he returned the packet of messages that censured his position. His name was removed from the *Enquirer*'s masthead, and Virginia delegates were told that they did not need to honor their commitment to him at the convention.

Jackson, mortified by Van Buren's letter yet filled with deep anguish in having to differ with his friend and protégé, publicly took the New Yorker to task for having failed to realize the danger that Great Britain would pose to the nation if annexation were not accomplished at once. No time ever had been more propitious than the present, Jackson insisted. If action were postponed, Texas would feel "insulted and neglected," and the opportunity for annexation would be lost.

Clay's glee over the turn of events was boundless. "I do not think I ever witnessed such a state of utter disorder, confusion, and decomposition as that which the Democratic party now presents," he happily wrote to Thurlow Weed. Clay was absolutely certain that his own opinion on the Texas question would do him "no prejudice at the South." But in the South there were calls for "Texas meetings in every town and hamlet." "Agitate, agitate, agitate" was the growing cry. Even though the Democratic party might be breaking into factions, Ritchie believed that the current of public sentiment in the South could not be stopped. Among southern Whigs there were those who found the possibility of extending the area of slavery, and hence the power of the South, attractive. Others feared that the Texas question would herald the breakup of the Union, so they denounced the fervent agitators for annexation.[28]

Waddy Thompson, completely reversing his earlier position, now was convinced that the ratification of the treaty "would be tantamount to a declaration of war on Mexico," and this he found objectionable. During his years of residency in that country, he had developed a great affection for the nation and its people. Furthermore, the Walker thesis disturbed him. With Texas a part of the Union, Thompson believed that southern agriculture would be faced with greater competition in the cotton market than if Texas were to remain separate and independent. Production in the Old South would decline, slaves would be sold to planters in the newly acquired territory, and life in the southeastern states would be utterly changed. Although he disliked Calhoun, Thompson agreed with him on the positive good of slavery. Because Thompson could no longer accept the administration's policy on annexation, he resigned his position as minister to Mexico and declared his support for Clay in the upcoming election. There were other strong declarations for Clay among southern Whigs, yet there was cause for concern. Clay might hold southern Whig senators in line against the treaty, but how southern Whigs, in general, would express themselves at the polls was another matter.

While the Whigs had no trouble in deciding on their candidate, the Democrats were not so fortunate. There was no dearth of aspirants. Cass, Buchanan, Richard M. Johnson (who had been vice-president during Van Buren's administration), and several others were ready and willing. Van Buren still had many supporters. Silas Wright was mentioned, but being loyal to Van Buren, he rejected all such suggestions. The very eager Cass appeared to be the most likely choice if Van Buren was abandoned. Cass was an ardent immediate annexationist, and as a resident of Michigan, his candidacy could temper the appearance of a sectional split in the party. Among South Carolina Democrats, along with other Calhoun admirers, there was an intense desire to raise again the standard for the secretary of state. Theirs was the extremist point of view. "Is it impossible," James Hammond asked, "yet to rally your friends so as at least to get your name into the House?" No one could better lead the Slave States. The Texas question had to be pushed, and "if the Union is to break there could be no better pretext" than the failure of ratification. Furthermore, if, separated from the North, the Slave States could unite with Texas, "a *first rate power*" could be formed, "one that under a free trade system would flourish beyond any on the Globe—immediately and forever." The tariff, sectional hostility, and the growing zeal and impertinence of the abolitionists—all showed clearly, Hammond was convinced, that the North and the South could not exist united as one country.[29]

If Calhoun was not a possible candidate, there were some southern Democrats who wondered about "hoisting the flag for Tyler." But usually his name was mentioned as a last resort, with the comment that "even Tyler" would be better than Van Buren or any other northern candidate. A group of the president's supporters, consisting mostly, it was said, of officeholders, planned to meet in Baltimore on 27 May 1844, at the same time as the Democratic convention, and to name Tyler as an independent candidate. This they did, probably with the idea that if the Democratic convention deadlocked, the delegates might turn to their man.

The Tyler convention was a small affair. Tyler thought perhaps a thousand delegates were present, but the unsympathetic *Niles' Register* reported the "room was not crowded and a large portion of the persons within were spectators." The theme was "Reannexation of Texas—Postponement Is Rejection." After a brief debate on whether or not to wait until the Democratic convention had named a candidate, Tyler was nominated by acclamation. The entire procedure lasted less than an hour. Tyler's acceptance, on the following day, attracted slight attention.

All eyes were on the Democratic convention, where the anti–Van Buren faction successfully promoted the rule, which had been used by the party in 1832 and 1836, of requiring a two-thirds majority of the delegate vote for nomination. In all probability, Van Buren could have carried a simple majority but not two-thirds. His opponents also were able to elect their man for presiding officer. Further skillful behind-the-scenes manipulations on the part of Gideon J. Pillow of Tennessee, George Bancroft of Massachusetts, and Benjamin Butler of New York rocketed James K. Polk to the top of the list of potential candidates and finally secured his nomination on a platform calling for the reannexation of Texas and the reoccupation of Oregon—all of Oregon—"at the earliest practicable period," which could be interpreted as meaning immediately or at a later, more auspicious period. To Polk's enthusiastic followers it meant "at once." George M. Dallas of Pennsylvania, another of Robert Walker's relatives who was a strong proponent of annexation, was selected as the vice-presidential candidate after Silas Wright had refused to accede to the convention's unanimous desire to place him on the ticket.

The Whigs chanted their belittling question, "Who is James K. Polk?" But the Democratic nominee was not a political unknown. He had served six terms in the House of Representatives and had been Speaker of the House during the Twenty-fourth and Twenty-fifth Congresses. From 1839 to 1841 he had been governor of Tennessee, and within the Democratic party he had been considered a serious vice-presidential possibility in 1844. Yet, to the Whig senator from North Carolina, Willie P. Mangum, Polk's presidential nomination was unbelievable. "We will literally crush the ticket," he assured his brother.[30]

There was no doubt now that the battle for the presidency would be fought on the issues of expansion and slavery. Clay's plan to center the campaign on domestic matters and presidential usurpation had been foiled, but within the halls of Congress, usurpation remained a burning concern, the administration's promise of military aid to Texas being the most recent incident. "You may have seen in the papers," Alexander Stephens fumed, "that he [Tyler] has actually called out the military forces and stationed two regiments on the confines of *Texas* and several sail in the Gulph—a virtual declaration of war—without consulting Congress. This is true, and a greater outrage upon the Constitution has never been committed by any President. I should not be surprised if he is impeached." A number of Whigs were "impatient" to take such action, but John Quincy Adams dissuaded them, saying impeachment proceedings during the excitement and differences over annexation would not be advisable. Like "a cracked gun-barrel," any attempt to unseat the president at this time would only "explode in the hand of him who would use it."

Besides, the Senate was too busy debating the treaty, which had been reported out of the Committee on Foreign Affairs on 10 May. Three days later, Senator Benton began his determined effort to defeat annexation. His first major speech lasted three days. Ratification, he thundered, would bring war, an "unjust war upon a peaceable neighbor in violation of treaties and of pledged neutrality," a war that had been "unconstitutionally made," because the war power was an exclusive responsibility of the legislative, not the executive, branch. And why had the treaty been exploded upon the country "like a ripened plot and a charged bomb"? This was to make Tyler "a new Texas candidate, anointed with gunpowder." Tyler, Benton charged, wanted to "play Jackson"; but how ridiculous. Jackson was a hero; Tyler, a harlequin.[31]

Many of the resolutions that Benton offered were related to what he termed "mistaken and unfounded" information sent to the president and the secretary of state by "a private citizen from Maryland," who, of course, was Duff Green. Benton particularly wanted one letter, written by this "private citizen" to Secretary Upshur, delivered to the Senate. It contained, he said, erroneous information that was being used to create the climate of fear on which the administration based its arguments in favor of annexation. Benton raised many questions. Was Green employed by the president? If so, out of what fund was he being paid? What were his instructions? Was he told to discover reasons, real or fictitious, to justify annexation? These were logical questions, and they were embarrassing to Tyler, who had allowed himself to be pressured by Upshur, or rather by Calhoun working through Upshur, into employing Green as an "executive agent," supposedly to foster better trade relations with England and France. The president was responsible for the appointment. It was he who had by-passed Webster and sent a personal letter to Everett, introducing Green.

On Benton's request, the Senate asked the president to produce the Green letter, mentioned in a communication from Upshur to Murphy, which detailed Britain's desire to eliminate slavery in Texas. After a "diligent inquiry," Calhoun said he had not been able to locate the letter in the State Department files. Benton also recommended that Green be called before "the bar of the Senate to be examined on oath" about the veracity of the information that he had sent to the president, Upshur, and Calhoun. The Senate approved the resolution, along with others requesting that the president provide information on a temporary armistice between Mexico and Texas and on the sending of a special messenger to Mexico in an attempt to obtain that government's consent to annexation.

Benton also submitted three declaratory resolutions, to which the Senate "listened with approval." One stated that ratification would amount to a declaration of war against Mexico; another stated that Congress alone could declare war; but certainly in this instance, the executive's treaty-making power infringed on legislative prerogatives. The third resolution stated that Texas should not be annexed until the consent of the people of the United States, the people of Texas, and the government of Mexico had been obtained.

Day after day, as the Senate probed the origin of negotiations with Texas, any hope for ratification, which had always been slight despite Upshur's optimistic reports, faded. Tyler, who was forced to defend himself against the current charge of presidential usurpation, tried to justify the promise of military aid to Texas; but his argument was not convincing. He said that when the treaty was signed, the United States, in reality, acquired Texas. Only Senate ratification was needed in order to make this official, and although there was no serious threat of a Mexican invasion of Texas, the administration believed it was logical to take precautionary measures to protect America's newly acquired territory. He complied with the Senate's request for copies of his orders to units of the army and the navy.[32]

Even though the treaty and the accompanying documents had been made public by Tappan's illicit action, for which he was lightly reprimanded, the Senate debated the treaty in secret executive session until, acting on protests from antiannexation groups, the secrecy was lifted. Certainly, Benton and others argued, the American people should be made aware of the objections to ratification. However, there was to be some selectivity in deciding what should be revealed. The "people's right to know" was honored mainly by releasing materials that were considered particularly embarrassing to the president. Some extraordinary methods were employed. For example, twenty thousand copies of Tyler's 31 May message, in which he admitted that military assistance had been promised to Texas, were ordered for distribution, along with the same number of the message acknowledging that the State Department could not locate the "private letter" written by "the citizen of Maryland." On the other hand, communications or documents from the president that could be interpreted as justifications for ratification or which placed the treaty in a favorable light were labeled propaganda and were not released. The Senate majority, it can be concluded, did all it could to convince the public of the executive branch's deviousness; but of course, the executive branch had not been chary in its use of propaganda tactics.[33]

The debate over ratification lasted from 16 May to 8 June. The most important Democratic speeches that were in favor of accepting the treaty were made by Levi Woodbury of New Hampshire, James Buchanan of Pennsylvania, George McDuffie of South Carolina, and Robert Walker of Mississippi. Whigs who spoke against the treaty included Virginia's two senators: William Rives and William Archer, chairman of the Committee on Foreign Relations. Archer attacked the "now or never" argument that if Texas were not annexed now, it would be lost forever. "Let it resound through this land—reverberate from Texas—Never! oh, never!" Interestingly, however, sizable numbers of Whigs were willing to concede, at least in private, that the rejection of annexation need not be permanent, but "just not now," when the credit for it would go to Tyler. Three days before the final decision, Senator Preston said to Crittenden, "When Clay is in and Mexico consents, the matter can be reviewed."

On 6 June, Rives spoke against the immediate approval of the treaty, and he introduced a resolution asking the president to reopen negotiations with Texas in order to extend the period allotted for ratification, thus allowing time to obtain Mexico's concurrence and to give the American people an opportunity for more serious consideration of the issue. No action was taken on the Rives resolution.

When the vote was taken on 8 June, thirty-five senators opposed ratification, while sixteen approved. Benton was the only Democrat from a Slave State who voted in the negative. The six other Democrats who opposed were from the North. All the Whigs, with the exception of John Henderson of Mississippi, cast their ballots against annexation, at least for the present. If Calhoun's objective in writing the letter to Pakenham was to arouse the ire of southern Whig senators in defense of slavery, he seemed, for the moment, to have failed.

Needless to say, Clay was euphoric over the defeat of "Mr. Tyler's abominable treaty," which Clay described as "a bubble blown up . . . in the most exceptionable manner, for sinister purposes, and its bursting has injured no body but Mr. Van Buren."[34]

14

"THE APOPLEXY
OF THE CONSTITUTION"

The Senate's refusal to ratify the treaty to annex Texas did not deter the president. On 10 June 1844 he notified the House of Representatives that he was sending to it, for its information and consideration, the treaty, together with all correspondence and documents that had been submitted to the Senate in its executive session. Included were not only the papers that the Senate had already made public but also those which that body had chosen to keep "under the veil of secrecy." He informed the House that Congress was fully empowered to accomplish all that a formal treaty ratification would have succeeded in doing, and because the subject of Texas had created no ordinary degree of excitement and interest among the populace, he believed he would be remiss if he failed to lay before the House all the materials in his possession. These would enable the House to act "with full light upon the subject," should it desire to do so.

Texas, Tyler reminded the House, was an independent republic, both de facto and de jure. By entering into a negotiation with that nation, the United States would not be violating any treaty stipulations with Mexico. Nor was annexation in any way a sectional or a local issue; rather, it "addressed itself to the interests of every part of the country and made its appeal to the glory of the American name." The Senate's rejection of the treaty need not mean the final defeat of annexation if the full Congress were now to act quickly. The great question was, not the manner in which annexation was to be accomplished, but whether "it shall be accomplished." The president's invitation was strong and clear.

He wanted Texas to enter the Union as a state, under Article IV, section 3, of the Constitution, which stipulates: "New States may be admitted by the Congress into this Union," implicitly with a majority of both houses agreeing by joint resolution, rather than as territory acquired by treaty, under Article II, section 2, which gives the president "power, by and with the advice and consent of the Senate, to make treaties, provided two-thirds of the senators present concur."[1]

On the day that the House received Tyler's message, Thomas Hart Benton, in the Senate, savagely denounced the president and instigated another bitter exchange between those who were either for or against annexation. The Missourian, who early in May had spoken so forcefully against the treaty, calling it nothing but a slave conspiracy to break up the Union, was now in a difficult position. Although crushed by the repudiation of Van Buren, he had to salvage some rapport with the Polk Democrats; but he could not bring himself to support annexation that had been brought to fruition by the use of the joint-resolution ploy. Instead, he moved for opening new treaty negotiations, which would include Mexico as well as Texas. The defeated treaty, he maintained, was fraught with difficulties at home and abroad: namely, "war and loss of trade with Mexico, slavery controversies and dissolution of the Union at home." Calhoun and Tyler had not served the nation well by allowing such an agreement to see the light of day. The letter to Pakenham had been disastrous. Reannexation, as Benton now termed it, had merit, but "the treaty was a wrong and criminal way of doing a right thing." His proposal would right the wrong.

His bill contained several specific and complex items, designed to prevent war with Mexico and protect trade with that nation. To eliminate internal disputes, Benton proposed that in the event of annexation, a half and half division of Texas be made between slave and free soil. This was reasonable, he maintained, because half of the area was not adapted to slave labor and would eventually be formed into nonslaveholding states.

Benton's plan did not please the immediate annexationists. Senator McDuffie of South Carolina, who was incensed by the Missourian's superior attitude, called him "Sir Oracle," who, when he opened his mouth to speak, ordered no dogs to bark. Benton, McDuffie said, had no right to "play schoolmaster to the Senate." Benton had no prerogative to teach experienced statesmen the lessons of their trade. Benton was disloyal to his party and would be "thrown out of the Democratic position he has so ably occupied."

Benton's reply was explosive: he declared that he opposed the treaty because disunion was at the bottom of "this long-concealed Texas machination. . . . A separate confederacy, stretching from the Atlantic to California . . . , is the cherished vision of disappointed ambition [apparently Calhoun's]; and for this consummation every circumstance has been carefully and artfully controlled." Benton categorized the circumstances: the secret negotiations; the abolition quarrel that had been provoked with Great Britain; the Pakenham letter; the clandestine concentration of ships and troops near Texas. All, he declared, betrayed the objective of the extremists who surrounded Tyler, those whose desire was disunion, just as it had been during the nullification crisis of the 1830s. In his rage, Benton pounded his fist on McDuffie's desk. For one hour, Adams observed, Benton's speech "was so merciless and personal that nothing but bodily fear could have withheld the hand of McDuffie from a challenge; but he put up with it, quiet as a lamb."[2]

Andrew Jackson, according to George Harris, editor of the Nashville (Tenn.) Union, "was a good deal excited at Benton's course—and said 'he [Benton] shall hear from me soon'; and asserts that ever since the explosion of the big gun [aboard the Princeton] Benton has not been in his right mind." Benton's skepticism about the British menace in Texas irritated Francis Blair, as it did many a good Jacksonian, but Blair said he agreed with Benton that Calhoun and his associates had plotted the defeat of the treaty in order to pave the way for secession.[3] In spite of Tyler's many declarations about the treaty's benefits to the nation, accusations of sectionalism and disunion persisted among the Democrats as well as the Whigs.

Tyler did not help the situation when, with the resignation of John Spencer in May and after the Senate had refused to confirm the appointment of James Green of New Jersey, he had named George Bibb of Kentucky as secretary of the treasury. Although the Senate had approved Bibb's nomination, Tyler had received considerable criticism because, with the exception of Wilkins in the War Department, all cabinet posts now were being held by men from the South.

Whenever possible, Congress demonstrated its displeasure with Tyler. Before the first session of the Twenty-eighth Congress had come to a close, the Senate, in essence, rejected another treaty, which Tyler considered to be of importance to the further development of international trade. Negotiated by Henry Wheaton, the United States minister in Berlin, according to instructions from the president and the secretary of state, with the German Customs Union, or Zollverein, it reduced duties on tobacco and lard that were shipped by the United States, placed raw cotton on the free list, and created a low rate for rice. In turn, the United States lowered the tarriff for certain German products that, for the most part, were not in competition with American manufactured goods. The arrangement promised great advantages to agricultural interests of the South and the West.

In his annual message of December 1843, Tyler notified Congress of the negotiation in progress, pointing out the importance of commercial relations with the Zollverein, which had been established in 1823 and had grown in twenty years to be a customs union of more than twenty German states, with a total population of 27 million people. When Tyler transmitted the treaty to the Senate in April 1844, he again stressed "the important benefits to the great agricultural, commercial, and navigating interests of the United States." This, he said, was the first instance in which attempts to reduce the heavy duties on tobacco, which were imposed by various countries, had been successful. Tyler tried to be very careful. Certain provisions in the treaty, he realized, conflicted with existing tariff laws; therefore, he acknowledged that it would be necessary for him to send a copy of the treaty to the House so that it could take proper legislative action should the Senate ratify the treaty.

Because the Senate was occupied with the debate on the Texas issue, the Zollverein treaty was not reported out of the Foreign Relations Committee until 14 June 1844. The committee's decision was unfavorable. There was no criticism of the substance of the treaty, but the report noted that it infringed on the right of Congress to pass tariff legislation. The committee contended that the Constitution conferred the power to make commercial regulations upon Congress alone. No matter how beneficial the treaty might be, Congress had no intention of allowing the president to take the initiative in such a matter. Here was another opportunity to lecture the executive, as well as the nation in general, on the evils of presidential usurpation and to spell out the appropriate functions of the chief executive, which, said the Foreign Relations Committee, were "to follow, not to lead, to fulfill, not to ordain the law; to carry into effect, by negotiation and compact with foreign Governments, the legislative will, when it has been announced, upon great subjects of trade and revenue, not to interpose with controlling influence, not to go forward with too ambitious enterprises."

These remarks undoubtedly were directed more at the Texas treaty than at the agreement with the Zollverein, but they expressed the philosophy of the Clay-Whig school on how a president should conduct himself. He should not presume to negotiate a treaty until the legislative branch had given him permission to do so. He should follow the directions of Congress and not implement his own ideas, his "too ambitious enterprises."

On the last day of the session, the Senate voted 26 to 18 to table the treaty. As a four-month's time limit on ratification was written into the treaty, this virtually meant rejection. "There never was," Jackson told Polk, "such treachery to the laborers of the South and West, as the rejection of this treaty." The dastardly vote of the Senate should be "fully exposed to the people." Undoubtedly there were political reasons, in addition to sensitivity to presidential usurpation, for the Senate's decision. The treaty, with its agricultural benefits, could well attract presidential support from some southern Whigs.

After dispensing with the Zollverein treaty, the Senate adjourned. "Moloch and Mammon have sunk into momentary slumber," Adams disgustedly wrote in his diary; "the Texas treason is blasted for the hour, and the first session of the most perverse and worthless Congress that ever disgraced this Confederacy has closed." No action had been taken on Benton's Texas bill, but annexation was not a dead issue. Across the nation the debate continued, and there was talk of a special session of Congress in August or September to consider a joint resolution.[4]

In Texas the defeat of the annexation treaty created concern and turmoil. Sam Houston ordered General Henderson to leave Washington, which he did. Van Zandt resigned as chargé but did not return to Texas until September. Houston was angry. As he had feared, his country again had been rebuffed by the United States. From Mexico came renewed threats of hostilities. Antonio López de Santa Anna, its erratic and dictatorial president, vowed horrible vengeance on Texas and on anyone who might aid that republic.

To add to the confusion in Texas, a presidential election was slated there for September, and Houston, who was constitutionally barred from being a candidate, was hostile toward Anson Jones, the secretary of state, who was favored to succeed him. The two split over how to proceed now that the treaty had been rejected and over whether or not assurances from Jackson, Tyler, and others that the matter was not closed could be believed. Houston, upset and disappointed, appeared to oppose further consideration of the subject; he wanted to turn again to Great Britain for aid in seeking Mexico's recognition of Texas' independence. Jones preferred to wait and see what the United States might do. If the Tyler administration failed to persuade Congress to act favorably on a joint resolution, then there should be another attempt to obtain Mexico's recognition of his country's independence.[5]

To further complicate relations between Texas and the United States, William S. Murphy, a recess appointment as United States chargé d'affaires in Texas, was refused confirmation by the same Senate that had rejected the treaty. Murphy, some charged, had been overly zealous in pursuing annexation; he had promised and actually ordered military aid for Texas. Murphy informed President Houston: "The treaty is rejected and so is my nomination. The tail went with the hide." Before Murphy could return to the United States, he died in the yellow-fever epidemic that was sweeping the coast of Texas. To fill the post, Tyler appointed Tilghman A. Howard of Indiana. Originally from Tennessee, Howard was a friend of both Jackson's and Houston's and was expected to be able to persuade Houston to stand firm for annexation, if anyone could. Unfortunately, by mid August, Howard, too, had become a victim of yellow fever.

The American legation in Mexico City was in worse condition. In the spring of 1844, Wilson Shannon, who had twice been governor of Ohio, was named United States minister to Mexico to replace Waddy Thompson. Shannon was a most unfortunate choice. As a diplomat, he was a rank amateur; moreover, he lacked tact and was completely devoid of common sense. Later, as governor of Kansas Territory during the Buchanan administration, he contributed significantly to the unrest in that area. Perhaps it was well that he did not arrive in Mexico City until the end of August, but in the meantime, the legation was in the hands of Benjamin Green, Duff Green's son, who had been promoted from secretary to chargé d'affaires.[6]

On the United States political scene, Texas and Oregon, but particularly Texas, obliterated all other issues. Whig anxieties were expressed at a mass meeting in Lexington, Kentucky, where it was said that scheming politicians were using the Texas issue to divert the populace from proper consideration of the far-more-important domestic questions that alone should decide the presidential election. Clay, no longer as certain about where southern Whigs would stand, was worried. Even in Kentucky there were increasing calls for immediate annexation and expressions of dissatisfaction about their candidate's statements in his *National Intelligencer* letter. On 1 July, Clay tried either to clarify or to modify his position in a letter to the *Tuscaloosa Monitor,* which later became known as his first "Alabama Letter." In it he denied that he had any personal objection to annexation, but because of opposition from a considerable number of northern states, he feared that a move at this time would jeopardize the Union. This did not satisfy the growing number of proannexationists in the Deep South. Would not refusal to see the matter their way also jeopardize the Union? Why was Clay pandering to the North? The letter only inflamed the issue. On 27 July, Clay wrote a second "Alabama Letter," in which he again stressed the danger of insisting upon immediate annexation. Repeating some statements from his *National Intelligencer* letter, he said he would be happy to have Texas become a part of the Union if this could be accomplished without dishonor or war, with the consent of all concerned, and upon fair and just terms. Clay seemed almost to be echoing Robert Walker when he said slavery should not enter into a consideration of whether or not the nation should encompass Texas. Slavery was destined, at some distant day, for extinction "by the operation of the inevitable laws of population." It would be unwise to refuse a permanent acquisition, which would exist as long as the globe remained, on account of a temporary institution.

This was an attempt to please southerners by saying that northerners should not oppose annexation because of slavery, but in certain sections of the South the idea of slavery's becoming extinct was not acceptable. If elected and faced with the Texas issue, Clay promised to be governed by public opinion and the duty of preserving the Union. This generalization gave no comfort to either side. Clay's biographer Glyndon G. Van Deusen has contended: "Clay's position was consistent throughout—a consistent straddle. No one could be sure from these letters what would be his future attitude toward annexation." Moreover, the Liberty party, with James Birney again heading the ticket, was attracting antislavery Whigs who felt uncomfortable about voting for a southern slaveholder whose position on annexation was nebulous.[7]

Within the Democratic party, divisiveness also was a serious problem. Van Buren Democrats were bitter about the treatment that their candidate had received at the national convention. Silas Wright thought the consequences could be unpleasant. "In my deliberate judgment," he told Polk, "our Union was never in so much danger as at this moment." Northern Democrats had no confidence "in the faith and fidelity of their southern brethren." Words of a similar nature had been voiced by Calhoun, regarding southerners' feelings about their northern brethren. However, both Calhoun and Van Buren and those who followed them took heart when Polk, after receiving the official notification of his nomination, wrote in his letter of acceptance that if elected, it was his settled purpose not to be a candidate for reelection. At the convention there had been rumors of a one-term Polk presidency. Now the declaration was public, and with the passage of four years, those who had been disappointed in 1844 might again be able to pursue their presidential dreams. For the present, Calhoun's goal was to stay on in the State Department if Polk was victorious.

To defeat Clay, Polk had to keep the fragments of his party together. The task was not easy. Robert Walker assured Polk that the Texas issue would carry the South, and because Pennsylvania was crucial, Polk should indicate his willingness to go along with a tariff increase, at least for "incidental protection." Polk did so in a letter to John K. Kane of Philadelphia, a letter that enraged Robert Barnwell Rhett of South Carolina, already overwrought by the defeat of the Texas treaty and the "treachery" committed by Tyler and northern Democrats in the passage of the tariff of 1842. Southern Democratic reaction to the letter made Polk realize the folly of making public statements, and for the remainder of the campaign, he kept silent on sensitive issues. Unfortunately for the Whigs, their candidate failed to see the wisdom of doing so.[8]

By mid July, Calhoun had decided that Polk was a fine candidate, the best nomination "that could be made under all the circumstances." He urged his friends everywhere to give the ticket their hearty support. He had strong hopes of its success, but in order for it to succeed, unity was mandatory. One of the more perplexing problems was what to do about Tyler's candidacy. Was the president serious in accepting the nomination of the splinter group in Baltimore? In his letter of acceptance, Tyler interpreted the nomination as a vindication of his presidency, and he chronicled all the abuses that had been heaped upon him by both Whigs and Democrats. Whether or not he truly believed in it, he professed to see a grass-roots desire for his candidacy: "I have not been an inattentive observer of the course of public opinion in my favor, as manifested in numerous primary assemblies and resolutions of lay masses of the people, in most States of the Union." But he intimated that his main reason for accepting was the better leverage it would give him in his pursuit of annexation, a goal of greater importance than the presidency. However, with Polk committed to immediate annexation, Tyler's bid for reelection appeared extraneous. Yet, his "party" went ahead with plans for an active campaign.

Tyler's entire attention was not on politics. His romance with Julia Gardiner had prospered, and on 26 June, in a ceremony that was kept secret from the public, they were married in the Episcopal Church of the Ascension on Fifth Avenue in New York. Two days later, a wedding reception was held in the Blue Room of the White House, and Julia entered upon her short, but most enjoyable, grand tenure as undoubtedly the most conspicuous First Lady the nation had yet seen. "I have commenced my auspicious reign and am in quiet possession of the Presidential Mansion," she wrote to her mother. But the presidential mansion was in disgraceful condition; it was run-down and dirty. Throughout the Tyler administration, the House of Representatives had refused to vote funds even to keep the White House in a "minimum state of cleanliness."

Early in July the newlyweds left Washington for a month's stay in a cottage at Old Point Comfort, Virginia, on the shore of Hampton Roads, with brief visits to Sherwood Forest, Tyler's plantation on the James River, and to Norfolk. The president's marriage to a vivacious lady at least thirty years younger than he caused endless comments, which kept Washington society amused for the remainder of his term. In recording the event in his diary, Philip Hone referred to the president as "the old fool." Others were less kind. Julia seemed not to mind; she made no move to hide her delight in her new position, which some found offensive and unbecoming. Jessie Benton Frémont remarked that Julia's "dress and her demeanor were much commented on by the elders who had seen other President's wives take their new state more easily."

After their return to Washington, the Tylers entertained lavishly, at their own expense, and introduced their guests to the latest dance fad, the polka. This and the risqué waltz were featured at the frequent White House balls, which shocked more conservative members of the populace. Julia was enthusiastic, bright, and well informed. She was, the historian Robert Seager II has said, "a born ballroom lobbyist"; she took great interest in the affairs of state, particularly the annexation issue and her husband's bid for the presidency, a bid that she fully expected him to continue to the November election.[9]

Tyler was not so certain. From various Democratic quarters came urgent messages asking him to withdraw. It was not that experienced politicians thought he had a chance to defeat Polk and Clay; realizing that the election would be a close contest, however, they feared that he could draw enough votes away from Polk to give the victory to Clay—an outcome that Tyler surely would not relish. During June and July, Thomas Ritchie's editorials in the *Richmond Enquirer* repeatedly exhorted Tyler to unite with the Democrats in support of Polk. Some concerned party members even hinted at a possible Polk-Tyler Union ticket, if George Dallas could be persuaded to withdraw, but this was not in any way a serious consideration of the majority.

Robert Walker was anxious enough that he sought out Tyler at Sherwood Forest, where Walker undertook the "most disagreeable duty" of prevailing upon Tyler not to do anything to harm Polk's chances. Alarmed by movements on the part of Tyler's Philadelphia friends to run separate Tyler tickets for congressional, state, and county offices, as well as for members of the electoral college, Walker was convinced that the president must withdraw. Pennsylvanians were encouraging Tylerites in other states to adopt similar measures, and these efforts could spell defeat for Polk.

Tyler listened courteously to Walker's plea, and later, the president admitted that it had given him considerable satisfaction to realize how deeply the Democrats felt "the great necessity of my cooperation." During the several hours that Walker spent at Sherwood Forest, Tyler acknowledged that he had no expectation of winning the presidency in the 1844 election. He was willing to take himself out of the race at once, but only on certain conditions. His followers, whose number he estimated at about 150,000, were chiefly former Jacksonian Democrats who, like himself, had left the Democratic party and had become Whigs. Tyler wanted assurance, "on reliable authority," that they would be welcomed back into the Democratic party, where they would be "treated as brethren and equals." Tyler feared that if he were to withdraw without obtaining such an assurance, either his followers would remain neutral in the election or they would vote for Clay. If the promise were given, presumably by Polk, Tyler pledged that he would unite in support of the party's candidate, and he had no doubt that his supporters would follow his lead "zealously and efficiently."

"The importance of this union and cooperation," Walker informed Polk, "*cannot be over-rated*," and Walker asked Polk to write a private letter to Tyler, welcoming Tyler and his friends back into the party. Perhaps, Walker also suggested, Jackson might write a letter, one that could be published, to some friend, praising Tyler's presidential accomplishments and expressing the party's "cordiality and joy" at his return to the fold.

When Polk forwarded Walker's suggestions to Jackson, the former president was irate, saying they displayed a "great want of common sense." If Polk were to write to Tyler, welcoming the latter's return and expressing Polk's gratitude for the cooperation of Tyler and his friends, political opponents could seize upon it as a bargain, an intrigue for the presidency, just like the Adams-Clay "corrupt bargain" of 1825. This would destroy Polk. Furthermore, Jackson had no intention of writing to anyone in praise of Tyler. It would be better to play on Tyler's vanity, his "sagacity" and "fondness for popularity," by telling him how important he was to Democratic success and how grateful the party would be if he would withdraw. "No letter from you or your friends must be written or published upon any such subject," Jackson warned.

There was another matter bothering Tyler, one that he also made a condition for his leaving the presidential race. Blair's *Washington Globe* and other Van Buren–Benton papers were assailing Tyler at every turn, charging that Democrats held him in as much contempt as did the Whigs. Tyler wanted this stopped. "Support the cause of Polk and Dallas," Jackson directed Blair, "and let Tyler alone." Jackson then sent messages to William B. Lewis, his long-time friend, and to Secretary of the Navy John Y. Mason, which Jackson intended to be conveyed to Tyler in one way or another. These messages let it be known that if the president did not retire from the race, he would be responsible for a Democratic defeat; however, he did have an opportunity to save the party and to leave office with greater popularity than he had ever possessed. Moreover, Polk was willing to say, if elected, he would have no prejudice or unkind feelings toward any portion of the party. Although Blair never was reconciled to the idea of telling "good men & true, that Tyler & his handful of prostituted followers" should be welcomed back, he did comply with Jackson's directive to "let Tyler alone."[10]

On 18 August, Tyler informed Jackson that he intended to withdraw from the canvass. Two days later the *Madisonian* carried Tyler's letter "To My Friends throughout the Union," explaining why he had accepted the nomination and why, now, he was withdrawing. In the congressional election of 1842, Tyler contended, the Democratic party had been victorious because the people had desired to sustain him in what he had done, in the stand he had taken. Yet, those who controlled the party had made no friendly gestures toward him. Rather, they had "exhibited the bitterest hostility and most unrelenting spirit of opposition," and their chief objective seemed to have been to deprecate and disgrace him in every way possible. The individuals and groups who wanted him to be a candidate in 1844 did so in a "self-sacrificing spirit," and Tyler said he was grateful. "An indistinct hope that the great question of annexation" could, in some degree, be furthered by his candidacy had been another reason for his acceptance of the nomination.

A large portion of his letter was addressed to the former Jacksonians who, during the late 1830s, had left the Democratic party and joined the Whigs but who were clearly distinct from Clay and his supporters, who had designed, "in the first instance, to drive me from the government, and in the last to overwhelm me with obloquy and reproach." Tyler asked these "synthetic" Whigs, as Clay regarded them, to judge the state of the nation in 1844. Had the currency ever been sounder or the rates of exchange lower? A well-supplied exchequer now gave evidence of the expansion of trade and of the stable basis upon which public credit rested. Stocks, for which no bidders could at one time be found, were now selling for respectable sums. All this had been accomplished without a Bank of the United States and without weakening the executive branch by surrendering to Congress' determination to make its will supreme. Checks and balances had been preserved, and the right of veto had been protected, despite all attempts to overturn these constitutional provisions. In foreign affairs, longstanding problems that had threatened the peace had been adjusted. Efforts had been made to create markets for American goods throughout the world. Tyler deplored the rejection of the Zollverein treaty, but much more tragic, he believed, had been the Senate's refusal to approve the treaty with Texas. What upset him even more were the motives that had been ascribed to him for negotiating the treaty. Benton, Tyler said, had accused him of having two prominent ones: personal ambition and the dissolution of the Union. Clay, in a recent letter (one of the Alabama Letters), had called the treaty infamous and said that it had been entered into with sinister objectives. Clay, Tyler recalled, had tried to acquire Texas in 1827, when he was secretary of state. What was there now to have rendered a treaty infamous that had not existed then? Clay had dealt with Mexico for the annexation of Texas while Spain still considered Mexico its province, but the United States had recognized Mexico's independence and had claimed a perfect right to treat with Mexico for Texas. "Eight years ago we recognized Texas as independent, and surely our right to negotiate with her implied no worse faith than in 1827, to negotiate with Mexico for Texas, without consulting Spain."

Tyler denied any desire to dissolve the Union: "I regard the preservation of the Union as the first great American interest. I equally disapprove of all threats of its dissolution, whether they proceed from the North or the South. The glory of my country, its safety, and its prosperity alike depend on Union; and he who would contemplate its destruction, even for a moment, and form plans to accomplish it, deserves the deepest anathemas of the human race." He was certain that Texas would increase the nation's strength, and he intended to exert his best efforts in securing its annexation, "either now or at a future date." In closing, he asked his countrymen candidly to review his presidency and impartially to compare the condition of the country now with what it had been three years earlier.[11]

The letter was forceful, and Tyler's points were apt. It was an opportunity for him to make a public defense of his actions and principles and to answer his critics. He did not have a press secretary or an important news medium as significant as the *National Intelligencer* or the *Washington Globe* through which he could speak to the general public. His wife was more progressive. She employed a part-time correspondent of the *New York Herald*, mainly to give her social events favorable publicity—"to sound Julia's praises far and wide," according to her sister. The president, however, believed it would be unseemly for him to indulge in such a practice.

Also clearly indicated in Tyler's letter was that he had not accepted the nomination under any delusion that he would be elected. Partly, he wanted to prove to himself and to the country that he had some support, and he understandably needed to salve the wounds inflicted upon him by Whigs and Democrats alike. Tyler took pleasure in saying that if Polk were elected, "his administration will be a continuance of my own, since he will be found the advocate of most of my measures."[12]

Clay was uncomfortable. Early in the summer he had been sure enough of his election to be sarcastically demeaning about Polk and Dallas: "Are our Democratic friends serious in the nominations which they have made at Baltimore? . . . No matter how many candidates or who they bring out, we must beat them with ease if we do one half our duty." As late as mid September, the *Intelligencer* announced that Polk would be fortunate to carry seven states. By that time, however, Clay had become worried. He wrote another letter on the Texas issue, this time addressed to Gales and Seaton, editors of the *Intelligencer*. Previously, Clay had vowed not to permit another letter on public affairs to be drawn from him, but now he felt it necessary "to correct the erroneous interpretation of one or two of those which I had previously written." This was a mistake. The Democrats were quick to increase their taunts about Clay's fence-straddling. He was in a difficult position. His own state of Kentucky had a warm interest in annexation, and people there were perplexed about where he stood. Then, when Cassius M. Clay, a strong antislavery man, began to campaign for his distant relative, saying Henry Clay's feelings were with the cause of emancipation, there was an outcry from the South. Clay's attempt to explain that he was neither proslavery nor an abolitionist caused a number of antislavery northern Whigs, especially in New York, to declare their support for the Liberty party. Clay "wires in and wires out, and leaves the people still in doubt," a Missouri editor jibed.[13]

In New York there was great excitement. In the city, both the Whigs and the Democrats held nightly meetings. The Whigs trotted out their most important personages. Webster campaigned diligently for the party throughout the Northeast, but he rarely mentioned Clay's name. The Whigs bent every effort, but the New York Democrats gained an advantage by making a significant decision to nominate Silas Wright as their gubernatorial candidate. Highly respected and superbly qualified, Wright attracted strong support for the Democratic ticket. An important Whig moaned that the Democrats were "exerting themselves to the utmost and have certainly made a great hit in the nomination of Silas Wright, while our friends picked one of their feeblest men in Fillmore, who has no personal popularity and labors under the disadvantage of not being generally known." For the Whigs, there was "nothing like the enthusiasm that was displayed here in 1840," when the party's appeal, while superficial, had been optimistic, with songs, hard cider, and good cheer. Now there was a tendency to be negative—to be against foreigners, against Catholics or Jews, or against annexation and slavery. True, Harrison had equivocated on nativism, but the issue was not as significant then as it was to be four years later. The Native American party—or the American Republican party, which it became—had grown rapidly during 1843 and 1844, and northeastern Whigs were taking advantage of this attitude. Theodore Frelinghuysen, Clay's running mate, was especially popular with the nativists, and in New York and Massachusetts the movement was exceptionally strong. Meanwhile, the Democrats were adept at getting immigrants to the polls, whether or not they were qualified to vote.[14]

Before Tyler withdrew from the campaign, his brother-in-law Alexander Gardiner and other partisans of the president saw to it that Whigs were removed from various positions in order to make way for the "faithful." Even Edward Curtis, whose appointment as collector of the port of New York had caused so much trouble between Harrison and Clay, was purged, to be replaced by Cornelius Peter Van Ness, a Tyler admirer. However, David Lambert, an ardent Whig, said there could be no question about Van Ness's qualifications. "Capt. Tyler made an excellent appointment. . . . I know not when so large a portion of the public revenues could be deposited in safer or more competent hands." After Tyler took himself out of contention, his followers immediately campaigned and wielded patronage for Polk, for the Democratic party, and especially for Texas. Robert Tyler was busy in Philadelphia, attempting to win Pennsylvania's substantial electoral vote for the Democratic candidate. For himself, Alexander Gardiner wanted a colonelcy and an appointment as Tyler's honorary aide-de-camp, but on this, Tyler drew the line and stood firm, even against Julia's fervent pleading.

Francis P. Blair, who stifled his criticism of the president on instructions from Jackson, was upset with the number of appointments that were being made by the outgoing chief executive. Tyler, Blair complained to Jackson, was filling as many offices as possible with "reconverted Democrats" before Polk could have a chance to make his own selections. Furthermore, Tyler expected the appointees not only to be treated as brethren but also to be retained in a Polk administration. Jackson relayed the message to Polk with the comment, "I have said to my friend Blair that you have sufficient energy to give yourself elbow room, whenever it becomes necessary."

Tyler's withdrawal may or may not have had an impact on the outcome of an election that was beset by innumerable crosscurrents. It is impossible to isolate one reason for Clay's defeat in an exceptionally close contest which shocked Whigs to the depth of their beings. Polk's popular vote was 1,337,243 and Clay's, 1,299,062, giving Polk 170 electoral votes to Clay's 105. Compared with 1840, Birney appreciably increased his support, with 62,300 ballots cast for the abolitionist candidate. The new House of Representatives would have 143 Democrats and 77 Whigs, and the Democrats gained control of the Senate. The result, said the Whig *National Intelligencer,* was "wholly unexpected, the event took us by surprise. . . . The blow came upon us with a staggering force."[15]

Without question, Texas had much to do with the outcome. The issue deprived Van Buren of the nomination, and by many accounts, Clay could have defeated Van Buren. Certainly, slavery and expansion would have had less importance in a contest between those two. Clay would not have been moved to write so many letters and to have been as equivocal on controversial matters. Early on, Clay had thought he could defeat Polk with ease, "if we do one half our duty," but his fence-straddling had proved fatal. Clay blamed "a most extraordinary combination of adverse circumstances" for his failure to attain the goal he so persistently had sought. "If there had been no Native party," he rationalized, "or if all its members had been truer to their principles; or if the recent foreigners had not been all united against us; or if the foreign Catholics had not been arrayed on the other side; or if the Abolitionists had been true to their avowed principles; or if there had been no frauds, we should have triumphed."

Clay's "wiring in and out" on annexation cost the Whigs votes in the South. Alabama Whigs deserted their party in large numbers. In order to save the Whig party in Georgia, Alexander Stephens abandoned his opposition to annexation, and James Lyons, a leading Virginia Whig, spoke in its favor. Georgia, Louisiana, and Mississippi, which had been in the Harrison column in 1840, cast their electoral votes for Polk, as did Maine and the very crucial states of New York and Pennsylvania. In the Deep South there was desire not only for Texas but also for the preservation of a way of life and for strengthening the position of the South in the nation. In the North, foreigners, who were fearful of what would happen to them in the event of a Whig victory, swarmed to the polls in large numbers and voted Democratic.[16]

"You and the holy cause," Hone lamented to Clay, "have been sacrificed to fraud, corruption and misrepresentation, and the instruments used to effect the object were foreign voters made to order. . . .

Foreigners who have 'no lot or inheritance' in the matter have robbed us of our birthright. Ireland has reconquered the country which England lost." A North Carolinian insisted that there should be no citizens of the United States except those born within its borders. "Had that been the law, we should not now be like men in a thunder squall waiting with trembling anxiety for the next clap." Clay admitted he had great sympathy for the Native American party, but he warned the Whigs not to absorb it or allow themselves to be absorbed by the organization. Perhaps, he said, petitions should be presented to alter the naturalization laws.[17]

Publicly, Webster declared that the Whigs had been defeated by southern determination to expand slave territory; but to his friends, he expressed the belief that Clay had destroyed his chance for the presidency by his obstinate and vindictive opposition to Tyler. Leslie Coombs, a close Kentucky friend and associate of Clay's, was convinced that annexation was the rock upon which Clay's hopes had been wrecked. Polk had carried seven Free States and eight Slave States, Coombs noted, and Tennessee had gone for Clay by the narrowest of margins. Candidly, Coombs said, "but for our great attachment to Henry Clay, we would not have saved Kentucky," and he now thought the Whig party could no longer sustain its opposition to annexation. "We opposed Tyler's treaty mainly because of its secrecy and the people's ignorance of its negotiation. But the people have been appealed to and have elected a mere Tom Tit over the old Eagle." Fraud, falsehoods, and foreigners had also contributed to Clay's defeat. "Our strongest man has been beaten by a mere John Doe." Oscar D. Lambert, in *Presidential Politics in the United States, 1841–1844*, has expressed the belief that the nomination of Silas Wright as the Democratic gubernatorial candidate carried New York for the party. Wright, Lambert has contended, was the "secret hero of the Polk victory."

"For the present," William Preston told Clay, "the Whig party of the South is dispersed, and we cannot know our position until the heat and smoke of the conflict have passed away." Thomas Giles of Richmond, Virginia, reported that the Whig party of his city was "utterly destroyed," that the leaders were "completely prostrated, done up, quite chap-fallen." Although the Polk victory was not decisive "for our purposes," Giles thought it was time to come to a favorable determination on the subject of annexation.[18]

Tyler preferred to believe that the people had spoken, that the election was a mandate for annexation; and as soon as Congress had convened in December, he planned to press for a joint resolution. Calhoun was impatient. For weeks prior to the election, in fact all during the summer, he had been troubled by the uncertain future of the Texas project. In his own state there was serious talk of secession. Robert Barnwell Rhett was a main instigator. Disturbed by the tariff of 1842 and the defeat of the annexation treaty, Rhett was calling for a convention of southern states to consider what steps should be taken if whoever was elected in November did not advocate the repeal of the 1842 tariff or if abolitionists were to succeed in keeping Texas out of the Union. Many of Rhett's statements were not unlike those that Calhoun had made at one time or another; but at this juncture, with annexation still pending, Calhoun concluded that it was better to soften his approach. James Hammond could see no future for the South within the Union; he believed Calhoun was "endeavoring to sacrifice the South . . . on the altar of his ambition."[19]

Calhoun, concerned about the restiveness among people in his own state as well as in other southern regions, wanted quick action on Texas. He thought Tyler should call a special session; but the president, a majority of the cabinet, and Polk all agreed that this would be unwise. Extended debates so close to the election could spell trouble for the Democratic candidate.

There were other reasons for Calhoun's nervousness. He was convinced that Britain was again meddling in affairs south of the border—making promises to Mexico in return for California, while at the same time urging Texas to reject any attachment to the United States. It was true that the new British minister to Mexico, Charles Bankhead, had made friendly overtures to Santa Anna. This was enough to encourage the Mexican president to announce again that he was planning a reconquest of Texas. In England, Lord Aberdeen, heartened by the Senate's defeat of annexation, was occupied with developing a formal convention to be signed by Texas, Mexico, England, and France, a "Diplomatic Act" whereby Texas would be guaranteed independence and appropriate boundaries and whereby Britain and France would have the right to intervene to prevent violations of the guarantees, including further United States attempts at annexation.

William King, in Paris, proved to be an able diplomat in frustrating Aberdeen's plan. With help from Calhoun, King warned Louis Philippe about British plans to attain commercial control of the Western World. King stressed the importance of friendship with the United States, a country that had the warmest feelings for France and that wanted to annex Texas so as to prevent British control of that republic.

From Washington, Pakenham cautioned his government against interfering in Texas. If Britain again appeared to be threatening United States interests there, Clay's election could be in jeopardy, and Britain wanted Clay to be elected. Incidents in other areas of the world created sufficient Anglo-French tensions to cause rising resentment among the French people, which deterred Louis Philippe from joining Britain in the suggested agreement. He and his foreign minister, Guizot, were anxious to cultivate better relations with England, King informed Tyler, "but such is the hostile feeling of the French people, that they dare not. In this state of things, we have nothing to fear from any union of action between these governments."[20]

In the meantime, however, Texas' fears of a Mexican invasion raised again the matter of military aid from the United States. In late August, Calhoun received a dispatch from Tilghman Howard saying the Houston administration wanted reassurance that such assistance would be forthcoming if needed. On 10 September, not knowing that Howard had succumbed to yellow fever on 16 August, Calhoun sent the chargé a somewhat evasive reply. The president, Calhoun wrote, wanted Howard to assure the government of Texas that he, Tyler, felt the full force of the obligation to protect Texas while annexation was pending. "As far as it relates to the Executive Department, he [Tyler] is prepared to use all his powers for that purpose," but the Constitution prescribed "narrow limits" that would be impossible for the president to transcend. All Tyler could do would be to protest to the Mexican government against the renewal of war and "to recommend to Congress to adopt measures to repel any attacks which may be made."

Charles Raymond, who had replaced Van Zandt in Washington, informed Anson Jones, now the president-elect of Texas, that the Tyler administration was prepared to do more to protect Texas than it could publicly say. Discretion was necessary, because congressional cooperation on annexation soon would be sought, and it would be unwise to irritate members of Congress by the president's seeming to infringe on war powers, claimed by senators and representatives as their constitutional prerogative. In the cabinet, Mason, Nelson, and Wilkins wanted Tyler to tread softly. Calhoun was more bold. "Had he [Calhoun] the power," Raymond told Jones, "the army would doubtless be ordered right into Texas, to repel any attack upon her."[21]

Calhoun did not have the power, but there were things he could do. On 12 September 1844, Duff Green, who had returned to the United States from England early in the year, was appointed consul at Galveston in the Republic of Texas. As consuls were expected to glean their livelihood from the fees they collected, there was no salary attached to the position. Again, Tyler obviously must have acceded to an appointment for Green, but it is problematical whether or not he realized that the consulship was merely a cover for Green's real assignment.

On 13 September, Calhoun again wrote to Tilghman Howard, informing him that Green "leaves here tomorrow direct for Vera Cruz via Galveston." Green was to go to Mexico as a courier, to deliver messages to Wilson Shannon. In the summer of 1843, it will be recalled, Calhoun had approached Secretary of State Upshur with the idea of sending Green to Mexico "in some official capacity." Upshur had replied that he could not employ another person at the legation in Mexico but had suggested that Green could go as a bearer of dispatches. Green had not gone then, but now, in the fall of 1844, Calhoun resurrected the plan, and sent Green off to Mexico. "At his [Calhoun's] request," Green later recorded, "I went to Mexico to aid in conducting the negotiation for the acquisition of Texas, New Mexico, and California, and upon handing me his letter of instructions, he [Calhoun] remarked: 'If you succeed in this negotiation our commerce in the Pacific will in a few years, be greatly more valuable than in the Atlantic.'"

Shortly after Calhoun had penned his 13 September letter to Howard, he had learned about the chargé's death. At once the position had been offered to Andrew Jackson Donelson, a namesake and nephew-by-marriage of the former president. Because of this relationship, Donelson was expected to have considerable influence with Sam Houston. Although in a few months, Houston would no longer head the Texas government, it was thought his views for or against annexation would continue to sway a large portion of the populace. The appointment, Calhoun told Donelson, was of great importance, "one of the very first magnitude." The fate of annexation could "depend on him who shall fill the Mission now tendered to you."[22]

Tyler appealed to Jackson to urge his nephew to accept. It was vital to the Texas cause to persuade Houston, "if he entertains any feeling antagonistical to the U. States and favourable to England, to pause ere he decides against annexation." Tyler also informed Jackson of the instructions that had been dispatched to the United States minister in Mexico, directing him to oppose, in the strongest terms, any renewal of hostilities against Texas. "We have declared that we cannot look upon the war as other than offensive in the highest degree to this govt., seeing that Texas entered into that Treaty [annexation treaty] upon our invitation and that if any one should be singled out as the peculiar object of Mexican vengeance it should be the U. States." Tyler labeled as "atrocious and barbarous" and "anti-Christian and savage" Santa Anna's threats as to the manner in which he intended to conduct the war against Texas.

If the objective was a negotiation with Mexico in the hope of settling the annexation of Texas and of acquiring New Mexico and California, sending Green to Mexico City was an incredible act. Among Calhoun's opponents in Washington there were suspicions that the secretary intended to goad Mexico into making arrogant and insulting threats against the United States which could be used to rouse congressional support for a joint resolution. Calhoun may have had a more grandiose plan—namely, of provoking a war with Mexico and thereby not only protecting Texas but also obtaining New Mexico, California, and even Mexico itself, or at least the northern provinces.

Calhoun's instructions to Shannon, delivered by Green, were in no way conciliatory. The secretary gave the minister every indication that the United States was in no mood to be friendly. Diplomacy played no part in Calhoun's denunciation of Mexico and its threats of war against Texas. "Shall we stand by, and witness in silence the renewal of the war by Mexico, and its prosecution in this bloodthirsty and desolating spirit?" Should Mexico be permitted to defeat annexation, "a measure long cherished, and indispensable alike to the safety and welfare of the United States and Texas?" Shannon was to protest, in strong language, the renewal of war "and the barbarous and bloody manner in which it is proclaimed it will be conducted." These, Calhoun said, were Tyler's views. Nevertheless, if annexation were achieved, the United States would be prepared to consult with Mexico on the adjustment of "all questions growing out of it, including that of boundary, on the most liberal terms."[23]

With Green there to urge him on, Shannon used "rash and insulting" language in warning the Mexican government that any unwarranted reconquest of Texas would not be tolerated. Mexico's new foreign minister, Manuel Rejón, countered with a protest against United States aid to Texan rebels. Increasingly heated messages flew back and forth until Shannon called Rejón a liar and foolishly, without permission from the State Department, issued a statement saying that until Rejón had retracted his derogatory remarks, he, Shannon, would sever relations with the government of Mexico. Rejón had no intention of backing down, and Shannon sat in the legation with little to do except send dispatches to Calhoun calling for war with Mexico.

Duff Green, who was busily writing long letters to Calhoun explaining why he had been detained in Mexico longer than anticipated, described the situation as hastening to a crisis. Santa Anna, Green said, was in great disfavor with the Mexican congress and with the governors of the northern provinces, but the opposition had no leadership, and there was no prospect of Santa Anna's being overthrown. Moreover, any party that might come into power on Santa Anna's downfall would be compelled to take as strong or stronger ground against the United States than Santa Anna had done. The only solution was war with Mexico. "They have so long bullied, insulted and plundered us with impunity that they have lost all respect for us as a nation, altho they fear us as a people." It was up to the United States to teach decent behavior to Mexico, "and the advantage of a war with Mexico will be that we can indemnify ourselves while chastizing Mexico." Such a war would show other nations what the United States could and would do. This would command their respect. "If you could go abroad as I have done you would feel that we have lost caste and nothing but a war can regain the position we have lost." Shannon echoed Green. Nothing could resolve the difficulties with Mexico until the United States either had whipped Mexico or made that country believe that it would do so. "I think we ought to present to Mexico an *ultimatum*." On his return to Galveston, Green continued to press for war with Mexico, recommending the seizure of Vera Cruz as the first step. British creditors, he reported, held a mortgage on California, and if this was not repaid by 1847, the creditors would take possession of the region. The Mexican government refused to discuss United States acquisition of Texas, California, or any part of the Mexican domain; therefore, according to Green, there was "one way and but one in which all that our Government desires and much more than you asked for can be had." The British minister in Mexico City, he warned, was openly supporting Santa Anna.[24]

Anson Jones was not happy to have Green in Texas; Jones suspected that Green had been sent to excite the populace, even to the extent of creating an uprising against that republic's government if it should opt not to become a part of the United States. Fortunately, Donelson arrived in Galveston on 11 November, en route to the Texas capital. In contrast with Green and Shannon, Donelson was an ideal diplomat who refused to listen seriously to Green's gossip and rumors, although like his uncle, Donelson was a pronounced Anglophobe who was convinced that the British were constantly plotting to undermine the best interests of the United States. His initial observations in Texas, concerning the dissatisfaction with pledges of United States military protection and concerning Houston's tendency to talk about friendship with England, prompted Donelson to stress to Calhoun the necessity of quick congressional action. "Every day's delay is adding strength to the hands of those who are playing the game for the ascendancy of British influence in this Republic." When Houston, in his final address to the Texas congress, did not make any encouraging remarks about annexation but instead emphasized the splendid future that Texas could have as an independent nation, Donelson was uneasy. His anxiety increased when Jones, in his inaugural address, made no mention of annexation.

Tyler did not have to be convinced of the need for haste in concluding the acquisition of Texas. He had opposed a special session only because it might endanger Polk's election. With the election achieved, Tyler was ready to use every means possible to induce the House and the Senate to act on a joint resolution during the final session of the Twenty-eighth Congress, which opened on 2 December. He had been preparing his message since October, attempting "to make it strong and decided."[25]

Shortly before Congress received Tyler's annual message, John Quincy Adams presented another sensitive item to the House. For years, Adams had led the fight for the right of antislavery advocates to have their petitions received and debated by the people's representatives. Year after year he had tried various ways to loosen the gag that was strangling the requested deliberations. In 1843 he had an opportunity to try another approach in attacking the proslavery forces. He introduced a resolution, drafted by his son Charles Francis and passed by the legislature of Massachusetts, to amend Article I, section 2, of the Constitution, which allowed slaveholding states to determine the number of representatives they were entitled to have in the House by including their slave population, with five slaves equaling three white persons. For all of his political life, the three-fifths ratio had bothered Adams. The thought that the South was rewarded in this manner for holding human beings in bondage galled him. Even though he was well aware that such an amendment could not command a two-thirds vote of both houses and that it did not have any chance of being approved by the necessary three-fourths of the states, he doggedly pushed the resolution. A select committee of the House brought in a majority report against the proposal; and the House adopted the report by a vote of 156 to 13. The reasoning was that the framers of the Constitution had believed that the three-fifths compromise was essential to the formation of the Union and that, in order to preserve the Union, it was now necessary to retain the compromise.

Three times during 1844, the Massachusetts legislature sent the resolution to Adams, who presented it to the House. Three times the House refused to receive it. For the moment, Adams conceded, this was a lost cause, but eliminating the gag rule was another matter. Only a majority of the House was needed to accomplish that. In December 1843, Adams's motion to revoke the rule came close to being approved. The political climate was changing. The abolition movement was gaining momentum. Coupling opposition to the gag rule, on the one hand, with protests against violations of the right of petition, on the other hand, had been a master stroke. Also, when the Texas issue and the Pakenham letter had made slavery a political matter, many northerners who had supported the gag rule in order to keep peace in Congress or because they heeded southern fears of slave rebellion if the topic was agitated no longer saw a need for silence on the House floor.

On 3 December 1844, when Adams, as he had done for many years, offered his motion to repeal the gag rule, the motion was immediately approved by a vote of 108 to 80. All the northern Whigs, 4 southern Whigs, and 20 percent more northern Democrats than ever before voted with the majority. Calhoun reported to R. M. T. Hunter that with few exceptions, "the votes of the two sections, slave holding and non slave holding, arrayed against each other. They appear to me to be coming daily, more and more into deadly conflict." For the nation's good or evil, debates on slavery would, from this time on, widen the breach between the North and the South.[26]

Significantly, the president, in his annual message, the reading of which was postponed until action had been taken on the gag rule, mentioned the wonderful freedoms guaranteed to the American people by the Bill of Rights. Tyler listed freedom of religion, the press, and speech; the right of trial by jury; and habeas corpus; but he said nothing about the right of petition. Perhaps it was a deliberate omission, but the inevitable connection between Texas and slavery had already made the gag rule an anachronism.

Most of Tyler's message dealt with Texas and the Senate's failure to ratify the treaty, chiefly because, as many senators argued, the question of whether or not there should be a treaty had not been submitted to the "ordeal of public opinion." This, he declared, was an untenable objection. A president unquestionably had the constitutional power to negotiate a treaty without a popular referendum. But now the matter was moot, public sentiment had been expressed, and Tyler claimed, "a controlling majority of the people and a large majority of the States have decided in favor of immediate annexation." Constituents of representatives and senators had made their wishes known "in terms most emphatic," leaving no doubt that action should be taken without delay, by joint resolution. Collateral issues should be postponed until later.

Along with his message, Tyler sent to Congress all correspondence relating to Texas and to Mexico's threats of a "war of desolation" that had been received or sent during the summer and fall of 1844. Although he denounced Mexico's belligerent attitude, Tyler did not accommodate Green and Shannon by seconding their call for a war with Mexico. All that Tyler requested was annexation.[27]

The House, which began debate on 12 December, soon encountered complications. The first annexation resolution that was introduced contained terms identical with those that had been included in the rejected treaty. This led to protracted arguments over the boundary, the assumption of the Texas debt, and other collateral issues, which Tyler and Calhoun wanted to defer until after annexation. Debates were long and acrimonious over these matters and over whether or not it was possible to annex a foreign power and admit it as a state. The question of annexation, Calhoun told R. M. T. Hunter, had to be "properly pressed," without consideration of complicated issues. All Calhoun wanted was merely a yes or no on whether to bring Texas into the Union. If this could be done, he believed the House would support it. The Senate might be more difficult to convince.

Albert Gallatin, a survivor of the generation that had produced the Constitution, pronounced that the resort to annexation by a joint resolution would be a travesty. Territory, he said, could be acquired only by treaty or by conquest. A joint resolution to admit Texas, a foreign nation, into the Union as a state, without first annexing it by treaty and admitting it as a territory, would be unconstitutional. The Constitution expressly and exclusively vested the treaty-making power in the president, with the consent of two-thirds of the Senate. Therefore, the House resolution, in its present form, was a violation of the Constitution. After Texas had been annexed by treaty, Congress would have the right to decide whether or not Texas qualified for statehood. When taking such action, a joint resolution would be the proper procedure; but to substitute the approval of a majority of both houses of Congress for two-thirds of the Senate when annexing territory would require an amendment to the Constitution.[28]

While discussions were continuing inside and outside of Congress, Donelson pleaded for haste: "Let us get annexation on any terms we can, [only] taking care not to have any thing in form or substance that would render doubtful its ratification by Texas." All other matters could be decided after the simple act of annexation, "when there will be no danger of loss of the Territory from British intrigue, or other causes."

However, the entire annexation project came very close to collapsing when Duff Green managed to incur the wrath of President Anson Jones and much of the Texas government. While Donelson was away from his post on a brief visit to the United States, Green turned the duties of his Galveston office over to the vice-consul, journeyed to the Texas capital, and engaged members of the legislature in private conversations about land companies that he hoped to establish. From the lawmakers he wanted support for his schemes and their assurances that land-company charters would be granted that would guarantee various privileges and rights. Included in the charter that he had in mind for the Texas Land Company was the "power and capacity to monopolize the exclusive and perpetual use" of all the navigable streams in Texas. For the Del Norte Company he had even-more-fantastic plans. Part of this company's objective would be the conquest and occupancy, for Texas, of the Californias and the northern provinces of Mexico by an army, the composition of which was vague, assisted by around sixty thousand Indian warriors who would be brought from the western frontiers of the United States.

On several occasions, Green approached Jones with the proposals. The president was not impressed. Green then offered Jones a bribe in the form of portions of the corporate stock of the projected companies. The offer was accompanied by a threat: If Jones refused to cooperate, Green would instigate a revolution to overthrow his government. This, Green boasted, could be accomplished without difficulty. The people of Texas were unhappy because their officials had not been more enthusiastic about becoming a part of the United States. The extremely angry Jones called a meeting of his cabinet and directed the acting secretary of state, Ebenezer Allen, to inform Donelson of the revocation of Green's consular certification (his exequatur) and of the subsequent expulsion of Green from Texas. President Jones believed that Green was completely unqualified for his station.[29]

Immediately upon his return to Texas, Donelson notified Calhoun about all of this and then attempted to control the damage, informing Allen that Green was in no way authorized to commit the government of the United States to the conquest of California or any other region or to supply Indian warriors for such a purpose. Donelson explained that Green actually was a private citizen, that soon after Green had returned from Mexico, he had informed Donelson of his intention to become a legal resident of Texas and had turned the duties of his office over to the vice-consul, saying he did not want his name presented to the Senate for confirmation of his appointment. Therefore, Donelson contended that there was no reason for him to take cognizance of Green's absence from Galveston or to be responsible for his actions. "In this light then," Donelson assured Calhoun, "the objectionable conduct imputed to him [Green] ceases to have any higher importance than what belongs to an individual, private, character"; it should not injure the United States relationship with Texas. As consul, Donelson considered that Green was "out of his sphere" but perhaps was not as obnoxious as Jones and his administration portrayed him. Green was overly zealous in the cause of annexation and "approached the President [Jones] too familiarly," expecting his ideas to be considered "in a spirit of kindness," whereas, Texan governmental officials had watched Green "with suspicion from the beginning."[30]

Without a doubt, Green should never have been given authority to contact foreign nations, whether England, France, Mexico, or Texas. One explanation could be that some individuals in the United States government secretly promoted and condoned his activities. Green's appointment to the Galveston consulate at first puzzled Charles Elliot, the British chargé in Texas; but after reading in the papers about Green's proposals and his threats against Jones, Elliot decided the reason for Green's presence was clear. "He speaks of his expectation 'to encounter the combined influence of the British Minister, and the President of Texas, acting in concert for the purpose of defeating the wishes of a majority of the people of Texas and the United States.' . . . It is plain, in short, that he has some official mission *behind* Major Donelson's chair. . . . If he [Green] and Mr. Calhoun do not blow up annexation, it is *fire-proof*, that's all." Peel told Aberdeen that the expulsion of Green could have been made "a pretext with the U.S. for direct hostility against Texas—and annexation by that means instead of by amicable arrangement."[31] Territory could be acquired, Gallatin had said, only by treaty or conquest. If the Senate blocked a treaty and if a joint resolution was unconstitutional, had thought been given to the possibility of conquest? This raises other intriguing but unanswerable questions: Precisely what instructions did Calhoun give to Green? What did Tyler know about them? Or was Green, in his inimitable fashion, acting on his own, far exceeding any basic instructions he may have received from the secretary of state?

On 4 February 1845, a Whig senator from New Jersey, William L. Dayton, presented a resolution, calling upon the president to answer a number of questions, if the request was not inconsistent with the public interest. "Does Mr. Green hold, or has lately held, any diplomatic or official station near the government of Texas; and, if so, what, when appointed, at what salary, and with what instructions?" Tyler referred the questions to Calhoun, who replied that Green had been appointed consul at Galveston on 12 September 1844 and had received from the State Department the ordinary printed instructions given to all persons filling such a position, "and none other." No salary was attached to the position, and Green did not currently hold any diplomatic or official position in Texas. Calhoun's letter, according to Merk, "contained scarcely a word of untruth, but was filled with truth of the kind that concealed the truth." No mention was made of the instructions that

Green claimed to have received from Calhoun when Green was made bearer of dispatches to the United States minister in Mexico City.

In *The Diplomacy of Annexation: Texas, Oregon, and the Mexican War,* David Pletcher has offered the opinion that Green, "with his flare for invective and for attributing the most sinister motives to foreigners," was the worst possible person to send to Mexico, where the inexperienced Shannon, who was naturally inclined to bluster and blunder, was eager for advice. Green's appointment, says Pletcher, "is actually one more example of the erratic judgment that affected Calhoun in all matters connected with the Texas question."[32]

Throughout December and January the House and Senate debated annexation and how to accomplish it. Resolution after resolution was offered. Finally, in mid January, Congressman Milton Brown, a Whig from Tennessee, suggested a compromise plan that, after some alteration, included the admission of Texas as a state by joint resolution; boundary settlements would be the responsibility of the United States after Texas had become a part of the Union; Texas' debt would not be assumed by the United States; but Texas' public lands would remain in the possession of the new state; and the proceeds from the sale of the lands would be used to pay the public debt. With the consent of the state of Texas, four additional states could be created from the area. Those lying south of thirty degrees, thirty minutes, could become states with or without slavery, as the populace should decree, and those lying north of the line would be Free States.

The Brown resolution was approved by the House on 25 January by a vote of 120 to 98. Eight southern Whigs voted with the majority, including Alexander Stephens of Georgia. "I am no defender of slavery in the abstract," he announced to the House; "if the annexation of Texas were for the sole purpose of extending slavery where it does not now and would not otherwise exist, I should oppose it." But because slavery already existed in Texas, he had decided to support annexation in the national interest. No longer did he call annexation a "miserable humbug," devised to break up the Whig party.

The day before the House vote was to be taken, Robert Toombs, also of Georgia, told Stephens he did not know if it was constitutional to admit Texas as a state without first having acquired the area by treaty, but since it was a matter of doubt, "I would decide it in favour of the popular will and, I honestly believe, the public safety and the safety of the Union."[33]

In the Senate's decision, popular will also played a large part. Ephraim Foster, another Tennessee Whig, introduced a resolution of annexation similar to Brown's House version, but its reception was not enthusiastic. Rufus Choate, a Massachusetts Whig and a member of the Foreign Relations Committee, insisted that there was no way a foreign nation could be annexed to the United States without a constitutional amendment to that effect. William Rives and William Archer of Virginia and John Berrien of Georgia were convinced that annexation would divide the nation into two hostile sections. Annexation by resolution might be expedient, said Archer, but it was not lawful, not constitutional. "Perish all thought of illegitimate acquisition!"

The Foreign Relations Committee, under the guidance of Archer, discussed the matter until 4 February, when it reported negatively on annexation by joint resolution. On 5 February, Benton introduced a resolution stating simply that "a state formed out of the present republic of Texas" should be admitted as soon as a new treaty with Texas could be negotiated. Abandoning his earlier insistence on Mexico's consent, he now said the negotiators could decide if this was necessary. Some suspected that Benton was still deliberately using delaying tactics. Senate action seemed to be at a standstill.

The situation changed, however, when Polk arrived in Washington on 13 February and at once exerted pressure for a compromise measure between the House resolution and the one introduced by Benton. "The arrival of the President elect has given a powerful impulse to party action on this subject," Mangum observed; "he is for Texas, Texas, Texas; & talks of but little else, as I learn." As leverage, Polk used hints of patronage, and because he had not yet named his cabinet, those who hoped for a place were anxious to cooperate in whatever he desired. The Whigs knew the battle was lost. Washington Hunt sadly admitted to Thurlow Weed: "Texas will be brought into the Union. We must prepare for it. There is no escape. It is idle to think of resisting the current. It will sweep over every obstacle."[34]

Robert J. Walker, eager to head the Treasury Department, proposed a Senate amendment to the House resolution, which would give the president, unquestionably Polk, the choice of annexing Texas according to the House version or by opening new treaty negotiations with Texas, as specified in Benton's resolution. Archer countered by proposing that the Senate accept the report of the Foreign Relations Committee which rejected the House resolution and, in effect, made annexation a dead issue, at least for this session of Congress. Archer's motion was voted down, and Walker's compromise was approved by a vote of 27 to 25. The Democrats had closed ranks. Six northern Democrats who had voted against the treaty now supported the Walker amendment, including Benjamin Tappan and William Allen of Ohio, Benton, and Silas

Wright, but at least five probably did so because they believed Polk had declared his support for the Benton plan. The House agreed to accept the Walker compromise, 132 to 75.

To John Quincy Adams the passage of the joint resolution was "a signal triumph of the slave-representation in the Constitution of the United States. . . . The heaviest calamity that ever befell myself and my country was this day consummated. . . . I regard it as the apoplexy of the Constitution."[35]

On 1 March 1845, with only three days remaining of his presidency, Tyler signed the joint resolution. If the choice between immediate annexation, as spelled out by the House resolution, and the alternative of opening new negotiations with Texas was his to make, there was no doubt about his preference. But was it ethical for him to implement either? Should not the decision be left to Polk?

Calhoun was emphatic. Tyler should act and act quickly, opting for immediate annexation. The South Carolinian had hoped to be kept on as Polk's secretary of state, but now he knew the place would go to James Buchanan; therefore, he was determined to consummate the great measure, at least to the extent of having the United States approve annexation and officially notify Texas that this had been accomplished. Calhoun wanted to leave no loose ends. If there were a few left, he feared the possibility that the Blair-Benton faction would gain an upper hand and that Polk would give in to pressure to start the negotiation process all over. This could seal the doom of the acquisition of Texas for the near future, if not for all time. Great Britain was straining every effort to obtain a Texas pledge to remain independent.

Still Tyler hesitated, feeling it would not be proper for him, with so little time left in office, to make the decision; but Calhoun had an answer for every reason that Tyler gave for postponing action until after the inauguration. The Walker resolution, Calhoun reminded Tyler, did not specify which president should make the choice. Until noon on 4 March, John Tyler had the legal authority to do so.

At a cabinet meeting on Sunday, 2 March, the departmental heads unanimously agreed with Calhoun. Delay could be fatal to the Texas cause. To ease Tyler's conscience, it was agreed that Calhoun would call on Polk immediately at the close of the meeting and inform him of Tyler's decision and his reasons for having taken such action. Polk received the information without comment. He undoubtedly was surprised. George McDuffie, a confidant of Calhoun's who supposedly had inside knowledge of administration affairs, had assured Bentonians that Tyler "would not have the audacity to meddle with" making a choice between the House resolution and the Benton plan. There were rumors that Polk had instigated the Walker compromise himself, believing, of course, that it would be left to him to select the proper procedure. Benton Democrats were convinced that they had Polk's word to go along with their preference for a new Texas treaty.[36]

On 3 March, instructions were sent to Donelson, informing him of congressional approval to admit the Republic of Texas into the Union as a state, but there was a certain amount of confusion. The day after his inauguration, Polk sent a message directing Donelson not to act on the instructions that he had received from the Tyler administration. However, when Polk's cabinet met, common sense prevailed. Congress had left the choice to the president, and the president had acted. Even though the decision had come from Tyler, not Polk, it had been made according to the letter of the law. Polk's cabinet unanimously approved Tyler's action, and a third message was sent off to Donelson, who was waiting in New Orleans for his orders. Fortunately, all three messages were received on the same day, 24 March, and Donelson hurried to the Texas capital with the news before further British moves could be made. Polk's biographer Charles Sellers has stated that Polk preferred the House resolution and that he sent the first message, revoking Tyler's instructions, probably because he needed the votes of the Bentonian senators in order to confirm his appointments.[37]

Tyler considered that the passage of the joint resolution was the crowning achievement of his administration, and he deeply resented Calhoun's later claim to authorship of the entire project. This, said Tyler, chafed him more than anything else, because it narrowed annexation "to the comparatively contemptible ground of Southern and local interest" and "converted the executive into a mere Southern agency in place of being what it truly was—the representative of American interests, whether those interests were North, South, East or West; and if ever there was an American question, the Texas was that very question."

Calhoun also declared it was he who made the choice between the alternative resolutions. How ridiculous, exclaimed Tyler. If Calhoun had made the selection, then Texas was not legitimately a state in the Union, for Congress had given the power of choice to the president, not to the secretary of state. Calhoun had given advice, Tyler admitted, but it would be "too small game" for Calhoun to appear merely as an advisor. "He is the great 'I am,' and myself and cabinet have no voice in the matter."[38] In reality, of course, Calhoun—aided and abetted by Upshur, Gilmer, Green, Hunter and others—had forced the Texas issue, but not in the manner or with the national emphasis that Tyler had desired.

Polk was not deprived of all the glory of annexation. He was the one who presided over the final procedure of admitting Texas to the Union as the twenty-eighth state, a Slave State, on 29 December 1845. The Tyler administration also bequeathed to the incoming president the settlement of the Oregon controversy.

In the waning hours of the Tyler administration, in fact after the Tyler presidency legally had ended, Congress had the symbolic last word in the long and bitter struggle between the legislative and the executive branches, when it overrode Tyler's veto of a rather insignificant revenue-cutter bill by stunning majorities, 41 to 1 in the Senate and 127 to 30 in the House. The House debate of 3 March continued past midnight when, someone observed, the Twenty-eighth Congress legally had ceased to exist. For a few minutes, the calling of the roll was stopped, but uproarious shouts of "Go on, Go on," forced the clerk to complete the task. For the first time in the nation's history, Congress passed a law "in defiance" of a president's veto. Tyler seemed not to notice.[39]

Julia and John Tyler were ending his presidency in style. A farewell presidential ball was held on 18 February, and Julia was determined it would be an occasion to remember. The guest list numbered over two thousand, but more than three thousand came. Thousands of candles illuminated the East Room and other chambers that were set aside for dancing. A Marine band played polkas, waltzes, and cotillions. "Wine and champagne flowed like water." The Polks were invited, but declined to come. Mrs. Polk was indisposed. Vice-president-elect Dallas was there; however, not surprisingly, few Whigs were present. Tyler enjoyed himself immensely, and when someone congratulated him on the brilliant gathering, he laughingly replied, "Yes, they cannot say *now* that I am a President *without a party.*"

On 2 March, the Tylers hosted a gala cabinet dinner to celebrate the passage of the joint resolution. James and Sarah Polk were honored guests. On the following afternoon the White House was opened to all who wished to bid good-bye to the president and his family. The crowds were large and enthusiastic in their praises. On the next morning, Tyler called for Polk at Coleman's Hotel, and together, in an open carriage, they led the inaugural procession to the capitol.[40]

15

★ ★ ★ ★ ★

A FLAWED PRESIDENCY

"Mankind, it seems, makes a poorer performance of government than of almost any other human activity," says Barbara Tuchman.[1] Certainly, this has been the generally accepted verdict on the Tyler administration. First voiced by Whig historians of the nineteenth century, this viewpoint has been repeated by numerous scholars in the twentieth, among whom Tyler's reputation has been that of a mediocre president, at best.

American historians, who throughout the years have indulged in rating presidents on a scale from excellent to failure, invariably have placed Tyler in the low-average to below-average category, along with Calvin Coolidge, Millard Fillmore, Zachary Taylor, James Buchanan, and Franklin Pierce. Among such historians, Clinton Rossiter is an exception. Writing in the mid 1950s, he thought Tyler was more on a par with the two Adamses (a conclusion that would have caused John Quincy to wince), James Madison, Martin Van Buren, William McKinley, William Howard Taft, and Herbert C. Hoover, and a slot above Fillmore, Benjamin Harrison, and Coolidge. The British political scientist and economist Harold J. Laski, in his classic study *The American Presidency*, placed Tyler in the company of Theodore Roosevelt, Andrew Jackson, Woodrow Wilson, and Franklin Roosevelt, as a strong president, self-willed, courageous, stubborn, and of dominant personality.

However, in a 1962 poll, seventy-five American historians relegated Tyler to "below-average" status, while rating Polk "near-great" for extending "the national borders until they embraced what is now the great Southwest and all the country lying between the Rocky Mountains and the Pacific Ocean.'' Obviously, the Tyler presidency received no credit for having paved the way for expansion. Twenty years later, in a poll taken by Robert K. Murray and Tim H. Blessing, Tyler and Polk remained in their respective positions.[2]

For nearly a century and a half, Tyler has been depicted variously as a political apostate; as a man whom the Whigs elevated to the vice-presidency but who, when he claimed the presidency as his own after the death of Harrison, refused to carry out the policies of the party that had elected him; as a president whose entire focus was on states' rights; and as one who obstinately rejected legislation that was not compatible with his own ideas. He, it is said, betrayed the Whigs, violated the Constitution, destroyed Clay's chance for the presidency in the 1844 election, and led the nation into wild expansionism, the results of which were the Mexican War, pronounced sectionalism, and finally, disunion. He is charged with the responsibility for four years of tumult, tension, and struggle between the executive and the legislative branches of the government. Such conclusions are exaggerated and unfair. Shortcomings there were, and Tyler was not without fault, but a presidency is more than just a president. It is a complex combination of individuals working either together or against one another, all having a part in the success, the failure, or the flawing of a presidency.

Indications of trouble surfaced during Harrison's month in office. Expecting him to be merely a figurehead, the Whigs had intended firmly to establish their concept of congressional supremacy. Never again did they want another Andrew Jackson to occupy the White House. Clay—bitterly disappointed by the dashing of his 1840 presidential aspirations and locked in competition with Webster for the leadership of the Whig party—was determined to direct the decisions of the Harrison administration. Part of the plan was to impress the president with the advisability of having all important matters decided by a majority of a pro-Clay cabinet, in which each member, including the president, would have one vote. This, said Attorney General Crittenden, was the proper procedure. Harrison concurred, but he soon became restive; and when Clay challenged certain of the president's appointments and virtually forced him to call a special session of Congress, antagonisms arose which were to continue long after Harrison's demise.

Clay had a plan—a program for America's future—and he meant to have that program enacted for the good of the nation and to ensure his election to the presidency the next time around. Clay is often quoted as having said he would rather be right than president; but as Daniel Howe has so aptly stated, ''Though never president, he was often right; and he would have been right even more often had he wanted to be president less. . . . Clay was a victim of his own ambition."[3] Had Harrison lived, his relations with Clay undoubtedly would have been contentious, but perhaps not nearly so vehement as the hostility that developed between Tyler and Clay. Harrison was not quite as strong-minded, and he had pledged to serve only one term. Tyler was much younger, stubborn, and proud; and given a fair amount of success during his tenure, there was a chance he could be a candidate in 1844. Clay could not allow this to happen. When Tyler assumed, not just the duties of the presidency as an acting substitute for Harrison, but the office and title as well, Clay was very disturbed, and his anxiety manifested itself in even greater arrogance and imperiousness. He was fighting for his American System, the future of the Whig party, and, with it, the Clay presidency; but his tactics were injurious to all three. It is not known for certain whether Harrison actually said to Clay, "Mr. Clay, you forget that *I* am the President," or whether Tyler exclaimed: "Go you now, then, Mr. Clay, to your end of the avenue, where stands the Capitol, and there perform your duty to the country as you shall think proper. So help me God, I shall do mine at this end as I shall think proper."[4] The sentiment, however, most assuredly did exist.

Tyler had a long history of opposing as unconstitutional the creation or the recreation of a Bank of the United States. However, he conceivably would have been willing to meet Clay halfway had Clay been less presumptuous about the establishment of branch banks within the states without their consent. The nationalistic Webster blamed Clay more than Tyler for the impasse. In the tariff-distribution controversy of 1842, it was Tyler who saw the necessity of compromise. Clay was willing to have the nation deprived of needed revenue rather than surrender distribution, while Tyler, to whom a departure from the Compromise Tariff of 1833 was distasteful, realized that revenue from a higher tariff was mandatory in order to stave off complete economic collapse. Clay declared that Tyler should either accept the actions of Congress or resign. Tyler was adamant in his belief that the president had the right to disagree. The Constitution conferred upon him the prerogative of veto. While threats of impeachment came from the floor of the House, Clay moved to amend the Constitution to make it easier for Congress to override the veto. For lack of grounds, threats of impeachment were not carried to fruition, but attempts to drive Tyler from office, to "head the president," continued.

In spite of their differences in political philosophy, Tyler, for much of his political life, admired Clay; but with Tyler in the presidency, Clay was in no mood to be friendly. Rather, he treated Tyler as a subordinate who should act on his, Clay's, command; and Tyler's resentment increased accordingly.

Not all Whigs were in favor of Clay's stance. Thurlow Weed, in an editorial in the *Albany* (N.Y.) *Evening Journal,* expressed concern that Clay's hostility toward the president and the manner in which he exercised control over other Whigs in Congress could endanger the future of the party. "The Whig members of Congress, instead of taking the President 'for better or for worse,' . . . array themselves against his administration. This is a source of interminable mischiefs and evils. And what is worse, it's a warfare that will not only bring defeat and disgrace to both parties [the Whigs and Tyler] but is proving destructive to the public interests."[5]

Tyler's presidency was flawed by the imperiousness of Clay, by the actions of Abel P. Upshur and John C. Calhoun, Duff Green, Henry Wise, and others and, some believe, by his own lack of decisive leadership. To his contemporaries, Tyler appeared to vacillate. This criticism was expressed repeatedly in letters throughout the period. Ashburton was of this opinion. Tyler, he told Aberdeen, was "weak and vacillating though essentially an honest man," who allowed persons of "rather ominous character" to collect about him.[6] Tyler vacillated on the bank issue. Upshur thought he was too hesitant about Texas. Tyler wavered about whether or not he had the power to deploy troops and naval vessels to defend Texas. On this, of course, the Constitution is not clear, but neither was it specific on what position a vice-president should assume when a president dies in office; however, on this issue, Tyler was not indecisive. Neither was he irresolute in recommending the dubious device of joint resolution for the purpose of annexation or in taking a stand on distribution or deciding when or when not to comply with requests or demands from the House and Senate for information from the executive branch. He was firm in his conviction that the president was not required to relinquish all discretion in deciding what to do, but on most occasions he cooperated with Congress in delivering the materials it requested. He acknowledged that executive privilege was not absolute.

Even after he had left office, Tyler willingly responded to a congressional subpoena to appear before a House Select Committee investigating charges against Daniel Webster for the "fraudulent misapplication and personal use of public funds" when, as secretary of state, Webster had attempted to influence Maine to accept a compromise settlement of the boundary dispute with New Brunswick. Webster's detractors accused him of improperly using funds from the president's secret-service account to induce Maine to give up land to which the state had a rightful claim and of having failed to account for all the moneys he had at his disposal.

Payments from the president's secret contingency fund, Tyler testified, had been made with his knowledge and by his order, and they had been used to "secure and advance the public good" by taking steps to preserve peace with Great Britain. Tyler, a good administrator, had not condoned Webster's carelessness in having failed to keep adequate records of his expenditures and in not having obtained the necessary vouchers or receipts. As his administration drew to a close, Tyler had pressured Webster to produce receipts and vouchers for all expenditures, but several still were missing. As a result, Webster reimbursed the government approximately one thousand dollars from his own personal funds. "When Tyler left the White House in 1845, there were no loose ends," and in his testimony Tyler generously defended his former secretary of state against charges of wrongdoing. Webster may have been negligent, but he was not dishonest. While in Washington to appear before the congressional committee, Tyler called on President Polk, who voiced regret that the former president had been subjected to "unjust annoyance."[7]

Tyler's presidency was flawed as, to a greater or lesser extent, all presidencies are, but it was not a failure. On numerous occasions he demonstrated exemplary executive skill and common sense. Dorr's Rebellion is a case in point. Tyler handled this delicate situation with restraint. What could have had a tragically violent outcome was resolved without bloodshed and with eventual benefit to the democratic process. A hostile Congress, investigating the incident, found no grounds for censure. Likewise, he responded to several sensitive naval courts-martial decisions with discretion and sound judgment, meting out justice by reducing punishments or sentences that seemed to him extreme and by fostering badly needed social reforms throughout this branch of the military. As a man of learning, Tyler was interested in promoting the advancement of science and letters. He welcomed the information brought to the nation by the return of the Wilkes expedition, and he willingly supported the explorations of John Charles Frémont, although some accused Tyler of having done so to mollify Thomas Hart Benton and the Democratic Party.

The greatest advances came in the area of foreign affairs. The Webster-Ashburton Treaty; the Treaty of Wanghia; the "Tyler Doctrine"; the Sulu agreement, allowing a shorter passage to Manila and Canton; and various other actions elevated the position of the United States among the nations of the world, encouraged international trade, and improved the economy. Surprisingly, while the animosity between

Tyler and Congress brought domestic legislation to a virtual standstill, the Senate found much of the president's conduct of foreign affairs acceptable. Of fifteen treaties that he submitted to the Senate, only two—the Texas treaty and the Zollverein treaty—were rejected. Two others were so amended by the Senate that they were unacceptable to the other signatory countries, and one was not acted upon.[8]

Much of the success in foreign affairs was due to Tyler's able and aggressive secretaries of state, who frequently overshadowed the man in the White House. Tyler gave them significant latitude, and he considered the head of the State Department the premier of the cabinet. As long as Webster occupied the post, this posed no problem. He worked well with Tyler; he treated the president with respect; and he expressed gratitude for Tyler's collaboration. Upshur and Calhoun were more inclined to manipulate the president or to operate behind his back; into the Texas issue they injected matters of sectionalism and slavery that Tyler considered detrimental to a successful outcome and injurious to the nation. By placing Upshur and later Calhoun in the State Department and by bowing to their pressures—especially in allowing Duff Green to wander at will in France, England, and Mexico, sending reports that were designed to inflame public opinion against England to sympathetic and eager recipients in the United States—Tyler seemed to lose control of his government.

Without a doubt, the president wanted to add the large and valuable area of Texas to the Union to improve the nation's economic and strategic prowess. He also had a natural interest in strengthening the South, but he was not as obsessed with this aspect of annexation as were Upshur and Calhoun. By his letter to Pakenham, Calhoun widened the breach between the North and the South, a development that Tyler deplored. While Tyler wanted to balance the acquisition of Texas with a settlement of the Oregon question, Upshur had no patience with this, and Calhoun had little. Their attitudes were characteristic of extremists in the South, Whig as well as Democrat: Texas was important, but Oregon was peripheral and should not be a matter of concern until annexation had been accomplished, if at all. The opinion of George D. Phillips, a prominent Georgia Democrat, was typical: "I never would favour any project for the occupation of Oregon until we had got Texas, but on the contrary throw every impediment in the way, even give it up to England or the devil. . . . For a foot of Maine I was willing to fight; for Texas I would fight the world, because the world would be impertinently interfering with our concerns, but for Oregon north of 49, I would not quarrel." Robert Toombs, a leading Georgia Whig, was more emphatic: "I don't want a foot of Oregon or an acre of any other country, especially without 'niggers.' "[9]

By remaining in the cabinet after the mass resignation of all the other department heads in the fall of 1841, Webster severely hurt himself politically, but his historical reputation was immeasurably enhanced by his accomplishments as Tyler's secretary of state and by the manner in which he deported himself. If Webster had resigned in 1841, very likely there would have been no treaty with Great Britain. Without such an accord, the possibility of war between the two nations would have been great. Upshur and Calhoun were pronounced Anglophobes. Tyler initially may have leaned in that direction, but tempered by Webster and anxious for diplomatic achievements, he welcomed the opportunity to settle problems with England, even if this necessitated compromises that upset states'-rights southerners. Webster preached moderation and forbearance, and Tyler frequently listened. By contrast, the actions of Clay and Calhoun during this period added no luster to their names.

Tyler incurred the wrath of many southerners when he, without hesitation, vigorously supported Webster's recommendation to make Edward Everett minister to England. "The President was friendly, decided, and immovable," the secretary told Everett.[10] At the behest of Webster and George Ticknor, Tyler also wholeheartedly agreed to appoint Washington Irving as minister to Spain. Fortuitously, Charles Dickens was in Washington in the spring of 1842, shortly after Irving's appointment, and the president hosted a levee in honor of the two authors. Dickens was pleased to observe that "in all the madness of American politics," there were "noisy orators and officers of state" who took pride in the appointment of Irving, "a man of quiet pursuits." Dickens concluded that not all of America's governmental officials were without "some refinement of taste and appreciation of intellectual gifts," although he found their ill-mannered and incessant tobacco spitting, with universal "disregard of the spittoon," very offensive when he visited the House of Representatives.

The president impressed the British visitor as decidedly a civilized person. "He looked somewhat worn and anxious,—and well he might: being at war with everybody,—but the expression of his face was mild and pleasant, and his manner was remarkably unaffected, gentlemanly, and agreeable. I thought that, in his whole carriage and demeanor, he became his station singularly well."[11]

Tyler had reason to look worn and anxious. No other president during the pre–Civil War period faced such congressional hostility and defiance. He had no party base, and few in the House or the Senate were willing to speak in his behalf. Expressions of the most acerbic bitterness against him came from extreme states' righters, many of whom were from his own state. They were angry with Tyler for having even briefly considered the Exchequer Plan, or a fiscal corporation, for having signed the Tariff Act of 1842, for having accepted the provisions of the Webster-Ashburton agreements that dealt with aspects of slavery, for having stressed the national attributes of the acquisition of Texas, for not having moved enthusiastically enough in accomplishing annexation. The extreme states' righters had expected much from Tyler; therefore, they felt betrayed. So did the Whigs, and the Democrats could not forgive Tyler for his "traitorous" behavior in leaving their party, becoming a Whig, and finally accepting that party's vice-presidential nomination.

Among Virginia's extreme states' righters, Beverley Tucker was Tyler's most caustic critic. Late in 1844, Tucker asked Calhoun to recommend him to Polk for a diplomatic mission to Texas. Tucker had large land interests there and was anxious to press for annexation, but he did not want to request a position until Tyler had left office: "At Mr. Tyler's hands I wouldn't receive it. As his minister I could have no weight." John Strode Barbour, another Virginian, also confided in Calhoun: "I agree with you perfectly as to Tyler. His ambition has warped a candid mind, that nature and early education put in a true place and gave it true direction."[12]

Virginia Whigs were no less disillusioned. As well as he knew Tyler, Benjamin Watkins Leigh said he earlier had had no idea of the "unscrupulousness, the folly and knavery of his ambition, and I do not believe he had the least consciousness of it himself" when he accepted the vice-presidential nomination. Leigh blamed Henry Wise for "putting the idea of succession to the presidency into his head." Wise had done this, Leigh contended, not to benefit Tyler, but "to cross the Whig party in Congress" because its members refused to make Wise the Speaker of the House and to thwart Clay, who had somehow injured Wise's pride. Wise said that Webster sided with Tyler because of Webster's jealousy of Clay. Leigh and other Virginia Whigs were exceedingly anxious to bring the "most perplexing" Tyler administration to a close. Perhaps Calhoun was more correct than any of the others when he characterized Tyler as "essentially a man for the middle ground, and will attempt a middle position now when there is none. . . . If he should he will be lost."[13]

Reflecting on his years as chief executive, Tyler hoped that future vice-presidents who succeeded to the presidency would benefit from the course he had pursued in insisting on assuming the title of president as well as the powers and duties of that office and that they would be encouraged to stand their ground. Otherwise, they would be nothing more than mere instruments "in the hands of ambitious and aspiring demagogues; the executive power will be completely in abeyance, and the Congress will unite the legislative and executive functions." Marcus Cunliffe believes that Tyler, by establishing this precedent, "went a long way toward establishing the Presidency as an institution independent of death," assuring "that there would never be an automatic diminution in executive prestige, either at home or abroad, when a Vice President had to take over." Tyler wanted neither the president nor Congress to usurp the rights, privileges, and responsibilities that the Constitution relegated to each branch.[14]

With the judiciary, Tyler had little trouble. Of the nine members of the Supreme Court, the two most important were Chief Justice Roger B. Taney and Associate Justice Joseph Story. Taney had been appointed to the Court by President Jackson as a reward for Taney's willingness, as secretary of the treasury, to remove governmental deposits from the Bank of the United States, an action that had brought from Senator John Tyler a heated charge of flagrant assumption of power. As a member of the Senate Finance Committee, Tyler had opposed rechartering the bank, but he believed Jackson had overstepped his authority in ordering the removal of deposits before the charter had expired. This, Tyler declared, was a breach of faith, a violation of contract; and when Taney's nomination as secretary of the treasury (a recess appointment) came before the Senate, Tyler voted against confirmation. Had Tyler not resigned from the Senate, he undoubtedly would have cast a negative vote in regard to Taney's appointment as chief justice.

During Tyler's presidency, however, mutual Whig enemies brought the two men closer, and they became friends. Taney attended Tyler's farewell ball on 18 February 1845; he later wrote to his wife: "You know the President and I are good friends, and he and Mrs. President received me with great kindness; and I met there more old friends, and spent a more pleasant evening than I expected." Both Tyler and Taney were devoted to the South, and while neither was zealous in defense of slavery, each feared absolute northern domination of the nation, and each feared possible disunion if steps were not taken to equalize the political strength of the two sections.[15]

Joseph Story, a Massachusetts Federalist, had been appointed to the Supreme Court by President Madison in 1811, and since the demise of Chief Justice John Marshall in 1835, Story believed that the Court and the country had declined in prestige and power. Story deplored the rise of Jacksonian democracy and the burgeoning of slaveocracy; he declared that the annexation of Texas, which had been brought about by the forces of slavery, was "grossly unconstitutional." He held Tyler in great disdain.

The Taney Court has been depicted as leaning toward the acknowledgment of the power of the states more than had been the case in Marshall's time, but this was not as true of the Court during the Tyler administration as it may have been later. In the first half of the 1840s, signals that came from the Court were mixed. In *Swift* v. *Tyson*, the Court attempted to bring greater uniformity among courts of the various states in deciding cases concerning commercial law. Cases that were essentially alike, the Court declared, should not be decided in different ways in different states, and when the Supreme Court deemed that a uniform rule was preferable to separate state statutes, it could override the state laws. This led for a time to the development of a national common law of commercial relations. In *Groves* v. *Slaughter*, however, it was decided that the federal government did not have exclusive control over interstate commerce and, therefore, that Mississippi could ban the importation of slaves from other states. The reasons for this decision were so varied that it is impossible to interpret this as reflecting the philosophy of the Taney Court. The decision that caused the greatest controversey was *Prigg* v. *Pennsylvania*, in which the Court concluded that the Constitution and the federal Fugitive Slave Act of 1793 gave the federal government the exclusive power to deal with fugitive slaves and that, as a consequence, individual states had no authority to pass laws on the subject, even if such laws were not in conflict with federal statutes.[16]

Story, on the verge of retirement, was confident that Henry Clay would be elected in 1844 and, as president, would name stalwart nationalists to the Court. Whig Senators were of the same mind, so they refused to allow Tyler to fill the vacancy left by the death of Henry Baldwin. But Clay's defeat ended all hope for "suitable appointments," and Story was distressed. "In every way which I look to the future," he sadly commented to Charles Sumner, "I can see little or no ground of hope for our country. We are rapidly on the decline. Corruption and profligacy, demagogism, and recklessness characterize the times, and I for one am unable to see where the thing is to end."[17]

Tyler, on the other hand, believed the nation was in better condition when he left office than it had been four years earlier. Certainly it was more prosperous. Some observers denied that this was the result of any effort by his administration, but others thought improved international trade and the Tariff Act of 1842 had helped the economy. In his final annual message, Tyler took pleasure in categorizing the achievements of his presidency. Along with the soundness of the currency and the surplus in the treasury, he pointed with pride to the opening of trade avenues in the Pacific and the Far East; to the continued development of a steam navy, improved coastal fortifications, and a stronger military; to the revival of commerce and manufacturing; and to the rapid growth of cities. Moreover, he announced, "a desolating and wasting war with savage tribes" had been brought to a close. He was referring to his termination of the second Seminole War (1835–42), "the vexatious, harassing, and expensive war which so long prevailed with the Indian tribes inhabiting the peninsula of Florida" had been "happily terminated."

A young lieutenant, William T. Sherman, believed it was absurd to call raids upon Indian villages a war. It was part of a ferreting out process—rounding up the Indians and driving them westward from their lands in the Southeast. Long after the "happy termination," the practice continued. Tyler advocated both "rigid justice" toward the Indian tribes that were residing within the territorial limits of the United States and "a parental vigilance over their interests." He looked forward to their introduction to "the arts of civilized life." Chitwood may have been correct in saying that "Tyler favored a policy of justice and fairness to the Indians"; but unfortunately, Tyler's administration did not end the practices that contributed to an inglorious and shameful chapter in American history.[18]

Although Tyler made concessions to the growth of nationalism, he ended his presidential tenure with his states'-rights philosophy intact. Each state, he told the Congress in his last annual message, had the privilege (which could be judiciously exerted only by itself) "of consulting the means best calculated to advance its own happiness."[19]

Tyler must have been gratified to know that the *Richmond Enquirer* believed his administration had ended "in a blaze of glory." "Erroneous as his policy may have been in several particulars," Thomas Ritchie wrote, "yet his presidency was responsible for a number of brilliant events. Posterity at least will do him justice in these respects, if the present age denies it."[20]

Unfortunately, Ritchie's prophecy was not correct. Posterity did not do Tyler justice, even though the achievements of the Tyler presidency, operating under tremendous difficulties, were astonishingly significant. As the first "accidental president," Tyler faced greater challenges to his executive authority than had any of his predecessors and few of his successors, but he refused to accept the idea that his only responsibility was to carry out the directives of an omnipotent Congress. A president, he maintained, had prerogatives of his own, granted to him by the

Constitution, and while his powers could be checked and balanced, they could not be obliterated by the legislative branch.

Although it has been said that the Polk administration was ''the one bright spot in the dull void between Jackson and Lincoln,''[21] Tyler found his own presidency anything but dull.

NOTES

PREFACE

1. Henry Adams, *The Great Secession Winter of 1860–61 and Other Essays*, ed. George Hochfield (New York: Sagamore Press, 1958), pp. 197, 100.

2. Edward S. Corwin, *The President: Office and Powers, 1787–1957* (New York: New York University Press, 1957), pp. 3–5.

3. Clinton Rossiter, *1787: The Grand Convention* (New York: Macmillan, 1966), p. 223.

CHAPTER 1
THE GROPINGS OF A GROWING NATION

1. Niles is quoted by George Rogers Taylor in *The Transportation Revolution, 1815–1860* (1951; reprint, New York: Harper Torchbook, 1968), p. 4.

2. Ray Allen Billington, *The Protestant Crusade, 1800–1860: A Study of the Origins of American Nativism* (1938; reprint, Chicago: Quadrangle Books, 1964), pp. 124–25, 193–94, 205–8.

3. Emerson is quoted by Henry Steele Commager in *The Era of Reform, 1830–1860* (Princeton, N.J.: D. Van Nostrand, Anvil Books, 1960), p. 7.

4. Gerda Lerner, *The Grimké Sisters from South Carolina: Pioneers for Women's Rights and Abolition* (New York: Schocken Books, 1971), p. 1.

5. Russel B. Nye, *Fettered Freedom: Civil Liberties and the Slavery Controversy, 1830–1860*, rev. ed. (East Lansing: Michigan State University Press, 1963), pp. 49–51.

6. William F. Gordon to James Barbour, 18 Feb. 1820, in John Tyler Papers, Manuscripts Division, Library of Congress.

7. John C. Miller, *The Federalist Era, 1789–1801* (New York: Harper Torchbook, 1963), pp. 55–62, 81, 115–16.

8. James Sterling Young, *The Washington Community, 1800–1828* (New York: Columbia University Press, 1966), pp. 185–89, 233–37—Story is quoted on p. 188; John Quincy Adams, *Memoirs of John Quincy Adams,* ed. Charles Francis Adams, 12 vols. (1874–77; reprint, New York: AMS Press, 1970), 5:324; Wilfred E. Binkley, *President and Congress* (New York: Alfred A. Knopf, 1947), p. 63.

9. Andrew Jackson to William B. Lewis, 14 Feb. 1825, in Andrew Jackson, *Correspondence of Andrew Jackson,* ed. John Spencer Bassett, 7 vols. (1926–35; reprint, New York: Kraus, 1969), 3:276.

10. Martin Van Buren, *The Autobiography of Martin Van Buren,* ed. John C. Fitzpatrick, vol. 2 of *Annual Report of the American Historical Association for the Year 1918* (Washington, D.C.: Government Printing Office, 1920), p. 514; Robert V. Remini, *Andrew Jackson,* 3 vols. (New York: Harper & Row, 1977–84), 2:114.

11. John C. Calhoun to James Monroe, 10 July 1828, in John C. Calhoun, *Correspondence of John C. Calhoun,* ed. J. Franklin Jameson, vol. 2 of *Report of the American Historical Association for the Year 1899* (Washington, D.C.: Government Printing Office, 1900), pp. 437–38.

12. John William Ward, *Andrew Jackson: Symbol for an Age* (New York: Oxford University Press, Galaxy Book, 1962), pp. 208, 213.

13. Richard R. Stenberg, "The Jefferson Birthday Dinner, 1830," *Journal of Southern History* 4 (1938): 337; Remini, *Andrew Jackson,* 2:234–37, 3:42–43.

14. Veto message, 10 July 1832, in *A Compilation of the Messages and Papers of the Presidents, 1789–1902,* comp. James D. Richardson, 10 vols. (Washington, D.C.: Bureau of National Literature and Art, 1903), 2:567–91.

15. Van Buren, *Autobiography,* p. 625.

16. Glyndon G. Van Deusen, *The Life of Henry Clay* (Boston, Mass.: Little, Brown, 1937), pp. 278–86.

17. *National Intelligencer,* 14 and 15 July 1836, quoted in Remini, *Andrew Jackson,* 3:328.

CHAPTER 2
"THIS DISCORDANT COMBINATION"

1. *Richmond Enquirer,* 22 Jan. 1835.

2. John Quincy Adams, *Memoirs of John Quincy Adams,* ed. Charles Francis Adams, 12 vols. (1874–77; reprint, New York: AMS Press, 1970), 7:530. Information on Harrison's background is from Dorothy B. Goebel, *William Henry Harrison: A Political Biography* (Indianapolis: Historical Bureau of the Indiana Library and Historical Department, 1926), and Freeman Cleves, *Old Tippecanoe: William Henry Harrison and His Times* (New York: Charles Scribner's Sons, 1939).

3. Adams, *Memoirs,* 7:530.

4. Information on Tyler's background is from Oliver Perry Chitwood, *John Tyler: Champion of the Old South* (New York: D. Appleton-Century, 1939), and Robert Seager II, *And Tyler Too: A Biography of John and Julia Gardiner Tyler* (New York: McGraw-Hill, 1963).

5. Adams, *Memoirs*, 10:469; Chitwood, *John Tyler*, p. 106; Norma Lois Peterson, *Littleton Waller Tazewell* (Charlottesville: University Press of Virginia, 1983), p. 200.

6. *Register of Debates*, 22d Cong., 2d sess., p. 371.

7. Glyndon G. Van Deusen, "The Whig Party," in *History of U.S. Political Parties*, ed. Arthur M. Schlesinger, Jr., 4 vols. (New York: Chelsea House, 1980), 1:338–39; William C. Preston to Willie P. Mangum, 14 Oct. 1837, in Willie P. Mangum, *The Papers of Willie Person Mangum*, ed. Henry T. Shanks, 5 vols. (Raleigh, N.C.: State Department of Archives and History, 1950–56), 2:508–10.

8. Norman D. Brown, *Daniel Webster and the Politics of Availability* (Athens: University of Georgia Press, 1969), p. 162.

9. Philip Hone, *The Diary of Philip Hone, 1828–1851*, ed. Allan Nevins, 2 vols. (1927; reprint, New York: Kraus, 1969), 1:254–55; Samuel Rezneck, "The Social History of an American Depression, 1837–1843," *American Historical Review* 40 (1935): 662–67—Greeley is quoted on p. 665.

10. James D. Richardson, comp., *A Compilation of the Messages and Papers of the Presidents, 1789–1902*, 10 vols. (Washington, D.C.: Bureau of National Literature and Art, 1903), 3:324–46.

11. Maurice G. Baxter, *One and Inseparable: Daniel Webster and the Union* (Cambridge, Mass.: Harvard University Press, 1984), p. 262.

12. Hone, *Diary*, 1:385.

13. Levi Woodbury to Richard Rush, 8 Jan. 1838, quoted by James C. Curtis in *The Fox at Bay: Martin Van Buren and the Presidency, 1837–1841* (Lexington: University Press of Kentucky, 1970), p. 175.

14. Clay to Mangum, 31 May 1838, in Mangum, *Papers*, 2:525–26.

15. William Graham to Mangum, 11 Oct. 1839, ibid., 3:18–20.

16. Van Deusen, "Whig Party," 1:343; John Tyler to Clay, 16 Sept. 1839, in *The Letters and Times of the Tylers*, ed. Lyon G. Tyler, 3 vols. (1884–96; reprint, New York: Da Capo Press, 1970), 3:75–76.

17. Webster to Samuel Jaudon, 29 Mar. 1839, in Daniel Webster, *The Private Correspondence of Daniel Webster*, ed. Fletcher Webster, 2 vols. (Boston, Mass.: Little, Brown, 1857), 2:44–45.

18. Glyndon G. Van Deusen, *The Life of Henry Clay* (Boston, Mass.: Little, Brown, 1937), p. 334.

19. Thurlow Weed Barnes, *Memoir of Thurlow Weed* (vol. 2 of *Life of Thurlow Weed*) (Boston, Mass.: Houghton Mifflin, 1884), p. 77.

20. Chitwood, *John Tyler*, pp. 167–72; Seager, *And Tyler Too*, pp. 131–36; Calhoun to Andrew Pickens Calhoun, 20 Dec. 1839, in John C. Calhoun, *Correspondence of John C. Calhoun*, ed. J. Franklin Jameson, vol. 2 of *Report of the American Historical Association for the Year 1899* (Washington, D.C.: Government Printing Office, 1900), pp. 437–38.

21. *National Intelligencer,* 29 Jan. 1840; Sydney Nathans, *Daniel Webster and Jacksonian Democracy* (Baltimore, Md.: Johns Hopkins University Press, 1973), p. 147.

22. Henry Clay, speech delivered at Hanover Court House, Virginia, 27 June 1840, in *The Life, Correspondence, and Speeches of Henry Clay,* ed. Calvin Colton, 6 vols. (New York: P. O'Shea, 1864), 6:211; Van Deusen, *Life of Henry Clay,* pp. 335–36; Webster to John P. Healy, 31 Jan. 1840, quoted by Baxter in *One and Inseparable,* p. 269; Webster to Samuel Coffin, 11 June 1840, in Webster, *Private Correspondence,* 2:44–45, 82–86.

23. Chitwood, *John Tyler,* pp. 184–86; Seager, *And Tyler Too,* pp. 137–38.

24. Van Buren is quoted by Arthur M. Schlesinger, Jr., in *The Age of Jackson* (Boston, Mass.: Little, Brown, 1945, Book Find Club ed.), p. 51.

25. Robert G. Gunderson, *The Log-Cabin Campaign* (1957; reprint, Westport, Conn.: Greenwood Press, 1977), pp. 121–24; Webster to Samuel Coffin, 11 June 1840, in Webster, *Private Correspondence,* 2:82–86; Hone, *Diary,* 2:652.

26. George Rawlings Poage, *Henry Clay and the Whig Party* (1936; reprint, Gloucester, Mass.: Peter Smith, 1965), p. 14.

27. Ritchie is quoted by Chitwood in *John Tyler,* p. 196.

CHAPTER 3

THE SHORT MONTH

OF HARRISON'S PRESIDENCY

1. John Quincy Adams, *Memoirs of John Quincy Adams,* ed. Charles Francis Adams, 12 vols. (1874–77; reprint, New York: AMS Press, 1970), 10:366.

2. Nicholas Biddle to Webster, 13 Dec. 1840, in Nicholas Biddle, *The Correspondence of Nicholas Biddle Dealing with National Affairs, 1807–1844,* ed. Reginald C. McGrane (Boston, Mass.: Houghton Mifflin, 1919), pp. 337–38.

3. Harrison to Clay, 15 Nov. 1840, in Henry Clay, *The Private Correspondence of Henry Clay,* ed. Calvin Colton (New York: A. S. Barnes, 1855), p. 446.

4. George Rawlings Poage, *Henry Clay and the Whig Party* (1936; reprint, Gloucester, Mass.: Peter Smith, 1965), pp. 16–17.

5. Ibid., pp. 16–19; Harrison to Webster, 1 Dec. 1840, in Daniel Webster, *The Private Correspondence of Daniel Webster,* ed. Fletcher Webster, 2 vols. (Boston, Mass.: Little, Brown, 1857), 2:90–91, 93–94.

6. Clay to Francis Brooke, 8 Dec. 1840, in Clay, *Private Correspondence,* pp. 446–47.

7. John C. Calhoun to James Edward Calhoun, 26 Dec. 1840, in John C. Calhoun, *Correspondence of John C. Calhoun,* ed. J. Franklin Jameson, vol. 2 of *Report of the American Historical Association for the Year 1899* (Washington, D.C.: Government Printing Office, 1900), pp. 469–70; Poage, *Henry Clay,* pp. 21–22.

8. Sydney Nathans, *Daniel Webster and Jacksonian Democracy* (Baltimore, Md.: Johns Hopkins University Press, 1973), pp. 150–52; Claude Moore Fuess, *Daniel Webster,* 2 vols. (Boston, Mass.: Little, Brown, 1930), 2:93.

9. Van Buren is quoted by Freeman Cleves in *Old Tippecanoe: William Henry Harrison and His Times* (New York: Charles Scribner's Sons, 1939), p. 334; Philip Hone, *The Diary of Philip Hone, 1828–1851*, ed. Allan Nevins, 2 vols. (1927; reprint, New York: Kraus, 1969), 2:529.

10. Calhoun to Mrs. T. G. Clemson, 17 Feb. 1841, in Calhoun, *Correspondence*, pp. 474–75; Dorothy B. Goebel, *William Henry Harrison: A Political Biography* (Indianapolis: Historical Bureau of the Indiana Library and Historical Department, 1926), p. 370.

11. Glyndon G. Van Deusen, *The Life of Henry Clay* (Boston, Mass.: Little, Brown, 1937), pp. 338–39; Poage, *Henry Clay*, pp. 20–21; Nathans, *Daniel Webster*, pp. 152–53.

12. Robert Seager II, *And Tyler Too: A Biography of John and Julia Gardiner Tyler* (New York: McGraw-Hill, 1963), pp. 141–42; Tyler to Henry Wise, 25 Nov. and 20 Dec. 1840, in *The Letters and Times of the Tylers*, ed. Lyon G. Tyler, 3 vols. (1884–96; reprint, New York: Da Capo Press, 1970), 3:84–88.

13. Cleves, *Old Tippecanoe*, pp. 335–36.

14. Adams, *Memoirs*, 10:439–40; Oliver Perry Chitwood, *John Tyler: Champion of the Old South* (New York: D. Appleton-Century, 1939), pp. 200–201; *National Intelligencer*, 5 Mar. 1841.

15. James D. Richardson, comp., *A Compilation of the Messages and Papers of the Presidents, 1789–1902*, 10 vols. (Washington, D.C.: Bureau of National Literature and Art, 1903), 4:5–21 (hereafter cited as *Messages and Papers*).

16. Biddle to Webster, 13 Dec. 1840, in Biddle, *Correspondence*, pp. 337–39; Webster to Washington Irving, 16 Mar. 1841, in Daniel Webster, *The Papers of Daniel Webster, Correspondence*, ed. Charles M. Wiltse, Harold D. Moser, and Michael J. Birkner, 7 vols. (Hanover, N.H.: University Press of New England, 1974–86), 5:95–96; Duff Green to Harrison, 28 Feb. 1841, in William Henry Harrison Papers, Manuscripts Division, Library of Congress.

17. Van Deusen, *Henry Clay*, pp. 339–42; Maurice G. Baxter, *One and Inseparable: Daniel Webster and the Union* (Cambridge, Mass.: Harvard University Press, 1984), pp. 297–300.

18. Nathans, *Daniel Webster*, pp. 157–58; Poage, *Henry Clay*, p. 28.

19. Harrison to Clay, 13 Mar. 1841, quoted by Poage in *Henry Clay*, p. 31.

20. Nathan Sargent, *Public Men and Events, from the Commencement of Mr. Monroe's Administration, in 1817, to the Close of Mr. Fillmore's Administration, in 1853*, 2 vols. (Philadelphia: J. B. Lippincott, 1875), 2:115–16.

21. Clay to Harrison, 15 Mar. 1841, in Clay, *Private Correspondence*, pp. 452–53.

22. Nathans, *Daniel Webster*, pp. 160–61; *Messages and Papers*, 4:21.

23. Leonard D. White, *The Jacksonians: A Study in Administrative History, 1829–1861* (New York: Macmillan, 1954), pp. 336–38; Webster to Ewing, 20 Mar. 1841, in Webster, *Correspondence*, 5:96–97.

24. White, *Jacksonians*, pp. 309–11; Nathans, *Daniel Webster*, p. 160; Willie P. Mangum, *The Papers of Willie Person Mangum*, ed. Henry T. Shanks, 5 vols. (Raleigh, N.C.: State Department of Archives and History, 1950–56), 3:128–29;

Thomas Ewing, "Diary of Thomas Ewing, August and September, 1841," *American Historical Review* 18 (1912): 98.

25. Cleves, *Old Tippecanoe*, p. 341; White, *Jacksonians*, pp. 310–11.

26. Dumas Malone, *Jefferson and His Time*, 6 vols. (Boston, Mass.: Little, Brown, 1948–81), 2:269–70, 4:51; Jefferson to William Short, 12 June 1807, in Thomas Jefferson, *The Works of Thomas Jefferson*, ed. Paul L. Ford, 12 vols. (New York: G. P. Putnam's Sons, 1905), 10:414–15.

27. James Sterling Young, *The Washington Community, 1800–1828* (New York: Columbia University Press, 1966), pp. 240–47.

28. White, *Jacksonians*, pp. 47–48, 93; Ben Perley Poore, *Perley's Reminiscences of Sixty Years in the National Metropolis*, 2 vols. (Philadelphia: Hubbard Brothers, 1886), 1:258.

29. Cleves, *Old Tippecanoe*, pp. 341–43; Adams, *Memoirs*, 10:457; Baxter, *Daniel Webster*, pp. 300–301.

30. Seager, *And Tyler Too*, pp. 147–48; "The Vice-President Receives Bad News in Williamsburg: A Letter of James Lyons to John Tyler [April 3, 1841]," ed. Fred Shelley, *Virginia Magazine of History and Biography* 76 (1968): 337–39.

31. Adams, *Memoirs*, 10:456.

32. Henry Alexander Wise, *Seven Decades of the Union: The Humanities and Materialism, Illustrated by A Memoir of John Tyler* (Philadelphia: J. B. Lippincott, 1881), p. 180.

CHAPTER 4
THE SUCCESSION

1. Blair to Jackson, 4 Apr. 1841, in Andrew Jackson, *Correspondence of Andrew Jackson*, ed. John Spencer Bassett, 7 vols. (1926–35; reprint, New York: Kraus, 1969), 6:98.

2. Nathan Sargent, *Public Men and Events, from the Commencement of Mr. Monroe's Administration, in 1817, to the Close of Mr. Fillmore's Administration, in 1853*, 2 vols. (Philadelphia: J. B. Lippincott, 1875), 2:122–23.

3. *The Letters and Times of the Tylers*, ed. Lyon G. Tyler, 3 vols. (1884–96; reprint, New York: Da Capo Press, 1970), 2:12.

4. The various commentaries are quoted by Ruth C. Silva in *Presidential Succession* (Ann Arbor: University of Michigan Press, 1951), pp. 39–41.

5. Ibid., pp. 16–17.

6. Carl Brent Swisher, *Roger B. Taney* (1936; reprint, Hamden, Conn.: Archon Books, 1961), pp. 269–72, 449.

7. George Ticknor Curtis, *Life of Daniel Webster*, 2 vols. (New York: D. Appleton, 1893), 2:67; James D. Richardson, comp., *A Compilation of the Messages and Papers of the Presidents, 1789–1902*, 10 vols. (Washington, D.C.: Bureau of National Literature and Art, 1903), 4:31–32 (hereafter cited as *Messages and Papers*).

8. John Quincy Adams, *Memoirs of John Quincy Adams*, ed. Charles Francis Adams, 12 vols. (1874-77; reprint, New York: AMS Press, 1970), 10:463-64; Edward S. Corwin, *The President: Office and Powers, 1787-1957* (New York: New York University Press, 1957), pp. 344-45.

9. Arthur M. Schlesinger, Jr., *The Cycles of American History* (Boston, Mass.: Houghton Mifflin, 1986), pp. 337-45.

10. Silva, *Presidential Succession*, p. 47; Edward S. Corwin, *The Constitution and What It Means Today* (Princeton, N.J.: Princeton University Press, 1974), pp. 454-55.

11. Silva, *Presidential Succession*, p. 37.

12. Ibid., pp. 22-23.

13. Stephen W. Stathis, "John Tyler's Presidential Succession: A Reappraisal," *Prologue* 8 (1976): 223-36.

14. Tyler to Thomas Gilmer, 7 Jan. 1834, and Tyler to Littleton Waller Tazewell, 3 Dec. 1833, in *Letters and Times of the Tylers*, 1:479-81.

15. Clinton Rossiter, *1787: The Grand Convention* (New York: Macmillan, 1966), p. 223.

16. Tyler to William C. Rives, 9 Apr. 1841, in *Letters and Times of the Tylers*, 2:20.

17. Robert J. Morgan, *A Whig Embattled: The Presidency under John Tyler* (Lincoln: University of Nebraska Press, 1954), pp. 57-62; Tyler to N. B. Tucker, 28 July 1841, in *Letters and Times of the Tylers*, 2:53-54.

18. Thomas W. Gilmer to Frank Minor, 1 Jan. 1841, in Tyler Papers, Earl Gregg Swem Library, College of William and Mary, Williamsburg, Va.

19. Oliver Perry Chitwood, *John Tyler: Champion of the Old South* (New York: D. Appleton-Century, 1939), pp. 269-72; Robert Seager II, *And Tyler Too: A Biography of John and Julia Gardiner Tyler* (New York: McGraw-Hill, 1963), p. 149.

20. Sydney Nathans, *Daniel Webster and Jacksonian Democracy* (Baltimore, Md.: Johns Hopkins University Press, 1973), pp. 161-62.

21. *National Intelligencer*, 7 Apr. 1841.

22. *Messages and Papers*, 4:36-39; Chitwood, *John Tyler*, p. 204.

23. *National Intelligencer*, 12 Apr. 1841.

24. Webster to William Graham, 12 Apr. 1841 in William A. Graham, *The Papers of William Alexander Graham*, ed. J. G. deRoulhac Hamilton and Max R. Williams, 6 vols. to date (Raleigh, N.C.: State Department of Archives and History, 1957-), 2:186-87; George Badger to Graham, 28 Apr. 1841, ibid., 2:189; John Bell to R. P. Letcher, 2 May 1841, *Tyler Quarterly Historical and Genealogical Magazine* 8 (1927): 178.

25. Preston to Willie P. Mangum, 3 May 1841, in Willie P. Mangum, *The Papers of Willie Person Mangum*, ed. Henry T. Shanks, 5 vols. (Raleigh, N.C.: State Department of Archives and History, 1950-56), 3:155-57.

26. Clay to N. B. Tucker, 15 Apr. 1841, in *Letters and Times of the Tylers*, 2:30.

27. Lambert to Mangum, 14 Apr. 1841, in Mangum, *Papers*, 3:152-54.

28. S. Jones to Tyler, 14 Apr. 1841, Tyler Papers, Swem Library, College of William and Mary.

29. Chitwood, *John Tyler*, pp. 270–71; Glyndon G. Van Deusen, *The Life of Henry Clay* (Boston, Mass.: Little, Brown, 1937), pp. 343–44; Oscar Doane Lambert, *Presidential Politics in the United States, 1841–1844* (Durham, N.C.: Duke University Press, 1936), pp. 8–9.

30. Adams, *Memoirs*, 10:465; Clay to E. M. Letcher, 11 June 1841, in *The Life of John Crittenden, with Selections from His Correspondence and Speeches*, ed. Mrs. Chapman Coleman, 2 vols. (1871; reprint, New York: Da Capo Press, 1970), 1:156–57; Calhoun to Thomas G. Clemson, 13 June, 1841, in John C. Calhoun, *Correspondence of John C. Calhoun*, ed. J. Franklin Jameson, vol. 2 of *Report of the American Historical Association for the Year 1899* (Washington, D.C.: Government Printing Office, 1900), pp. 477–78.

31. Seager, *And Tyler Too*, pp. 172–76; Chitwood, *John Tyler*, pp. 390–95; Elizabeth Tyler Coleman, *Priscilla Cooper Tyler and the American Scene, 1816–1889* (University: University of Alabama Press, 1955), pp. 84–107.

32. Adams, *Memoirs*, 10:464.

CHAPTER 5
THE SPECIAL SESSION

1. Clay to John Berrien, 20 Apr. 1841, quoted by William R. Brock in *Parties and Political Conscience: American Dilemmas, 1840–1850* (Millwood, N.Y.: KTO Press, 1979), p. 81; Oliver Perry Chitwood, *John Tyler: Champion of the Old South* (New York: D. Appleton-Century, 1939), p. 210 n. 31.

2. Brock, *Parties and Political Conscience*, p. 81; Maurice G. Baxter, *One and Inseparable: Daniel Webster and the Union* (Cambridge, Mass.: Harvard University Press, 1984), p. 300; Thomas Payne Govan, *Nicholas Biddle: Nationalist and Public Banker, 1786–1844* (Chicago: University of Chicago Press, 1959), pp. 383, 392; Bray Hammond, *Banks and Politics in America from the Revolution to the Civil War* (Princeton, N.J.: Princeton University Press, 1957), p. 439.

3. Carroll to Mangum, 7 Apr. 1841, in Willie P. Mangum, *The Papers of Willie Person Mangum*, ed. Henry T. Shanks, 5 vols. (Raleigh, N.C.: State Department of Archives and History, 1950–56), 3:132–35; Hammond, *Banks and Politics*, p. 522; Samuel Rezneck, "The Social History of an American Depression, 1837–1843," *American Historical Review* 40 (1935): 664, 676–81.

4. Tyler to N. B. Tucker, 25 Apr. 1841, in *The Letters and Times of the Tylers*, ed. Lyon G. Tyler, 3 vols. (1884–96; reprint, New York: Da Capo Press, 1970), 2:53–54; Robert J. Brugger, *Beverley Tucker: Heart over Head in the Old South* (Baltimore, Md.: Johns Hopkins University Press, 1978), pp. 140–41.

5. Tyler to Clay, 30 Apr. 1841, Henry Clay Papers, Alderman Library, University of Virginia, Charlottesville; Glyndon G. Van Deusen, *The Life of Henry Clay* (Boston, Mass.: Little, Brown, 1937), pp. 344–45; Ewing to Clay, 8 May 1841, quoted by Chitwood in *John Tyler*, p. 210; Clay to Francis Brooke, 14 May 1841, in Henry Clay, *The Private Correspondence of Henry Clay*, ed. Calvin Colton (New York: A. S. Barnes, 1855), pp. 453–54.

6. Preston to Mangum, 3 May 1841, Mangum, *Papers*, 3:155–57.

7. James D. Richardson, comp., *A Compilation of the Messages and Papers of the Presidents, 1789–1902*, 10 vols. (Washington, D.C.: Bureau of National Literature and Art, 1903), 4:40–51 (hereafter cited as *Messages and Papers*).

8. Carl Brent Swisher, *American Constitutional Development* (Boston, Mass.: Houghton Mifflin, 1943), pp. 183–85; Baxter, *One and Inseparable*, pp. 261–66, 302–3.

9. Tyler to Clay, 30 Apr. 1841, Clay Papers, University of Virginia; Robert J. Morgan, *A Whig Embattled: The Presidency under John Tyler* (Lincoln: University of Nebraska Press, 1954), pp. 30–31; *Messages and Papers*, 4:40–51.

10. George Rawlings Poage, *Henry Clay and the Whig Party* (1936; reprint, Gloucester, Mass.: Peter Smith, 1965), pp. 43–45; Norman D. Brown, *Edward Stanly: Whiggery's Tarheel "Conqueror"* (University: University of Alabama Press, 1974), pp. 75–76; Brock, *Parties and Political Conscience*, p. 93.

11. Sydney Nathans, *Daniel Webster and Jacksonian Democracy* (Baltimore, Md.: Johns Hopkins University Press, 1973), p. 174; Tyler to N. B. Tucker, 28 June 1841, in *Letters and Times of the Tylers*, 2:53–54; "Extract from Secretary Ewing's Report," ibid., 2:38; Clay to E. M. Letcher, 11 June 1841, in *The Life of John J. Crittenden, with Selections from His Correspondence and Speeches*, ed. Mrs. Chapman Coleman, 2 vols. (1871; reprint, New York: Da Capo Press, 1970), 1:156–57.

12. *National Intelligencer*, 14, 15, 16, and 17 June 1841.

13. Duncan Cameron to William Graham, 7 June 1841, in William A. Graham, *The Papers of William Alexander Graham*, ed. J. G. deRoulhac Hamilton and Max R. Williams, 6 vols. to date (Raleigh, N.C.: State Department of Archives and History, 1957–), 2:192–93; Brown, *Edward Stanly*, pp. 76–77; Graham to Priestly H. Mangum, 12 June 1841 in Mangum, *Papers*, 3:163.

14. Noah to Willie P. Mangum, 13 June 1841, in Mangum, *Papers*, 3:166–67; Silas Wright and *Herald* correspondent are quoted by Chitwood in *John Tyler*, p. 217.

15. Oscar Doane Lambert, *Presidential Politics in the United States, 1841–1844* (Durham, N.C.: Duke University Press, 1936), pp. 27–31; Clement Eaton, *Henry Clay and the Art of American Politics* (Boston, Mass.: Little, Brown, 1957), p. 150; Wilfred E. Binkley, *President and Congress* (New York: Alfred A. Knopf, 1947), p. 69.

16. Van Deusen, *Life of Henry Clay*, pp. 345–51; Mangum to Duncan Cameron, 26 June 1841, in Mangum, *Papers*, 3:181–88.

17. Eaton, *Henry Clay*, p. 147; Calhoun to Mrs. T. G. (Anna Calhoun) Clemson, 28 June 1841, in John C. Calhoun, *Correspondence of John C. Calhoun*, ed. J. Franklin Jameson, vol. 2 of *Report of the American Historical Association for the Year 1899* (Washington, D.C.: Government Printing Office, 1900), pp. 437–38; Chitwood, *John Tyler*, p. 222; Albert D. Kirwan, *John J. Crittenden: The Struggle for the Union* (Lexington: University of Kentucky Press, 1962), pp. 150–51.

18. Baxter, *One and Inseparable*, p. 303; Calhoun to T. G. Clemson, 11 July 1841, in Calhoun, *Correspondence*, pp. 480–81; Willie P. Mangum to Charity

Mangum, 11 July 1841, and M. M. Noah to D. Lambert, 18 July 1841, in Mangum, *Papers,* 3:196–97, 200–202.

19. Webster to Hiram Ketchum, 17 July 1841, cited by George Ticknor Curtis in *Life of Daniel Webster,* 2 vols. (New York: D. Appleton, 1893), 2:75–77. Curtis includes many of Webster's letters in their entirety. Poage, *Henry Clay and the Whig Party,* pp. 63–65; *Letters and Times of the Tylers,* 2:70.

20. Calhoun to Andrew Pickens Calhoun, 26 July 1841, and Calhoun to Hammond, 1 Aug. 1841, in Calhoun, *Correspondence,* pp. 482–85; Chitwood, *John Tyler,* p. 224 n. 19.

21. Johnson to Mangum, 28 July 1841, in Mangum, *Papers,* 3:207–8; Tyler to N. B. Tucker, 28 July 1841, in *Letters and Times of the Tylers,* 2:53–54.

22. Thomas Gilmer to Franklin Minor, 7 Aug. 1841, in *Letters and Times of the Tylers,* 2:706–9; Webster to Mrs. C. L. R. Webster, 18 Aug. 1841, in Daniel Webster, *The Private Correspondence of Daniel Webster,* ed. Fletcher Webster, 2 vols. (Boston, Mass.: Little, Brown, 1857), 2:107–8.

23. Nathans, *Daniel Webster,* p. 172; Morgan, *Whig Embattled,* pp. 63–65; *National Intelligencer,* 14 Aug. 1841; Mangum to C. L. Hinton, 13 Aug. 1841, in Mangum, *Papers,* 3:215–16.

24. Poage, *Henry Clay and the Whig Party,* pp. 79–80; Nathans, *Daniel Webster,* p. 173; Chitwood, *John Tyler,* pp. 240–41.

25. *Messages and Papers,* 4:63–68; Baxter, *One and Inseparable,* pp. 304–5; "Draft of Editorial for the *National Intelligencer,*" Daniel Webster, in *The Papers of Daniel Webster, Correspondence,* ed. Charles M. Wiltse, Harold D. Moser, and Michael J. Birkner, 7 vols. (Hanover, N.H.: University Press of New England, 1974–86), 5:142–43; *National Intelligencer,* 17 Aug. 1841.

26. Crittenden to Clay, 16 Aug. 1841, in Coleman, *Life of John J. Crittenden,* 1:159–60.

27. Baxter, *One and Inseparable,* p. 306; Chitwood, *John Tyler,* pp. 263–64, 469–70.

28. Thomas Ewing, "Diary of Thomas Ewing, August and September, 1841," *American Historical Review* 18 (1912): 99–103; "Memorandum on the Banking Bills and Vetoes," Webster, *Papers, Correspondence,* 5:177–78; Nathans, *Daniel Webster,* pp. 174–76.

29. Nathans, *Daniel Webster,* p. 177.

CHAPTER 6
THE WHIGS EXPEL A PRESIDENT

1. Henry Clay, "On Mr. Tyler's Veto of the Bank Bill," in *The Life, Correspondence, and Speeches of Henry Clay,* ed. Calvin Colton, 6 vols. (New York: P. O'Shea, 1864), 6:275–96.

2. John M. Botts to Coffee House, Richmond, Va., 16 Aug. 1841, in *The Letters and Times of the Tylers,* ed. Lyon G. Tyler, 3 vols. (1884–96; reprint, New York: Da Capo Press, 1970), 2:112; Daniel Webster, "Memorandum on the

Banking Bills and the Vetoes, 1841," in Daniel Webster, *The Papers of Daniel Webster, Correspondence,* ed. Charles M. Wiltse, Harold D. Moser, and Michael J. Birkner, 7 vols. (Hanover, N.H.: University Press of New England, 1974–86), 5:177–79.

3. Webster to Hiram Ketchum, 22 Aug. 1841, and Webster to Bates and Choate, 25 Aug. 1841, in *Papers of Daniel Webster, Correspondence,* 5:146–48.

4. Robert J. Morgan, *A Whig Embattled: The Presidency under John Tyler* (Lincoln: University of Nebraska Press, 1954), pp. 173–74; Thomas Ewing, "Diary of Thomas Ewing, August and September, 1841," *American Historical Review* 18 (1912): 105–6; Maurice G. Baxter, *One and Inseparable: Daniel Webster and the Union* (Cambridge, Mass.: Harvard University Press, 1984), p. 307; *Congressional Globe,* 27th Cong., 1st sess., p. 346.

5. "Extract from a Letter Addressed by President Tyler to the Norfolk Democratic Association, Dated September 2, 1844," Wise to Tucker, 29 Aug. 1841, in *Letters and Times of the Tylers,* 2:95–96, 90–91.

6. Tyler to Tucker, 25 Apr. 1841, ibid., 2:32; Webster to Edward Everett, 24 July 1841, in Daniel Webster, *The Private Correspondence of Daniel Webster,* ed. Fletcher Webster, 2 vols. (Boston, Mass.: Little, Brown, 1857), 2:105–6; Robert J. Brugger, *Beverley Tucker: Heart over Head in the Old South* (Baltimore, Md.: Johns Hopkins University Press, 1978), p. 142.

7. Upshur to Tucker, 19 Oct. 1841, quoted by Brugger in *Beverley Tucker,* p. 245 n. 16; Reverdy Johnson to Crittenden, 30 Aug. 1841, in *The Life of John J. Crittenden, with Selections from His Correspondence and Speeches,* ed. Mrs. Chapman Coleman, 2 vols. (1871; reprint, New York: Da Capo Press, 1970), 1:160.

8. George Rawlings Poage, *Henry Clay and the Whig Party* (1936; reprint, Gloucester, Mass.: Peter Smith, 1965), pp. 87, 96–98; Charles M. Wiltse, *John C. Calhoun,* 3 vols. (Indianapolis, Ind.: Bobbs-Merrill, 1944–51), 3:37. Greeley's letter, dated 8 Sept. 1841, was quoted in the *National Intelligencer,* 16 Sept. 1841.

9. John A. Munroe, *Louis McLane: Federalist and Jacksonian* (New Brunswick, N.J.: Rutgers University Press, 1973), pp. 491–92; Baxter, *One and Inseparable,* pp. 577–78 n. 55; Oliver Perry Chitwood, *John Tyler: Champion of the Old South* (New York: D. Appleton-Century, 1939), pp. 279–80.

10. Upshur to Tucker, 28 July and 7 Sept. 1841, and Wise to Tucker, 18 and 27 June 1841, in *Letters and Times of the Tylers,* 2:46, 47, 115, 122; Claude H. Hall, *Abel Parker Upshur: Conservative Virginian, 1790–1844* (Madison: State Historical Society of Wisconsin, 1963), pp. 116–18.

11. Ewing, "*Diary,*" pp. 107, 109–11; Poage, *Henry Clay and the Whig Party,* pp. 88–89; John Quincy Adams, *Memoirs of John Quincy Adams,* ed. Charles Francis Adams, 12 vols. (1874–77; reprint, New York: AMS Press, 1970), 10:544–45.

12. James D. Richardson, comp., *A Compilation of the Messages and Papers of the Presidents, 1789–1902,* 10 vols. (Washington, D.C.: Bureau of National Literature and Art, 1903), 4:68–72; Chitwood, *John Tyler,* pp. 244–46; Poage, *Henry Clay and the Whig Party,* pp. 100–101.

13. Webster to Ketchum, 11 Sept. 1841, in Webster, *Papers, Correspondence,* 5:149–50; Webster to Ketchum, 10 Sept. 1841, in Webster, *Private Correspondence,* 2:110; Morgan, *Whig Embattled,* pp. 68–69; Baxter, *One and Inseparable,* pp. 310–11; *National Intelligencer,* 14 Sept. 1841; Glyndon G. Van Deusen, *The Life of Henry Clay* (Boston, Mass.: Little, Brown, 1937), pp. 351–55; Poage, *Henry Clay and the Whig Party,* p. 102.

14. *National Intelligencer,* 13 Sept. 1841; Mary Louise Hinsdale, *A History of the President's Cabinet* (Ann Arbor, Mich.: G. Wahr, 1911), pp. 115–17; Crittenden to R. P. Letcher, 11 Sept. 1841, in Coleman, *Life of John J. Crittenden,* 1:165–66; *National Intelligencer,* 13 and 15 Sept. 1841.

15. Hinsdale, *History of the President's Cabinet,* p. 118; Michael O'Brien, *A Character of Hugh Legaré* (Knoxville: University of Tennessee Press, 1985), pp. 165–66, 183, 238–39, 241, 264–66, 274; Marvin Cain, "A Reappraisal of Hugh Swinton Legaré and the Tyler Presidency," *South Carolina Historical Magazine* 79 (1978): 268–70.

16. John C. Calhoun, *Correspondence of John C. Calhoun,* ed. J. Franklin Jameson, vol. 2 of *Report of the American Historical Association for the Year 1899* (Washington, D.C.: Government Printing Office, 1900), pp. 487–88; Morgan, *Whig Embattled,* pp. 160–61; R. P. Letcher to Crittenden, 8 Sept. 1841, in Coleman, *Life of John J. Crittenden,* 1:164; Webster to McLean, 11 Sept. 1841, in Webster, *Papers, Correspondence,* 5:150–51; Glyndon G. Van Deusen, *William Henry Seward* (New York: Oxford University Press, 1967), p. 80.

17. Hall, *Abel Parker Upshur,* p. 118.

18. R. P. Letcher to Crittenden, 3 Sept. 1841, and Crittenden to Letcher, 11 Sept. 1841, in Coleman, *Life of John J. Crittenden,* 1:160–62, 165–66; *National Intelligencer,* 15 and 16 Sept. 1841; Chitwood, *John Tyler,* pp. 249–50.

19. Norman D. Brown, *Edward Stanly: Whiggery's Tarheel "Conqueror,"* (University: University of Alabama Press, 1974), pp. 1–2, 80–81; *National Intelligencer,* 21 and 23 Sept. 1841.

20. Claude M. Fuess, *The Life of Caleb Cushing,* 2 vols. (1923; reprint, Hamden, Conn.: Archon Books, 1965), 1:323–26; Letcher to Crittenden, 3 Sept. 1841, in Coleman, *Life of John J. Crittenden,* 1:160–62.

21. *National Intelligencer,* 16 Aug. 1841; William E. Ames, *A History of the "National Intelligencer"* (Chapel Hill: University of North Carolina Press, 1972), pp. 259–62; Constance McLaughlin Green, *Washington, Village and Capital, 1800–1878* (Princeton, N.J.: Princeton University Press, 1962), p. 160; Chitwood, *John Tyler,* p. 251; Robert Seager II, *And Tyler Too: A Biography of John and Julia Gardiner Tyler* (New York: McGraw-Hill, 1963), p. 160; Tyler to Thomas Cooper, 4 Oct. 1841, Tyler Papers, Manuscripts Division, Library of Congress.

22. Gaston to Graham, 19 Aug. 1841, in William A. Graham, *The Papers of William Alexander Graham,* ed. J. G. deRoulhac Hamilton and Max R. Williams, 6 vols. to date (Raleigh, N.C.: State Department of Archives and History, 1957–), 2:230–32; Webster to Ketchum, 22 Aug. 1841, in Webster, *Papers, Correspondence,* 5:146.

23. William J. Cooper, Jr., *The South and the Politics of Slavery, 1828–1856* (Baton Rouge: Louisiana State University Press, 1978), pp. 149–65; Charles G. Sellers, Jr., "Who Were the Southern Whigs?" *American Historical Review* 59 (1954): 335–46; Oscar Doane Lambert, *Presidential Politics in the United States, 1841–1844* (Durham, N.C.: Duke University Press, 1936), pp. 46–48; Morgan, *Whig Embattled*, pp. 23–28.

CHAPTER 7
THE TRYING SUMMER OF 1842

1. Crittenden to R. P. Letcher, 13 Sept. 1841, in *The Life of John J. Crittenden, with Selections from His Correspondence and Speeches*, ed. Mrs. Chapman Coleman, 2 vols. (1871; reprint, New York: Da Capo Press, 1970), 1:166–67.

2. Ralph Waldo Emerson, *The Heart of Emerson's Journals*, ed. Bliss Perry (Boston, Mass.: Houghton Mifflin, 1926), pp. 168–69; Webster to Thurlow Weed, 20 Sept. 1841, in Thurlow Weed Barnes, *Memoir of Thurlow Weed*, vol. 2 of *Life of Thurlow Weed* (Boston, Mass.: Houghton Mifflin, 1884), p. 95.

3. George Rawlings Poage, *Henry Clay and the Whig Party* (1936; reprint, Gloucester, Mass.: Peter Smith, 1965), p. 107; Clay to Francis Brooke, 28 Oct. 1841, in Henry Clay, *The Private Correspondence of Henry Clay*, ed. Calvin Colton (New York: A. S. Barnes, 1855), p. 455; Tyler to Tazewell, 2 Nov. 1841, *The Letters and Times of the Tylers*, ed. Lyon G. Tyler, 3 vols. (1884–96; reprint, New York: Da Capo Press, 1970), 2:129–31.

4. Spencer to Webster, 16 Oct. 1841, in Daniel Webster, *The Papers of Daniel Webster, Correspondence*, ed. Charles M. Wiltse, Harold D. Moser, and Michael J. Birkner, 7 vols. (Hanover, N.H.: University Press of New England, 1974–86), 5:168; Upshur to N. B. Tucker, 5 Nov. 1841, in *Letters and Times of the Tylers*, 2:155; First Annual Message, 7 Dec. 1841, in James D. Richardson, comp., *A Compilation of the Messages and Papers of the Presidents, 1789–1902*, 10 vols. (Washington, D.C.: Bureau of National Literature and Art, 1903), 4:74–89 (hereafter cited as *Messages and Papers*).

5. Upshur to N. B. Tucker, 12 Jan. 1842, in *Letters and Times of the Tylers*, 2:154–55; Webster to John Wilson, 9 Feb. 1842, in Webster, *Papers, Correspondence*, 5:188; Greeley to Cushing, 29 Dec. 1841, quoted by Claude M. Fuess in *The Life of Caleb Cushing*, 2 vols. (1923; reprint, Hamden, Conn.: Archon Books, 1965), 1:339–40; Weed to Webster, 18 Dec. 1841, in Webster, *Papers, Correspondence*, 5:175–76; Sydney Nathans, *Daniel Webster and Jacksonian Democracy* (Baltimore, Md.: Johns Hopkins University Press, 1973), p. 188; *Congressional Globe*, 27th Cong., 2d ses., pp. 75–78.

6. Daniel Webster, "Speech Delivered in Faneuil Hall," 30 Sept. 1842, in Daniel Webster, *The Works of Daniel Webster*, ed. Edward Everett, 6 vols. (Boston, Mass.: Little, Brown, 1851), 2:117–40; Calhoun to James H. Hammond, 31 Dec. 1841, in John C. Calhoun, *The Papers of John C. Calhoun*, ed. Robert L. Meriwether, W. Edwin Hemphill, and Clyde N. Wilson, 16 vols. to date

(Columbia: University of South Carolina Press, 1959–), 16:28–29; *Messages and Papers*, 4:81–82; William A. Graham to James W. Bryan, 22 Dec. 1841, in William A. Graham, *The Papers of William Alexander Graham*, ed. J. G. deRoulhac Hamilton and Max R. Williams, 6 vols. to date (Raleigh, N.C.: State Department of Archives and History, 1957–), 2:245–46.

7. William R. Brock, *Parties and Political Conscience: American Dilemmas, 1840–1850* (Millwood, N.Y.: KTO Press, 1979), pp. 102–4; Upshur to N. B. Tucker, 23 Dec. 1841, in *Letters and Times of the Tylers*, 2:153–55.

8. Clement Eaton, *Henry Clay and the Art of American Politics* (Boston, Mass.: Little, Brown, 1957), p. 151; Calhoun to Thomas G. Clemson, 23 Jan. 1842, and Calhoun to James H. Hammond, 4 Feb. 1842, in John C. Calhoun, *Correspondence of John C. Calhoun*, ed. J. Franklin Jameson, vol. 2 of *Report of the American Historical Association for the Year 1899* (Washington, D.C.: Government Printing Office, 1900), pp. 502–4.

9. *Messages and Papers*, 4:102, 106–11; Henry Clay, "Speech on the Abolition of the Veto Power," 24 Jan. 1842, in *The Life, Correspondence, and Speeches of Henry Clay*, ed. Calvin Colton, 6 vols. (New York: P. O'Shea, 1864), 6:301–19; Upshur to N. B. Tucker, 6 Mar. 1842, in *Letters and Times of the Tylers*, 2:165.

10. Albert D. Kirwan, *John J. Crittenden: The Struggle for the Union* (Lexington: University of Kentucky Press, 1962), p. 161; Poage, *Henry Clay and the Whig Party*, p. 114; Calhoun to Duff Green, 2 Apr. 1842, in Calhoun, *Correspondence*, pp. 506–8; Crittenden to R. P. Letcher, 1 May 1842, in Coleman, *Life of John J. Crittenden*, 1:177–79.

11. Calhoun to Robert Carter Nicholas, 7 May 1842, in Calhoun, *Papers*, 16:273–74; Upshur to N. B. Tucker, 6 and 28 Mar. 1842, in *Letters and Times of the Tylers*, 2:156–58; Robert J. Brugger, *Beverley Tucker: Heart over Head in the Old South* (Baltimore, Md.: Johns Hopkins University Press, 1978), p. 142.

12. Michael O'Brien, *A Character of Hugh Legaré* (Knoxville: University of Tennessee Press, 1985), p. 269–70; Oliver Perry Chitwood, *John Tyler: Champion of the Old South* (New York: D. Appleton-Century, 1939), p. 299; Charles M. Wiltse, *John C. Calhoun*, 3 vols. (Indianapolis, Ind.: Bobbs-Merrill, 1944–51), 3:82–83; *Messages and Papers*, 4:180–83; Mangum to Clay, 15 June 1842, in Willie P. Mangum, *The Papers of Willie Person Mangum*, ed. Henry T. Shanks, 5 vols. (Raleigh, N.C.: State Department of Archives and History, 1950–56), 3:358–60; R. P. Letcher to Crittenden, 21 June 1842, Crittenden to Letcher, 23 June 1842, and Crittenden to Clay, 2 July 1842, in Coleman, *Life of John J. Crittenden*, 1:182–86.

13. Chitwood, *John Tyler*, p. 303; Robert J. Morgan, *A Whig Embattled: The Presidency under John Tyler* (Lincoln: University of Nebraska Press, 1954), pp. 53–54; Crittenden to Clay, 15 July 1842, and Clay to Crittenden, 16 and 21 July 1842, in Coleman, *Life of John J. Crittenden*, 1:187–90.

14. Clay to Mangum, in Mangum, *Papers*, 3:367–68; Webster to Bates, 16 July 1842, and Webster to Tyler, 8 Aug. 1842, in Webster, *Papers, Correspondence*, 5:223–26, 235–36.

15. *Messages and Papers*, 4:183–89.

16. Samuel Flagg Bemis, *John Quincy Adams*, 2 vols. (New York: Alfred A. Knopf, 1949-1956), 2:440-42; Morgan, *Whig Embattled*, pp. 48-51; Chitwood, *John Tyler*, pp. 297-303; Tyler to a gathering of his friends in Philadelphia, 19 Feb. 1842, typecopy from the *Philadelphia Ledger*, 25 Feb. 1842, in Tyler Papers, Alderman Library, University of Virginia, Charlottesville; Tyler to Philadelphia friends, 2 July 1842, in *Letters and Times of the Tylers*, 2:170-71; Carlton Jackson, *Presidential Vetoes, 1792-1945* (Athens: University of Georgia Press, 1967), pp. 71-72.

17. *Messages and Papers*, 4:190-93; Wiltse, *John C. Calhoun*, 3:86; Nathans, *Daniel Webster*, pp. 181-89; Robert V. Remini, *Andrew Jackson*, 3 vols. (New York: Harper & Row, 1977-84), 3:154-55.

18. Crittenden to Clay, 12 Aug. 1842, and Crittenden to R. P. Letcher, 18 Aug. 1842, in Coleman, *Life of John J. Crittenden*, 1:192-95; Calhoun, *Papers*, 16:392-93; Edward Everett to Webster, 3 Aug. 1842, and Webster to Everett, 25 Aug. 1842, in Webster, *Papers, Correspondence*, 5:232-33, 238.

19. *Congressional Globe*, 27th Cong., 2d sess., pp. 912, 923-26; Wiltse, *John C. Calhoun*, 3:86-87; Calhoun, *Papers*, 16:434; Arthur C. Cole, *The Whig Party in the South* (1914; reprint, Gloucester, Mass.: Peter Smith, 1962), p. 99 n. 112; Kirwan, *John J. Crittenden*, pp. 164-66.

20. Tyler to Tazewell, 26 Aug. and 24 Oct. 1842, in *Letters and Times of the Tylers*, 2:183-84, 248-49; Calhoun to Thomas G. Clemson, 13 June 1841, in Calhoun, *Correspondence*, pp. 477-78.

21. The background on Dorr and the movement is taken largely from George M. Dennison, *The Dorr War: Republicanism on Trial, 1831-1861* (Lexington: University Press of Kentucky, 1976), and from Morgan, *Whig Embattled*, pp. 97-105.

22. The King-Tyler correspondence regarding the Dorr's Rebellion is found in *Messages and Papers*, 4:286-307; Morgan, *Whig Embattled*, p. 101.

23. William Graham to Paul C. Cameron, 20 May 1842, in Graham, *Papers*, 2:313.

24. Brugger, *Beverley Tucker*, p. 143; George T. Strong, *The Diary of George Templeton Strong*, ed. Allan Nevins and Milton H. Thomas, 4 vols. (New York: Macmillan, 1952), 1:184; Jackson to Francis P. Blair, 23 May 1842, in Andrew Jackson, *Correspondence of Andrew Jackson*, ed. John Spencer Bassett, 7 vols. (1926-35; reprint, New York: Kraus, 1969), 6:153.

25. *Luther v. Borden*, 7 Howard 1 (1849); *Messages and Papers*, 4:283-86; *House Report 546*, 28th Cong., 1st sess., "Interference of the Executive in the Affairs of Rhode Island"; Webster to Tyler, 18 Apr. 1844, in Daniel Webster, *The Private Correspondence of Daniel Webster*, ed. Fletcher Webster, 2 vols. (Boston, Mass.: Little, Brown, 1857), 2:189-90.

26. Tyler to Mary Tyler Jones, 6 July 1842, in *Letters and Times of the Tylers*, 2:172; Chitwood, *John Tyler*, pp. 395-96; *Richmond Enquirer*, 16 Sept. 1842.

CHAPTER 8
THE PEACEMAKERS

1. Howard Jones, *To the Webster-Ashburton Treaty: A Study in Anglo-American Relations, 1783–1843* (Chapel Hill: University of North Carolina Press, 1977), pp. 19, 37–47.

2. Ibid., pp. 20–31, 48–56; Samuel Flagg Bemis, *John Quincy Adams*, 2 vols. (New York: Alfred A. Knopf, 1949, 1956), 2:452.

3. Sydney Nathans, *Daniel Webster and Jacksonian Democracy* (Baltimore, Md.: Johns Hopkins University Press, 1973), pp. 189–90; Ashburton to Webster, 2 Jan. 1842, in Daniel Webster, *The Papers of Daniel Webster, Diplomatic Papers*, ed. Charles M. Wiltse, Kenneth E. Shewmaker, and Kenneth R. Stevens, 1 vol. to date (Hanover, N.H.: University Press of New England, 1983–), 1:486–88.

4. John Quincy Adams, *Memoirs of John Quincy Adams*, ed. Charles Francis Adams, 12 vols. (1874–77; reprint, New York: AMS Press, 1970), 11:47.

5. Richard N. Current, *Daniel Webster and the Rise of National Conservatism* (Boston, Mass.: Little, Brown, 1955), p. 119; Webster to Edward Everett, 25 Apr. 1842, in Webster, *Papers, Diplomatic*, 1:539–42.

6. Lady Ashburton to Webster, 12 Jan. 1842, Webster, *Papers, Diplomatic*, 1:490; Webster to Everett, 25 Apr. 1842, ibid., 1:539–42; Ashburton to Aberdeen, 25 and 26 Apr. and 12 and 29 May, 1842, quoted by Jones in *To the Webster-Ashburton Treaty*, p. 118.

7. Gallatin to Ashburton, 20 Apr. 1842, in Albert Gallatin, *The Writings of Albert Gallatin*, ed. Henry Adams, 3 vols. (1879; reprint, New York: Antiquarian Press, 1960), 2:596–97.

8. Seward to Crittenden, 31 May 1842, in *The Life of John J. Crittenden, with Selections from His Correspondence and Speeches*, ed. Mrs. Chapman Coleman, 2 vols. (1871; reprint, New York: Da Capo Press, 1970), 1:154–55; Glyndon G. Van Deusen, *William Henry Seward* (New York: Oxford University Press, 1967), pp. 77–78; Robert J. Morgan, *A Whig Embattled: The Presidency under John Tyler* (Lincoln: University of Nebraska Press, 1954), pp. 110–12.

9. Webster to John E. Denison, 26 Apr. 1842, in Daniel Webster, *The Papers of Daniel Webster, Correspondence*, ed. Charles M. Wiltse, Harold D. Moser, and Michael J. Birkner, 7 vols. (Hanover, N.H.: University Press of New England, 1974–86), 5:199–201; Calhoun to Anna Calhoun Clemson, 22 Apr. 1842, in John C. Calhoun, *The Papers of John C. Calhoun*, ed. Robert L. Meriwether, W. Edwin Hemphill, and Clyde N. Wilson, 16 vols. to date (Columbia: University of South Carolina Press, 1959–), 16:238–39.

10. Ashburton to Webster, 28 July 1842, in Webster, *Papers, Diplomatic*, 1:651–52; Maurice G. Baxter, *One and Inseparable: Daniel Webster and the Union* (Cambridge, Mass.: Harvard University Press, 1984), pp. 351–52.

11. Frederick Merk, *Fruits of Propaganda in the Tyler Administration* (Cambridge, Mass.: Harvard University Press, 1971), pp. 3, 39–58; Nathans, *Daniel Webster*, p. 192; Jones, *To the Webster-Ashburton Treaty*, pp. 90–91.

12. Francis O. J. Smith to Webster, 7 June 1841 and 12 Aug. 1842, in Webster, *Papers, Diplomatic,* 1:94–96, 681–82; Merk, *Fruits of Propaganda,* pp. 59–64. President Polk's Message to the House of Representatives, 10 Apr. 1846, in connection with the investigation of Webster's probable "official misconduct" in the use of the secret fund, James D. Richardson, comp., *A Compilation of the Messages and Papers of the Presidents, 1789–1902,* 10 vols. (Washington, D.C.: Bureau of National Literature and Art, 1903), 4:431–36; Merk, *Fruits of Propaganda,* pp. 57, 63–65, 191–98; Jones, *To the Webster-Ashburton Treaty,* pp. 91–94; Baxter, *Webster,* pp. 340–41.

13. Jones, *To the Webster-Ashburton Treaty,* pp. 102–11, 128, 132; Baxter, *One and Inseparable,* pp. 343, 586 n. 27; Sparks to Webster, 15 Feb. and 19 May 1842, and Webster to Sparks, 4 Mar. and 14 May 1842, in Webster, *Papers, Diplomatic,* 1:513, 523, 556–57, 564–65; Merk, *Fruits of Propaganda,* pp. 65–66, 70–72.

14. Ashburton to Webster, 1 and 2 July 1842, in Webster, *Papers, Diplomatic,* 1:604–5; Webster to Everett, 28 June 1842. This letter, marked Private, accompanied an official letter, found ibid., 1:592. The private letter is published in its entirety in George Ticknor Curtis's *Life of Daniel Webster,* 2 vols. (New York: D. Appleton, 1893), 2:104–7.

15. Baxter, *One and Inseparable,* pp. 346–47; Merk, *Fruits of Propaganda,* pp. 74–77; Webster to Maine Commissioners, 15 July 1842, in Webster, *Papers, Diplomatic,* 1:620–24; *National Intelligencer,* 25 July 1842.

16. Merk, *Fruits of Propaganda,* p. 75; Jones, *To the Webster-Ashburton Treaty,* pp. 133–36; Thomas LeDuc, "The Webster-Ashburton Treaty and the Minnesota Iron Range," *Mississippi Valley Historical Review* 51 (1964): 476–81.

17. Webster to Everett, 29 Jan. 1842, in Webster, *Papers, Diplomatic,* 1:177–85; Jones, *To the Webster-Ashburton Treaty,* pp. 145–48.

18. Samuel J. May and Edward Morton, of the Massachusetts Anti-Slavery Society, to Webster, 29 Mar. 1842, in Webster, *Papers, Diplomatic,* 1:528–29; *Congressional Globe,* 27th Cong., 2d sess., pp. 110, 203–4.

19. Michael O'Brien, *A Character of Hugh Legaré* (Knoxville: University of Tennessee Press, 1985), pp. 268–70; Leonard L. Richards, *The Life and Times of Congressman John Quincy Adams* (New York: Oxford University Press, 1986), pp. 144–45; Charles M. Wiltse, *John C. Calhoun,* 3 vols. (Indianapolis, Ind.: Bobbs-Merrill, 1944–51), 3:69–71; Legaré to Webster, 29 July 1842, in Webster, *Papers, Diplomatic,* 1:656–57.

20. Jones, *To the Webster-Ashburton Treaty,* pp. 146–48; Van Deusen, *William Henry Seward,* pp. 66–67; Webster to Ashburton, 1 Aug. 1842, Ashburton to Webster, 6 Aug. 1842, and Tyler to Webster, 7 Aug. 1842, in Webster, *Papers Diplomatic,* 1:658–69, 671.

21. Peter Duignan and Clarence C. Clindenen, *The United States and the African Slave Trade, 1619–1862* (Palo Alto, Calif.: Hoover Institution, Stanford University, 1963), pp. 33–35; Everett to Webster, 3 Jan. 1842, in Webster, *Papers, Diplomatic,* 1:488–89.

22. Duff Green to Calhoun, 24 Jan. 1842, and Calhoun to Green, 2 Apr. 1842, in Calhoun, *Papers,* 16:83–86; Bemis, *John Quincy Adams,* 2:453–54; Adams,

Memoirs, 11:243; Webster to Everett, 26 Apr. 1842, Story to Webster, 19 Apr. 1842, and Webster to Cass, 25 Apr. 1842, in Webster, *Papers, Diplomatic,* 1:543, 537–39.

23. Jones, *To the Webster-Ashburton Treaty,* pp. 140–42; Everett to Webster, 29 Jan. 1842, in Webster, *Papers, Diplomatic,* 1:494–95; John Tyler to Robert Tyler, 29 Aug. 1858, in *The Letters and Times of the Tylers,* ed. Lyon G. Tyler, 3 vols. (1884–96; reprint, New York: Da Capo Press, 1970), 2:240–42. The text of the Webster-Ashburton Treaty can be found in Jones, *To the Webster-Ashburton Treaty,* pp. 181–87; Webster to Ashburton, 8 Aug. 1842, in Webster, *Papers, Diplomatic,* 1:673–79; Crittenden to Clay, 12 Aug. 1842, in Coleman, *Life of John J. Crittenden,* 1:192–93; Calhoun to James E. Calhoun, 18 Aug. 1842, in Calhoun, *Papers,* 16:392–93; Upshur to N. B. Tucker, 11 Aug. 1842, *Letters and Times of the Tylers,* 2:178–79.

24. Thomas Hart Benton, *Thirty Years' View,* 2 vols. (New York: D. Appleton, 1854, 1856), 2:424; Baxter, *One and Inseparable,* pp. 354–55; Calhoun's speech on the treaty, Calhoun, *Papers,* 16:393–409; Webster to Everett, 25 Aug. 1842, Webster to George Ticknor, 20 Aug. 1842, in Webster, *Papers, Diplomatic,* 1:695, 354–55; Jones, *To the Webster-Ashburton Treaty,* pp. 164–65, 216–17 n. 7.

25. Webster to John Tyler, 24 Aug. 1842, in Webster, *Papers, Diplomatic,* 1:695.

26. Tyler to Tazewell, 24 Oct. 1842, Upshur to N. B. Tucker, 11 Aug. 1842, in *Letters and Times of the Tylers,* 2:248–49, 178–79; Philip Hone, *The Diary of Philip Hone, 1828–1851,* ed. Allan Nevins, 2 vols. (1927; reprint, New York: Kraus, 1969), 2:618–619; Oliver Perry Chitwood, *John Tyler: Champion of the Old South* (New York: D. Appleton-Century, 1939), pp. 315–16; Claude Moore Fuess, *Daniel Webster,* 2 vols. (Boston, Mass.: Little, Brown, 1930), 2:118–19.

CHAPTER 9
PACIFIC-MINDEDNESS

1. See Cass-Webster and related correspondence in Daniel Webster, *The Papers of Daniel Webster, Diplomatic Papers,* ed. Charles M. Wiltse, Kenneth E. Shewmaker, and Kenneth R. Stevens, 1 vol. to date (Hanover, N.H.: University Press of New England, 1983–), 1:713–75. The Webster quote is from Webster to Cass, 20 Dec. 1842, ibid., 1:148.

2. Frank B. Woodford, *Lewis Cass: The Last Jeffersonian* (New Brunswick, N.J.: Rutgers University Press, 1950), pp. 217–28; Dickerson to Cass, 10 Dec. 1842, quoted by W. L. G. Smith in *Life and Times of Lewis Cass* (New York: Derby & Jackson, 1856), p. 483.

3. Thomas Hart Benton, *Thirty Years' View,* 2 vols. (New York: D. Appleton, 1854, 1856), 2:424; Webster to Everett, 25 Aug. 1842, in Webster, *Papers, Diplomatic,* 1:695–98; Philip Shriver Klein, *President James Buchanan: A Biography* (University Park: Pennsylvania State University Press, 1962), pp. 145–46; Samuel Flagg Bemis, *John Quincy Adams,* 2 vols. (New York: Alfred A. Knopf,

1949, 1956), 1:460–62, 478–81; Frederick Merk, *Fruits of Propaganda in the Tyler Administration* (Cambridge, Mass.: Harvard University Press, 1971), pp. 71–72; Howard Jones, *To the Webster-Ashburton Treaty: A Study in Anglo-American Relations, 1783–1843* (Chapel Hill: University of North Carolina Press, 1977), pp. 126–32.

4. William H. Goetzmann, *New Lands, New Men: America and the Second Great Age of Discovery* (New York: Viking, 1986), p. 168; Benton, *Thirty Years' View*, 2:426–30.

5. David M. Pletcher, *The Diplomacy of Annexation: Texas, Oregon, and the Mexican War* (Columbia: University of Missouri Press, 1973), pp. 102–6.

6. Ibid., p. 107; Goetzmann, *New Lands*, pp. 280–86, 297; E. Jeffrey Stann, "Charles Wilkes as a Diplomat," in *Magnificent Voyagers: The U.S. Exploring Expedition, 1838–1842*, ed. Herman J. Viola and Carolyn Margolis (Washington, D.C.: Smithsonian Institution Press, 1985), pp. 221–24; Philip K. Lundberg, "Ships and Squadron Logistics," ibid., pp. 160–62; Frederick Merk, *The Oregon Question: Essays in Anglo-American Diplomacy and Politics* (Cambridge, Mass.: Harvard University Press, 1967), pp. 196–97.

7. Ashburton to Aberdeen, 25 Apr. 1842, quoted by Merk, *Oregon Question*, pp. 205–6; Thompson to Webster, 20 Apr. 1842, quoted by Pletcher in *Diplomacy of Annexation*, p. 99, see also pp. 84–88; Thompson to Tyler, 9 May 1842, in Webster, *Papers, Diplomatic*, 1:422–23.

8. Webster to Everett, 29 Jan. 1843, in Webster, *Papers, Diplomatic*, 1:841–44; Merk, *Oregon Question*, p. 214; Daniel Walker Howe, in *The Political Culture of the American Whigs* (Chicago: University of Chicago Press, 1979), pp. 20–21, discusses ideas presented by Major L. Wilson in *Space, Time and Freedom: The Quest for Nationality and the Irrepressible Conflict* (Westport, Conn.: Greenwood Press, 1974); Clay to Crittenden, 3 Dec. 1843, in *The Life of John J. Crittenden, with Selections from His Correspondence and Speeches*, ed. Mrs. Chapman Coleman, 2 vols. (1871; reprint, New York: Da Capo Press, 1970), 1:207–10.

9. Merk, *Oregon Question*, p. 211; Webster, *Papers, Diplomatic*, 1:373–74.

10. John Quincy Adams, *Memoirs of John Quincy Adams*, ed. Charles Francis Adams, 12 vols. (1874–77; reprint, New York: AMS Press, 1970), 11:351, 353; Pletcher, *Diplomacy of Annexation*, pp. 100–1.

11. Pletcher, *Diplomacy of Annexation*, p. 106; William Nisbet Chambers, *Old Bullion Benton: Senator from the New West* (Boston, Mass.: Little, Brown, 1956), pp. 264–65.

12. For background on the "Tyler Doctrine" see Webster, *Papers, Diplomatic*, 1:851–57; James D. Richardson, comp., *A Compilation of the Messages and Papers of the Presidents, 1789–1902*, 10 vols. (Washington, D.C.: Bureau of National Literature and Art, 1903), 4:211–14.

13. Samuel Eliot Morison, *The Maritime History of Massachusetts, 1783–1860* (Boston, Mass.: Houghton Mifflin, Sentry ed., 1961), pp. 44–48, 76; Webster, *Papers, Diplomatic*, 1:879; Benton, *Thirty Years' View*, 2:510–22.

14. Webster to Everett, 10 Mar. 1843, Everett to Webster, 3 Apr. 1843, and Webster to Cushing, 8 May 1843, in Webster, *Papers, Diplomatic*, 1:880–82, 905–7,

922; Claude M. Fuess, *The Life of Caleb Cushing*, 2 vols. (1923; reprint, Hamden, Conn.: Archon Books, 1965), 1:397–454; Webster Circular, 20 Mar. 1843, John Murray Forbes et al. to Webster, 20 Apr. 1843, List of Articles for the Legation to China, with notations by Webster and Tyler, 11 Apr. 1843, and Webster to Cushing, 8 May 1843, in Webster, *Papers, Diplomatic*, 1:901–3, 917–26.

CHAPTER 10
THE PRESIDENT, THE CABINET,
AND THE WHITE HOUSE

1. Tyler to Daniel Webster, 15 May, 8 Sept. and 14 Oct. 1841, in Daniel Webster, *The Papers of Daniel Webster, Diplomatic Papers*, ed. Charles M. Wiltse, Kenneth E. Shewmaker, and Kenneth R. Stevens, 1 vol. to date (Hanover, N.H.: University Press of New England, 1983–), 1:75, 116–17, 320–21; Tyler to Webster, 10 July 1842 and 13 Feb. 1843, in *The Letters and Times of the Tylers*, ed. Lyon G. Tyler, 3 vols. (1884–96; reprint, New York: Da Capo Press, 1970), 2:258, 265.

2. Robert J. Morgan, *A Whig Embattled: The Presidency under John Tyler* (Lincoln: University of Nebraska Press, 1954), pp. 71–73.

3. Tyler to John C. Spencer, 13 May and 2 Sept. 1843, in Tyler Papers, Manuscripts Division, Library of Congress; Robert Seager II, *And Tyler Too: A Biography of John and Julia Gardiner Tyler* (New York: McGraw-Hill, 1963), pp. 224–27.

4. Oliver Perry Chitwood, *John Tyler: Champion of the Old South* (New York: D. Appleton-Century, 1939), pp. 270–72; Leonard D. White, *The Jacksonians: A Study in Administrative History, 1829–1861* (New York: Macmillan, 1954), pp. 95, 68, 82–83; Seager, *And Tyler Too*, pp. 226, 588–89 n. 82.

5. Tyler to Robert McCandlish, 10 July 1842, in *Letters and Times of the Tylers*, 2:172–73.

6. Chitwood, *John Tyler*, pp. 388–89, 392–93; John Quincy Adams, *Memoirs of John Quincy Adams*, ed. Charles Francis Adams, 12 vols. (1874–77; reprint, New York: AMS Press, 1970), 11:174.

7. Chitwood, *John Tyler*, pp. 394–95; Paul F. Boller, Jr., *Presidential Wives* (New York: Oxford University Press, 1988), pp. 78–87; Elizabeth Tyler Coleman, *Priscilla Cooper Tyler and the American Scene, 1816–1889* (University: University of Alabama Press, 1955), pp. 84–107; Claude H. Hall, *Abel Parker Upshur: Conservative Virginian, 1790–1844* (Madison: State Historical Society of Wisconsin, 1963), pp. 37, 121.

8. White, *Jacksonians*, pp. 215–16; Hall, *Abel Parker Upshur*, pp. 124–26; Harold Sprout and Margaret Sprout, *The Rise of American Naval Power, 1776–1918* (Princeton, N.J.: Princeton University Press, paperback ed., 1967), pp. 116–26.

9. White, *Jacksonians*, pp. 217–27, 232–41; Sprout and Sprout, *Rise of American Naval Power*, p. 114; James Fenimore Cooper, *The History of the Navy of the United States of America*, 2 vols. (Philadelphia: Lea & Blanchard, 1839), xxxiii–xxxvi; *Report of the Secretary of the Navy, December 4, 1841, Senate*

Document Number 1, 27th Cong., 2d sess., pp. 367–69; Hall, *Abel Parker Upshur*, pp. 125–46.

10. White, *Jacksonians*, p. 218; *Congressional Globe*, 29th Cong., 1st sess., p. 738.

11. Harold D. Langley, *Social Reform in the United States Navy, 1798–1862* (Urbana: University of Illinois Press, 1967), pp. 159–60.

12. Samuel Eliot Morison, *"Old Bruin": Commodore Matthew C. Perry, 1794–1858* (Boston, Mass.: Little, Brown, 1967), pp. 144–62; Hall, *Abel Parker Upshur*, pp. 164–71.

13. White, *Jacksonians*, pp. 188–94.

14. Glyndon G. Van Deusen, *William Henry Seward* (New York: Oxford University Press, 1967), p. 60; Philip Hone, *The Diary of Philip Hone, 1828–1851*, ed. Allan Nevins, 2 vols. (1927; reprint, New York: Kraus, 1969), 2:640; Adams, *Memoirs*, 11:336.

15. James D. Richardson, comp., *A Compilation of the Messages and Papers of the Presidents, 1789–1902*, 10 vols. (Washington, D.C.: Bureau of National Literature and Art, 1903), 4:268 (hereafter cited as *Messages and Papers*); White, *Jacksonians*, pp. 188–91; James P. Espy, "To the Friends of Science," 6 Dec. 1842, in William Graham, *The Papers of William Alexander Graham*, ed. J. G. deRoulhac Hamilton and Max R. Williams, 6 vols. to date (Raleigh, N.C.: State Department of Archives and History, 1957–), 2:387–89; Donald R. Whitnah, *A History of the United States Weather Bureau* (Urbana: University of Illinois Press, Illini Books, 1965), pp. 5–13.

16. Cushing to Henry Wise, 24 Sept. 1842, in *Letters and Times of the Tylers*, 3:105.

17. Webster to Joshua Bates, 30 Nov. 1843, in Daniel Webster, *The Papers of Daniel Webster, Correspondence*, ed. Charles M. Wiltse, Harold C. Moser, and Michael J. Birkner, 7 vols. (Hanover, N.H.: University Press of New England, 1974–86), 5:320–21.

18. *Messages and Papers*, 4:270, 346–47; Adams, *Memoirs*, 11:335–36, 12:60; White, *Jacksonians*, p. 490; William H. Goetzmann, *New Lands, New Men: America and the Second Age of Discovery* (New York: Viking, 1986), pp. 305–6.

19. Michael O'Brien, *A Character of Hugh Legaré* (Knoxville: University of Tennessee Press, 1985), pp. 264–65.

20. George Ticknor, *Life, Letters, and Journals of George Ticknor*, ed. George S. Hillard, 2 vols. (Boston, Mass.: James R. Osgood, 1876), 1:489.

21. O'Brien, *Character of Hugh Legaré*, pp. 266–73; Ticknor to William H. Prescott, 14 Aug. 1842, in Ticknor, *Life, Letters, and Journals*, 2:209.

22. Tyler to John Nelson, 28 June 1843, and Wickliffe to Tyler, 25 Mar. 1845, Tyler Papers, Library of Congress; Seager, *And Tyler Too*, pp. 4, 42.

23. Peter T. Rohrbach and Lowell S. Newman, *American Issue: The U.S. Postage Stamp, 1842–1869* (Washington, D.C.: Smithsonian Institution Press, 1984), pp. 22–53.

24. White, *Jacksonians*, pp. 456–57.

25. Goetzmann, *New Lands*, pp. 289–90.

26. Russel B. Nye, *William Lloyd Garrison and the Humanitarian Reformers* (Boston, Mass.: Little, Brown, 1955), pp. 142–43; Leonard L. Richards, *The Life and Times of Congressman John Quincy Adams* (New York: Oxford University Press, 1986), p. 144.

CHAPTER 11
MODERATION GONE AWRY

1. Richard N. Current, *Daniel Webster and the Rise of National Conservatism* (Boston, Mass.: Little, Brown, 1955), p. 134.

2. Abbott Lawrence to Webster, 20 July 1842, in Daniel Webster, *The Papers of Daniel Webster, Correspondence,* ed. Charles M. Wiltse, Harold D. Moser, and Michael J. Birkner, 7 vols. (Hanover, N.H.: University Press of New England, 1974–86), 5:232; Webster to Edward Everett, 25 Aug. 1842, in Daniel Webster, *The Papers of Daniel Webster, Diplomatic Papers,* ed. Charles M. Wiltse, Kenneth E. Shewmaker, and Kenneth R. Stevens, 1 vol. to date (Hanover, N.H.: University Press of New England, 1983–), 1:694–98; R. P. Letcher to J. J. Crittenden, 8 Aug. 1842, in *The Life of John J. Crittenden, with Selections from His Correspondence and Speeches,* ed. Mrs. Chapman Coleman, 2 vols. (1871; reprint, New York: Da Capo Press, 1970), 1:192.

3. Webster to John Plummer Healy, 24 and 26 Aug. 1842, in Webster, *Papers, Correspondence,* 5:237–39; Sydney Nathans, *Daniel Webster and Jacksonian Democracy* (Baltimore, Md.: Johns Hopkins University Press, 1973), pp. 196–97; Maurice G. Baxter, *One and Inseparable: Daniel Webster and the Union* (Cambridge, Mass.: Harvard University Press, 1984), p. 361.

4. For the Faneuil Hall speech see Daniel Webster, *The Works of Daniel Webster,* ed. Edward Everett, 6 vols. (Boston, Mass.: Little, Brown, 1851), 2:111–40; George Ticknor Curtis, *Life of Daniel Webster,* 2 vols. (New York: D. Appleton, 1893), 2:142–46; John Quincy Adams, *Memoirs of John Quincy Adams,* ed. Charles Francis Adams, 12 vols. (1874–77; reprint, New York: AMS Press, 1970), 11:256.

5. Webster to Fletcher Webster, 19 Oct. 1842, in Webster, *Papers, Correspondence,* 5:246; Webster to Fletcher Webster, 8 Nov. 1842, in Daniel Webster, *The Private Correspondence of Daniel Webster,* ed. Fletcher Webster, 2 vols. (Boston, Mass.: Little, Brown, 1857), 2:152; Webster to Everett, 28 Nov. and 28 June 1842, in Webster, *Papers, Diplomatic,* 1:834–37, 592.

6. Webster to Everett, 25 Aug. 1842, in Webster, *Papers, Diplomatic,* 1:695–98; Oliver Perry Chitwood, *John Tyler: Champion of the Old South* (New York: D. Appleton-Century, 1939), p. 371; Baxter, *One and Inseparable,* pp. 363–66; William Graham to James Webb, 14 Jan. 1843, in William A. Graham, *The Papers of William Alexander Graham,* J. G. deRoulhac Hamilton and Max R. Williams, 6 vols. to date (Raleigh, N.C.: State Department of Archives and History, 1957–), 2:414–15; Nathans, *Daniel Webster,* pp. 194–97.

7. Chitwood, *John Tyler,* p. 303; Claude M. Fuess, *The Life of Caleb Cushing,* 2 vols. (1923; reprint, Hamden, Conn.: Archon Books, 1965), 1:365–66; Philip Hone, *The Diary of Philip Hone,* ed. Allan Nevins, 2 vols. (1927; reprint, New York: Kraus, 1969), 2:645.

8. James D. Richardson, comp., *A Compilation of the Messages and Papers of the Presidents, 1789–1902,* 10 vols. (Washington, D.C.: Bureau of National Literature and Art, 1903), 4:101 (hereafter cited as *Messages and Papers*); Arthur M. Schlesinger, Jr., *The Imperial Presidency* (Boston, Mass.: Houghton Mifflin, 1973), pp. 16–17.

9. *Messages and Papers,* 4:105–6; Robert J. Morgan, *A Whig Embattled: The Presidency under John Tyler* (Lincoln: University of Nebraska Press, 1954), pp. 87–88.

10. *Messages and Papers,* 4:220–25; Morgan, *Whig Embattled,* pp. 94–95; Leonard D. White, *The Jacksonians: A Study in Administrative History, 1829–1861* (New York: Macmillan, 1954), pp. 145–46; Bernard Schwartz, *From Confederation to Nation: The American Constitution, 1835–1877* (Baltimore, Md.: Johns Hopkins University Press, 1973), pp. 71–73; Schlesinger, *Imperial Presidency,* pp. 46–57.

11. Scott to Stevens, 24 May 1842, quoted by George Rawlings Poage, in *Henry Clay and the Whig Party* (1936; reprint, Gloucester, Mass.: Peter Smith, 1965), p. 108; Scott to Crittenden, 5 Apr. and 29 June 1843, in Coleman, *Life of John J. Crittenden,* 1:201–3; Alphonso Taft to Webster, 7 Apr. 1843, in Webster, *Papers, Correspondence,* 5:291–94.

12. Calhoun to Thomas G. Clemson, 6 Feb. 1843, in John C. Calhoun, *The Papers of John C. Calhoun,* ed. Robert L. Meriwether, W. Edwin Hemphill, and Clyde N. Wilson, 16 vols. to date (Columbia: University of South Carolina Press, 1959–), 16:659–60; Robert J. Brugger, *Beverley Tucker: Heart over Head in the Old South* (Baltimore, Md.: Johns Hopkins University Press, 1978), p. 139; Chitwood, *John Tyler,* pp. 367–72; *Richmond* (Va.) *Enquirer,* 26 Feb. 1842; Robert Seager II, *And Tyler Too: A Biography of John and Julia Gardiner Tyler* (New York: McGraw-Hill, 1963), pp. 170–71.

13. *Niles' National Register,* 19 Aug. 1843, p. 394; Tazewell to John Wickham II, 30 Apr. 1843, in Papers of John Wickham, microfilm copy, Alderman Library, University of Virginia, Charlottesville; Nathans, *Daniel Webster,* pp. 201–2.

14. Tyler to J. B. Jones, 13 Sept. 1843 and 16 Jan. 1844, in *The Letters and Times of the Tylers,* ed. Lyon G. Tyler, 3 vols. (1884–96; reprint, New York: Da Capo Press, 1970), 3:113–14; Calhoun to Thomas G. Clemson, 6 Feb. 1843, in Calhoun, *Papers,* 16:659–60; Charles Sellers, ''The Election of 1844,'' in *History of American Presidential Elections, 1789–1968,* ed. Arthur M. Schlesinger, Jr., 4 vols. (New York: Chelsea House, 1971), 1:751; Waddy Thompson to Tucker, 13 Sept. 1841 and 13 Mar. 1842, and Upshur to Tucker, 15 Nov. 1841, in *William and Mary Quarterly,* 1st ser. 12 (1904): 145–46, 152–54, 148–50; Brugger, *Beverley Tucker,* pp. 148–51.

15. Tyler to Webster, 11 Oct. 1841, in *Letters and Times of the Tylers,* 2:126; Thompson to Tucker, 13 Mar. 1842, in *William and Mary Quarterly,* 1st ser. 12 (1904): 152–54; Craig Simpson, *A Good Southerner: The Life of Henry A. Wise*

(Chapel Hill: University of North Carolina Press, 1985), pp. 56–57. Wise's speech in the House of Representatives, 13 Apr. 1842, and Gilmer's editorial in the *Baltimore Sun and Argus*, 19 Jan. 1842, are reprinted in the "Documents" section of Frederick Merk's *Slavery and the Annexation of Texas* (New York: Alfred A. Knopf, 1972), pp. 192–204.

16. David M. Pletcher, *The Diplomacy of Annexation: Texas, Oregon, and the Mexican War* (Columbia: University of Missouri Press, 1973), pp. 86–88; Chitwood, *John Tyler*, p. 344; Upshur to Tucker, 7 Aug. 1841, quoted by Merk, in *Slavery and the Annexation of Texas*, p. 18.

17. Merk, *Slavery and the Annexation of Texas*, pp. 12–14; Green to William Henry Harrison, 28 Feb. 1841, in Harrison Papers, Manuscripts Division, Library of Congress; Green to Tyler, 24 Jan. 1842, and Green to Upshur, 24 Jan. 1842, in "Documents" section of Merk, *Slavery and the Annexation of Texas*, pp. 187–92. For evidence of Green's commitment to Calhoun see Green to Calhoun, 3 and 24 Jan., 16 Sept., and 10 Nov. 1842, and Calhoun to Green, 2 Apr., 31 Aug., and 27 Oct. 1842, in Calhoun, *Papers*, 16:33–34, 83–86, 458–60, 540–41, 209–10, 437–38, 516–18.

18. Frank B. Woodford, *Lewis Cass: The Last Jeffersonian* (New Brunswick, N.J.: Rutgers University Press, 1950), pp. 209–17; Adams, *Memoirs*, 11:243; Webster to Cass, 14 Nov. 1842, and Everett to Webster, 3 Nov. 1842, in Webster, *Papers, Diplomatic*, 1:721–34; Everett to Webster, 20 May 1842, in "Private & confidential, for yourself alone," Webster, *Papers, Correspondence*, 5:209–10.

19. Everett to Webster, 3 Dec. 1842, in Webster, *Papers, Correspondence*, 5:253–55; Tyler to Everett, 27 Apr. 1843, in "Documents" section, Merk, *Slavery and the Annexation of Texas*, pp. 211–12.

20. Webster to Everett, 12 May 1843, in Webster, *Papers, Diplomatic*, 1:27; Merk, *Slavery and the Annexation of Texas*, pp. 14–15; Biddle to Webster, 27 Feb. 1843, in Nicholas Biddle, *The Correspondence of Nicholas Biddle Dealing with National Affairs, 1807–1844*, ed. Reginald C. McGrane (Boston, Mass.: Houghton Mifflin, 1919), p. 344; Shaw to Webster, 28 Feb. 1843, in Webster, *Papers, Correspondence*, 5:276–77.

21. Webster to Biddle, 11 Mar. 1843, in Biddle, *Correspondence*, pp. 345–46; Webster to Everett, 28 Apr. 1843, in Webster, *Papers, Diplomatic*, 1:916; *National Intelligencer*, 13 May 1843.

22. Webster to Everett, 12 May 1843, in Webster, *Papers, Correspondence*, 5:303–4. Although in Webster's letter the antecedent is confusing, the "He" in the quotation refers to Legaré. In the *Private Correspondence of Daniel Webster*, 2:173, Fletcher Webster, ed., misquotes the original letter by stating, "Mr. Upshur is an accomplished lawyer." In May 1843, Upshur still was secretary of the navy. For the original letter see Daniel Webster Papers, microfilm, reel 19, frame 25076. Michael O'Brien, *A Character of Hugh Legaré* (Knoxville: University of Tennessee Press, 1985), p. 275.

23. George T. Strong, *The Diary of George Templeton Strong*, ed. Allan Nevins and Milton H. Thomas, 4 vols. (New York: Macmillan, 1952), 1:205; Adams,

Memoirs, 11:382–83; Russel B. Nye, *George Bancroft: Brahmin Rebel* (New York: Alfred A. Knopf, 1944), pp. 126–27.

24. Nicholas Carroll to W. P. Mangum, 21 June 1843, in Willie P. Mangum, *The Papers of Willie Person Mangum,* ed. Henry T. Shanks, 5 vols. (Raleigh, N.C.: State Department of Archives and History, 1950–56), 3:457; O'Brien, *Character of Hugh Legaré,* pp. 277–80; Adams, *Memoirs,* 11:386.

25. Mary Louise Hinsdale, *A History of the President's Cabinet* (Ann Arbor, Mich.: G. Wahr, 1911), pp. 119–20; Chitwood, *John Tyler,* pp. 283–84; Fuess, *Life of Caleb Cushing,* 1:387–88; Simpson, *Good Southerner,* p. 57.

26. Webster to Tyler, 29 Aug. 1843, in Webster, *Papers, Correspondence,* 5:311–13.

CHAPTER 12
TEXAS: MISINFORMATION,
RUMORS, AND SECRECY

1. *Niles' National Register,* 4 Nov. 1843, pp. 149–50; Upshur to W. S. Murphy, 8 Aug. 1843, quoted by Frederick Merk in *Slavery and the Annexation of Texas* (New York: Alfred A. Knopf, 1972), pp. 12–13; Tyler to Everett, 21 July 1843, quoted by Sydney Nathans in *Daniel Webster and Jacksonian Democracy* (Baltimore, Md.: Johns Hopkins University Press, 1973), p. 212.

2. Claude H. Hall, *Abel Parker Upshur: Conservative Virginian, 1790–1844* (Madison: State Historical Society of Wisconsin, 1964), p. 196; Green to Tyler, 31 May and 3 July 1843. The letters are found in the "Documents" section of Merk's *Slavery and the Annexation of Texas,* pp. 217–24.

3. Van Zandt to Anson Jones, 15 Mar. and 5 Apr. 1843, in *The Letters and Times of the Tylers,* ed. Lyon G. Tyler, 3 vols. (1884–96; reprint, New York: Da Capo Press, 1970), 3:129–30.

4. Oliver Perry Chitwood, *John Tyler: Champion of the Old South* (New York: D. Appleton-Century, 1939), pp. 373–74; Charles Henry Ambler, *Thomas Ritchie: A Study in Virginia Politics* (Richmond, Va.: Bell Book & Stationery Co., 1913), p. 232; Charles M. Wiltse, *John C. Calhoun,* 3 vols. (Indianapolis, Ind.: Bobbs-Merrill, 1944–51), 3:114.

5. John Quincy Adams, *Memoirs of John Quincy Adams,* ed. Charles Francis Adams, 12 vols. (1874–77; reprint, New York: AMS Press, 1970), 11:380; Leonard L. Richards, *The Life and Times of Congressman John Quincy Adams* (New York: Oxford University Press, 1986), pp. 166–67.

6. Smith to Jones, 2 and 31 July 1843, in George P. Garrison, ed., *Diplomatic Correspondence of the Republic of Texas, Annual Report of the American Historical Association for the Year 1908,* 2 vols. (Washington, D.C.: Government Printing Office, 1911), 2(pt. #3):1099–1103, 1116–17.

7. Smith to Calhoun, 19 June 1843, quoted by David M. Pletcher in *The Diplomacy of Annexation: Texas, Oregon, and the Mexican War* (Columbia: University of Missouri Press, 1973), pp. 122–23.

8. Jones to Van Zandt, 6 July 1843, in *Diplomatic Correspondence of the Republic of Texas,* 2(pt. #2):195.

9. Van Zandt to Jones, 18 Sept. 1843, ibid., pp. 207–8; Pletcher, *Diplomacy of Annexation,* p. 122; Merk, *Slavery and the Annexation of Texas,* p. 23.

10. Green to Calhoun, 2 Aug. and 2 Sept. 1843, in John C. Calhoun, *Correspondence of John C. Calhoun,* ed. J. Franklin Jameson, vol. 2 of *Report of the American Historical Association for the Year 1899* (Washington, D.C.: Government Printing Office, 1900), pp. 846–49, 871–72; Green to Tyler, 29 Aug. 1843, Green to Upshur, 17 Oct. 1843, and Green to editors of the *Boston Post,* 18 Sept. and 14 and 15 Dec. 1843, Merk, "Documents," *Slavery and the Annexation of Texas,* pp. 225–36, 258–64.

11. Tyler to Thompson, 28 Aug. 1843, in *William and Mary Quarterly,* 1st ser. 12 (1904): 140–41.

12. Upshur to Calhoun, 14 Aug. 1843, ibid., 2d ser. 16 (1936): 554–57.

13. Van Zandt to Jones, 18 Sept. 1843, in *Diplomatic Correspondence of the Republic of Texas,* 2(pt. #2):207–10, Frederick Merk, *The Monroe Doctrine and American Expansion, 1843–1849* (1966; reprint, New York: Vintage Books, 1972), pp. 19–20; Merk, *Slavery and the Annexation of Texas,* pp. 26–27; Hall, *Abel Parker Upshur,* pp. 199–200.

14. Hunter to Calhoun, 10 Oct. 1843, in *Correspondence Addressed to John C. Calhoun, 1837–1849,* ed. Chauncey S. Boucher and Robert P. Brooks, *Annual Report of the American Historical Association for the Year 1929* (Washington, D.C.: Government Printing Office, 1930), pp. 186–88; Van Zandt to Jones, 16 Oct. 1843, in *Diplomatic Correspondence of the Republic of Texas,* 2(pt. #2):221–24; Hall, *Abel Parker Upshur,* pp. 203–4; Tyler to Calhoun, 5 June 1848 in Calhoun, *Correspondence,* pp. 1172–76.

15. Upshur to Tucker, 10 and 26 Oct. 1843, in Merk, "Documents," *Slavery and the Annexation of Texas,* pp. 234, 244; Everett to Upshur, 2 Nov. 1843, quoted by Hall in *Abel Parker Upshur,* p. 203.

16. Everett to Upshur, 3 and 16 Nov. 1843, and an excerpt from Everett's diary, quoted by Merk in *Slavery and the Annexation of Texas,* pp. 27–29.

17. Jones to Van Zandt, 13 Dec. 1843, in *Diplomatic Correspondence of the Republic of Texas,* 2(pt. #2):232–35; Jesse S. Reeves, *American Diplomacy under Tyler and Polk* (1907; reprint, Gloucester, Mass.: Peter Smith, 1967), p. 133.

18. Maxcy to Calhoun, 10 Dec. 1843, in Calhoun, *Correspondence,* pp. 900–904; James D. Richardson, comp., *A Compilation of the Messages and Papers of the Presidents, 1789–1902,* 10 vols. (Washington, D.C.: Bureau of National Literature and Art, 1903), 4:257–72; Webster to Everett, 30 Nov. 1843, in Daniel Webster, *The Papers of Daniel Webster, Correspondence,* ed. Charles M. Wiltse, Harold D. Moser, and Michael J. Birkner, 7 vols. (Hanover, N.H.: University Press of New England, 1974–86), 5:321–23; Pletcher, *Diplomacy of Annexation,* pp. 129–30.

19. Jackson to William B. Lewis, 15 Dec. 1843, in Andrew Jackson, *Correspondence of Andrew Jackson,* ed. John Spencer Bassett, 7 vols. (1926–35; reprint, New York: Kraus, 1969), 6:249. The Jackson letter to which Wise referred was

written to Aaron V. Brown, 9 Feb. 1843, ibid., 6:201–2; it was published in the *Richmond Enquirer* and in the *Madisonian* in Mar. 1844. Ambler, *Thomas Ritchie*, pp. 236–37; Pletcher, *Diplomacy of Annexation*, pp. 141–42; James C. N. Paul, *Rift in the Democracy* (1951; reprint, New York: A. S. Barnes, a Perpetua Book, 1961), p. 81.

20. Calhoun to Gilmer, 28 July 1843, in *William and Mary Quarterly*, 1st ser. 20 (1911): 9–10; Calhoun to Hunter, 12 Sept. 1843, and Hunter to Calhoun, 19 Dec. 1843, in Calhoun, *Correspondence*, pp. 547–49, 906–8; Gilmer to Calhoun, 13 Dec. 1843, in *Letters and Times of the Tylers*, 3:130–32.

21. Charles Sellers, "The Election of 1844," in *History of American Presidential Elections, 1789–1968*, ed. Arthur M. Schlesinger, Jr., 4 vols. (New York: Chelsea House, 1971), 1:758.

22. Wiltse, *John C. Calhoun*, 3:144–47; Richard P. McCormick, *The Presidential Game: The Origins of American Presidential Politics* (New York: Oxford University Press, 1982), pp. 188–89; Van Zandt to Jones, 20 Jan. 1844, in *Diplomatic Correspondence of the Republic of Texas*, 2(pt. #2):240; Chitwood, *John Tyler*, pp. 373–74; Ambler, *Thomas Ritchie*, pp. 231–33; Rives to Edmund Fontaine, 1 Jan. 1844, published in the *Richmond Enquirer*, 12 Jan. 1844.

23. Tyler to George Roberts, 28 Sept. 1843, in *William and Mary Quarterly*, 1st ser. 19 (1911): 216; Tyler to _____, 13 Sept. 1843, in Tyler Papers, Manuscripts Division, Library of Congress.

24. Hall, *Abel Parker Upshur*, p. 258 n. 22; Biddle to Tyler, 21 Nov. 1843, quoted by Thomas Payne Govan, in *Nicholas Biddle: Nationalist and Public Banker, 1786–1844* (Chicago: University of Chicago Press, 1959), p. 410.

25. Hall, *Abel Parker Upshur*, p. 205; Russel B. Nye, *George Bancroft: Brahmin Rebel* (New York: Alfred A. Knopf, 1944), p. 129; Mary Louise Hinsdale, *A History of the President's Cabinet* (Ann Arbor, Mich.: G. Wahr, 1911), p. 120; Chitwood, *John Tyler*, p. 284; Wiltse, *John C. Calhoun*, 3:105–6.

26. Upshur to Murphy, 16 Jan. 1844, in *Letters and Times of the Tylers*, 2:283–84; Van Zandt to Jones, 20 Jan. 1844, Jones to Van Zandt, 27 Jan. 1844, and Jones to Henderson, 15 Feb. 1844, in *Diplomatic Correspondence of the Republic of Texas*, 2(pt. #2):239–43, 248–57; Merk, *Slavery and the Annexation of Texas*, p. 38; Pletcher, *Diplomacy of Annexation*, pp. 131–33; Hall, *Abel Parker Upshur*, pp. 208–9.

CHAPTER 13

"MR. TYLER'S ABOMINABLE TREATY"

1. Harold Sprout and Margaret Sprout, *The Rise of American Naval Power, 1776–1918* (Princeton, N.J.: Princeton University Press, 1966), pp. 125–26; Samuel Eliot Morison, *"Old Bruin": Commodore Matthew C. Perry, 1794–1858* (Boston, Mass.: Little, Brown, 1967), pp. 131–32; Claude H. Hall, *Abel Parker Upshur: Conservative Virginian, 1790–1844* (Madison: State Historical Society of Wisconsin, 1964), pp. 209–10.

2. Robert Seager II, *And Tyler Too: A Biography of John and Julia Gardiner Tyler* (New York: McGraw-Hill, 1963), pp. 196, 203.

3. Thomas Gilmer to _____, 16 Feb. 1844, in Tyler Papers, Manuscripts Division, Library of Congress.

4. Seager, *And Tyler Too*, pp. 204-5; Thomas Hart Benton, *Thirty Years' View*, 2 vols. (New York: D. Appleton, 1854, 1856), 2:567-69; *National Intelligencer*, 29 Feb. 1844; *Richmond* (Va.) *Enquirer*, 1 and 5 Mar. 1844.

5. Henry Alexander Wise, *Seven Decades of the Union: The Humanities and Materialism, Illustrated by A Memoir of John Tyler* (Philadelphia: J. B. Lippincott, 1881), pp. 220-25; Calhoun to Green, 31 Aug. 1842, in John C. Calhoun, *Correspondence of John C. Calhoun*, ed. J. Franklin Jameson, vol. 2 of *Report of the American Historical Association for the Year 1899* (Washington, D.C.: Government Printing Office, 1900), pp. 515-16.

6. Frederick Merk, *Fruits of Propaganda in the Tyler Administration* (Cambridge, Mass.: Harvard University Press, 1971), p. 104; idem, *Slavery and the Annexation of Texas* (New York: Alfred A. Knopf, 1972), p. 54; Charles M. Wiltse, *John C. Calhoun*, 3 vols. (Indianapolis, Ind.: Bobbs-Merrill, 1944-51), 3:161-62, 504 n. 12.; Seager, *And Tyler Too*, p. 217; Oliver Perry Chitwood, *John Tyler: Champion of the Old South* (New York: D. Appleton-Century, 1939), pp. 286-88; Margaret L. Coit, in *John C. Calhoun: American Portrait* (Boston, Mass.: Houghton Mifflin, 1950), pp. 361-62, also accepts Wise's rendition. For Robert Barnwell Rhett's letter see *American Historical Review* 13 (1908): 311-12.

7. Norma Lois Peterson, *Littleton Waller Tazewell* (Charlottesville: University Press of Virginia, 1983), pp. 191-93; Chitwood, *John Tyler*, pp. 114-15; Seager, *And Tyler Too*, pp. 92-93.

8. Chitwood, *John Tyler*, pp. 140-43; Seager, *And Tyler Too*, pp. 54, 215-16; William R. Brock, *Parties and Political Conscience: American Dilemmas, 1840-1850* (Millwood, N.Y.: KTO Press, 1979), p. 117; Tyler to Calhoun, 6 Mar. 1844, in Calhoun, *Correspondence*, pp. 938-39; Van Zandt to Anson Jones, 5 Mar. 1844, in *Diplomatic Correspondence of the Republic of Texas*, ed. George P. Garrison, *Annual Report of the American Historical Association for the Year 1908*, 2 vols. (Washington, D.C.: Government Printing Office, 1911), 2 (pt. #2):261-62.

9. George Ticknor Curtis, *Life of Daniel Webster*, 2 vols. (New York: D. Appleton, 1893), 2:230-35; Maurice G. Baxter, *One and Inseparable: Daniel Webster and the Union* (Cambridge, Mass.: Harvard University Press, 1984), pp. 373-74; *National Intelligencer*, 16 Mar. 1844; John Quincy Adams, *Memoirs of John Quincy Adams*, ed. Charles Francis Adams, 12 vols. (1874-77; reprint, New York: AMS Press, 1970), 11:528-29; Robert F. Dalzell, Jr., *Daniel Webster and the Trial of American Nationalism, 1843-1852* (Boston, Mass.: Houghton Mifflin, 1973), pp. 87-88.

10. Stephens to James Thomas, 7 Mar. 1844, quoted by E. Ramsay Richardson in *Little Aleck: A Life of Alexander Stephens* (New York: Grosset & Dunlap, 1938), p. 90.

11. Walker's letter is published in its entirety in Merk, *Fruits of Propaganda*, pp. 221-52; see also pp. 97-104.

12. Seager, *And Tyler Too*, p. 215; James P. Shenton, *Robert Walker: A Politician from Jackson to Lincoln* (New York: Columbia University Press, 1961), pp. 11-15, 31-39; Ritchie to Silas Wright, 20 Mar. 1844, in "Unpublished Letters of Thomas Ritchie," ed. Charles H. Ambler, in *The John P. Branch Historical Papers of Randolph-Macon College* 3 (1911): 249-50; Charles Henry Ambler, *Thomas Ritchie: A Study in Virginia Politics* (Richmond, Va.: Bell Book & Stationery Co., 1913), pp. 236-37.

13. Clay to Crittenden, 24 Mar. 1844, in *The Life of John J. Crittenden, with Selections from His Correspondence and Speeches*, ed. Mrs. Chapman Coleman, 2 vols. (1871; reprint, New York: Da Capo Press, 1970), 1:217-18; Benjamin Watkins Leigh to Willie P. Mangum, 28 Mar. 1844, in Willie P. Mangum, *The Papers of Willie Person Mangum*, ed. Henry T. Shanks, 5 vols. (Raleigh, N.C.: State Department of Archives and History, 1950-56), 4:79-83; Adams, *Memoirs*, 11:538; Chitwood, *John Tyler*, pp. 284-85; Charles G. Sellers, *James K. Polk*, 2 vols. (Princeton, N.J.: Princeton University Press, 1957, 1966), 2:48.

14. Letcher to Crittenden, 22 Jan. 1844, and Clay to Crittenden, 24 Jan. 1844, in Coleman, *Life of John J. Crittenden*, 1:213-15; Mangum to Paul Cameron, 10 Feb. 1844, in Mangum, *Papers*, 4:41-43; Adams, *Memoirs*, 12:60; Henry J. Abraham, *Justices and Presidents: A Political History of Appointments to the Supreme Court* (New York: Oxford University Press, 1974), pp. 96-98.

15. Van Zandt and Henderson to Anson Jones, 12 Apr. 1844, in *Diplomatic Correspondence of the Republic of Texas*, 2 (pt. #2):269-73; Jesse S. Reeves, *American Diplomacy under Tyler and Polk* (1907; reprint, Gloucester, Mass.: Peter Smith, 1967), pp. 136-37; David M. Pletcher, *The Diplomacy of Annexation: Texas, Oregon, and the Mexican War* (Columbia: University of Missouri Press, 1973), pp. 137, 204-7.

16. Van Zandt to Anson Jones, 20 Jan. 1844, and Van Zandt and Henderson to Jones, 12 Apr. 1844, in *Diplomatic Correspondence of the Republic of Texas*, 2 (pt. #2):242, 269-73; Merk, *Slavery and the Annexation of Texas*, pp. 40-41; Nelson's letter to Murphy, 11 Mar. 1844, is quoted ibid., pp. 42-43.

17. Van Zandt and Henderson to Anson Jones, 12 Apr. 1844, in *Diplomatic Correspondence of the Republic of Texas*, 2 (pt. #2):269-73.

18. The Pakenham-Calhoun correspondence can be found in John C. Calhoun, *The Works of John C. Calhoun*, ed. Richard K. Crallé, 6 vols. (New York: D. Appleton, 1854-57), 5:330-47. Merk, *Slavery and the Annexation of Texas*, pp. 68-69.

19. James D. Richardson, comp., *A Compilation of the Messages and Papers of the Presidents, 1789-1902*, 10 vols. (Washington, D.C.: Bureau of National Literature and Art, 1903), 4:307-13 (hereafter cited as *Messages and Papers*); Wiltse, *John C. Calhoun*, 3:171; Reeves, *American Diplomacy*, pp. 150-51; Pletcher, *Diplomacy of Annexation*, p. 144.

20. George Rawlings Poage, *Henry Clay and the Whig Party* (1936; reprint, Gloucester, Mass.: Peter Smith, 1965), p. 131; Brock, *Parties and Political Conscience*, pp. 132-35; Calhoun to James H. Hammond, 5 Mar. 1844, in Calhoun, *Correspondence*, p. 572; Lewis to Richard Crallé, 19 Mar. 1844, quoted

by Eugene I. McCormac in *James K. Polk: A Political Biography* (Berkeley: University of California Press, 1922), p. 615.

21. Calhoun to Francis Wharton, 28 May 1844, in Calhoun, *Correspondence,* pp. 592-94; Sydney Nathans, "The Southern Connection: Slaveholders and Antebellum Expansion," *Reviews in American History* 1 (1973): 394-95 n. 2.; Benton, *Thirty Years' View,* 2:189-90.

22. Blair to Andrew Jackson, 7 July 1844, in Andrew Jackson, *Correspondence of Andrew Jackson,* ed. John Spencer Bassett, 7 vols. (1926-35; reprint, New York: Kraus, 1969), 6:299-302; Pletcher, *Diplomacy of Annexation,* p. 144; Calhoun to James Hammond, 17 May 1844, and Calhoun to Anna Calhoun Clemson, 10 May 1844, in Calhoun, *Correspondence,* pp. 585, 588-89.

23. Bertram Watt-Brown, *Lewis Tappan and the Evangelical War against Slavery* (Cleveland, Ohio: Case Western Reserve University Press, 1969), pp. 276-77; Arthur M. Schlesinger, Jr., *The Imperial Presidency* (Boston, Mass.: Houghton Mifflin, 1973), pp. 334-35; Clay to Crittenden, 5 Dec. 1843, and R. P. Letcher to Crittenden, 18 Jan. 1844, in Coleman, *Life of John J. Crittenden,* 1:207-10, 213; Adams, *Memoirs,* 11:348-49; Poage, *Henry Clay and the Whig Party,* pp. 125-26.

24. McCormac, *James K. Polk,* pp. 224-25; Paulding to Van Buren, 16 Apr. 1844, in James K. Paulding, *The Letters of James Kirke Paulding,* ed. Ralph M. Aderman (Madison: University of Wisconsin Press, 1962), pp. 364-66; John Niven, *Martin Van Buren: The Romantic Age of American Politics* (New York: Oxford University Press, 1983), pp. 526-28.

25. Clay to Crittenden, 17 Apr. 1844, in Coleman, *Life of John J. Crittenden,* 1:219; Clay to Willie P. Mangum, 14 Apr. 1844, in Mangum, *Papers,* 4:102-3; Albert D. Kirwan, *John J. Crittenden: The Struggle for the Union* (Lexington: University of Kentucky Press, 1962), p. 176; Glyndon G. Van Deusen, *The Life of Henry Clay* (Boston, Mass.: Little, Brown, 1937), pp. 359-60, 365.

26. Poage, *Henry Clay and the Whig Party,* p. 139.

27. Numerous letters of this nature are to be found in the Ritchie-Harrison Papers, Earl Gregg Swem Library, College of William and Mary, Williamsburg, Va.

28. Ambler, *Thomas Ritchie,* pp. 237-40; Ritchie to Van Buren, 5 May 1844, in *John P. Branch Historical Papers* 3 (1911): 250-52; Niven, *Martin Van Buren,* p. 532; Jackson to Francis P. Blair, 7 May 1844, in Jackson, *Correspondence,* 6:283-87; Clay to Weed, 6 May 1844, in Thurlow Weed Barnes, *Memoir of Thurlow Weed,* vol. 2 of *Life of Thurlow Weed* (Boston, Mass.: Houghton Mifflin, 1884), 2:119-20.

29. Ritchie to Howell Cobb, 6 May 1844, in *Correspondence of Robert Toombs, Alexander H. Stephens, and Howell Cobb,* ed. Ulrich B. Phillips, *Annual Report of the American Historical Association for the Year 1911,* 2 vols. (Washington, D.C.: Government Printing Office, 1913), 2:56-57; Arthur C. Cole, *The Whig Party in the South* (1914; reprint, Gloucester, Mass.: Peter Smith, 1962), p. 109; Charles Sellers, "The Election of 1844," in *History of American Presidential Elections, 1789-1968,* ed. Arthur M. Schlesinger, Jr., 4 vols. (New York: Chelsea House, 1971), 1:762-63. Thompson's views were expressed in a letter to the *National*

Intelligencer, 6 July 1844; Hammond to Calhoun, 10 May 1844, in Calhoun, *Correspondence,* pp. 953-54.

30. James Gadsden to Calhoun, in Calhoun, *Correspondence,* pp. 952-53; Chitwood, *John Tyler,* pp. 376-77; Willie P. Mangum to Priestly Mangum, 29 May 1844, in Mangum, *Papers,* 4:127-28.

31. Stephens to James Thomas, 17 May 1844, in *Correspondence of Robert Toombs, Alexander H. Stephens, and Howell Cobb,* 2:57-58; Adams, *Memoirs,* 12:37; William Nisbet Chambers, *Old Bullion Benton: Senator from the New West* (Boston, Mass.: Little, Brown, 1956), pp. 275-76.

32. Merk, *Slavery and the Annexation of Texas,* pp. 70-71; Upshur to Murphy, 8 Aug. 1843, quoted ibid., pp. 12-13; *Messages and Papers,* 4:316-18, 321.

33. Merk, *Slavery and the Annexation of Texas,* pp. 81-82; Robert J. Morgan, *A Whig Embattled: The Presidency under John Tyler* (Lincoln: University of Nebraska Press, 1954), p. 141.

34. Archer is quoted by Merk in *Slavery and the Annexation of Texas,* p. 81. Preston is quoted by Cole in *Whig Party in the South,* p. 111 n. 27; Reeves, *American Diplomacy,* p. 166; Clay to Stephen Miller, 1 July 1844, in Henry Clay, *The Private Correspondence of Henry Clay,* ed. Calvin Colton (New York: A. S. Barnes, 1855), pp. 490-91.

CHAPTER 14
"THE APOPLEXY OF THE CONSTITUTION"

1. James D. Richardson, comp., *A Compilation of the Messages and Papers of the Presidents, 1789-1902,* 10 vols. (Washington, D.C.: Bureau of National Literature and Art, 1903), 4:323-27 (hereafter cited as *Messages and Papers*); Frederick Merk, *Slavery and the Annexation of Texas* (New York: Alfred A. Knopf, 1972), pp. 83-84.

2. Thomas Hart Benton, *Thirty Years' View,* 2 vols. (New York: D. Appleton, 1854, 1856), 2:619-24; *Congressional Globe,* 28th Cong., 1st sess., pp. 568-90; John Quincy Adams, *Memoirs of John Quincy Adams,* ed. Charles Francis Adams, 12 vols. (1874-77; reprint, New York: AMS Press, 1970), 12:56.

3. Harris to George Bancroft, 25 June 1844, quoted by Eugene I. McCormac in *James K. Polk: A Political Biography* (Berkeley: University of California Press, 1922), p. 257 n. 22; see also Jackson to Polk, 29 June 1844, and Blair to Jackson, 7 July 1844, in Andrew Jackson, *Correspondence of Andrew Jackson,* ed. John Spencer Bassett, 7 vols. (1926-35; reprint, New York: Kraus, 1969), 6:298-302.

4. *Messages and Papers,* 4:260, 314; Robert J. Morgan, *A Whig Embattled: The Presidency under John Tyler* (Lincoln: University of Nebraska Press, 1954), pp. 132-33; Wheaton to Tyler, 27 Mar. 1844, and Jackson to Polk, 2 Sept. 1844, in *The Letters and Times of the Tylers,* ed. Lyon G. Tyler, 3 vols. (1884-96; reprint, New York: Da Capo Press, 1970), 2:326-28, 3:149; Adams, *Memoirs,* 12:57.

5. Jesse S. Reeves, *American Diplomacy under Tyler and Polk* (1907; reprint, Gloucester, Mass.: Peter Smith, 1967), pp. 164-65, 167; Van Zandt and Henderson to Jones, 10 June 1844, in *Diplomatic Correspondence of the Republic of Texas,* ed.

George P. Garrison, *Annual Report of the American Historical Association for the Year 1908*, 2 vols. (Washington, D.C.: Government Printing Office, 1911), 2 (pt. #2): 284–87.

6. Murphy to Houston, 3 July 1844, quoted by Reeves in *American Diplomacy*, pp. 159–60; David M. Pletcher, *The Diplomacy of Annexation: Texas, Oregon, and the Mexican War* (Columbia: University of Missouri Press, 1973), p. 166.

7. George Rawlings Poage, *Henry Clay and the Whig Party* (1936; reprint, Gloucester, Mass.: Peter Smith, 1965), pp. 142–47. Portions of Clay's letter of 27 July 1844 can be found in *History of American Presidential Elections, 1789–1968*, ed. Arthur M. Schlesinger, Jr., 4 vols. (New York: Chelsea House, 1971), 1:855–56; Glyndon G. Van Deusen, *The Life of Henry Clay* (Boston, Mass.: Little, Brown, 1937), pp. 374–75; Daniel Walker Howe, in *The Political Culture of the American Whigs* (Chicago: University of Chicago Press, 1979), p. 144, has expressed the belief that "on expansion, as on most subjects, Clay was a genuine Centerist, not a mere trimmer."

8. Wright to Polk, 2 June 1844, quoted by Charles Sellers in *James K. Polk*, 2 vols. (Princeton, N.J.: Princeton University Press, 1957, 1966), 2:110, 113–14; idem, "The Election of 1844," in *History of American Presidential Elections*, 1:780–784; Robert B. Rhett to R. M. T. Hunter, 30 Aug. 1844, in R. M. T. Hunter, *Correspondence of Robert M. T. Hunter, 1826–1876*, ed. Charles H. Ambler, *Annual Report of the American Historical Association for the Year 1916* (1918; reprint, New York: Da Capo Press, 1971), pp. 70–71; Francis Wharton to Calhoun, 21 Aug. 1844, in *Correspondence Addressed to John C. Calhoun, 1837–1849*, ed. Chauncey S. Boucher and Robert P. Brooks, *Annual Report of the American Historical Association for the Year 1929* (Washington, D.C.: Government Printing Office, 1930), pp. 245–46.

9. Calhoun to Francis Wharton, 14 July 1844, in John C. Calhoun, *Correspondence of John C. Calhoun*, ed. J. Franklin Jameson, vol. 2 of *Report of the American Historical Association for the Year 1899* (Washington, D.C.: Government Printing Office, 1900), p. 601; Tyler to the Nominating Committee, 30 May 1844, in *Letters and Times of the Tylers*, 2:319–21; Robert Seager II, *And Tyler Too: A Biography of John and Julia Gardiner Tyler* (New York: McGraw-Hill, 1963), pp. 1–14, 228, 244–48; Philip Hone, *The Diary of Philip Hone, 1828–1851*, ed. Allan Nevins, 2 vols. (1927; reprint, New York: Kraus, 1969), 2:707–8; Constance McLaughlin Green, *Washington, Village and Capital, 1800–1878* (Princeton, N.J.: Princeton University Press, 1962), pp. 153–54; Jesse Benton Frémont is quoted by Oliver Perry Chitwood in *John Tyler: Champion of the Old South* (New York: D. Appleton-Century, 1939), p. 404.

10. Seager, *And Tyler Too*, pp. 230–31; Walker to Polk, 10 July 1844, in *Letters and Times of the Tylers*, 3:139–40; Jackson to Polk, 26 July 1844, Jackson to Blair, 26 July 1844, Jackson to Lewis, 1 Aug. 1844, and Jackson to Mason, 1 Aug. 1844, in Jackson, *Correspondence*, 6:303–8; Sellers, *James K. Polk*, 2:136–37.

11. Tyler to Jackson, 18 Aug. 1844, in Jackson, *Correspondence*, 6:315; Tyler's letter to the *Madisonian* is in *Letters and Times of the Tylers*, 2:342–49.

12. Seager, *And Tyler Too*, p. 245; Tyler to Elizabeth Tyler Waller, 13 Sept. 1844, in *Letters and Times of the Tylers*, 3:155.

13. Clay to Willie P. Mangum, 7 June 1844, in Willie P. Mangum, *The Papers of Willie Person Mangum*, ed. Henry T. Shanks, 5 vols. (Raleigh, N.C.: State Department of Archives and History, 1950-56), 4:134; *National Intelligencer*, 17 Sept. 1844; Poage, *Henry Clay and the Whig Party*, pp. 146-50.

14. David Lambert to Willie P. Mangum, 29 Sept. 1844, in Mangum, *Papers*, 4:199-200; Maurice G. Baxter, *One and Inseparable: Daniel Webster and the Union* (Cambridge, Mass.: Harvard University Press, 1984), pp. 370-71; Robert G. Gunderson, *The Log-Cabin Campaign* (1957; reprint, Westport, Conn.: Greenwood Press, 1977), p. 169; Ray Allen Billington, *The Protestant Crusade, 1800-1860: A Study of the Origins of American Nativism* (1938; reprint, Chicago: Quadrangle Books, 1964), pp. 200-201; Sydney Nathans, *Daniel Webster and Jacksonian Democracy* (Baltimore, Md.: Johns Hopkins University Press, 1973), p. 222.

15. Seager, *And Tyler Too*, pp. 237-40; David Lambert to Mangum, 29 Sept. 1844, in Mangum, *Papers*, 4:199-200; Sellers, *James K. Polk*, 2:135-36; Jackson to Polk, 13 Dec. 1844, in *Letters and Times of the Tylers*, 3:155-56; *National Intelligencer*, 26 Nov. 1844.

16. Arthur C. Cole, *The Whig Party in the South* (1914; reprint, Gloucester, Mass.: Peter Smith, 1962), pp. 112-16; Howe, *Political Culture of the American Whigs*, p. 242; Clay is quoted by Sellers in "Election of 1844," p. 798.

17. Hone to Clay, 28 Nov. 1844, and E. Pettigrew to Clay, 1 Jan. 1845, in Henry Clay, *The Private Correspondence of Henry Clay*, ed. Calvin Colton (New York: A. S. Barnes, 1855), pp. 507-9, 518-20; Clay to J. J. Crittenden, 28 Nov. 1844, in *The Life of John J. Crittenden, with Selections from His Correspondence and Speeches*, ed. Mrs. Chapman Coleman, 2 vols. (1871; reprint, New York: Da Capo Press, 1970), 1:223-25.

18. Nathans, *Daniel Webster*, p. 223; Coombs to John M. Clayton, 20 Nov. 1844, quoted by Cole in *Whig Party in the South*, p. 115 n. 48; Oscar Doane Lambert, *Presidential Politics in the United States, 1841-1844* (Durham, N.C.: Duke University Press, 1936), p. 196. Preston to Clay, 23 Nov. 1844, in Clay, *Private Correspondence*, p. 503; Thomas Giles to John N. Tazewell,—November 1844, in Tazewell Papers, Virginia State Library, Richmond.

19. Charles M. Wiltse, *John C. Calhoun*, 3 vols. (Indianapolis, Ind.: Bobbs-Merrill, 1944-51), 3:187-92; Drew Gilpin Faust, *James Henry Hammond and the Old South: A Design for Mastery* (Baton Rouge: Louisiana State University Press, 1982), pp. 247-48.

20. Pletcher, *Diplomacy of Annexation*, pp. 156-65; King to Tyler, 13 Sept. 1844, in *Letters and Times of the Tylers*, 2:328-29.

21. Calhoun to Howard, 10 Sept. 1844, in John C. Calhoun, *The Works of John C. Calhoun*, ed. Richard K. Crallé, 6 vols. (New York: D. Appleton, 1854-57), 5:377-79; Raymond to Jones, 13 Sept. 1844, quoted by Wiltse in *John C. Calhoun*, 3:203.

22. Calhoun to Howard, 13 Sept. 1844, Calhoun to Donelson, 16 Sept. 1844, in Calhoun, *Correspondence,* pp. 612, 614–15; Upshur to Calhoun, 14 Aug. 1843, *William and Mary Quarterly,* 1st ser. 12 (1904): 140–41; Duff Green, *Facts and Suggestions, Biographical, Historical, Financial, and Political* (New York: Union Printing Office, 1866), p. 85.

23. Tyler to Jackson, 17 Sept. 1844, in Jackson, *Correspondence,* 6:319–20; Pletcher, *Diplomacy of Annexation,* p. 167 n. 75; Calhoun to Shannon, 10 Sept. 1844, in Calhoun, *Works,* 5:364–73.

24. Pletcher, *Diplomacy of Annexation,* p. 167; Green to Calhoun, 28 Oct. and 12 and 29 Nov. 1844, in Calhoun, *Correspondence,* pp. 975–80, 991–5, 1000–1002.

25. Reeves, *American Diplomacy,* pp. 179–81; Donelson to Calhoun, 23 Nov. 1844, quoted by Reeves, p. 181; Tyler to Alexander Gardiner, 18 Oct. 1844, in Tyler Papers, Earl Gregg Swem Library, College of William and Mary, Williamsburg, Va.

26. Merk, *Slavery and the Annexation of Texas,* p. 132; Leonard L. Richards, *The Life and Times of Congressman John Quincy Adams* (New York: Oxford University Press, 1986), pp. 176–78; Samuel Flagg Bemis, *John Quincy Adams,* 2 vols. (New York: Alfred A. Knopf, 1949, 1956), 2:446–47; Adams, *Memoirs,* 12:115–16; Calhoun to Hunter, 29 Dec. 1844, in Calhoun, *Correspondence,* pp. 636–37.

27. *Messages and Papers,* 4:340–46, 353–56.

28. Calhoun to Hunter, 29 Dec. 1844, in Calhoun, *Correspondence,* pp. 636–37; Merk, *Slavery and the Annexation of Texas,* p. 154; Gallatin to D. Dudley Field, 17 Dec. 1844 and 10 Feb. 1845, in Albert Gallatin, *The Writings of Albert Gallatin,* ed. Henry Adams, 3 vols. (1879; reprint, New York: Antiquarian Press, 1960), 2:605–10.

29. Donelson to Calhoun, 26 Dec. 1844, in Calhoun, *Correspondence,* pp. 1011–13; Allen to Donelson, 4 Jan. 1845, in *Diplomatic Correspondence of Texas,* 2 (pt. #2): 332–34.

30. Donelson to Allen, 6 Jan. 1845, in *Diplomatic Correspondence of Texas,* pp. 335–37; Donelson to Calhoun, 27 Jan. 1845, in Calhoun, *Correspondence,* pp. 1019–22.

31. Elliot and Peel are quoted by Merk in *Slavery and the Annexation of Texas,* p. 165.

32. Calhoun to Tyler, 6 Feb. 1845, in Calhoun, *Correspondence,* p. 643; Merk, *Slavery and the Annexation of Texas,* p. 166; Pletcher, *Diplomacy of Annexation,* p. 167.

33. *Congressional Globe,* 28th Cong., 2d sess., pp. 190 and app. 309–14; Howe, *Political Culture of the American Whigs,* p. 242; Adams, *Memoirs,* 12:153; Toombs to Stephens, 24 Jan. 1845, in *Correspondence of Robert Toombs, Alexander H. Stephens, and Howell Cobb,* ed. Ulrich B. Phillips, *Annual Report of the American Historical Association for the Year 1911,* 2 vols. (Washington, D.C.: Government Printing Office, 1913), 2:61.

34. *Congressional Globe,* 28th Cong., 2d sess., pp. 378–82; William R. Brock, *Parties and Political Conscience: American Dilemmas, 1840–1850* (Millwood, N.Y.:

KTO Press, 1979), pp. 135–36; Mangum to Tod R. Caldwell, 20 Feb. 1845, and Mangum to William Graham, 21 Feb. 1845, in Mangum, *Papers*, 4:267–71; Washington Hunt to Thurlow Weed, 15 Feb. 1845, in Thurlow Weed Barnes, *Memoir of Thurlow Weed*, vol. 2 of *Life of Thurlow Weed* (Boston, Mass.: Houghton Mifflin, 1884), p. 130.

35. Sellers, *Polk*, 2:218; Adams, *Memoirs*, 12:173–74.

36. Wiltse, *John C. Calhoun*, 3:214; Sellers, *James K. Polk*, 2:207.

37. Chitwood, *John Tyler*, pp. 363–64; Wiltse, *John C. Calhoun*, 3:214–15; Sellers, *James K. Polk*, 2:216–18.

38. Tyler to Alexander Gardiner, 11 Mar. and 17 June 1847, and Tyler to the editors of the *Richmond Enquirer*, n.d., in *Letters and Times of the Tylers*, 2:420–26.

39. *Messages and Papers*, 4:366–67; Carlton Jackson, *Presidential Vetoes, 1792–1945* (Athens: University of Georgia Press, 1967), pp. 83–85; Adams, *Memoirs*, 12:177.

40. Seager, *And Tyler Too*, pp. 262–65, 290–91; "Reminiscences of Mrs. Julia G. Tyler," in *Letters and Times of the Tylers*, 3:200; *Richmond* (Va.) *Enquirer*, 28 Feb. 1845; Sellers, *James K. Polk*, 2:208–9.

CHAPTER 15
A FLAWED PRESIDENCY

1. Barbara W. Tuchman, *The March of Folly: From Troy to Vietnam* (New York: Alfred A. Knopf, 1984), p. 4.

2. Thomas A. Bailey, *Presidential Greatness: The Image and the Man from George Washington to the Present* (New York: Appleton-Century, 1966), pp. 24–25; Arthur M. Schlesinger, Jr., "Our Presidents: A Rating by 75 Historians," *New York Times Magazine*, 29 July 1962, p. 12; Robert M. Murray and Tim H. Blessing, in "The Presidential Performance Study: A Progress Report," *Journal of American History* 70 (1983): 535–55, analyze the various polls. See also Daniel L. Bratton, "The Rating of Presidents," *Presidential Studies Quarterly* 13 (1983): 400–404; Clinton Rossiter, *The American Presidency* (New York: New American Library, 1956), p. 78; Harold J. Laski, *The American Presidency: An Interpretation* (1940; reprint, New York: Grosset & Dunlap, University Library, n.d.), pp. 14, 200.

3. Daniel Walker Howe, *The Political Culture of the American Whigs* (Chicago: University of Chicago Press, 1979), p. 124.

4. Lyon G. Tyler, ed., *The Letters and Times of the Tylers*, 3 vols. (1884–96; reprint, New York: Da Capo Press, 1970), 2:10, 33–34.

5. Weed is quoted by William R. Brock in *Parties and Political Conscience: American Dilemmas, 1840–1850* (Millwood, N.Y.: KTO Press, 1979), p. 106.

6. Ashburton to Aberdeen, 10 May 1842, in Daniel Webster, *The Papers of Daniel Webster, Diplomatic Papers*, ed. Charles M. Wiltse, Kenneth E. Shewmaker, and Kenneth R. Stevens, 1 vol. to date (Hanover, N.H.: University Press of New England, 1983–), 1:569–70.

7. Stephen W. Stathis, "Former Presidents as Congressional Witnesses," *Presidential Studies Quarterly* 13 (1983): 458–59; Maurice G. Baxter, *One and Inseparable: Daniel Webster and the Union* (Cambridge, Mass.: Harvard University Press, 1984), pp. 380–86; James K. Polk, *The Diary of James K. Polk*, ed. Miles Milton Quaife, 4 vols. (Chicago: A. C. McClurg, 1910), 1:431.

8. Robert J. Morgan, *A Whig Embattled: The Presidency under John Tyler* (Lincoln: University of Nebraska Press, 1954), p. 129.

9. Phillips to Cobb, 21 and 25 Feb. 1845, and Toombs to George W. Crawford, 6 Feb. 1846, in *Correspondence of Robert Toombs, Alexander H. Stephens, and Howell Cobb*, ed. Ulrich B. Phillips, *Annual Report of the American Historical Association for the Year 1911*, 2 vols. (Washington, D.C.: Government Printing Office, 1913), 2:65–68, 72–75.

10. Webster to Everett, 20 Nov. 1841, in Webster, *Papers, Diplomatic*, 1:20–22.

11. Charles Dickens, *American Notes: A Journey* (1842; reprint, Fromm International Publishing Corp., 1985), pp. 121, 124–26.

12. Tucker to Calhoun, 13 Nov. 1844, and Barbour to Calhoun, 16 May 1844, in *Correspondence Addressed to John C. Calhoun, 1837–1849*, ed. Chauncey S. Boucher and Robert P. Brooks, *Annual Report of the American Historical Association for the Year 1929* (Washington, D.C.: Government Printing Office, 1930), pp. 258–62, 229–30.

13. Leigh to Willie P. Mangum, 28 Mar. 1844, in Willie P. Mangum, *The Papers of Willie Person Mangum*, ed. Henry T. Shanks, 5 vols. (Raleigh, N.C.: State Department of Archives and History, 1950–56), 4:79–83; William Wickham to Littleton Waller Tazewell, 30 Aug. 1844, in Tazewell Papers, Virginia State Library, Richmond; Calhoun to Thomas G. Clemson, 13 June 1842, in John C. Calhoun, *Correspondence of John C. Calhoun*, ed. J. Franklin Jameson, vol. 2 of *Annual Report of the American Historical Association for the Year 1899* (Washington, D.C.: Government Printing Office, 1900), pp. 477–78.

14. Tyler to Robert Tyler, 12 Mar. 1848, in *Letters and Times of the Tylers*, 2:107; Marcus Cunliffe and the Editors of *American Heritage, The American Heritage History of the Presidency* (New York: American Heritage Publishing Co., 1968), pp. 132–33.

15. Taney to Mrs. Taney, 24 Feb. 1845, quoted by Carl Brent Swisher in *Roger B. Taney* (New York: Macmillan, 1935), p. 448–49.

16. *Swift* v. *Tyson*, 16 Peters 1 (1842), *Groves* v. *Slaughter*, 15 Peters 449 (1841), *Prigg* v. *Pennsylvania*, 16 Peters 539 (1842); R. Kent Newmyer, *The Supreme Court under Marshall and Taney* (New York: Thomas Y. Crowell, 1968), pp. 111–12, 123–26.

17. Story to Sumner, 4 Jan. 1845, quoted by Gerald T. Dunne in *Justice Joseph Story and the Rise of the Supreme Court* (New York: Simon & Schuster, 1970), p. 426.

18. James D. Richardson, comp., *A Compilation of the Messages and Papers of the Presidents, 1789–1902*, 10 vols. (Washington, D.C.: Bureau of National Literature and Art, 1903), 4:198–99, 348 (hereafter cited as *Messages and Papers*); Oliver Perry Chitwood, *John Tyler: Champion of the Old South* (New York: D.

Appleton-Century, 1939), p. 330; Edwin C. McReynolds, *The Seminoles* (Norman: University of Oklahoma Press, 1957), pp. 235-36; Alvin M. Josephy, *The Indian Heritage of America* (New York: Alfred A. Knopf, 1969), p. 324.

19. *Messages and Papers,* 4:336.
20. *Richmond* (Va.) *Enquirer,* 4 Mar. 1845.
21. Rossiter, *American Presidency,* p. 78.

BIBLIOGRAPHICAL ESSAY

In the summer of 1858, the "Old Log Cabin" at North Bend, Ohio, and almost all of Harrison's papers and correspondence that were housed there were destroyed by fire. The small portion of the papers that survived, plus others that throughout the years have turned up elsewhere, constitute the nine volumes (984 pieces) of the William Henry Harrison Papers in the Library of Congress. As part of the Presidential Series, these are available on microfilm (3 reels) from the library's Photoduplication Service. *The Messages and Letters of William Henry Harrison,* ed. Logan Esarey, 2 vols. (Indianapolis: Indiana Historical Commission, 1922), does not cover the Harrison candidacy or presidency. Dorothy B. Goebel, *William Henry Harrison: A Political Biography* (Indianapolis: Historical Bureau of the Indiana Library and Historical Department, 1926), pp. 383–88, lists Harrison materials that are scattered in other collections.

Most of John Tyler's papers were destroyed when Union forces invaded southeastern Virginia during the Civil War. His plantation home, Sherwood Forest, was ransacked several times, and many letters and documents were either pilfered or ruined. The ones that Mrs. Tyler had placed for safekeeping in the Farmers' Bank of Richmond were lost in the great fire of 1865, during the last days of the Civil War. The Tyler papers that survived at Sherwood Forest, plus others that were later collected from Tyler's associates and friends by his son Lyon G. Tyler, are now in the Library of Congress. These, too are available on microfilm from the library's Photoduplication Service (3 reels), and most have been published with careful authenticity in *The Letters and Times of the Tylers,* ed. Lyon G. Tyler, 3 vols. (1884–96; reprint, New York: Da Capo Press, 1970). However, in his eulogistic interpretation of his father's place in history, Lyon Tyler is understandably biased. Smaller collections of Tyler Papers are in the Alderman Library, University of Virginia, Charlottesville; the Earl Gregg Swem

Library, College of William and Mary, Williamsburg; and the Virginia State Library, Richmond. Other collections in Virginia that are important to the Tyler presidency are the Tucker-Coleman Papers and the Abel Parker Upshur Papers, also in the Earl Gregg Swem Library; but the Thomas Ritchie Papers, located there, are of little significance to this study. A larger collection of Ritchie Papers is in the Library of Congress, as are others of importance to the Tyler administration, including those of Daniel Webster, Henry Clay, John C. Calhoun, Duff Green, Caleb Cushing, John J. Crittenden, and Thomas Ewing. Microfilm of Calhoun's Papers is available from the Library of Congress.

The most comprehensive and reliable collection of the Webster Papers currently is being published by the University Press of New England, under the sponsorship of Dartmouth College. When finished, the project will consist of four series: *Correspondence*, 7 vols., covering the years 1798 to 1852 and edited by Charles M. Wiltse, Harold D. Moser, and Michael J. Birkner, is complete; *Diplomatic Papers*, 1 vol. (1841–43) to date, edited by Charles M. Wiltse, Kenneth E. Shewmaker, and Kenneth R. Stevens; *Speeches and Formal Writings*, 1 vol. (1800–33) to date, edited by Charles M. Wiltse; *Legal Papers*, 2 vols. to date, edited by Alfred S. Konefsky and Andrew J. King. One volume is yet to be published in each of the last three series.

In addition to the letterpress edition of the Webster Papers, Dartmouth College has sponsored the microfilm edition of the letters (holograph) and documents in 41 reels. *A Guide and Index to the Microfilm of the Papers of Daniel Webster*, edited by Charles M. Wiltse (Ann Arbor, Mich.: University Microfilms, 1971), gives detailed information about major Webster collections and their locations, with a reel-by-reel description of their contents and a valuable index.

Older published editions of Webster's papers are not as reliable. *The Private Correspondence of Daniel Webster*, edited by Fletcher Webster, 2 vols. (Boston, Mass.: Little, Brown, 1857); *The Letters of Daniel Webster, from Documents Owned Principally by the New Hampshire Historical Society*, edited by C. H. Van Tyne (1902; reprint, St. Clair Shores, Mich.: Scholarly Press, 1970); *The Works of Daniel Webster*, edited by Edward Everett, 6 vols. (Boston, Mass.: Little, Brown, 1851); and *The Writings and Speeches of Daniel Webster*, edited by J. W. McIntyre, 18 vols. (Boston, Mass.: Little, Brown, 1903), are in varying degrees less responsibly edited. George Ticknor Curtis's *Life of Daniel Webster*, 2 vols. (New York: D. Appleton, 1893), contains many letters in their entirety.

The Papers of Henry Clay, edited by James F. Hopkins, Mary Hargreaves, Robert Seager II, Robert Winslow III, and Melba Porter Hay, 8 vols. to date (Lexington: University Press of Kentucky, 1959–), has not yet reached the 1840s. For that period one must still rely on *The Private Correspondence of Henry Clay*, edited by Calvin Colton (New York: A. S. Barnes, 1855), and *The Life, Correspondence, and Speeches of Henry Clay*, edited by Calvin Colton, 6 vols. (New York: P. O'Shea, 1864).

Like the writings of Clay and Webster, those of Calhoun currently are being published in a new edition: *The Papers of John C. Calhoun*, edited by Robert L.

Meriwether, W. Edwin Hemphill, and Clyde N. Wilson, 16 vols. to date (Columbia: University of South Carolina Press, 1959–). Volume 16 (1841–43) proved very helpful, as did older published collections: *Correspondence of John C. Calhoun*, edited by J. Franklin Jameson, vol. 2 of *Annual Report of the American Historical Association for the Year 1899* (Washington, D.C.: Government Printing Office, 1900); *Correspondence Addressed to John C. Calhoun, 1837–1849*, edited by Chauncey S. Boucher and Robert P. Brooks, *Annual Report of the American Historical Association for the Year 1929* (Washington, D.C.: Government Printing Office, 1930); *The Works of John C. Calhoun*, edited by Richard K. Crallé, 6 vols. (New York: D. Appleton, 1853–55).

The Papers of Willie Person Mangum, edited by Henry Thomas Shanks, 5 vols. (Raleigh, N.C.: State Department of Archives and History, 1950–56), and *The Papers of William Alexander Graham*, edited by J. G. deRoulhac Hamilton and Max R. Williams, 6 vols. to date (Raleigh, N.C.: State Department of Archives and History, 1957–), give indications of the thinking of two loyal southern Clay Whigs. The opinions and reactions of a northern Clay Whig are found in *The Diary of Philip Hone, 1828–1851*, edited by Allan Nevins, 2 vols. (1927; reprint, New York: Kraus, 1969); those of a Webster, but pro-Texas-annexation, Whig are found in *The Correspondence of Nicholas Biddle Dealing with National Affairs, 1807–1844*, edited by Reginald C. McGrane (Boston, Mass.: Houghton Mifflin, 1919).

The views of three Georgians—two Whigs and one Democrat—are contained in *Correspondence of Robert Toombs, Alexander H. Stephens, and Howell Cobb*, edited by Ulrich B. Phillips, *Annual Report of the American Historical Association for the Year 1911*, 2 vols. (Washington, D.C.: Government Printing Office, 1913). *The Life of John J. Crittenden, with Selections from His Correspondence and Speeches*, edited by Mrs. Chapman Coleman, 2 vols. (1871; reprint, New York: Da Capo Press, 1970), includes letters that reveal Clay's attitudes and motivations as well as the strategy of the 1841 resignations from Tyler's cabinet. "The Diary of Thomas Ewing, August and September, 1841," *American Historical Review* 18 (1912): 97–112, gives a detailed two-months account of the anguish caused by the bank issue. The despair of New York Whigs is disclosed in Thurlow Weed Barnes, *Memoir of Thurlow Weed*, vol. 2 of *Life of Thurlow Weed* (Boston, Mass.: Houghton Mifflin, 1884). Bias and sarcasm aside, *Memoirs of John Quincy Adams*, edited by Charles Francis Adams, 12 vols. (1874–77; reprint, New York: AMS Press, 1970), constitute an indispensable, almost day-by-day, guide to happenings during the Harrison-Tyler years.

Correspondence of Andrew Jackson, edited by John Spencer Bassett, 7 vols. (1926–35; reprint, New York: Kraus, 1969), is being updated by a projected 15-volume publication of the *Papers of Andrew Jackson* by the University of Tennessee Press, under the editorship of Harold D. Moser, Sharon MacPherson, and Charles F. Bryan, Jr. To date the first two volumes, covering the years through 1813, are available. For other Democratic viewpoints see Thomas Hart Benton, *Thirty Years' View*, 2 vols. (New York: D. Appleton, 1854, 1856), and "Unpublished Letters of Thomas Ritchie,'' edited by Charles H. Ambler, in *The John P. Branch Historical Papers of Randolph-Macon College* 3 (1911): 199–252.

Essential to the Texas issue is the *Diplomatic Correspondence of the Republic of Texas*, edited by George P. Garrison, *Annual Report of the American Historical Association for the Year 1908*, 2 vols. (Washington, D.C.: Government Printing Office, 1911).

Henry Alexander Wise's *Seven Decades of the Union: The Humanities and Materialism, Illustrated by A Memoir of John Tyler* (Philadelphia: J. B. Lippincott, 1881) is of questionable reliability, as is Duff Green's, *Facts and Suggestions, Biographical, Historical, Financial, and Political* (New York: Union Printing Office, 1866).

Numerous letters relating to the Tyler presidency can be found in the *William and Mary Quarterly*, series 1 and 2, and in *Tyler's Quarterly Historical and Genealogical Magazine*. The newspapers that I consulted most frequently were the *National Intelligencer, Niles' National Register,* and the *Richmond* (Va.) *Enquirer.*

In addition to the Harrison biography by Dorothy Goebel, mentioned above, Freeman Cleves's *Old Tippecanoe: William Henry Harrison and His Times* (New York: Charles Scribner's Sons, 1939) provides good background information. No major work on Tyler has appeared in the last two decades. Oliver Perry Chitwood's *John Tyler: Champion of the Old South* (New York: D. Appleton-Century, 1939) is considered the standard political biography. Robert Seager II, *And Tyler Too: A Biography of John and Julia Gardiner Tyler* (New York: McGraw-Hill, 1963), is very readable; it focuses in greater detail on Tyler's second marriage and his personal life, as well as on his political career. Robert J. Morgan's *A Whig Embattled: The Presidency under John Tyler* (Lincoln: University of Nebraska Press, 1954), is an insightful topical analysis of the Tyler presidency.

In attracting the attention of scholars in more recent years, Webster has fared better than the other two members of the illustrious trio—Clay and Calhoun. Maurice G. Baxter's *One and Inseparable: Daniel Webster and the Union* (Cambridge, Mass.: Harvard University Press, 1984) is the latest full-length biography. This was preceded by Baxter's specialized study of *Daniel Webster and the Supreme Court* (Amherst: University of Massachusetts Press, 1966). Other works on Webster that have been published during the past approximately twenty years include Irving H. Bartlett, *Daniel Webster* (New York: W. W. Norton, 1978); Robert F. Dalzell, Jr., *Daniel Webster and the Trial of American Nationalism, 1843–1852* (Boston, Mass.: Houghton Mifflin, 1973); and Norman Brown, *Daniel Webster and the Politics of Availability* (Athens: University of Georgia Press, 1969). In its relation to the Harrison-Tyler presidencies, special mention must be made of Sydney Nathans's superb *Daniel Webster and Jacksonian Democracy* (Baltimore, Md.: Johns Hopkins University Press, 1973). Older volumes on Webster that are valuable are Richard N. Current, *Daniel Webster and the Rise of National Conservatism* (Boston, Mass.: Little, Brown, 1955), and the earlier mentioned George Curtis, *Life of Daniel Webster.*

The most detailed biography of John C. Calhoun is Charles M. Wiltse's *John C. Calhoun*, 3 vols. (Indianapolis, Ind.: Bobbs-Merrill, 1944–51). Another fine study is Margaret L. Coit's *John C. Calhoun: American Portrait* (Boston, Mass.: Houghton Mifflin, 1950). More critical is Gerald M. Capers's *John C. Calhoun, Opportunist* (Gainesville: University of Florida Press, 1960). The best biography of Henry Clay is Glyndon G. Van Deusen's *The Life of Henry Clay* (Boston, Mass.: Little, Brown, 1937). Good interpretations of Clay's political career are George Rawlings Poage's *Henry Clay and the Whig Party* (1936; reprint, Gloucester, Mass.: Peter Smith, 1965) and Clement Eaton's *Henry Clay and the Art of American Politics* (Boston, Mass.: Little, Brown, 1957). Although Merrill D. Peterson's *The Great Triumvirate: Webster, Clay, and Calhoun* (New York: Oxford University Press, 1987) appeared after I had completed this manuscript, no bibliography of this period should omit it.

Other biographies of individuals who were important to the 1840s are three by Glyndon G. Van Deusen, *William Henry Seward* (New York: Oxford University Press, 1967), *Thurlow Weed: Wizard of the Lobby* (Boston, Mass.: Little, Brown, 1947), and *Horace Greeley: Nineteenth-Century Crusader* (Philadelphia: University of Pennsylvania Press, 1953); Claude H. Hall, *Abel Parker Upshur: Conservative Virginian, 1790–1844* (Madison: State Historical Society of Wisconsin, 1963); Michael O'Brien, *A Character of Hugh Legaré* (Knoxville: University of Tennessee Press, 1985); Albert D. Kirwan, *John J. Crittenden: The Struggle for the Union* (Lexington: University of Kentucky Press, 1962); Norma Lois Peterson, *Littleton Waller Tazewell* (Charlottesville: University Press of Virginia, 1983); Thomas Payne Govan, *Nicholas Biddle: Nationalist and Public Banker, 1786–1844* (Chicago: University of Chicago Press, 1959); Robert J. Brugger, *Beverley Tucker: Heart over Head in the Old South* (Baltimore, Md.: Johns Hopkins University Press, 1978); Norman D. Brown, *Edward Stanly: Whiggery's Tarheel "Conqueror"* (University: University of Alabama Press, 1974); Craig Simpson, *A Good Southerner: The Life of Henry A. Wise* (Chapel Hill: University of North Carolina Press, 1985); Drew Gilpin Faust, *James Henry Hammond and the Old South: A Design for Mastery* (Baton Rouge: Louisiana State University Press, 1982); James P. Shenton, *Robert Walker: A Politician from Jackson to Lincoln* (New York: Columbia University Press, 1961); Charles Henry Ambler, *Thomas Ritchie: A Study in Virginia Politics* (Richmond, Va.: Bell Book & Stationery Co., 1913); Carl Brent Swisher, *Roger B. Taney* (1935; reprint, Hamden, Conn.: Archon Books, 1961); John A. Garraty, *Silas Wright* (New York: Columbia University Press, 1949); William Nisbet Chambers, *Old Bullion Benton: Senator from the New West* (Boston, Mass.: Little, Brown, 1956); Samuel Flagg Bemis, *John Quincy Adams*, 2 vols. (New York: Alfred A. Knopf, 1949, 1956); Leonard L. Richards, *The Life and Times of Congressman John Quincy Adams* (New York: Oxford University Press, 1986); Frank B. Woodford, *Lewis Cass: The Last Jeffersonian* (New Brunswick, N.J.: Rutgers University Press, 1950); Claude M. Fuess, *The Life of Caleb Cushing*, 2 vols. (1923; reprint, Hamden, Conn.: Archon Books, 1965); John A. Munroe, *Louis McLane: Federalist and Jacksonian* (New Brunswick, N.J.: Rutgers University Press, 1973); Russel B. Nye, *George Bancroft: Brahmin Rebel* (New York: Alfred A. Knopf, 1944). See also Marvin Cain, "Return of Republicanism: A Reappraisal of Hugh Swinton Legaré and the Tyler Presidency," *South Carolina Historical Magazine* 79 (1978):

264–80; and Fletcher M. Green, "Duff Green, Militant Journalist of the Old School," *American Historical Review* 52 (1947): 247–64.

Ruth C. Silva, in *Presidential Succession* (Ann Arbor: University of Michigan Press, 1951), questions the constitutionality of Tyler's assumption of the presidential office. Arthur M. Schlesinger, Jr., in *The Cycles of American History* (Boston, Mass.: Houghton Mifflin, 1986), in an excellent chapter, explores the origin of the vice-presidency, Tyler's "constitutional coup," the complexities of succession, the fallacies of the Twenty-fifth Amendment, and the future of the vice-presidency. Stephen W. Stathis, in "John Tyler's Presidential Succession: A Reappraisal," *Prologue* 8 (1976): 223–36, expressed the belief that almost from the moment that Tyler learned of Harrison's death, he set his sights on the 1844 election and seized the presidential office in order to outmaneuver Clay.

Among the numerous books and articles abut the presidency, many of which deal mainly with the twentieth century, the following were most beneficial to this study: Edward S. Corwin, *The President: Office and Powers, 1787–1957* (New York: New York University Press, 1957); Edward Stanwood, *A History of the Presidency*, 2 vols. (1928; reprint, Clifton, N.J.: Augustus M. Kelley, 1975); and Arthur M. Schlesinger, Jr., *The Imperial Presidency* (Boston, Mass.: Houghton Mifflin, 1973), which contains references to the Tyler administration. An older but useful work is George Fort Milton's *The Use of Presidential Power, 1789–1943* (Boston, Mass.: Little, Brown, 1944). Bernard Schwartz, *From Confederation to Nation: The American Constitution, 1835–1877* (Baltimore, Md.: Johns Hopkins University Press, 1973), contains valuable chapters on the presidency and on the relationship between Congress and the executive. Wilfred E. Binkley's *President and Congress* (New York: Alfred A. Knopf, 1947) is a revision of Binkley's earlier work, *The Powers of the President: Problems of American Democracy* (1937; reprint, Russell & Russell, 1973). Other aspects of the presidency are covered by Carlton Jackson in *Presidential Vetoes, 1792–1945* (Athens: University of Georgia Press, 1967); by Stephen W. Stathis in "Former Presidents as Congressional Witnesses," *Presidential Studies Quarterly* 13 (1983): 458–81; by Mary Louise Hinsdale in *A History of the President's Cabinet* (Ann Arbor, Mich.: G. Wahr, 1911); and by Henry B. Learned in *The President's Cabinet* (New Haven, Conn.: Yale University Press, 1912).

For interesting theories on the presidency see Harold J. Laski, *The American Presidency: An Interpretation* (1940; reprint, New York: Grosset & Dunlap, the University Library, n.d.); Clinton Rossiter, *The American Presidency* (New York: New American Library, 1956); James Deakin, "A Modest Political Theory," a review of *Presidents, Politics, and Policy*, by Erwin C. Hargrove and Michael Nelson, *Virginia Quarterly Review* 61 (1985): 713–18; Erwin C. Hargrove and Michael Nelson, *Presidents, Politics, and Policy* (Baltimore, Md.: Johns Hopkins University Press, 1984); Richard E. Neustadt, *Presidential Power: The Politics of Leadership* (New York: John Wiley & Sons, 1961); Edward Pessen, *The Log Cabin Myth: The Social Backgrounds of the Presidents* (New Haven, Conn.: Yale University Press, 1984). George E. Reedy, in "Discovering the Presidency," *New York Times Book Review*, 20 Jan. 1985, pp. 1, 22–23, discusses various authors' characterizations of the presidency. James Sterling Young, in *The Washington Community, 1800–1828* (New York: Columbia University Press, 1966), and Michael Nelson, in *"The Washington Community* Revisited," *Virginia Quarterly Review* 61 (1985): 189–210, provide invaluable background on the struggle between the president and Congress, as does Leonard D. White in *The Jacksonians: A Study in Administrative History, 1829–1861* (New York: Macmillan, 1954).

Views on parties, political issues, and campaigns are found in Oscar Doane Lambert, *Presidential Politics in the United States, 1841–1844* (Durham, N.C.: Duke University Press, 1936); William R. Brock, *Parties and Political Conscience: American Dilemmas, 1840–1850* (Millwood, N.Y.: KTO Press, 1979); Richard P. McCormick, *The Second American Party System: Party Formation in the Jacksonian Era* (Chapel Hill: University of North Carolina Press, 1966), and *The Presidential Game: The Origins of American Presidential Politics* (New York: Oxford University Press, 1982); James C. N. Paul, *Rift in the Democracy* (1951; reprint, New York: A. S. Barnes, a Perpetua Book, 1961); Arthur C. Cole, *The Whig Party in the South* (1914; reprint, Gloucester, Mass.: Peter Smith, 1962); Daniel Walker Howe, *The Political Culture of the American Whigs* (Chicago: University of Chicago Press, 1979); E. Malcolm Carroll, *Origins of the Whig Party* (1925; reprint, Gloucester, Mass.: Peter Smith, 1964); Michael F. Holt, "The Democratic Party, 1828–1860"; and Glyndon G. Van Deusen, "The Whig Party," in *History of U.S. Political Parties,* edited by Arthur M. Schlesinger, Jr., 4 vols. (New York: Chelsea House, 1980); Charles G. Sellers, Jr., "Who Were the Southern Whigs?" *American Historical Review* 59 (1954): 335–46; Edward Pessen, *Jacksonian America: Society, Personality, and Politics* (Homewood, Ill.: Dorsey Press, 1969); William Cooper, Jr., *The South and the Politics of Slavery, 1828–1856* (Baton Rouge: Louisiana State University Press, 1978); Glyndon G. Van Deusen, *The Jacksonian Era, 1828–1848* (New York: Harper, 1959); John McCardell, *The Idea of a Southern Nation: Southern Nationalists and Southern Nationalism, 1830–1860* (New York: W. W. Norton, 1979).

For aspects of the judicial branch during the Tyler administration see Gerald T. Dunne, *Justice Joseph Story and the Rise of the Supreme Court* (New York: Simon & Schuster, 1970); John P. Frank, *Justice Daniel Dissenting: A Biography of Peter V. Daniel, 1784–1860* (Cambridge, Mass.: Harvard University Press, 1964); G. Edward White, *The American Judicial Tradition: Profiles of Leading American Judges* (New York: Oxford University Press, 1976); Henry J. Abraham, *Justices and Presidents: A Political History of Appointments to the Supreme Court* (New York: Oxford University Press, 1974); and Carl Brent Swisher, *Roger B. Taney,* cited previously.

On diplomacy and foreign affairs, two indispensable books by Frederick Merk, *Fruits of Propaganda in the Tyler Administration* (Cambridge, Mass.: Harvard University Press, 1971) and *Slavery and the Annexation of Texas* (New York: Alfred A. Knopf, 1972), are valuable not only for the ideas presented but also for the inclusion of numerous documents, letters, and newspaper editorials. Other volumes by Merk that are essential to an understanding of foreign affairs and the westward expansion during this period are *The Oregon Question: Essays in Anglo-*

American Diplomacy and Politics (Cambridge, Mass.: Harvard University Press, 1967), *The Monroe Doctrine and American Expansion, 1843–1849* (1966; reprint, New York: Vintage Books, 1972), and *Manifest Destiny and Mission in American History: A Reinterpretation* (New York: Alfred A. Knopf, 1970). Howard Jones's *To the Webster-Ashburton Treaty: A Study in Anglo-American Relations, 1783–1843* (Chapel Hill: University of North Carolina Press, 1977) is a comprehensive study. Also on the treaty see Thomas LeDuc, "The Webster-Ashburton Treaty and the Minnesota Iron Range," *Mississippi Valley Historical Review* 51 (1964): 476–81; and Richard N. Current, "Webster's Propaganda and the Ashburton Treaty," ibid., 34 (1947): 187–200. David M. Pletcher's *The Diplomacy of Annexation: Texas, Oregon, and the Mexican War* (Columbia: University of Missouri Press, 1973) is first-rate. See also Jesse S. Reeves, *American Diplomacy under Tyler and Polk* (1907; reprint, Gloucester, Mass.: Peter Smith, 1967), and two almost encyclopedic studies by Justin Smith: *The Annexation of Texas* (1911; reprint, New York: Barnes & Noble, 1941) and *The War with Mexico*, 2 vols. (1919; reprint, Gloucester, Mass.: Peter Smith, 1963). Sydney Nathans, in "The Southern Connection: Slaveholders and Antebellum Expansion," *Reviews in American History* 1 (1973): 389–95, explores Calhoun's reasons for writing the Pakenham letter.

Explorations and scientific progress are discussed brilliantly by William H. Goetzmann in *New Lands, New Men: America and the Second Age of Discovery* (New York: Viking, 1986). *Magnificent Voyagers: The U.S. Exploring Expedition, 1838–1842*, edited by Herman J. Viola and Carolyn Margolis (Washington, D.C.: Smithsonian Institution Press, 1985), covers the ambitious undertaking in a series of essays. William Stanton's *The Great United States Exploring Expedition of 1838–1842* (Berkeley: University of California Press, 1975) and Daniel C. Haskell's *The United States Exploring Expedition, 1838–1842 and Its Publications, 1844–1874* (1942; reprint, New York: Greenwood Press, 1968) are fine works. A first-hand account is Charles Wilkes's *Narrative of the United States Exploring Expedition during the Years 1838, 1839, 1840, 1841, 1842*, 5 vols. (Philadelphia: Lea & Blanchard, 1845). John Charles Frémont's *Report of the Exploring Expedition to the Great Rocky Mountains in the Year 1842, and to Oregon and North California in the Years 1843–1844* (Washington, D.C.: Gales & Seaton, Printers, 1845) is another narrative of exploration during the Tyler years. For studies of scientific and technological developments see George Rogers Taylor, *The Transportation Revolution, 1815–1860* (1951; reprint, New York: Harper Torchbook, 1968); Brooke Hindle and Steven Lubar, *Engines of Change: The American Industrial Revolution, 1790–1860* (Washington, D.C.: Smithsonian Institution Press, 1986); Harold Sprout and Margaret Sprout, *The Rise of American Naval Power, 1776–1918* (Princeton, N.J.: Princeton University Press, paperback ed., 1966); Charles L. Lewis, *Matthew Fontaine Maury: The Pathfinder of the Sea* (1927; reprint, New York: AMS Press, 1969); and Donald R. Whitnah, *A History of the United States Weather Bureau* (Urbana: University of Illinois Press, Illini Books, 1965).

From the vast literature on society, culture, and reform movements, the following have been consulted in detail: Russell B. Nye, *Society and Culture in America, 1830–1860* (New York: Harper & Row, Torchbook ed., 1974); Ray Allen

Billington, *The Protestant Crusade, 1800–1860: A Study of the Origins of American Nativism* (1938; reprint, Chicago: Quadrangle Books, 1964); Russel B. Nye, *Fettered Freedom: Civil Liberties and the Slavery Controversy, 1830–1860*, rev. ed. (East Lansing: Michigan State University Press, 1963); Alice Felt Tyler, *Freedom's Ferment* (New York: Harper, Torchbook ed., 1967); George M. Dennison, *The Dorr War: Republicanism on Trial, 1831–1861* (Lexington: University Press of Kentucky, 1976); Harold D. Langley, *Social Reform in the United States Navy, 1798–1862* (Urbana: University of Illinois Press, 1967); Merton L. Dillon, *The Abolitionists: The Growth of a Dissenting Minority* (New York: W. W. Norton, paperback ed., 1979); Samuel Rezneck, "The Social History of an American Depression, 1837–1843," *American Historical Review* 40 (1935): 662–86; Edwin C. McReynolds, *The Seminoles* (Norman: University of Oklahoma Press, 1957); and Alvin M. Josephy, *The Indian Heritage of America* (New York: Alfred A. Knopf, 1969).

Intellectual developments during the pre–Civil War period are discussed by Perry Miller in *The Life of the Mind in America: From the Revolution to the Civil War* (New York: Harcourt, Brace, 1965) and by Ralph Gabriel in *The Course of American Democratic Thought*, 2d ed. (New York: Roland Press, 1956). The second volume of Vernon L. Parrington's three-volume study *Main Currents in American Thought: An Interpretation of American Literature from the Beginnings to 1920* (New York: Harcourt, Brace, 1927) includes vignettes of several figures who were associated with the Tyler administration, such as John C. Calhoun, Alexander H. Stephens, and Hugh S. Legaré.

INDEX